WEBER, IRRATIONALITY, AND SOCIAL ORDER

WEBER, IRRATIONALITY, AND SOCIAL ORDER

Alan Sica

University of California Press
Berkeley · Los Angeles · London

University of California Press
Berkeley and Los Angeles, California

University of California Press, Ltd.
London, England

Library of Congress Cataloging-in-Publication Data
Sica, Alan, 1949–
    Weber, irrationality, and social order.
    Bibliography: p.
    Includes index.
    1. Weber, Max, 1864–1920—Views on rationalism.
2. Pareto, Vilfredo, 1848–1923.   3. Irrationalism
(Philosophy).   4. Hermeneutics.   I. Title.
HM22.G3W4576   1988   301'.01   88–14330
ISBN 0–520–06149–7 (alk. paper)

Printed in the United States of America
1 2 3 4 5 6 7 8 9

La Famiglia

Man's nature is irrational and the love of wonders and magic so deeply rooted in his whole being that it can never be completely eradicated.

George Sarton

And I compared myself to a palimpsest; I tasted the scholar's joy when he discovers under more recent writing, and on the same paper, a very ancient and infinitely more precious text. What was this occult text? In order to read it, was it not first of all necessary to efface the more recent one?

André Gide

Contents

Preface

Those who observe that too many monographs about Weber or his ideas have been appearing in English lately do not speak idly. The specialist has had to read about five new books a year over the past half-decade, in addition to whatever articles come to hand. Already by the mid-1970s over 2,400 items of Weberiana had been listed by two German bibliographers. We are awash in Max Weber—his mighty *Gesamtausgabe* is also begun in Germany—and one wonders why. Thirty years ago conventional wisdom held that his ideas and studies were rapidly being subsumed by empirical research or grand theory, so that Weber's obsolescence was in sight. And a glance at the corpus of American or English Weber studies from that period reveals very little, in either number or lasting importance. Then without warning, in the last ten years, historians, sociologists, political scientists, economists, even some stray literati, have turned out serious reanalyses and extensions of his material, first shaped between 1904 and 1920, in that period of social science so often deemed "pre-modern." This being the case, every new entrant into the Weber circle must justify its claim to attention from an already weary group of scholars and their students known, somewhat unhappily, as the Weber industry.

Despite immediate appearances, this book is not primarily a hermeneutical exercise in which the superiority of one interpretation of canonical texts is championed against others. Its origin lies elsewhere, near the overlap of history, psychoanalysis, aesthetics, and social theory of the usual kind. Weber, Pareto, Freud, W. I. Thomas, Max Scheler, Karl Mannheim, and many others of similar stature long ago wondered and wrote much about the interplay between societal rationalization and individual rationality, between collective furor and private psychopathology—in short, about the strange and worrisome union of "character and social structure" (to recall Gerth and Mills). Pondering the history of social thought in this century can lead to the unpleasant realization that such large-scale questions slipped away, especially from sociologists, sometime before World War II. Or, if not entirely lost, they were so transformed in range and rhetoric that a gap opened between contemporary theorizing and its European background. Perhaps this partly explains Weber's continuing appeal. By dealing with him, one might again broach topics long at odds with "social science" of the last forty years.

If there is a weakness in the founding fathers of social thought—Tocqueville, Marx, Spencer, Durkheim, Weber—it lies in their pre-theorized notions about consciousness and its development through social life. Certainly Simmel, Mead, Husserl, Cooley, James, and others can be brought in, as they often are, for enlightenment. Yet a "Jamesian Weberianism," for instance, is not very practical, nor a "Meadian Marxism," though something can be said for the effort to join micro and macro along these lines. Perhaps the most successful early theorist in this regard, one who paid serious attention to structure but never allowed it to cloud his acute vision of the singular, was Pareto. The irrational and nonrational fascinated him, and he worked miracles of labor documenting their role in human history. It is not intellectually feasible or even politically desirable to rebuild Pareto's reputation to its former height. But it is another thing entirely to take a page from his text and lay it beside Weber's, as it were, imitating in a sense Weber's own addiction to Italian life and culture: that sharp cynicism about ideals and idealizations of the sort which grew without bounds in his homeland.

Weber's underdeveloped theory of social action is brittle and artificial when compared with his comparative studies, of law, religion, and music. Marginal utility theory urged him and other theorists of his time to hypostatize rational action, even when done with exquisite qualification, as in his ideal-types. The "residual" mass of individual behavior, even as a product of interaction, was slowly lost to sociology and became the property, redefined and carefully guarded, of various psychologies. This was a momentous error for everyone concerned, since by so doing sociology lost touch with the fundamental unit of social life, and her sister disciplines became caged in scientistic laboratories, trying to hunt down and capture the quantifiable essence of humanness. Now with positivism largely deposed throughout the social sciences, it is time to reappropriate selectively some of what has been forgotten over the last half-century. And with the help of contemporary hermeneutics, such a project has more chance of succeeding than in the past when similar efforts were made. The goal of this book, then, becomes twofold: to stimulate Weber's theory of social action with Pareto's adroit analytical concern for the irrational; and also to open up current opinion regarding what social theory ought to take in before it hauls up the drawbridge on disciplinary limits and scholarly adventure. To have succeeded at both objectives would be more than one could ask. But at least a start has been made, more or less in Weber's form, but with the spirit of his noisy colleague to the south.

Acknowledgments

Charles H. Page postponed retirement to help with this, which is typical of his big-heartedness and remarkable sense of professional duty. He also showed me that clear writing beats bluster, and that generosity of spirit among scholars (and regular folk, too) makes for a social world worth inhabiting. Norman Birnbaum pointed out useful European writers and showed that hedging one's bets while writing social theory is pointless. Dick Martin—friend, master editor, intellectual—prompted me to think again when I thought I had finished.

My typists were Peggy O'Connor, Pat Johnston, and Lori Houk-Stephens, without whom not.

If William Julius Wilson had not invited me to Chicago, and if therefore Wendy Espeland had not told Paul Hirsch about the manuscript, he would not have mentioned it to Naomi Schneider—gifted and effective editor at the University of California Press—and it would still be in the drawer where it had lain for six years. I also want to thank Mary Renaud and Jane-Ellen Long for turning the manuscript into a book.

Alexandra Mason and her staff at the Spencer Research Library opened their unique setting to me, a haven for scholars in a noisy world. Praise be to Room 284.

For inspiring intellectual give and take I must thank Robert Antonio, Clint Howard, and Karl Morrison.

Assistance with languages came from my foreign agents, Hanna Margarethe Meyer and her associate, E. Giuseppe Sica.

For welcome *scriptum interruptum*, deepest ambivalence goes to Paolo, Enzo, and Carlo. And the balance of appreciation—and there is plenty left—all belongs to Anne.

1

Rationality and Irrationality
in Modern Thought

The Problem: Weber Versus Pareto on Irrationality

No matter how apparently grand when finished, social theories resemble most people in their humble origins. What follows is an attempt to enlarge contemporary social thought by reexamining a component of action and sentiment which since the 1930s has been cast in the humblest of all positions: simply dismissed from theorizing and research. The motive for this query is empirically immediate, an outgrowth of pre-theorized experience. It does not "test" a specific theory, which adds, one might argue, to the project's initial modesty. The history of social thought and its ties to current preoccupations give rise to the question: Why does so much social theory—of personality, organizations, social change, even of deviance—lay such emphasis upon, even itself rely on, the notion of rationality in human action? And why has it therefore suppressed or judged irrelevant systematic tracking of "irrationality" as a factor in social behavior, as, moreover, an essential, invariant element of lived experience?

With Vilfredo Pareto's death in 1923, the century's last major social theorist to set irrational factors as central to communal life was silenced. Save for a brief, intense period at Harvard in the 1930s, his theories have been slighted in the United States except for obligatory historical reference.[1] Meanwhile Max Weber, Pareto's

---

1. Arun Sahay's *Sociological Analysis* is meant to serve, as is much of John Rex's "International Library of Sociology," as a primer on methods and theory. It explicates the "sociological imagination" with alternating chapters on Weber and Pareto. Yet, Sahay, for all his welcome and unorthodox use of Pareto, seems to enter the debate about the proper theoretical place of irrationality only to succumb, with some elegance, to an uncommonly reflective "scientific" spirit. As usual, this relegates irrationality to the residual, "unknowable" category. He discusses Pareto not for his own sake, but to compare Weber with the "lesser" Italian, and at times falls into

contemporary, became the standard-bearer of American sociology. It is difficult to recall that at one time these two were similarly valued by sociologists in America and abroad. Weber's scholarly and personal complexity undoes pat characterization. It could be strongly argued, though, that he comprehended the place of irrationality in social action, even to the point of fascination. Yet he carefully imitated classical economics, theoretically and substantively, by focusing on rational acts, letting them fill up the familiar *zweckrational* and, somewhat less, *wertrational* categories in his typology of social action. The "irrational" *affektuell* and traditional spheres were thus left aside.[2]

Weber's preference has been thoroughly incorporated into American sociology and political science, but in most cases without his abundant stipulations and reservations concerning the rational

---

false dichotomies between the two theorists, in the process shortchanging Pareto considerably.

Warren Samuels's long, intelligent book, *Pareto on Policy*, fuses Pareto's equilibrium theory with contemporary interests in social planning. Samuels is totally committed to the hyper-positivist Pareto, the engineer and scientist, and consequently has little interest in irrationality, either individual or cultural.

These two volumes comprise the total recent sociological oeuvre that incorporates Pareto in other than a strictly historical manner into ongoing theorizing. (Economists still frequently write on Pareto, occasionally in entire monographs such as Vincent Tarascio's *Pareto's Methodological Approach to Economics,* but, naturally, they emphasize his *Manual on Political Economy,* a book practically unknown to sociologists.) One older volume must be mentioned. In 1964 Charles Madge's *Society in the Mind* appeared in this country as part of a series ("Society Today and Tomorrow") designed and composed by British academics for their peers. The book's idiosyncratic and essayistic blend of Greek philosophy with classical social theory kept it from having much impact in the United States. This is unfortunate because Madge makes much use of the *Trattato,* concluding his brief, dense monograph with three exciting chapters: "The Rationality of Survival," "Other Rationalities?" and "The Aesthetic Utopia." Although Madge clearly writes from within the Peter Winch orbit regarding the "problem" of irrationality, he seems to consider irrationality more seriously, as a motor of social action, than do some of his positivist-rationalist colleagues.

A last note: in his *Human Nature, Class, and Ethnicity,* Milton Gordon published an essay, "Human Nature and Sociology," juxtaposing Weber and Pareto concerning rationality.

[All works that appear in abbreviated form in the footnotes are cited in full in the bibliography. Most works are cited by author and title; works by Weber, however, are cited by year of publication and are listed chronologically in a separate section of the bibliography.]

2. Weber 1968a, 1: 24–25. Historian of economic thought Günter Hartfiel succinctly locates Weber (as well as Pareto) in the nineteenth-century tradition of political economy in his *Wirtschaftliche und sozial Rationalität,* pp. 181–210.

model. This development forces many questions, for the sociology of knowledge, the history of social thought, and the future of social science. How adequate is our theorizing in the face of contemporary life? Do exchange theory, neo-functionalism, neo-structuralism, ethnomethodology, systems analysis, phenomenological sociology, neo-Marxism, network theory, or their rival perspectives account reasonably well for common behavior in industrial societies? These forbidding questions signal what I see as diminished theoretical power, that is, when theory is asked to illuminate, interpret, perhaps even predict, meaningful behavior.

I think Weber would have agreed that a strictly rational model applies best to formal, narrowly circumscribed milieux, the archetypes being complex organizations and exchange relations. Such a tool necessarily shunts much behavior—the "unrationalized" part—into a nether region, long ago stigmatized as the "residual category."[3] This behavior is thought to be linked, in some sociologically unexaminable way, to an irrational or nonrational (hence, unanalyzable) substrate of personality. This quasi-psychoanalytic observation becomes *sociologically* important because of the ubiquitous fact that subjectivity interacts, in its own formation, with commanding societal and cultural constraints. This is true no matter how structurally *or* morally "irrational" the social order may be. Most theorists apparently presume a fit between rationalized culture and rational personality, an assumption for which the evidence, especially at the social-psychological level, is inconclusive. Contemporary theorizing ought to complement the structurally oriented data on "rationalization" gathered since Weber's time, and in his shadow, with theory that more closely follows Pareto's objective of dissecting contemporary personality fully: rational, "rationalized," irrational, or "unrationalizable," as the case may be. The time is past when social theory could hand over untouched this bothersome "substrate" of personality to psychoanalysis and allied approaches. Certainly that majority of sociologists who do not use Freud as their theoretical foundation can help clarify the obscure connection of "character and social structure" in ways they have not for some time. Such a contribution, with correlated

---

3. Talcott Parsons, *The Structure of Social Action*, pp. 16ff., 201.

attention to the historical-structural development of institutions, *and* their intersection with personality as such, is the raison d'être of what follows.

This line of reasoning, and the charges against contemporary thought which it inspires, grew from a study of social theory's "maturation" since the philosophes. Particular emphasis was given the fathers of the discipline; however, Durkheim's positivism and his tendency toward philosophical realism and conceptual hypostasis made him unfit as a primary target of study. Of course, his work on suicide and religion is explicitly concerned with what are commonly known as irrational behaviors. Yet his methods, conceptualizations, and relatively unreflective understanding of "reason" vitiated, for my purposes, the substantive discoveries. Marx's use of the term *rationality* (and its opposite) is no longer theoretically compelling, for two reasons. First, he used such terms as polemical weapons, calling his enemies "irrational" or the apologists for "irrational" social forces.[4] Second, he owed much to the French Enlightenment, and from the philosophes we do not learn a great deal about the "darker" aspects of social psychology. After all, their political program rested upon the apotheosis of rational man: witness the vituperative relation of Voltaire and Rousseau on just these grounds. Of the founding triumvirate only Weber remains, and to him I add Pareto, as did Parsons in his first book some fifty years ago. By comparing their work and its effect on later writers, I hope to reintroduce into theory the seldom denied, yet more seldom confronted, fact of irrationality in human life—what Weber and his peers knew as *das Irrationalitätsproblem*.

I am quite aware that "rationality" has attained totemic status, having served more often during the past two centuries as slogan or symbol than as a convincing analytic concept. It connotes secularization and the eclipse of mythological explanation, what Daniel Bell, following Feuerbach, has called the "progressive disenchantment" of the West.[5] Of course, I support the political and cul-

4. For details of Marx's "reason," see Alan Sica, "Reasonable Science, Unreasonable Life," in *A Weber-Marx Dialogue*, ed. Robert J. Antonio and Ronald Glassman.

5. Daniel Bell, *The End of Ideology*, p. 370. However, for a stunning reanalysis of "secularization" that challenges most conventional accounts, see Hans Blumenberg, *The Legitimacy of the Modern Age*, and the companion volume, *Work on Myth*.

tural program that gives the word its power: that *rationality*, when it means predictability, is a social good and the sine qua non of liberal-democratic ethics. Yet wishing or theoretically demanding submission to rational consistency from social actors will not make it so. It will not lessen the empirical prevalence of irrationality in meaning-seeking activity. This, Pareto's major thesis, was boldly brushed aside by Weber and tends accordingly to be ignored or denied by today's researchers. My interest is both to bolster a realistic understanding—a "rational," accurate view—of behavioral influences and to delimit the range of social action we can properly attribute to rational capability. And it is important to consider, as much as practically possible, not only public, observable acts, but private, "pre-active" cognitive rehearsals of intended behavior as well.

"Rationality" and Modern Philosophy

Intellectual change in the West during the last two centuries can be interpreted in a number of ways without unduly distorting events as best we can know them. One might conceive of intellectual and, some would argue, political history as shifting between poles on a continuum, each representing a pure type of action and thought. One represents rationality, the other its opposite, however named. Consider from all the available definitions several that seem fairly bland:

Rationality: (1) The ability to ascertain and act upon cause-and-effect relationships toward achieving a precisely defined end; or (2) the willingness to forego idiosyncratic pleasures or valued experiences, privately created, on behalf of increased efficiency in securing ends, when pleasure and efficiency conflict, that is to say, the hedonistic versus bureaucratic calculus.

Irrationality: (1) A spring of action or belief that is not readily susceptible of rational explanation, invariably from the observer's position, and not infrequently from that of the subject as well. Such an impulse does not comprehend or employ causal analysis in attempts to secure ends (if the concept *ends* is even recognized as such), or uses inappropriate or nonsensical means as assessed post facto via a rational model of action; or

(2) a form of behavior or belief that controls the subject's action in gaining either pleasant, unpleasant, or ambivalent results, without the subject's absolute control or conscious wishes.

Nonrationality: (1) Behavior that is carried out in defiance of rational procedure; although the rational path may be strategically noted, it is then ignored in the interest of nonrational ends or means (which become, according to standard definitions, ends in themselves). However, the process is often done without *purely* rational consideration of costs consequent to abrogating rational procedure.

The partial parallel here to Weber's typology of social action is intentional. But divergence will become evident when these brief definitions are expanded into a fuller typology more adequate to the subject—the factor of irrationality expressed in and contributing to meaningful behavior.[6] I am especially dissatisfied with the sterile, needlessly restrictive Weberian use of "ends." The other critical definition, of "meaning" in social action, will also be developed at a later point.

Movement between the antipodes sketched above is usually interpreted as a broad cultural advance, slow and hardly inexorable, toward pervasive "societal rationality." This "growth of reason in the West," considered a moral good, has taken on an axiomatic quality, as if post-feudal history can be well represented as deliberate escape from bondage to irrational (and unrationalized) beliefs and acts. This encourages ignoring social behavior that does not observably subscribe to rationality, conceptually defined (or to aspects of its formal expression, logical positivism).[7]

---

6. *Meaning* for the time being can be understood as "whatever subjectively defined qualities of one's life make active persistence appealing." I do not have in mind any extrinsically judged, ontological, or historical characteristics when I use the word, as are often implied in neo-Hegelian, phenomenological, or Marxist texts. It is unfortunately the case, according to my research, that the concept *meaning* is not being used or explored *as such* in contemporary sociological or social-psychological theory. Studies of *meaning* seem to have crested in the 1950s with the work of Charles Osgood on the one hand, Parsons et al. on the other, and the term has disappeared from most research since then. I am retaining it because it plays such a prominent role in classical theory and because I value the term on theoretical grounds.

7. Documentation of this decisive attitudinal shift regarding irrationality is in Michel Foucault's *Madness and Civilization*, subtitled *A History of Insanity in the Age of*

Locke's epistemology announced what many consider the beginning of the modern Western character. His theories of government and human behavior posit as their fundament a human being capable of "rational action."[8] For Locke, and later for his French disciples—as they transformed his work[9]—widespread capability for rational decision, emancipated from supernatural and political mythology and directed at satisfying lucidly conceived ends through reliable means, provided the theoretical basis for a post-feudal enlightened monarchy. Republicanism and parliamentarianism rested, for them, upon this idealized human ability, which they wrote into their theories and polemics; yet they were each realistic enough to recognize it as more normatively desirable than empirically achieved.

Rousseau's attack on the likelihood of "reasonable" social organization and his championing of a fictive pre-modern social order were uncharacteristic of other philosophes. They ostracized him from their circle for several reasons, among them his pessimism about the masses attaining intellectual enlightenment and, relatedly, because in his social analyses he favored elements other than and contrary to "reason" in shaping a modern state.[10] Rousseau

---

Reason, pp. 38–64. In another Foucault book, *The Birth of the Clinic*, he points out the abruptness with which medieval "fools" were redefined as modern "madmen," taken from the village green, and cast into prison. This attitude is captured in the tone of W. E. H. Lecky's classic *History of the Rise and Influence of Rationalism in Europe* (1865), with a major chapter titled "The Declining Sense of the Miraculous." A more recent parallel is Keith Thomas's *Religion and the Decline of Magic*, a massive work culturally indicative of an epoch as was Lecky's book in its time, since Thomas's treatment of the "decline" is less celebrative.

8. Many make this claim, e.g., Robert Paul Wolff: "In the classical writings of the liberal political tradition, man is portrayed as a rational agent, engaged in the political arena either in actions dictated by the rational canons of prudence or in actions conforming to the rational principles of morality" ("Man as a Rational Political Agent," in *Women and Philosophy*, ed. Carol Gould and Marx Wartofsky, p. 129). Or, somewhat more obliquely, Victor Ferkiss, *The Future of Technological Society*, p. 25: "Northrop therefore would seem justified in making Locke the archetype and in large measure the originator of the modern worldview which attempts to reduce all knowledge to the laws of physics," physics serving as the apotheosis of the rational inductive method. F. S. C. Northrop himself refers to the "laissez-faire atomic individualism of Locke," which is, as I have suggested, the root of secularized revolutionary behavior in eighteenth-century France and America (*The Meeting of East and West*, p. 149).

9. George Sabine, *A History of Political Theory*, pp. 545–550.

10. Charles W. Hendel, *Jean-Jacques Rousseau*, 2: 1–38. In rejecting undefiled rationality, Rousseau was bucking a tradition among moralists and philosophers dat-

was perhaps too aware, for his time, that the benefits derived from "cool calculation" of means-ends relationships, already immortalized the century before by Molière, were outweighed by their costs. Among these costs he saw the intolerably arid quality of urbane social relations, the emptying from interaction of the warmth and sincerity that he hypothesized for primitive or pre-modern societies.

On the opposite tack we find Locke, whose social psychology, more circumspect than Rousseau's, is not conveyable in brief. Yet it is clear, in both his political and philosophical works, that his hope for libertarian government and the reasonable society it was to govern retained for him a problematic, somewhat utopian quality.[11] Among the polemicists of this era, perhaps Voltaire made the mightiest claims for the successful application of reason to the exigencies of social life, asserting that all societal difficulties (especially those of the ancien régime) were soluble through "modern" ratiocination. But even his rhetoric to this effect is marked with the clearest irony. And if he openly mocked Rousseau's proto-Romanticism vis-à-vis the place of reason in culture, he did so for polemical purposes, to further his social ethics and out of personal dislike for Rousseau, not because he could offer any apodictic assertions about the "essential" place of reason, in either social or ontological reality.

In simplified form, this philosophical triumvirate makes up a triangle, the sides of which enclose a "pure type" of rational action. All three are fixed around this ideal description of behavior, firmly distanced from one another but each relying on the "essential correctness" of the center as the source of their own propositions, whether merely social—the level of analysis and speculation at which they most often were content to rest—or ontological. Tension among the three, arising from ideological variance, is immense, contrary to the fact that now they are often grouped together as the philosophical/ideological fathers of the "democratic revolutions." This initial, unresolved discord among the sources

---

ing back some time, e.g., from Robert Burton's *Anatomy of Melancholy* (1628): "According to Chrysostom, the sequel of riches is pride, riot, intemperance, arrogancy, fury, and *all irrational courses*" (p. 509, emphasis added).

11. Sabine, *History*, pp. 537–540; also Frederick Copleston, *A History of Philosophy*, 5: 121–152.

of "light" two centuries ago was a harbinger of logically inescapable epistemological and methodological "tensions" that the philosophes unwittingly spawned in their theoretical encounter with modernity and that later received their most thorough exposition by the southwest German neo-Kantians.

This panoply of problems and associated tensions has since become institutionalized in modern social science, and, in a peculiar, somewhat sublimated way, largely through Weber's influence, whose methodological ambivalence and ambiguity we continue to debate. Many "bourgeois" social scientists pride themselves on maintaining this tension in their theories and substantive work, viewing it as the mark of trustworthy social analysis. Their opponents, the Left on the one hand, neo-idealists or phenomenologists on the other, feel differently, of course.

Social philosophers between the philosophes and Weber—notably Hegel, Fichte, Schopenhauer, Kierkegaard, and Nietzsche— proposed their own answers to the question of rationality in history, culture, and personality. Each in his own way resolved *philosophically* the tension that keeps the philosophes provocative. This series of conceptual resolutions, forced as they seem at points, has apparently rendered these five thinkers less inspiring to modern Anglo-American social science than are their French progenitors. This is difficult to explain when the general philosophical quality of nineteenth-century French and German thought is compared. Again, I think, social theory has taken a wrong turn in following the lucid where denser works contained the more fruitful thought.

Weber's Ambivalence

Theoretical "ambiguity," "ambivalence," "tension," whatever the designation, is a well-known characteristic of the Teutonic speculative tradition. Weber's commentators seldom fail to note this in his work as a whole and surrounding *das Irrationalitätsproblem* specifically. Among the most perceptive remarks ever written about Weber's fundamental uneasiness as he faced "fact" on one side, "value" on the other, are these by Hans-Georg Gadamer as part of a memoir on Karl Jaspers, Weber's friend and analyst:

> One can easily grasp that for a man of many interests [Jaspers], the demonic figure of Max Weber, the world's most recent polymath in

the cultural sciences, was the great model he admired and tried to emulate. In Weber he came face-to-face with the iron self-discipline of a researcher who productively drove his will to universal knowledge in all directions up to the limits forced upon him by his scientific asceticism and methodical integrity.

The deep irrationalism that lay behind the quixotic magnificence of the champion of sociology as a value-free science presented a true challenge to Jaspers' philosophical need to ground his thinking.

This philosophy [Jaspers's] . . . does not simply repeat the irrational split of Max Weber, who may have pushed back the limits of the scientific world orientation on all sides, but who pulled so hard that the decisions that life demands of the individual would have had to have been created out of depths other than that of knowledge. Precisely this—that the science embodied with imperial authority by Max Weber had delivered up what was truly worth knowing to irrational choice because that is what the asceticism of science demanded—had become unbearable to the generation to which Jaspers lent his voice.[12]

These reflections document Weber's unwillingness either to scrutinize *or* to ignore rationality in personal life, individualized social action, the wider social world, micro and macro, or its ontological meaning. Yet these troublesome terms, and the theoretical exasperation they denote, cannot be dropped from discourse for mere convenience.

English translations of Weber, seeking faithfulness to the original, are often crammed with qualifiers that reflect this tension. Gerth and Mills first noted this,[13] and Guenther Roth has seconded them: "Weber tended to overqualify his sentences, using terms such as 'perhaps,' 'more or less,' 'in general,' 'as a rule,' 'frequently, but not always,' etc. . . . Weber's sense of caution became a stylistic mannerism."[14] Compare the unevasive forthrightness of the mature Marx. This tension may have contributed to Weber's popularity in the United States and his lower status among social analysts on the "periphery" and among the European Left. They claim that profuse qualification can mask structural and intellectual contradictions of industrial society, assuming the role of ideology, not liberating science.

12. Hans-Georg Gadamer, *Philosophical Apprenticeships*, trans. R. Sullivan, pp. 160–161, 164. See also Reinhard Bendix, *Max Weber*, pp. passim, esp. 3, 494.

13. Weber 1946, pp. v–vii.

14. Guenther Roth, Introduction to Weber 1968a, 1: ci–cii. See also Bendix, *Max Weber*, p. xxi.

Unfortunately this very uneasiness—which was linked to a false resolution of the irrationality problem—is partially obscured from readers of English versions: "Our translation . . . conforms to the English convention: we have omitted what to the English reader would seem self-conscious reservations and manner of emphasis. The same holds for the accumulation of qualifying words, with which the English language dispenses without losing in exactitude, emphasis, and meaning." [15] These two early translators went even further in homogenizing Weber. They explain: "Weber pushes German academic tradition to its extremes. His major theme often seems to be lost in a wealth of footnoted digressions, exemptions, and comparative illustrations. We have taken some footnotes into the text and in a few instances we have relegated technical cross-references which stand in the original text to footnotes." [16]

As is demonstrated in general terms by Hans-Georg Gadamer, Paul Ricoeur, Jacques Derrida, and other hermeneutic theorists, convincing textual interpretation revolves around these sorts of discrepancies, trite as they seem to the conventional reader. Since my dual task is both to chart Weber's positions on irrationality and also to explain the peculiar favoritism accorded aspects of his work by Americans, it is dangerous to ignore even subtle inflections in his texts. Put less loftily, it is essential to care as much about Weber's expressive *form* in studying it as Weber cared for it himself: "boiling down" the content becomes heresy.

Nowhere in Weber's work are equivocations or blind spots more obvious and theoretically bothersome than where he struggled to deal with aspects of behavior about which he privately felt most strongly but which, as a scholar, he approached with trepidation and suspicion. H. Stuart Hughes, in his important study of Weber's epoch, notes that "Weber sought to curb the romanticism [he] discovered in himself," a stunningly crisp and correct remark which finds support in many other sources, including Marianne Weber, Karl Loewenstein, Paul Honigsheim, and Karl Jaspers. [17]

15. Weber 1946, pp. vi–vii.
16. Ibid.
17. H. Stuart Hughes, *Consciousness and Society*, p. 35; Marianne Weber, *Max Weber*; Karl Loewenstein, *Max Weber's Political Ideas in the Perspective of Our Time*, pp. 21–104; Paul Honigsheim, *On Max Weber*, pp. 1–112; Karl Jaspers, "Max Weber as Politician, Scientist, Philosopher," in his *Three Essays*, pp. 189–274.

Compare, for instance, the bold prose in those chapters in *From Max Weber*, "Structures of Power," "Class, Status, Party," and "Bureaucracy" (all originally from *Wirtschaft und Gesellschaft*), with two fascinating, slighted parts of "Religious Rejections of the World and Their Direction." First "The Erotic Sphere," which opens typically enough, full of uncertainty:

> The brotherly ethic of salvation is in profound tension [but what kind?] with the *greatest irrational force of life:* sexual love. . . . [E]roticism appeared to be like a gate into the most irrational and thereby *real kernel of life,* as compared with the mechanism of rationalization. (pp. 343, 345; emphasis added)

Second, "The Esthetic Sphere," which begins:

> The religious ethic of brotherliness stands in dynamic tension [undefined] with any purposive-rational conduct that follows its own laws. In no less degree, this tension occurs between the religious ethic and "this-worldly" life forces [undefined] whose character is nonrational or basically anti-rational. Above all, there is tension between the ethic of religious brotherliness and the sphere of esthetic and erotic life. (pp. 340–341)

Not only do we find Weber chronically reliant, in analyzing these murky matters, upon the word *tension*—and not very daring in exploring it as a concept—but also, and more interestingly, his work itself evolves into a study *in* tension that arose from a congeries of sources, scholarly and personal.[18] This fascinating dimen-

---

18. Hughes writes of himself: "A now familiar tension has established itself between a temperamental leaning toward the reasonable and humane ethics of England and France and a recognition of both the heady deceptions and unparalleled critical contribution of German philosophy" (*Consciousness and Society,* p. 26). Weber was himself subject to a very similar dualism. Perhaps one source for the overused word *Spannung* ("tension") was a popular historical-poetic work that prefigured Spengler in its literary and historical persuasiveness and its careless use of data: Karl Lamprecht's *Deutsche Geschichte* (1891–), a multivolume chronicle of the "stages" of societal and "sociopsychic" development from the ancients to the nineteenth century. Among the labels for epochs in Lamprecht's nomenclature is "the period since the Industrial Revolution . . . declared to be one of the 'nervous tension' in which mankind is still groping for a central idea of an organizing sociopsychic principle" (Harry Elmer Barnes, *Historical Sociology,* p. 116). Lamprecht's other stages were the "symbolic" (primitive), "typical" (early medieval), "conventional" (late medieval), and "individual" (Renaissance). Similar historical categories can be found in many popular histories of the period. Weber, at least formally, was contemptuous of this "appalling" popularization and "psychologizing" of history, obviously written to appeal to the self-aggrandizing propensities of the German middle class: see Max Weber 1975b, pp. 105, 111. But as is clear from p. 114 n. 10, Weber did read

sion of his work, because of its impact on subsequent theory, will be developed in more detail by examining particular texts and connecting the tension with his persona as presented in American and European monographs. H. Stuart Hughes's book is "concerned not so much with the formal enunciation of concepts as with what we may call styles of thought," a worthy model to follow.[19]

Part of the explanation for scholarly prose beset with equivocation, or excess definitional subtlety, comes from Weber himself, in his criticism of another scholar:

> His literary style is occasionally awkward to the point of unintelligibility. This is a consequence of the research method of the scholar, who packs a number of thoughts in a single sentence, piling dependent clause upon dependent clause, without considering whether the resulting sentence makes . . . sense. . . . His book resembles a mosaic made of stones of very different hue: they blend nicely when viewed in the large, but not always when viewed closely.[20]

Julien Freund's *The Sociology of Max Weber*, the most creative part of which is called "The Antagonism of Values," speaks directly to Weber's theoretical ambivalence:

> Despite the superficial progress they have brought about in all fields of human activity, rationalization and intellectualization have made no inroads on the empire of the irrational. On the contrary, as rationalization increases, the irrational grows in intensity. This is a key idea of Weber's, and although he never stated it in so many words, it *dominates his entire philosophy.* . . . The fact that it [*zweckrational Handeln*] is the most readily understandable kind of conduct does not, however, mean that it is the most frequent, although Weber would have liked it so. Nevertheless, his deep belief, which he expressed more than once . . . was that life and the world are *fundamentally irrational.*[21]

Unfortunately Freund did not develop these important assertions very fully.

Lamprecht, so his use of *tension* as a semi-category of both historical and social-psychological events may have influenced Weber.

Through psychoanalytic technique, Arthur Mitzman has made a great deal of Weber's personal dilemmas within his family and the supposed effects on his politics (*The Iron Cage*). Mitzman has many critics, e.g., Walter Struve (*Elites Against Democracy*, pp. 114–115).

19. Hughes, *Consciousness and Society*, p. 22.
20. "Knies and the Problem of Irrationality," in Weber 1975b, p. 94.
21. Julien Freund, *The Sociology of Max Weber*, p. 25 (emphasis added).

Yet no less a thinker than Merleau-Ponty has written persuasively on Weber's behalf, supporting his technique of dedicated qualifying, that desire to maintain shades of gray throughout analyses. In "The Crisis of the Understanding," Merleau-Ponty seconds Weber's cognizance of *Vielseitigkeit* ("the ambiguity of historical fact") and the related demands of subtlety.[22] Yet the essay leaves one feeling that his defender could have abetted Weber more effectively by extending or consolidating his analyses than by forcing a disparate selection of his ideas through an existentialist-phenomenological sieve. Nevertheless, Merleau-Ponty, with Jaspers, is among the very few important philosophers who have even begun assimilating Weber.

The fact, then, that so many nineteenth-century philosophers and social theorists exiled from discussion any rigorous concern for the relationship of rationality and irrationality reduces the interest of their work to the historical, particularly concerning the "tension" springing from the unresolved place of rationality in social action. By contrast, French thinkers maintain their role as inventors of modern social thought because they minimized the gap between theory and practice, which keeps them alive for pragmatic cultures, and because they skirted irrationality with a simplistic rationalist psychology. Serious consideration of what we know as the "darker sides" of personality would have crushed their ingrained optimism.

Yet although Weber was unable or unwilling to settle this theoretical difficulty[23] (attacked most tellingly by the advanced Left, e.g., Lukács in *History and Class Consciousness*), the very object of his scholarly study and personal concern—the modern citizen (*Bürger*) in his struggle for a "reasonable" life in late imperialist Europe—was forced by constraining necessity to accomplish this task

---

22. Maurice Merleau-Ponty, *The Primacy of Perception*, pp. 201ff.
23. Some do not consider these unresolved tensions in social theory to be virtues. Benedetto Croce (a "hero," in Hughes's *Consciousness and Society*, second only to Weber) writes of "the decline of the historical concept—the transition from history to sociology—from philosophy to empirical science. It is well worth meditating upon the fact that such a decline could occur in a country with a cultural tradition such as that of Germany. . . . These theorists [Dilthey, Weber, Troeltsch, etc.] formulated dualisms, insoluble and unsolved paradoxes. . . . They cling to these paradoxes as 'compromises' and multiply entities endlessly" (from Croce's foreword to Carlo Antoni, *From History to Sociology*, p. iii).

in everyday life.[24] Thus tension—for the theorist—translates into dualities of fact and value, theory and practice, that remain the most aggravating of many conceptual tangles in Western non-Marxist social theory.

I cannot, however, concur with Croce's verdict (see footnote 23, above) that these "insoluble and unsolved paradoxes" are entertained out of theoretical desperation, confusion, or sloth. The problems associated with twentieth-century social theory, if they are to be understood, demand finer perception, such as this:

> In evaluating the permanent significance of the generation of the 1890s, we need constantly to bear in mind the central paradox of their achievement: more often than not, their work encouraged an anti-intellectualism to which the vast majority of them were intensely hostile. Some of these thinkers never quite realized the implications of their own theories: they clung tenaciously to a set of philosophical presuppositions that their thought had long ago outgrown. A second group welcomed the advent of the irrational and sought to ground in "intuition" the social philosophy of the future. Finally there were a few thinkers—and I believe these were the greatest—who while fighting every step of the way to salvage as much as possible of the rationalist heritage decisively shifted the axis of that tradition to make room for the new definition of man as something more (or less) than a logically calculating animal.[25]

Hughes's intellectual Puritanism of the heroic mold is apparent, but the idea is a crucial one, nonetheless, and helps balance Croce's attack on early German sociology.

Hughes intimates that modern theory is inherently problematic, even for adept thinkers. Croce's remarks, satisfying as they may be to those exhausted by reflex equivocating, do not allow for the

24. This cultural coercion, which always demands the delicate but definite blending in life of rational with irrational tendencies (the constant struggle to rationalize the irrational), has been repeatedly commented on in the modern West. Kierkegaard and Schopenhauer reflected on this process, and so, of course, did Nietzsche, at great length. The latter two influenced Weber considerably, as we know from his heavily annotated copy of Georg Simmel's *Schopenhauer und Nietzsche*, kept at the Max Weber Institute in Munich. In addition, many studies by Germans delineate the kinship between Weber's thought and that of Nietzsche, notably as expressed in some of Weber's private letters discussing "philosophical" topics he considered inappropriate to his scholarly work. For a list of these works, see Arthur Mitzman, *Sociology and Estrangement*, p. 7n. Recently, after a generation-long lapse of interest, especially in the United States, Marcuse, Norman Brown, and others, with decidedly different approaches, have reincorporated this fascination with tension and irrationality (for Marcuse, "repressive desublimation") into social theory.

25. Hughes, *Consciousness and Society*, p. 17.

moralistically framed milieux in which early theorists worked—as if they could have resolved paradoxes, but chose not to. This ignores the world-historical situation at the beginning of the century, which did not provide an intellectual or political setting in which one might confidently draft robust theories in the style, say, of Spencer. Perhaps Weber felt the fin de siècle more than Croce, having adapted, if only theoretically, to a level of ambiguity, tension, and paradox that the neo-idealist found intolerable. Croce *may* not, in himself, be important to a critique of social theory, but his viewpoint is sharp, and hardly idiosyncratic. He speaks for the *Bürger* who *must* act and integrate abundant rationalities with the equally abundant irrationalities (structural and psychological) that marked recent history. Thus we see, oddly enough, the aesthetician/idealist philosopher railing against our empirically grounded, value-free social scientist, all in the interest of pragmatic vision.

The source, then, of this problematic lies in ambivalent theory about social reality which cannot itself be negotiated by worried, tentative action, but only by exactly its opposite, precise, "dogmatic" moves that humiliate rationalist, objectivist, and relativistic theories alike. That is, a fit is lacking between the mandatory clarity of behavior amid life's "constraining immediacy," and theories designed to interpret it, since, by its very nature, ambiguity can hardly be a part of action. It may be party to the cognitive and imaginative rehearsal preceding behavior, or its post facto explanation, but that is another matter, and one that falls beyond normal "positivist" study.

Thus, when broadly considering behavior, both objective social scientist and cultural relativist (who may be the same) are equally alien to daily intercourse because of their limiting concepts. They leave the field to Marxists with their improbable claims for a resolution, through historical action, of "paradox," "ambiguity," and "irrationality" in social existence *and* in theories designed to explain them.[26] This disparity between life-as-lived and the strictures

26. The attack was first mounted by Georg Lukács in *History and Class Consciousness* in 1922 with his discussion of "reification" (pp. 83–222). The translation of the book has stimulated younger American and British Marxists, along with "critical theorists," to imitate their European colleagues in attacking "bourgeois sociology" from a variety of angles, e.g., for its "methodological intractability . . . as with Max Weber" (ibid., p. 154). A spirited example is Jean Cohen's "Max Weber and the Dy-

of research and theorizing is the beginning of the subjectivist-objectivist controversy that has consumed so many scholarly hours. (It is known sociologically as the phenomenological/ethnomethodological versus behaviorist or systems-theory "dialogue," although everyone involved claims the "objectivist" title.) Perhaps it rests in some nonrational substratum of common human experience. But we progress too quickly.

Current Social Theory and Irrationality

The noted Dilthey expert H. A. Hodges has written a lucid, stimulating essay, "Lukács on Irrationalism,"[27] responding to Lukács's treatment of Dilthey and Mannheim in *Die Zerstörung der Vernunft*, a boisterous Marxist interpretation of "irrationalists" since Hegel. Hodges claims it severely distorts the evidence because of Lukács's unbending attack on thinking, which Hodges feels obscures or diminishes the liberating potential of "reason" as a Marxist concept. In one section of this essay, Hodges provides a summary of how irrationality and rationality interrelate in broad terms. He claims no originality for this, but his statement does possess a conciseness and an intellectual detachment that many others lack. It transmits rather well, on one level, my own opinion, and suggests one reason for this study. Let us allow it to serve as a point of departure in pursuing the vexing rationality-irrationality conundrum as far as possible.[28]

---

namics of Rationalized Domination," pp. 63–86, in which the "objectivity-as-bunk" argument, made famous by Herbert Marcuse (*Negations*, pp. 203ff.) and carried on among mainstream sociologists for more than a decade, is elaborated from a Marxist position. I find Cohen's argument strident but inaccurate, since to make her points she must distort Weber far more than Lukács did in his many theoretical writings. Perhaps his early, amiable personal relation with the Webers (cf. memoirs by Marianne Weber, Paul Honigsheim, and others, which describe Weber's esteem for the younger man) tempered (and made more "objective"?) Lukács's criticism of Weber's method and theories. This close, mutually sustaining intellectual friendship is well documented in *Georg Lukács: Selected Correspondence 1902–1920*, ed. J. Marcus and Z. Tar, which contains fourteen letters from Weber to Lukács between July 1912 and March 1920, and four in exchange from Lukács, including one to Marianne after Weber's death that is surely one of the most moving statements of its kind (p. 283).

27. In G. H. R. Parkinson, ed., *Georg Lukács*.

28. For the time being I will offer a few of the disparate notions, analyses, and uses made of the terms under consideration, reserving for later a more complete presentation—my own "typological reduction"—of the phenomena as they re-

Hodges's remarks are especially pertinent to my work, historically speaking, since Dilthey heavily influenced Weber, and because Mannheim knew Weber; in fact, Mannheim's most exciting notions in *Ideology and Utopia* were reactions to Weber's axiology and methodology. Through his works on Dilthey,[29] Hodges was intimately aware of the complex *Methodenstreit* and its effect on Weber, plus the subsequent growth of what are often labeled as more sophisticated methods. Much of what follows in my study could be interpreted as elaboration of Hodges's observations:

> There really is an irrationalist trend in nineteenth and twentieth century philosophy. [Hodges' understanding of "philosophy" is easily broad enough to include social theory.] It is not the only important trend in philosophy during this period . . . but it is real and deserving of serious study. It is also true that many of the doctrines advanced by writers belonging to this trend have had an unsettling effect upon the mind of the general public, in so far as it has come to know of them. It is not only Marxists who have seen in Nietzsche a dangerous thinker, as we are familiar with complaints so often brought in this country against the analytical philosophy which is associated with Oxford. Its doctrines could hardly be more different from those of German *Lebensphilosophie*, but the charge brought against them is the same: disintegration of the world-picture and a sense of meaninglessness of things.
>
> Unpleasing as this trend is to many people, it may yet be that it points to truths which need to be explored. Philosophy in the eighteenth century and earlier had tended to overemphasize the powers and achievements of reason, and the nineteenth and twentieth centuries have seen, perhaps, a necessary and healthy reaction against this lack of balance. There are many nonrational factors at work in human experience and activity—in aesthetic perception and imagination, in moral judgement, in political and religious belief and commitment, even in scientific and philosophical thinking itself. Rationalists may not like this, Marxists may suspect the motives of any who mention it, but it is true. Non-rational factors can in fact be detected in Marxism itself. Nay, the word "reason" or "rational" itself is often used emotively, as a cheer-word, and a careful examination of the ways in which it is applied might be disconcerting. At any rate not all would agree that devotion to the Marxist dialectic is a criterion of rationality.
>
> It has been given to our age to explore this aspect of human life more deeply and fully than was ever done before, and the result is indeed unsettling. But it is also laid upon us to face the music hon-

---

spond with and against social structure, and of suitable analytic tools in extending Weber, Pareto, and others.

29. H. A. Hodges, *The Philosophy of Wilhelm Dilthey;* idem, *Wilhelm Dilthey.*

estly, and to find a way to go on being human without yielding to a Leader or a Party, or a doctrine which is set above criticism.[30]

This position harmonizes with that of Vilfredo Pareto, who will serve hereafter as theoretical foil to Weber concerning irrationality in social life. Hodges's remarks, perhaps the product of a new age of scholarly self-consciousness among those who handle these unsavory matters, are much more refined than Pareto's, to the point of being indecisive. One need not go back even to 1916, when Pareto's *Trattato di sociologia generale* appeared, to find comments on nonrational behavior more robust and, by today's standards, more reckless than those of Hodges. Howard P. Becker's typology of values and social action, which blended Mead, Znaniecki, Thomas, and Weber, marks a theoretical highpoint for American sociology germane to this issue, and the last time a sustained interest was shown in the subject.[31] Becker meant to do more than frame irrationality in comprehensible terms, yet in the course of the book, he deals with it more skillfully than later writers. Reading his work today, however, is strange. His words are simple and direct, the illustrations literary or "homey," and the attempted grasp simultaneously broad and pragmatic. This absence of scholarly jargon may partly account for his work having been forgotten. It is unfortunate that Becker's theory of values is ignored and that his action (or "interaction") theory has been obliterated by that of Parsons; how ironic, though, that Becker's synthetic theorizing omitted Pareto while Parsons gave him pride of place.[32]

Hodges's reflections, perhaps through the influence of such writers as Morris Ginsberg, Peter Winch, Steven Lukes, and others on the English intellectual scene, are much less likely to incur surprise, acrimony, or boredom among European than American theorists.[33] An explanation for this blind spot is not easily provided. As

---

30. Hodges, "Lukács on Irrationalism," pp. 96–97.

31. Howard P. Becker, *Through Values to Social Interpretation*, pp. 22–35, analyzed in Roscoe Hinkle and Gisela Hinkle, *The Development of Modern Sociology*, p. 62.

32. Parsons, *Structure of Social Action*, pp. 178–300. The term *interaction theory* was coined by Charles H. Page, in the Introduction to Hinkle and Hinkle, *Development of Modern Sociology*, p. iv.

33. Morris Ginsberg, *The Psychology of Society*, pp. 29–38; idem, *Essays in Sociology and Social Philosophy*, pp. 271–314; Peter Winch, *The Idea of a Social Science*, pp. 95–120; Steven Lukes, "Some Problems about Rationality," in *Rationality*, ed. Bryan Wilson, pp. 194–213; John Torrance, "Rationality and the Structural Analysis

far back as 1879, William James dealt ingeniously with "The Sentiment of Rationality," and in 1937 Parsons wrote at length about what
had become a well-worn path through "philosophical" debate: the
place of reason in individual and collective behavior. In fact, non-
Marxist responses to fascism often stressed mass behavior as prone
to irrationality and manipulated by political formulae.[34]

Parsons's characterization of irrational, or, to use as he did Pareto's term, "nonlogical," action is interesting in its omissions. Although his interpretation of Pareto is more scrupulous and detailed
than many since, he sidesteps with the term *residual category* just
those aspects of his thought that are most pertinent here:

> Every system, including both its theoretical propositions, and its
> main relevant empirical insights, may be visualized as an illumi-
> nated spot enveloped by darkness. The logical name for the dark-
> ness is, in general, "residual categories." . . . The surest symptom of
> impending change in a theoretical system is increasing general inter-
> est in residual categories. . . . The utilitarian brand of positivistic
> thought . . . has focused upon a given range of definite empirical in-
> sights . . . the central fact of which—a fact beyond all question—is
> that in certain aspects and to certain degrees, and under certain con-
> ditions, *human action is rational.*[35]

Another fact "beyond all question" is that Parsons's broad, carefully plotted restrictions to his final clause are being ignored by
many sociologists today, as is reflected in the predominant view of
how sociology ought to be done. His impact in this regard *has*
been, despite his best early efforts to the contrary, to reinforce
schematic, unbending positivism, by which is meant, in part, pursuit of ever "harder" data, preferably of the interval-level type.
That positivism is undergirded by a psychology the unquestioned
a priori of which is a model of action exaggerating the rational.

---

of Myth"; I. C. Jarvie and J. Agassi, "The Problem of Rationality in Magic"; Martin
Hollis, "The Limits of Irrationality"; and, more recently, Thomas Luckmann, "On
the Rationality of Institutions in Modern Life." The discussion of rationality in
social processes, social research, and so on continues in Britain—witness S. I.
Benn and G. W. Mortimore, eds., *Rationality and Social Sciences*—and on the Conti-
nent—judging from the contributors to Anthony Giddens, ed., *Positivism and Sociology*—whereas in the United States it is rare to find an article on the subject in an
important journal.

34. Compare Franz Alexander's *Our Age of Unreason* with the leading Marxist
study, Franz Neumann's *Behemoth*, esp. p. 96.

35. Parsons, *Structure of Social Action*, pp. 17, 18, 19 (emphasis added).

This sort of social theory and the research it spawns speak "power-fully" only for behavior of "certain aspects, to certain degrees and under certain conditions."[36] My point of contention is precisely that *all* human behavior—except perhaps the most resolutely aso-cial and private, such as fantasies and reveries—should be exam-inable and explicable by sociological theories, and not merely "cer-tain" narrow and, I will continue to argue, relatively meaningless types.[37] Whether this counterproposal will become of increasing general interest in the direction I favor—a study of the "darkness" beyond the small "illuminated spot"—is left to the future. Aberra-tions in the last decades (preeminently ethnomethodology and phe-nomenology, at times apparently unbeknownst to themselves)[38]

36. Parsons's implicitly cautious claim for social science (that it must relinquish the great mass of phenomena to darkened "residual categories" and accept the humble task of explaining minor portions of social reality) is partly attributable to the intellectual and political *Zeitgeist* in the mid-1930s when he wrote. In 1930 Heisenberg's *The Physical Principles of Quantum Theory* appeared. Immediately the "metaphoricality" of the "uncertainty principle" (and Einstein's famous moral objection to quantum theory, "God does not play dice") suffused the academy, diluting those remnants of nineteenth-century "scientism" which had survived relativity theory and other cultural-political shocks of the early twentieth century. Parsons's position, given his lifelong enthusiasm for interdisciplinary study and model-building borrowed in form from economics and physical science, probably partly reflects his colleagues' newfound theoretical trepidation, inspired not only by scholastic discoveries but also by the world-historical uneasiness of the Depression era. But, to contradict Madame de Staël, in this case to understand is not to forgive. I sense in Parsons's writing of this period (and even more so in that of his associates later on, for example, Homans's), a *false* theoretical humility before the empirical facts of social life. I hope to demonstrate that it is time—*because* of the very nature of contemporary social structure—to become bolder. (The ideological, psychological, and intellectual sources of this "humbleness," definitively analyzed, I leave to an expansion on Robert Friedrichs's *A Sociology of Sociology* and Alvin Gouldner's *The Coming Crisis of Western Sociology*.) Details on the uncertainty principle appear in Werner Heisenberg's popularization, *Physics and Philosophy*, pp. 76–92, and in F. S. C. Northrop's Introduction to the book.
37. "There is indeed something to the often heard criticism that what is known with reasonable certainty in the social sciences is not interesting and what is in-teresting not known with reasonable certainty" (*W. Dilthey*, trans. H. P. Rick-man, p. 6).
38. In an article first published in 1960 that is remarkably puzzling, given his current reputation, Harold Garfinkel claims that "because sociologists find with such overwhelming frequency that effective, persistent, and stable actions and so-cial structures occur despite obvious discrepancies between the lay person's and the ideal scientist's knowledge and procedures, they have found that the rational prop-erties which their definitions discriminated are empirically uninteresting. They have preferred instead to study the features and conditions of non-rationality in hu-man conduct. The result is that in most of the available theories of social action and social structure rational actions are assigned residual status" ("The Rational Proper-ties of Scientific and Common-Sense Activities," reprinted in Giddens, *Positivism*

have indicated that the rationalist mythos may be losing its intellectual grip on American sociology.

In Parsons's terms, the aim of the present study is to expand the explanations we can give for types of actions, thought, motivation—meaning-giving experience—which have long been thought of as "residual." They were (1) expelled from discussion and study by Weber as he overturned Dilthey's methods, (2) treated only obliquely by Parsons,[39] and (3) dealt with by Pareto at length, yet unconvincingly, according to the canons of proof and argument respected today.

Parsons's influence on American theory has been decisive, both positively and negatively. Many, like Mills, decided after reading *The Social System* to avoid large-scale theorizing, whereas others fol-

---

and Sociology, pp. 53–54). Garfinkel's claim seems nonsensical. The "theory of social action" that gave rise to an important style of small-group research and theory, varieties of systems and cybernetic theories, opportunity theory (used in the field of deviance), game theory, exchange theory—all are solidly founded in a positive concern for the ability and willingness of the subjects involved to behave rationally. In the rest of the article Garfinkel outlines Schutz's categories of action, which he termed *rationalities*. To cite Schutz as a theorist concerned with rational action against so many others, unnamed, who putatively champion nonrationality in their theoretical perspectives seems to have very little justification at this point in the development of American social thought.

39. Throughout his work Parsons is more interested in and capable of explaining the "cognitive" and "evaluative" modes rather than the "cathectic"—terms which clearly spring from an extension and decisive "psychologizing" of Weber. Note the apparent congruence between Weber and Parsons in their scholarly approach to the irrational, and, one suspects, in their mutual intellectual and emotional discomfort at being confronted by examples of behavior which do not conform to rational models. Parsons's (and most functionalists') examination of art is pedestrian, in marked contrast to his shrewd study of formal, rigid, and "rational" behavior and structure. Likewise, Parsons's discussion of sexuality and its role in social interaction is limited to the bounds of rearranged Freudianism. Weber, for one, often remarked upon the imperviousness of the aesthetic and sexual (or "erotic," as he put it) to scientific categorization.

Robert Friedrichs claims that mere "aesthetic predilections" have much to say about how theories are created, and which of them are then absorbed (or rejected) by their intended audience. The "aesthetics of social theory" of Parsons's students are clearly constructed to exclude from study the aesthetics proper of art and culture, along with sexuality. (Cf. Friedrichs, *Sociology of Sociology*, p. 3.) By employing this "ascetic approach to his methodology" (Hans-Georg Gadamer, *Truth and Method*, p. 462, regarding Weber), Parsons aligns with Weber on scholarly/analytical and psychological grounds, intentionally or by happy accident. See Parsons, *Structure of Social Action*, chapter 16, p. 677, and chapter 19; idem, *The Social System*, pp. 408ff., and chapter 9 for a lame account of the aesthetic sphere; Talcott Parsons and Edward Shils, eds., *Toward a General Theory of Action*, chapter 3. Parsons loosens up a bit in the essays of *Social Structure and Personality* on Freud, but he was no longer actively interpreting the classics for American sociologists in the singular way he had thirty years before.

lowed Parsons's lead. But did his work itself give shape, tone, and intentions to our theories, or, rather, did it conform to existing expectations of what theory should take in? Znaniecki, Sorokin, Mannheim, and others have all contributed toward understanding the relation of irrationality and meaning sociologically.[40] Yet none is remembered or taken seriously today in this context, perhaps for two different reasons, each of which compounds the consequences of the other.

First, these writers to a man were virtuosi of linguistic or terminological "expansion," were all multilingual, and assumed from readers a willingness to follow involved conceptual distillations without numerical apparatus. Naturally, as the professional cynosure of American sociologists began to include more statistical than verbal competence, the appeal of these theorists waned. Second, Parsons had strongly urged, by his own example, that studying the nether world of human behavior be off limits, a decision anticipated by Weber, of course; or he has reserved it for some form of Freudianism. Parsons's intellectual and analytical choice is readily justifiable by the canons of the very positivism he hoped to transcend in his first book, and which to some degree he did. Yet Parsons could not resist the tug—of what is theoretically feasible or interesting—from classical economics, and it continues to bind the study of social relations in the same cognitive straitjacket that some contemporary economists are struggling to remove from their own discipline.[41] In addition, American theory faces the dilemma of grossly disproportionate social scientific and historical-cultural knowledge, the strife between old theorists and modern "users": a problem to be pursued in Chapter 2 and most properly confined to the realm of hermeneutics.

Social Thought, Politics, and Irrationality

It is almost as if Parsons were carrying on with European sources a venerable American theoretical tradition, one more recently noted

---

40. Florian Znaniecki, *Cultural Reality*, e.g., pp. 45ff., 53–55, 64ff.; Pitirim Sorokin, *Social and Cultural Dynamics*, 4: 12ff. on meaning, pp. 98–102; idem, *Ways and Power of Love*; Karl Mannheim, esp. *Man and Society in an Age of Reconstruction*, e.g., pp. 39–78; Ferdinand Tönnies, *Community and Society*, pp. 103–170—his analysis of "natural" versus "rational will" still merits study yet finds almost no audience.

41. E.g., Maurice Godelier's *Rationality and Irrationality in Economics* or Martin Hollis and Edward J. Nell's *Rational Economic Man*, two from the crop of critiques

by Morris Janowitz in an article on another lapsed concept, *social control:* "In fact, social control was one intellectual device for linking sociological analysis to the human values and philosophical orientations employed by some pioneer sociologists interested in 'social progress' and the *reduction of irrationality* in social behavior."[42] It seems possible that Parsons was as much following precedent in rejecting irrational processes for study as setting a new course for theory and research, as Friedrichs has claimed.[43] (Clearly, though, my theoretical interest is hardly synonymous with Parsons's, for he had other tasks besides investigating irrationality.)[44]

Even Mills, from a contrary position and with other goals, established "reason and freedom" as the ultimate good, whereas "unreason" (or what Peter Clecak calls "social irrationalities")[45] was to be extirpated from theory and politics—with luck, simultaneously. (This sentiment, as suggested above, is quite common in the British sociological tradition, culminating in the essays of writers like Morris Ginsberg who overtly associated "unreason" with fascism.) Irving Horowitz's remarks about Mills are telling in this context:

> The impulse to return sociology to the public from whence it emanated [a dubious assertion], to deprofessionalize it in fact, had as its basis Mills' recognition that in his natural state, *man is essentially irrational,* a creature who responds to impulses, political slogans, status symbols, etc. And sociology could provide that means by which man casts off an egoistic, sectarian, and mythic pride and grows to maturity. Sociology helps men "know where they stand, where they may be going and what—if anything—they can do about the present as history and the future as responsibility." Mills boldly employed the "neo-Machiavellians," the great sociologists of the Franco-Italian tradition, as no other American sociologist before him. The work of Mosca, Pareto, Michels, and Sorel deeply influenced his thinking on questions, not because they demonstrated that men are oftentimes irrational in their behavioral patterns. This he knew without them. What they did was to offer sociology what Freud and his circle offered psychology—a *rational explanation for irrational behavior.*[46]

---

that question the neoclassical model; and Harvey Lieberstein, *Beyond Economic Man,* pp. 72–99 on "selective rationality."

42. Morris Janowitz, "Social Theory and Social Control," p. 82 (emphasis added).

43. Friedrichs, *Sociology of Sociology,* pp. 11–22.

44. The most detailed yet uneven work on this subject is Gouldner, *Coming Crisis of Western Sociology,* pp. 167–338.

45. Peter Clecak, *Radical Paradoxes,* pp. 42ff.

46. From Irving Horowitz's Introduction to C. Wright Mills, *Power, Politics, and People,* p. 16 (emphasis added).

These are indeed interesting remarks, regardless of their simplifications. They well represent one of the strongest traditions in modern social theory vis-à-vis that congeries of notions, however sloppily defined, identified with irrationality. The wish to save humanity from itself, from its most "natural" predisposition, through the application of reason and logical analysis finds its own basis of persuasion in a thoroughly moralistic and nonrational belief: that once the solution to a societal dilemma is apprehended rationally, "consensus" or at least compliance will surely follow among those concerned.

Support for this hope has been particularly pronounced among the Left, as Hodges's remarks indicate. Marx attacked with visceral scorn any component of social reality which seemed to him anachronistic, resistant to change, or otherwise unprogressive, or which did not suit his theory of revolutionary progress.[47] In labeling these opponents "irrational," he set a tone for leftist radicals that has modulated little in 145 years. This attitude, in a paradoxical turn of political-intellectual events, corresponds closely to that of the extreme Right and also to the "apolitical" stance of proponents of pervasive rationalization.

One contingent on the right, the "literary" wing, is more at home with irrational processes and outcomes than others on the current ideological scene. This is the legacy of its "Romantic-Conservative" heritage, the anti-Enlightenment writers of the early nineteenth century.[48] The study of irrationality is thereby put on the defensive, because nowadays academic inquiry is so often tied to social implementation or sanctioning unless the researcher claims special status by pursuing antiquarian subjects. It is assumed, subliminally, I think, that the social theorist worthy of high liberal regard must ignore the blandishments of the "woolly" aspects of personality. This is because, the argument continues, irrationality in behavioral, spiritual, or social structural form has always been championed and utilized by politically reactionary, intellectually repressive ideologues and leaders. At this point Mussolini's relationship with Gentile and his mythical allegiance to Pareto or Hitler's fondness for certain Wagnerian and Nietzschean motifs is brought forward to

---

47. This is especially clear in Marx's youthful response to Hegel, as in his "Contribution to the Critique of Hegel's Philosophy of Right."

48. Among those who use this distinction is Irving Zeitlin, *Ideology and the Development of Sociological Theory*, pp. 35–55.

finalize the charge that irrationality is ipso facto the property of reaction and therefore evil; only reason is good.[49] This train of argument becomes genuinely grotesque when all that is reasonable
(thus, good) is attached, through the organs of popular culture and
government insinuation, to the Anglo-American worldview and its
politics. Meanwhile Asian, African, Portuguese, or Cuban *Weltanschauungen*, along with others that exist "out there somewhere," by
implication become "other-than-reasonable," "less-than-good."
That this style of cultural chauvinism is *somewhat* more a staple of
mass culture than of academic articles does not necessarily lessen its
impact on rarefied scholarly work.[50]

Mills's intellectual populism seems to have developed in awareness of this culturally specific understanding of the role of reason
in sociopolitical affairs. Gerth and Mills claimed that Weber's emphasis on *zweckrational* action was part of his intellectual flight from
Hegel and his conservative followers, a flight which I think is more
real to his commentators than it was to Weber.[51] They elaborate:

> Weber sees in the concept of "personality" a much abused notion
> referring to a *profoundly irrational center* of creativity, a center before
> which analytical inquiry comes to a halt. And he combats this poeti-
> cized and romantic element. For his conceptual nominalism and his
> pragmatic outlook are opposed to all reification of "unanalyzed"
> processes. The ultimate unit of analysis for him is the understand-
> able motivations of the single individual. His concepts are analytical
> tools with which he reconstructs various mechanisms. They are not
> descriptive categories, with which one tries to "taste" the color and
> grasp the surface image of the "spirit of the times." They are not
> concepts that contemplate the supposed substantives of great men
> and epochs. In fact, despite Weber's emphasis on charisma, he is not
> likely to focus on "the great figures of history."[52]

49. Some theorists *do* penetrate this veil of hope, but their works are typically
not well known. E.g., Gustav Ichheiser: "I also suggest we stop lamenting and de-
nouncing the 'irrational factors' in personality and society. These so-called 'irrational factors' are in the very core of our personality and many sacred meanings
and values of life are rooted in them. A society without irrational beliefs is an unknown entity and in practical terms a complete impossibility" (*Appearances and Realities*, p. 130).

50. Note Heidegger's brief but confusing relations with National Socialism in the
early 1930s; or, from the opposite pole, the bombast of those in the cabinets of presi-
dents Kennedy and Johnson regarding their decisions "on behalf of" the Third
World in the early to mid-1960s. For detailed explanations of how the myth of core
rationality and peripheral irrationality affects scholarship and international political
economics, see Harland Prechel and Alan Sica, "Demonstrating Dependency."

51. Bendix agrees on this: *Max Weber*, pp. 387, 487ff.

52. Weber 1946, p. 55 (emphasis added).

Gerth and Mills chose not to admit what they surely realized, that reification of concepts is by definition necessary to *any* form of conceptual analysis, as Weber repeatedly pointed out whenever discussing the problem of concept formation; and that *this* form of reification, not that of processes, unanalyzed or not, was what seemed to Weber the major obstacle to the progress of social knowledge.

This rather stiff and objectivist reading of Weber, presented to receptive American readers in 1946, might be called Althusserian or hard-nosed. Althusser tried to ossify Marxism into a "science" of structuralist qualities by minimizing *alienation*, the organizing idea of the early writings, and accentuating the "real" economistic, older Marx. Similarly, Gerth and Mills delivered to American sociology a sanitized Weber, confidently pragmatic, nominalist, and ontologically naive, as is indicated by most of the selections in *From Max Weber*. This image stands in contrary relation to that of the worried social theorist made familiar by Marianne Weber, Karl Jaspers, Paul Honigsheim, and others already mentioned. The "mushy" Marx of 1844 has not been effectively erased by Althusser and other *Capital* devotees, yet the Weber who wrote perceptively on the "aesthetic," "erotic," and "personal" has been obscured by codifiers dedicated to unambiguous precision.

Gerth and Mills's notion about Weber's "attachment to Western positivist thought" is simply wrong if *positivism* is taken in its standard meaning. As Parsons had shown ten years earlier and as compared with the works of any of the original positivists of nineteenth-century Europe, Weber's proclamations about method, as well as his working method itself (particularly his sponsorship of "ideal types" and other tools borrowed from the *Geisteswissenschaften* school), belie any attempt to make him sympathetic with the views of those such as Mach. In fact, Weber's grasp on reality contains more neo-Kantian (and some Hegelian) axioms, borrowed whole from the predominant German *Bildung* of the period, than any that could be called "nominalist" positivist. Had Weber been a positivist, he would of necessity also have been a relativist, and he was anything but.

Thus, while it is foolish to deny that Weber wished to remove from social science the baseless, emotionalistic rhetoric and pseudoscience of those like Treitschke, it is equally foolish to believe everything Weber wrote about methodology and the positivist quest for laws. Rather, one should look more directly at his substantive approach and applied conceptualizations, which are full of elements as truly philosophical and metaphysical as those in Hegel. One who presumably should know, Karl Jaspers—who psychoanalyzed Weber—has written about this:

> Max Weber was the greatest German of our age. . . . He was a man who actively fulfilled himself in a time of decline. Because, with exemplary clarity in word and action, he accepted this role—which he had not chosen—as his destiny, he was a *philosopher*. To be a philosopher is not at all times the same thing, but something original and new for every period. But all philosophers have one thing in common: they are what they know; every philosopher is the lucidity of an unconditional being. The being of other men, confused and unable to understand itself, can come to itself through him. This concrete philosophy is fully developed in Max Weber's work and only in his work; its medium is political judgement and scientific investigation. Similarly his life may be characterized as a philosophical response to the concrete situations that confronted him.
> If Max Weber was a politician, a scientist, and a philosopher, he was not the one *and* the other; rather, he was a whole man, who derived a vast vision of the world from the depth of his own being, which, indivisibly one, represents what a man can be: a seeker after truth. Both in his political thinking and in his scientific investigation he was above all a philosopher.[53]

Although Jaspers was Weber's friend, this is not hagiography but, rather, one of the wisest assessments we have of Weber, his "being," the most basic selfhood, as conveyed to the Heidelberg circle. And it certainly corrects the image of Weber as solely a positivist. Jaspers's Weber contrasts sharply with the version reflected in a composite of Bendix's, Parsons's, and Aron's studies. These writers were not incorrect to portray Weber the "scientist," but Weber was more than this. By speaking of his philosophical, uneasy side, Jaspers helps supplement an idealized Weber, freed from uncertainty over subjects resistant to positivist inquiry. This fuller vision of his being and aims is essential to the current study.

It is true that Weber at times supported nominalism and an "ascetic methodology": "For the purposes of a typological scientific analysis it is convenient to treat all irrational, affectually determined elements of behavior as factors of deviation from a conceptually pure type of rational action."[54] Today's American social

53. Karl Jaspers, "Max Weber as Politician, Scientist, and Philosopher," in *Three Essays*, pp. 189, 195.
54. Weber 1947/1964, p. 92. It is well known, however, that this epistemological or methodological position did not severely constrain Weber's empirical work. See

theorist or researcher feels comforted by this type of "conceptual nominalism," concurring with Weber's attachment to Western positivist thought as displayed in his scorn for philosophical or metaphysical elements in the social sciences.[55] And quite rightly. Over the last sixty years, through long introductions to heavily edited translations (by Gerth and Mills, Parsons, and many others),[56] Weber's prescription for fruitful social research has contributed as much as any other single factor to defining the perimeters of contemporary theory. The net effect of this preference—for the scientifically lucid, plain, and readily analyzable, in place of the more curious, macabre, implicitly undemocratic knowledge of modern "shamans"[57]—is to dilute social thought needlessly and to throw

---

Bendix, *Max Weber*, p. xxii.

55. Weber 1946, p. 59.

56. English translators of Weber's works include Henry A. Finch, Ephraim Fischoff, R. I. Frank, Bruce B. Frye, Hans Gerth, Jerome Gittleman, Edith Graber, A. M. Henderson, D. Hytch, Frank H. Knight, Donald Levine, Colin Loader, Christian Mackauer, Peter Markl, Don Martindale, J. P. Mayer, John Mikkelsen, C. Wright Mills, Benjamin Nelson, Gertrude Neuwirth, Guy Oakes, Talcott Parsons, Max Rheinstein, Johannes Riedel, Guenther Roth, Louis Schneider, H. P. Secher, Edward Shils, Keith Tribe, and Claus Wittich. Ascertaining the ultimate effect of the haphazard schedule of late-arriving, uneven translations on Weber's "image," and his pedagogical impact on American sociologists during the last sixty years, is a worthy project in itself, since an increasing proportion of social scientists lack the excellent German required to disentangle Weber's original; also, most European commentators—before *they* are translated—do use the German editions. In this, Weber is but another casualty of international scholarship and translation, which itself has been opened to analysis (e.g., George Steiner, *After Babel*, especially "The Hermeneutic Motion," pp. 296–413; Louis Kelly, *The True Interpreter*, esp. pp. 228–239).

57. Mannheim (*Man and Society*, pp. 44–49) points out that aristocratic societies value arcane knowledge, thought to emanate from aesthetic experiences, which by their nature are unsharable and undispersable. Democratic knowledges, known by symbols (often numerical), have been extracted from more comprehensive knowledge for mass communication. Mannheim thought this process was responsible for the shift from qualitative to quantitative assessment of social reality.

Some thinkers (e.g., Jung, Bergson, Hegelian sociologists, Freudian-Marxist radicals, phenomenologists) are frequently and foolishly discounted as sources of social knowledge, having become associated, correctly or not, with intellectual authoritarianism, cognitive obscurantism, and/or political totalitarianism. Such writers as Hayek, Popper, Shils, and Nisbet, in concert with political happenings since 1945, have given this negative "intellectual feeling" a rather secure place in American sociology. Social theorists are seldom read in the important American intellectual journals and opinion-makers, at least writing *as* theorists. For documentation, see Charles Kadushin's empirical breakdown of influential authors in *The American Intellectual Elite*. Daniel Bell heads the list, but Bell's audience is probably America's literary intellectuals, who can recognize in his essays enough of the humanist tradition, rather than social theorists. Kadushin's list includes few other social theorists, which is my point.

its practitioners into silence or equivocation when problems of modern sociopolitical existence arise, either in the public forum or as an outgrowth of officially sponsored research about the "quality of life."[58] Sociology and nonexperimental social psychology have not assumed their rightful places as interpreters of all social behavior that surfaces within modern societies. They remain fixed too securely to a scholastic vision, leaving interpretation of the most interesting (which often means nonrationalized) behavior to theologians, psychiatrists, and journalists, with anthropologists free to evaluate the even more fascinating cultural expressions of preindustrial cultures.[59]

The Politics of the Irrational

It is unfortunate that neither nineteenth-century theorists nor many today have taken to heart Schiller's admonitions about the fate of modern culture.[60] His conception in 1793 of a modern citizenry, still remarkably germane, is representative. He proposes that from the primary, physical being there be encouraged to evolve one who is attuned to moral-aesthetic discoveries, however attained or however catholic in content, so that the "truly social" creature, the

---

Those whose sociology apes the natural sciences do not find it disagreeable that American sociology "gets done" in professional journals, and only there. Sociology is not to be carried out for the benefit of the intelligent and politically animate upper middle class (or, as in Britain for many years, for the working class), for fear of academic degradation. This intellectualistic dodge helps guarantee sociology's impotence in public affairs.

58. Sociologists become nothing but technicians when they decide not to formulate judgments on desirable forms for contemporary living; if left to themselves, of course, the bureaucrats assemble these judgments without "expert" advice. See Richard A. Berk and Peter H. Rossi, "Doing Good or Worse," in *Evaluation Studies,* ed. Marcia Guttentag.

59. E.g., Clifford Geertz's celebrated essay on "deep play" in his *Interpretation of Cultures,* pp. 412–453.

60. Although Schiller has become an icon within Germanic culture, like Thomas Jefferson in America, he was forgotten by social theorists until very recently. Marcuse reintroduced Schillerian concepts without full citation in *Eros and Civilization* and has since shifted his theoretical ideas. Perhaps taking their cue from Marcuse, other writers have begun again to cite Schiller as the source of a growing rapprochement between theories of social organization and the "aesthetically informed" qualities of societies. Gadamer particularly emphasizes Schiller's work in *Truth and Method.* This represents a major thread in contemporary theorizing at the crossroads of hermeneutics, ethics, and social theory, plus aesthetics of a special sort, and will be discussed in the following chapter.

"moral person," may emerge.[61] Instead of this middle way between rationalism and obscurantism, theorists perpetuate a brittle, reformed positivism that very quickly, when applied in the social sciences, becomes tepidly liberal (from residues of earlier motives) or programmatically amoral. Contemporary theorists, then, have advanced a "rationalist" or "voluntarist nominalism."[62] Its limits are pronounced as an analytical framework *or* a professional ideology. One aim of this study is to expand these limits by including within analysis those behavioral characteristics that might enliven our models of social action, as they enliven otherwise tedious, "rationalized" lives.

It is also notable that the features of life with which political and theoretical conservatives often concern themselves—love, aesthetics, historicity, cultural terror, loneliness, death, and the like—are more interesting in our postmodern culture than what have come to be favorite subjects of the intellectual Left: the dissection of structures, power, domination, discrimination, irrationality, tradition, and the "bourgeois" arts.[63] The catchwords for conservatives, which sometimes are promoted to the status of concepts (organic unity, wholeness, continuity, tradition, stability, etc.), that provoke opposites in the radical vocabulary (plus still others: rational behavior, self-development or realization, alteration of consciousness, "men make their own history") all have their uses, to be sure, even as "cheer-words." But each set delineates, explicitly or otherwise, a philosophical anthropology and its *Weltanschauung*, which bars the insights of one group from the other. It is wisest to avoid

61. Many passages from Schiller's *The Aesthetic Education of Man* illustrate the point that blind rationalism cannot alone be responsible for the growth of a humanist society, e.g., "The intellectual enlightenment on which the refined ranks of society, not without justification, pride themselves, reveals on the whole an influence upon the disposition so little ennobling that it rather furnishes maxims to confirm depravity" (letter 5, p. 36).

62. Hinkle and Hinkle, *Development of Modern Sociology*, p. v.

63. I say "more interesting," but I also mean "less disheartening." The usual topics of radical research mentioned above have become so thoroughly knowable and demystified during the last two decades that despair results from contemplating them at length. After U.S. stratification, for example, is studied in detail, what more can be said but that inequality of every stripe persists, relatively unabated. With the collapse of 1960s tendencies, little room is left for hope that "more equality" (as Gans put it) is in the offing. As Theodor Adorno quipped, "Reality is no longer to be construed, because it would be all too thoroughly construable" (*Negative Dialectics*, p. 23).

the partisanship of either camp while exploiting the richness of both: the structural concerns of the radicals, the fidelity to a credible personality theory of their adversaries. Radicals have developed the sharpest tools for sociological and cultural analysis, but conservatives keep for themselves the most intriguing problems. In this as in other things, one can do worse than follow Weber's own path into eclecticism.

Irrationality in Social Action

The preceding has tried to show that *irrationality* as a concept or as the root of an ideology has not been greeted warmly by American or, indeed, Western social theorists for some time, no matter how presented. American sociology is unique in not sharing an intimate or official association with socialism, an association that would at least explain much of European sociology's distaste for investigating the irrational, in that their political affiliations demand rhetorical support for "reason." Among the last important American commentaries on the subject came around 1900 with William James's *The Varieties of Religious Experience* and essays written by his colleague George Santayana. But James's focus was on certain nonnormal states, which have become over the years, with the decline of religion as James knew it, increasingly arcane to theoretical interests.

I do not promote study of irrationality in human action and thought for its own sake, as some psychiatric theories that celebrate insanity apparently do. My primary motive is to broaden the competence of social theory and research concerning contemporary existence in industrial societies. On its face it seems absurd that one would hesitate to consult social theory in order to learn (1) why people often behave in ways other than predicted or expected "by reason"; (2) what factors in people's lives make, or fail to make, their existences important to them, that is, "meaningful"; or (3) what people might do to enhance their lives, the "eudaemonistic perspective" Weber rejected.[64] It is important to bring questions of this sort back into legitimacy as proper sociological problems—as they were among such men as Veblen, Mead, Park,

64. Marianne Weber, *Max Weber*, p. 217.

Small, Giddings, and Ward—to shore up weak theoretical ambition. Otherwise the discipline's future will darken even more than it recently has.

The clear-eyed "spirit of reason" dressed as inductive logic or method cannot account for enough of sociocultural reality to justify its use over and over again. I hope to find analytic concepts which are not in themselves alienated from the nature of *contemporary* humankind, a nature still apparently encumbered by demons of nonrationality.[65] Such concepts would help in theorizing about society with semi-scientific precision, yet without loss of heart. Social theory has swept irrationality in human life beneath the rug, and by Weber's explicit direction, yet partial answers to some of our most pressing and interesting problems reside in its study and explication.

This study, then, concerns itself with social action and meaningfulness as comprehended by modern social theory, with special emphasis on the classical origins of the current situation. It is commonly assumed that all behavior that is public (and therefore susceptible to study) is composed of both rational and irrational elements. As has repeatedly been noted, today's writers have followed Weber and others in slighting the irrational. This study examines the historical development of such "voluntarist nominalism" by hermeneutic analysis of Weber and Pareto, and by selective study of others who dealt in these matters, such as Mannheim, Mead, Becker, Habermas, and Adorno. Following this will come emendations to contemporary theory, with the ultimate goal of incorporating more of what is significant about the behavior of current humankind into models of personality and social action.

The substantive concept or problem that gives unity to the study is *das Irrationalitätsproblem*, as it was known in Weber's period, and its transformation over time. Connected with this is the existential *and* social question of meaning in life, as it is comprehended, formulated in context, and pursued by the subject (or social actor). Baldly stated, I propose two hypotheses. First, of historical interest, I argue that Pareto's understanding of human motivation and the search for meaning is more useful in some contexts than the

65. Youths most obviously manifest some sorts of nonrational behavior in their usual activities, but this reflects more, I believe, their *relative* lack of inhibitions than any decisive generational or age-specific quality linked to nonrationality per se.

version of Weber's underdeveloped view that has so saturated American sociology;[66] and furthermore, that Weber's more recently translated texts indicate that he disagreed with Pareto's position less than one might think based on his remarks regarding irrationality in *Wirtschaft und Gesellschaft*. Second, and more relevant to contemporary theorizing about industrialized societies: increasingly, rationality as a component of social action and as a valued quality of personality is becoming inversely related to meaning in human life; that is, *zweckrational* behavior and the major institutions it is usually thought to dominate no longer hold the appeal for social actors that they are believed to have held in an earlier period of Western development, especially among the middle classes.[67] In turn, those institutions previously deemed less vital to social order (e.g., the aesthetic, supernatural, or recreational) are being invested with much more personal energy—in the pursuit of meaningful experience—than is the case vis-à-vis so-called vital institutions (the economic, political-governmental, educational, stratificational, and so on).

Theory capable of portraying and analyzing life's meaning-structures (Husserl's "rich intersubjectivity") in addition to the even richer, socially engendered intrasubjectivity must begin with a more complete concern for personality, not merely for its rational component. Modern social structure, which other social sciences tend not to consider thoroughly, works with remarkable potency in determining personality, social behavior, and, particularly, the pursuit of meaning.[68] Social theory as presently pursued contains a miserly portion of all behavior, and it is not interpreting even the portion at the center of "human-ness" that gives vitality to the most prized features of self-presentation and intersubjective response. It is too often assumed that humankind's cosmically distinguishing characteristic is the use of reason, and whatever rational behavior flows from it. This antiquated image does not very well represent life as it is experienced. And to speak competently of life

66. For a provisional definition of *meaning,* see note 6, above.
67. For a sound and applicable treatment of American institutions and the broad types of behavior commonly ascribed to each, see Joyce Hertzler, *American Social Institutions;* also pertinent is Robin Williams, *American Society.*
68. If this seems a lame rehash of the message in Hans Gerth and C. Wright Mills, *Character and Social Structure,* it is because those advances have not been made that would render the book and its approach obsolete.

as a process, only partly subject to the willful manipulation of actors, whether individual or collective, should be the primary goal of theory.[69]

Social theory's initial project, in the last century, was enmeshed with the struggle to improve lives. For the most part, readily perceivable, material gains for those most wrenched by sudden industrialization were the center of concern. Many of those battles have since been won (and many of the rest may not be soon winnable) or have been transformed and psychologized out of awareness.[70] Now seems the time to revise and enrich the program, with attention to more elusive, and perhaps in the end more vital matters. This is what I wish to encourage. I start with Weber and Pareto because the confusion over and avoidance of irrationality as a theoretical problem in American theory began, I believe, with their different influences after the 1930s.

Addendum on Clarification of Concepts

Many current writers, especially in political, legal, and ethical theory (e.g., Robert E. Goodwin, *The Politics of Rational Man*, pp. 9–18, and John Rawls in his celebrated ethical treatise *A Theory of Justice*, pp. 408ff.), work at resolving the problem of irrationality. They assert that rationality is a subjectively disclosed and apprehended quality of action and thought, and any behavior, if assessed by the actor involved, is considered rational. Only the external observer's inability to analyze thoroughly enough another's actions leads to the appellation *irrational*.

69. Occasionally in American social science, someone will push for a radical widening of perspectives and aims. Ernest Becker did some of this in his works (most memorably in *The Structure of Evil*). Europeans who on their own ground are considered social theorists have for some time broadly understood the theorist's task and from them, more than from current American models, I receive my stimulus, e.g., Scheler on ethics, *ordo amoris*, sympathy, and so on; Ernst Bloch on hope; Horkheimer's definition of critical theory; plus a host of more current French writers from a number of fields who will be discussed presently. They have not proved very pertinent for my work in strictly theoretical terms, but as *approximate* models for ambitious, "synthetic" theorizing they serve well enough—perhaps because they seem to carry out the Weberian task in scope and depth, while their American colleagues as vigorously avoid broad sociological enterprises.

70. See Charles Anderson, *The Sociology of Survival*, for a catalogue of literature regarding nonsociological limits to societal development; and for problem-solving by redefinition, see Herbert Marcuse, *One-Dimensional Man*, and "The Affirmative

This is not, in my view, a legitimate resolution to the problem. This line of thought supposes, by logical extension, that when methodological techniques of observation and analysis become sufficiently developed all behavior will finally appear as it actually is, that is to say, rational. This position must be considered either as (1) a heuristic device or normative hope that facilitates debates over social ethics and political equality, or (2) a rationalistically inspired effort (perhaps of a Puritan legacy?) to rid the social world of "evil" (or inefficient) irrationality and demonic nonrationality. This same thinking is evident in a number of methodological manifestos, but with less of an evangelical tone.

This tendency assists in extracting from positivist-empiricist research whatever cogency and penetrative power it might otherwise claim. Again, it is not so much the techniques in themselves, with regard to irrationality, that deflate modern research (since the thought that irrational processes demand explanation does not figure in them). It is the general lack of scope that accomplishes this trivialization, and one small, but important, portion of this concerns *das Irrationalitätsproblem.*

The suggestion is occasionally made in overviews of American sociology that undue attention has for some time been given to nonrational aspects of behavior and that the discipline suffers for its attentiveness to these and not other behavioral characteristics. William J. Goode is but one example:

> Before World War I, sociology had carved out a set of distinct intellectual tasks and findings by focusing on the shared or group values and norms that molded human decisions and actions, in contrast with the focus on economics, and indeed much of social science, on individual seeking based on rational calculation. That break from the older, rationalistic, often positivistic and utilitarian social theory [Parsons' sentiments of 1937] was fruitful, even if it caused sociologists to overlook some of the truth in those quite ancient insights.
>
> Modern traditional sociology uncovered numerous regularities of considerable power. It emphasized groups and social systems rather than the individual; the influence of the nonrational (including religion) rather than the rational; the power of group norms and values rather than self-seeking profit; the commitment to norms and rules and the willingness to conform . . . sociology can now afford to turn

Character of Culture" in his *Negations*, pp. 88–133. Also cf. Richard Sennett's *The Fall of Public Man* and Christopher Lasch's *The Culture of Narcissism.*

back. . . . In theoretical terms we now need to explore . . . rational
and self-seeking calculations.[71]

In spite of immediate appearances, this view does not substantially
conflict with my own when I claim that American sociology does
not know or care much about irrationality and meaning in social
action. The "oversocialized conception of man" critique of the field
applies.

For modern (predominantly British) tastes, anthropological spec-
imens which came to be known between 1900 and 1925 seemed
"irrationally" bound by norms, *gemeinschaftlich* social control, and
"unscientific," mythical beliefs (Weber's "traditional behavior").
This may or may not have been a correct reading of pre-modern
cultures (since the matter of conscious, rational conformity for the
sake of inclusion in social life—ostracism being the ultimate negative sanction—was not so often studied as were hosts of amusing
"irrationalities," chronicled by Frazer and others). In any case, it is
no longer sensible to divide behavior broadly into the unthinkingly
norm-bound or religiously conditioned—the "nonrational"—and
the other—"rational," calculated action—which Goode thought
ought to become the focal point of study. The first type is historically defunct for my purposes. But *beyond* this dichotomy and
within behavior that can be considered rational (i.e., goal-directed
through efficient means) irrationality and meaning resolutely re-
appear and must be considered theoretically. In other words, the
equation "primitive mentality = nonrational behavior" along with
its conceptual opposite, "modernity = increased calculation," is
not the axis on which my study of irrationality turns. Irrational
components of *modern* behavior are at issue here. Thus, I am allowing that both traditional and *affektuell* action—in pure form—are
historically anachronistic, and not so currently prevalent as *wert-*
and *zweckrational* behavior. Yet the realm of the later two categories
contains irrational spurs to action and an intimate, necessary relation to meaning (part of which Weber knew of, but refused to
include, formally, in his theory and research). This fact renders
Goode's comments above true as far as they go (as well as Garfinkel's; see footnote 38, above), but for all that, not very important.

71. William J. Goode, "A Theory of Role Strain," pp. 97–98.

Thus it is not accurate to say that sociology has dedicated itself to studying irrationality, as I understand the term. Rather, it has studied what it thinks of as the doltlike, unthinkingly automatic behavior of the primitive or the "true believer" (in religion, politics, other forms of ritual, etc.), and from that light stuff seeks the reputation of having probed deeply into the nonrational. The very scholarly attitude that encourages "looking with a hard eye at the natives" runs counter to my task: to look with genuine perceptiveness upon the ultimate irrationality of those who wish most to appear rational—clearly a Paretian objective. This line of thought will surface repeatedly in the following pages, but I want to clear away at this point the claim that, contrary to my own opinion, sociology in America has been fascinated with the other side of the Millsian universe. A look at Dewey, Cooley, Mead, and Parsons quickly corrects this claim. Not only is it demeaning and condescending to the persons studied to make such an assertion—of their being "determined" like robots by norms that have perpetually escaped criticism—but such a position highlights more the student's own culture, and its demons, than that of the subjects being studied. We are reminded of Lévy-Bruhl's story of the Jesuits and the "savage" Iroquois who were unimpressed with the fundamental irrationality of Christian theology.[72]

72. Lucien Lévy-Bruhl, *Primitive Mentality*, pp. 21–22.

2

Toward a Hermeneutic of Weber

Limits of Contemporary Theorizing

Today's intellectuals are taught, some say trained, to plow a slim furrow, then urged to stay in it. This debilitates those hoping to understand and utilize Weber. The cause of this honed intellectual narrowness is obscure, but such an attitude fits with the encompassing awareness of axiological relativism that is pivotal to our era, yet difficult to abide. This skepticism about the ultimate truth-value of social knowledge has spawned the widespread "feeling" that knowledge is not so cumulative as it once was, or once was thought to be. We can recall wistfully when Dilthey built on Schleiermacher, Rickert on Dilthey, Weber on Rickert, then Parsons on Weber. Yet now the growth of knowledge is not so much artful ingestion and synthesis as selective forgetting and reapplication of what came before, often as prelude to facile transformation. Meanwhile the rate of rediscovery hastens,[1] even when managed only by fresh jargon.

1. As Thomas Kuhn, George Holton, and many others have explained, "cumulative knowledge" served as the idealized model of change in the physical sciences, but at the expense of understanding events as they occurred. "Paradigmatic breaks" are not based on even accumulations of information according to the revised history of physical science. But cumulative social thought is still possible, for the difference between physical and sociocultural sciences is decisive, although this distinction, belabored in the last century, has been undervalued by today's social scientists. *Geisteswissenschaften* study symbolic expressions of cultural groups, action that relates to them and by which it is reported, none of which is easily conveyed by what Znaniecki called mere "enumeration." Theorists' task, then, is to assimilate past theoretical and substantive contributions to the field in terms commensurate with the relevant documents. Merton (in, e.g., "On the History and Systematics of Sociological Theory" and *On the Shoulders of Giants*) has made this point, but it bears repeating. A small example appears in a letter to the editor of *Contemporary Sociology* by Jaroslav Moravec, giving an informed reading of Thomas Masaryk's classic, *Suicide and the Meaning of Civilization* (1881), in rebuttal to a review by Warren Breed of its reissue. The negative review was written without Moravec's knowledge of Masaryk's historical position and sociological achievement in context. "Special knowledge" such as this should surface more often to contradict received wisdom, which is frequently insensitive to anything but the boldest outlines of decontextualized argument and chronology.

For example, a recent Continental "discovery" amounts to a linguistic remodeling of Freud, who had already been widely denounced thirty years ago as an intellectual relic.

Knowledge is now distinct from *wisdom*, which, many believe, is no longer definable at all. Knowledge grows when a journal article reports results of highly specific research and refers lightly to an article of several years earlier that treated similar terrain or used like methods. In this intellectual climate, reference to work eighty years old that transcends a ritualized touching of bases seems antiquarian and dreamily remote from "advanced" practice. This cultural dilemma, expressed among academics as a worried refusal to think adventurously or to consider large problems—to confront rather than be bored by or ignore difficulties—has not left unaffected the scope of modern social thought. This trepidation, evident since World War II and the invention of computers, and by now too ingrained to arouse reflection, is founded in fear of baseless speculation. "Systems" of thought, it is supposed, are indefensible against the positivist requirement of publicly replicable proofs, often couched in probability theory.

Even beyond this set of inhibitions, subtler, more trying hurdles block those wishing to extend work of the past and promote genuinely cumulative social knowledge, not just glosses or counterfeit syntheses. These impediments must be examined as a prolegomenon to exegesis of Weber and Pareto, to set the limits of what can be expected from hermeneutic analysis.[2]

Since Weber's death in 1920, sociology in the United States, in tune to this extent with its sister disciplines, has lost a crucial share of the conceptual or moral-political unity its founders variously intended for it. Catholicity of knowledge and interests—now the cardinal point of contrast between early sociologists and their current descendants—has been traded for a dedication to narrow precision. The internal processes of such a mindset are not transparent; whether or not sociologists actually think in rigid dichotomies or

2. European social scientists often seem shackled by an outsized reverence for their classics. But if Americans examine past achievements at all, their commentaries on intellectual products composed in milieux alien to their own are marked by a breezy naiveté. This nonchalance may arise from the ahistoricity of American culture. It would seem that scholars on both sides of the Atlantic could learn from the others' expository skills and tastes.

use them in pursuit of small-scale research cannot easily be established. Yet time and again the discipline is characterized as existing within several polarities of theory and research: social organization versus social psychology; structure versus process; macro-structure versus personality's micro-events; and so on.

Though Weber labored strenuously in 500 pages of methodological essays—and, by example, in his monographs—to establish what he considered suitable limits of sociology,[3] I doubt whether he would quite understand why its range of subject matter has been so narrowly circumscribed, and often in his name. Weber's concepts and substantive contributions are today typically attached, or integrated with, only half of the sociological realm, the macro side: social structure, organization, collective change. This usage of Weber's ideas (to which Parsons's work stands in opposition) superficially represents his entire achievement. In fact, his macro, structural concerns were rooted in, often originated with, problems of theoretical explanation that are overtly micro or social-psychological. Weber's fascination with powerful sociocultural vectors *and* the individual's response to them set the tone of all his best sociological work. It is unjustified that "Weberian sociology" has come exclusively to mean macro or structural analysis.[4] "Rationalization" of the West cannot be simply equated with the growth of complex organizations or industrialization. It can as easily mean, as Weber so often pointed out, the rationalization of the "irrational," that is to say, the personal, unique, or unroutinized.

My principal theoretical concern is not with analyzing civilizational or cultural irrationality (an important stimulus for philosophically sensitive Marxists such as Lukács, Adorno, Horkheimer, Goldmann, Benjamin, and Marcuse). Such phenomena are usually thought of as structural in nature, reflected *in* irrational actors but not originating *with* them. More pertinent here is irrationality as it functions within the boundaries of what I will call "personal orga-

3. As late as 1904 he would mention sociology only in quotation marks; Jaspers quotes him: "Most of what goes by the name of sociology is a fraud" (Max Weber 1975b, pp. 63, 240, 251; Karl Jaspers, *Three Essays*, p. 191).
4. Randall Collins in *Weberian Sociological Theory* makes the latest and strongest statement about Weber of the macro-dimension. He divides his book into sections on economics, politics, culture, and sex; the index does not list *irrationality* and mentions *meaning* only twice. The book succeeds at what it sets out to do, but it leaves out most of the Weber that interests me.

nization," of values, motives, meaning, and so on.[5] Sociology expects pervasive interaction between these two realms, structure and personality, as Weber also recognized but his singular theoretical equal, Freud, failed to consider until late in his work. Before I can examine systematically Weber's perception of character and social structure, however, a preliminary catalogue of hurdles must be given. This begins with a discussion of textual interpretation or theory of reading—for present purposes, a theory of reading social theory.

Current Standards of Criticism as Applied to Weber

For a number of reasons, most readers of sociology no longer understand or adequately appreciate Weber's writings. I have found some support, post facto, for my own realization of this alarming claim.[6] This support is refreshing when contrasted with the opinion implicit in the endless "mainstream" articles and monographs depending on Weber. He personified the Faustian dilemma of modern intellectuality: demanding to know reality, driven to expose its

5. These terms, as I am aware, have fallen into disuse or misuse (and have been taken over by the media and debased) since the 1940s and 1950s, when they were given detailed analysis in social-psychological and social-structural research. It seems that their widespread, nonuniform use today has forfeited a great deal in precision and points to a need in sociology and social psychology for a generally accepted typology of human values, to include norms, ethics, ideologies, and so on.

6. Bryan Turner, Fredric Jameson, and Herbert Marcuse provide three of the starkest examples of a phenomenon which has become a regular part of Weber scholarship—astonishment at the difficulty of the sources. Turner wryly admits, "Unfortunately the longer one studies Weber's sociology, the more elusive, complex, and polychrome his sociology appears" (*Weber and Islam*, p. 1). This statement typifies the sentiments of scholars who do not begrudge the extreme effort needed to fathom Weber's meaning, holding that Weber's work, to the degree it is successfully interpreted, still bears forcefully upon current research. Herbert Marcuse's opinion (in "Industrialization and Capitalism in the Work of Max Weber," in his *Negations*, pp. 203ff.) was amplified by Fredric Jameson in a brilliant article about which more will be said: "the extraordinary intricacies attained by combinations between [*sic*] these various terms, particularly in late Weber where, as Herbert Marcuse has said, 'the method of formal definitions, classifications and typologies celebrates true orgies,' suggests that *to try to read Weber term by term*, to comprehend each semantic phenomenon in isolation, is an agonizing, and in the long run sterile, enterprise" (From "The Vanishing Mediator," p. 63; emphasis added). I agree with the adjective *agonizing* but not with its complement, *sterile*. I think it is perfectly clear that Weber must be comprehended as a scholarly, aesthetic-intellectual whole, and this must begin with meticulous, "term by term" analysis. Naturally, in so doing, "each semantic phenomenon" will *not* be considered "in isolation," which is precisely what occurs when the classics are "mined" for speedily utilized terms or phrases.

immanent mechanisms, yet hesitant to cast away the veil completely. Many of the forces Weber identified he was certain would destroy or reshape beyond recognition the *Geist* and achievements of the West. But it is at once more and less than this set of obstacles that hinders thorough understanding. Although these sorts of issues have some utility in assessing Weber's impact,[7] the major source of misreading, misunderstanding, and bowdlerization is less elevated; and the ease with which this barrier to interpretation is named does not make its elimination simple. When innovative ideas appear today, even if offered by eminent writers, they are assured of probing, even irreverent scrutiny by a large, eager group of professional readers. The better commentary evaluates the new argument in scientific or (Weber) "logical" terms and approaches its substantive consequences in like fashion. If this ideal is not always reached, its strength as a professional mos is not lessened. Yet behind it lies this unexamined assumption: *most* of the members of the guild are capable of criticizing a work, whether in review or as part of their own studies, no matter who wrote it or when. This anachronistic fiction has been welcomed into an academy no longer the intimate *Universität* of its origin. As Mannheim and others knew, the democratization of culture at large is not a uniform advance for human knowledge, nor for critical or interpretative proficiency.

Critical attention, then, is typically paid to whatever utility the claimed innovation may have for pure theory or research procedure, or, occasionally, to both. Several of Weber's works, none of them inconsequential, have only in the last decade been translated into English.[8] As I have already hinted, none of them—nor, I would

7. As is insisted by Arthur Mitzman, *The Iron Cage*, a psychohistory of Weber, and Martin Green, *The von Richthofen Sisters*, detailing the Else Jaffé affair.

8. Weber 1976, trans. R. I. Frank; Weber 1977, trans. Guy Oakes; Weber 1972, trans. Donald N. Levine; Weber 1975a, trans. Louis Schneider; "A Research Strategy for the Study of Occupational Careers and Mobility Patterns," trans. D. Hytch, in Weber 1971b, pp. 103–158; Weber 1973, trans. Jerome Gittleman; Weber 1971a, trans. Jerome Gittleman; Weber 1974, trans. Edward Shils; Weber 1975b, trans. Guy Oakes. Another translation of a section of *Knies und das Irrationalitaetsproblem* from Weber 1922a (3d ed. 1968, pp. 127–137) by Peter Markl and retitled "Subjectivity and Determinism" appeared in Anthony Giddens, ed., *Positivism and Sociology*, pp. 23–32. The essays that make up this book all speak to problems of method and substance which occupy the present study. Weber's article, not heretofore translated into English, leads the collection in discussing how one handles irrationality

argue, his previously translated works—is likely to be judged adequately,[9] or integrated properly into wider discourse, by any individual. The reasons for this are several.

First, no single reader knows enough economics, history, legal theory, philosophy, aesthetics, and epistemology, plus foreign languages, to pronounce definitively upon Weber's works in other than formal or logical terms.[10] That is, the construction of the argument may be attacked on its own terms (and even compared, cautiously, with later research), but not the *already synthesized* data that gave rise to it. Despite an ethic probably legitimated during collaborative efforts during World War II, when it was concluded that committees "think," the history of innovation demonstrates the obvious but forgotten truth that ideas invariably take useful form only in single minds.[11] As this truism repermeates the culture after having been obscured recently, even physical scientists are no longer expected to communicate or corroborate every detail of their creative experiences. Since committee appraisals of monographs

---

and intersubjective reality in social research. As one would expect, nearly all the contributors are European.

Other recent translations from Weber not yet assimilated into the secondary literature include Weber 1978a, trans. W. M. Davis; Weber 1979, trans. Keith Tribe; Weber 1980, trans. Keith Tribe; Weber 1981b, trans. Edith Graber; Weber 1984, trans. J. Mikkelsen and C. Schwarz; Weber 1985, trans. C. Loader; Weber 1986, trans. G. Wells.

9. This exact definition of an "adequate" critical judgment is difficult. If these new titles were reviewed in a professional journal, such reviews would be deemed adequate for the purposes of their intended audience. Yet most criticism of the classics, particularly Weber, fails to transmit the detail, careful thought, and theoretical suggestion of the original, only the thinnest reflection of which surfaces in today's appropriations. Lack of equivalent knowledge, brevity of remarks, speed of composition and delivery, disappearance of a multilingual audience, and a widespread lessening of verbal facility or trust in verbal exchange all contribute to a critical arena where treatises are gobbled up without much rumination; digestion suffers.

10. That is, individuals seldom have the means to practice Werner Stark's "method of significant detail" (*The Sociology of Religion* 5: vii). The lukewarm reception given Stark's magnum opus may perhaps be related to the "logic" of scholars less learned. Max Rheinstein, who studied with Weber, commented: "It is this universality of knowledge together with the author's gift of penetrating analysis, his objectivity, his passion for accurate formulation, and his genius for recognizing the essentials and the relations between seemingly remote phenomena which gives Weber's work its unique character" (Introduction to *Max Weber On Law in Economy and Society*, p. xxiv). The only living scholar who may well fit this description is the great classicist Arnaldo Momigliano (b. 1908), author of over seven hundred scholarly items, many on topics very similar to Weber's.

11. See Richard T. LaPiere, *Social Change*, and H. G. Barnett, *Innovation*.

are not done, the student of earlier theory encounters difficulties in his search for a definitive opinion, only one of which is the problem of how one, or a committee, can reappropriate those syntheses achieved by an author of difficult works in a bygone era.

It is not, however, merely the problem of accumulated knowledge, individually acquired, that makes intellectual continuity and reliable criticism problematic. For example, Weber had at his command no more "bits" of information than the venerable Lewis Mumford, and very similar bits at that (though, it is true, Mumford is hardly a "representative" modern). The more vexing problem lies with the imaginative reproduction of a *Zeitgeist* and a unique scholarly *Weltanschauung* within it, an exercise which, according to hermeneutics, precedes understanding. In discussing the progress of sociology, several authors have begun serious consideration of this issue,[12] but none has dealt with it at length. Perhaps literary critics or, better yet, phenomenological literary critics and aestheticians (Mikel Dufrenne and Paul Ricoeur, for instance) are more fully aware of the foibles of interpretation.[13] Such writers regard it

---

12. Alvin Gouldner, *The Coming Crisis of Western Sociology*, pp. 20–60; Robert Friedrichs, *A Sociology of Sociology*, pp. 135–166, 223–258; John O'Neill, *Sociology as a Skin Trade*, pp. 57–67, 177–208; Stanislav Andreski, *Social Sciences as Sorcery*, pp. 51–88, 187–197.

13. Mikel Dufrenne, *The Phenomenology of Aesthetic Experience*, and Paul Ricouer, *The Conflict of Interpretations*. The Polish philosopher Roman Ingarden (1893–1970) has fairly recently gained fame in the United States through translations of his two major works, *The Literary Work of Art*, trans. George Grabowicz, and *The Cognition of the Literary Work of Art*, trans. Ruth Crowley and Kenneth Olson. Still untranslated is *Untersuchungen zur Ontologie der Kunst*. Stefan Morawski, *An Inquiry into the Fundamentals of Aesthetics*, is also germane. Scott Sanders documents its usefulness to general problems of textual interpretation in a review in *Telos*.

Such works suggest how ill served the motley clientele for interpretative theory has been in allowing itself to be schooled mainly by exemplars of Anglo-American critical technique. By contrast, see Vernon Gras, ed., *European Literary Theory and Practice*. When American literary and aesthetic criticism walked away from the confines of formalism, it became the cross-disciplinary center of a conversation that has still not run its course. Suddenly philosophers, historians, economists, psychologists, even sociologists began to study literary critical technique for use in their own work. Cf. Denis Donoghue, *Ferocious Alphabets*; Edward Said, *The World, the Text, and the Critic*; Gerald Graff, *Literature Against Itself*; Geoffrey Hartman, *Criticism in the Wilderness*; and perhaps most useful, Frank Lentricchia's *After the New Criticism* and *Criticism and Social Change*. The self-consciousness of literary critics as important theorists in their own right comes to a head in Gerald Graff and Reginald Gibbons, eds., *Criticism in the University*, which asks whether criticism has not displaced literature as the locus of intellectual virtuosity. See Gary Shapiro and Alan Sica, eds., *Hermeneutics*, pp. 1–21.

as a mandatory element of sound criticism to reconstruct the interior world as the author under scrutiny perceived and then shaped it, at least to the limits of our ability.

The New Criticism movement of the 1930s (paralleling in spirit while preceding in time "value-free" American sociology) was founded on the notion that reaching into the past in the hope of evaluating a literary work as part of a cultural epoch betrayed a naive critical desire. The new method was to attack the text itself as a formally complete aesthetic expression, unmediated by cultural location and shorn of the writer's intentions, the audience to whom it was offered, and so on. This "methodological asceticism" (see Chapter 1, footnote 39) captured the American literary establishment of the time, a signal of the fear that interpretation, if allowed to evalute aspects of cultural reality other than the artifact itself, might tend toward the analytically forbidden: the personalistic, intuitive, and idiosyncratic judgment, more reflective of the critic's purpose than of the intrinsic qualities of the work at hand.

To return to more salient reasons for misinterpretation of Weber: it is notable that commentators effuse over his "magisterial," "unbelievable" learning. But the other side of that realization—the *relative* ignorance of contemporary academics—is politely left to intimation. Aside from his sheer intelligence and neurotic will to accumulate unwieldly information and then analyze it uniquely, both quite strange by today's lights, Weber had other advantages over today's scholar. He matured during a period of European intellectual life when one was expected to "know everything." Some mandarins of that era practically did—Dilthey, Max Mueller, Burckhardt, Mommsen, Gustav Schmoller, and others [14]—though it seems improbable now, given our feeble use of languages and lack of unencumbered time.

Plenty has been written about the Kantian epistemological and

14. Weber limited his inspiration for monumental scholarship to his German colleagues, for though he was aware of events in France and Italy, he went out of his way to omit the results of research there from his work. Especially notorious was his refusal to discuss in print the work of Durkheim or Pareto, the other members of the pantheon as conjured up by Parsons in 1937. According to one of his brother's students, Alfred Weber claimed Max was quite aware of Durkheim's work, but, as is well known, not one reference to him is to be found in Max's writings. See Edward A. Tiryakian, "A Problem for the Sociology of Knowledge." On Pareto, see Alan Sica, "Received Wisdom Versus Historical Fact."

ethical heritage of those Germans, about the "necessary" relation they thought self-evident among historical correctness and accuracy, personal morality, and knowledge of the *Geisteswissenschaften*—a relation of which Weber often spoke.[15] Whatever their scholarly motivations or mores, their published works and unforgettable lectures leave no doubt of their abilities and intentions toward this quasi-sacred pursuit of "objective truth."[16] They were, as Gerth and Mills put it, a "generation of universal scholars."[17] As we know too well, the psychic, material, and cultural preconditions for this sort of erudition on behalf of grand synthesis have vanished as totally as the Kaiser's noble cavalry.[18]

Weber as Scholar

Behind the most abstract presentations and analyses of his work, one senses profound admiration for Max Weber the man. It is this

15. Marianne Weber, *Max Weber*, pp. 105–106, 191–225. See Fritz K. Ringer, *The Decline of the German Mandarins;* Thomas E. Willey, *Back to Kant*, pp. 13–39, 153–181; and Arthur Mitzman, *Sociology and Estrangement*, pp. 6–38. Ernst Nolte remarks in the concluding pages of his *Three Faces of Fascism:* "Max Weber repeatedly shows a strange vacillation toward just those principal phenomena to which he gave his closest attention. In his eyes, rationalization is not merely typical of the West: it is also the root of his torturing anxiety as to whether man has even the strength to withstand the fearful rupturing effects of the irrevocable perversion of all natural conditions within the 'apparatus' of the modern world. The concept of 'progress' entirely loses its traditional positive accent; its use is frankly stated to be 'inopportune.' Most revealing of all, perhaps, is the use of the term 'disenchantment,' which in the total context of his work has a quite positive meaning and yet in one of Weber's best-known utterances is imbued with the melancholy sound of Stefan George's laments. This vacillation of such a man as Weber is possibly more indicative of the profound change in the intellectual climate favoring fascism than all the books written by Bergson or Klages. But at the same time it makes clear that there is more to this change than a purely sociological 'escape into irrationalism'" (pp. 562–563). For further details on the uncomfortable relation between Kantian individual morality and the fruits of political liberalism allied with it, see David R. Lipton, *Ernst Cassirer*, pp. 3–19. (Cassirer was introduced to Kant as a student by Simmel in 1894.)

16. Inter alia, see Gerhard Masur, *Prophets of Yesterday*, pp. vii, 159–203; Karl Loewenstein, *Max Weber's Political Ideas in the Perspective of Our Time*, pp. 91–104; Paul Honigsheim, *On Max Weber*, pp. 1–112.

17. Weber 1946, p. 23.

18. Hegel served as the initial model for "limitless" learning among scholars of the nineteenth century. He tried to establish that accretion and synthesis of cultural-historical information precedes credible large-scale speculation. His adumbration of Marxian themes (e.g., notes on the "Asiatic mode of production" in *The Philosophy of History*, pp. 111–138) and, in turn, those of later social thinkers is usually ascribed to a breadth and depth of knowledge in the human sciences that had no equal.

obvious attachment to his character that prompts most Weber scholarship, not disembodied theoretical interest alone. The key to his narrative is tension—*Spannung* or *Streckung*—and its defining theoretical and practical role in our age. He was not the first German social theorist or moralist to fasten on the term, but he pursued it, as it pursued him, further than any predecessor. Marx, by comparison, always claimed to know where science and politics met, and he tried to position himself at their nexus without much handwringing. Perhaps this is why today American and German ("bourgeois") theorists feel almost natural standing in the queue headed by Weber, with fact to one side, value to the other. Precisely what angered Lukács (in *Destruction of Reason*), this willingness to put on and take off the scientist's uniform rationally and apolitically, is the central characteristic of Weber, man and scholar, that guaranteed his symbolic sponsorship of Western sociology for a half-century. Voices against him are small, in compass and intensity, and his importance grows with time. *Against Weber* by Greg Philo was announced for publication, then did not appear, almost as if the presses refuse to commit sacrilege; meanwhile Bryan Turner's *For Weber,* a substantial book, raises no eyebrows unless one suspects more coals to Newcastle. In this happy spirit the Weber industry steams along, not pure hagiography to be sure, yet hardly tearing at its object's imperial robes. One wonders what the old man would think of this deference.

By now it is trite to see Weber as a charismatic leader of those upon whom he counted for Germany's political and cultural revivification. There were heroic qualities about Weber's life, and certainly enough to it of the tragic. Yet his productivity, learning, and personal grandeur are partially attributable to his bourgeois environment. Such pleasant quotodian arrangements helped succor extended works of scholarship so intense that interpretations of them often obscure more than illuminate, perhaps in unconscious imitation of the texts under review.[19] During this culturally orchestrated, politically coherent period (1890–1910), little pressure for early publishing was exerted on junior scholars, resulting in a fruitful waiting period until a scarce professorship became available.

19. Cf. the hoary quip that after studying James Stirling's *The Secret of Hegel* (1865), one learned the secret had been kept.

The obligatory political and analytical debate with Marxism insured attention to broad themes, though Weber's Marxist opponents, with the exception of Kautsky, were, unfortunately, too dogmatic to offer real theoretical opposition. Such scope demanded mighty collections of data, particularly historical and political-economic. Finally, an indispensable ally in sociological creation was Weber's wife, who gave him every encouragement in his work. Just as were the wives of Scheler, Simmel, Jaspers, and Mannheim, among others, she was intellectually equipped to play the accomplice in his quest for exhaustive knowledge.[20]

These preconditions of Wilhelmian scholarship are too well known perhaps to require repetition, having been thoroughly incorporated into our own academic sense of incompleteness. And yet the mountainous productivity of this period can be *too* handily acknowledged, thus trimming its impact upon later academic norms. Over time it has become a quiet part of our surroundings like a mighty tree that dominates a meadow, but this familiarity defuses its initial meaning. The legitimate import of the gap between their learning and ours is not honestly considered.

Theodor Adorno might say "it is no accident that" between 1650 and 1800 Germany "produced" the West's greatest composers. As Arnold Hauser and many others have shown, certain elusive characteristics of societies give rise to a recognizable range of cultural productions.[21] The modern composer does not compete with Mozart, since today's music cannot be held accountable for its historical place and the boundaries unique to it. Yet, strangely enough, when it is proposed that current conditions cannot foster analysts who match Weber, the line between art and science too often becomes a battlefront. Defenses are mustered, mostly consisting of sharp claims for techniques, not profound substance. The meaning today of Weber at twenty-eight publishing an 891-page analysis of survey research about agricultural laborers (among other activities) is not enough probed in this context.

This hardly means that one must be Weber to understand him,

20. In addition to her biography, see Marianne Weber, "Academic Conviviality," which describes the style of intellectual interchange in Heidelberg following Weber's death, a style clearly shaped in his memory.

21. Arnold Hauser, *Social History of Art;* also his *Sociology of Art* and *The Philosophy of Art History.*

but an appreciative sympathy with Weber's aims and skills forms the necessary foundation for reliable assimilation of his work into current research. A comparison of Reinhard Bendix's *Max Weber* with studies by younger American writers hoping to illuminate Weber for their peers illustrates this point. Bendix's Germanness is crucial to the success of his hermeneutics,[22] even if that success is, as I believe, only partial. The same can be said for Julien Freund's study of Weber. Whether membership in a cultural group is requisite to the best interpretation of works coming from that group is a question I dare not answer. But it does lead to another hurdle to understanding, the problem of reconstituting defunct *Weltanschauungen*. This process is both more and less than empathy, a term unfortunately and inaccurately used in relation to Dilthey's (hence, Weber's) method.[23] This argument will be rejoined momentarily.

Weber's Thought and Mannheim's Weltanschauungslehre

Those obstacles already named to adequate interpretation of classic texts are obvious. There exist others, however, less superficial, less often acknowledged or understood. Although elaboration must wait, they may be noted here. The first relates to those forms of social organization Weber most carefully studied: ancient agrarian civilizations, medieval Europe, the ancient Orient, and early capitalist Europe and America. Current analysts, in contrast, are obliged to evaluate existing social arrangements, either comparatively or in terms of individual nations somewhere on the developing-developed continuum. How Weber's penchant for qualification would have bloomed were he faced with Western civilization nearing the year 2000! When writing on the distant and empirically limited (e.g., medieval trading companies and the maritime laws which regulated their operations in the Mediterranean), he took extraordinary care in assigning causality and interpreting specific

22. See the Acknowledgments in *Work and Authority in Industry*, where Bendix credits his father, a "Dr. jur.," for having had him read in his youth "Karl Marx, Wilhelm Dilthey, Georg Simmel, Max Weber, and Karl Mannheim"; this helps explain Bendix's unique position within American sociology. See also Bendix's "A Memoir of My Father."

23. This widespread mistake is commented upon by Rudolf Makkreel, *Dilthey*, pp. 252n–253n.

events. Perhaps his powers of analysis might have been paralyzed if faced with Western civilization today.

The social orders Weber chose to examine, the research materials available to him, and the questions he wanted answered were all of a different complexity from those that inspire even the finest studies today. I doubt whether he had an easy time considering the Kaiser's foreign policy, about which he sometimes wrote topical commentaries. But at the macro level, the world seems more complex than it was before World War I, at least in available quantitative detail—the compilations of data recording this apparent complexity. And the questions social scientists are now asked, as a result of the pressing nature of contemporary affairs and the institutionalization of their disciplines, are of broader beam than many which Weber plied in his general social theory or more technical political-economic and comparative work.[24]

Weber was socialized to demand results from his scholarly work that are no longer sought today: a semblance of definitive conclusions, or at minimum some credible description of the matter at hand. I suspect that despite the mannered qualifying—perhaps reflected in its very use—his confidence in the ability to bring off convincing cultural analyses rested on a belief plausible in a pre-absurdist social world: that disciplined intelligence could master social reality, current and historical.[25]

So the initial hindrance to understanding is the joint result of two factors: first, Weber's objects of study seemed more susceptible to intellectualization, more fundamentally subject to rationalized understanding, than the miasma now confronting social science; and, second, his role as Wilhelmine mandarin called for less ritualized humility before empirical reality than is currently the case. These indicators of Weber's world-historical distance from us lead to the next interpretative difficulty.

The second occluded problem revolves around the Diltheyan theme, one which Weber avoided programmatically, yet regularly

24. Imagine Weber's hesitation, for instance, in titling a book *The Modern World-System* or *Politics and Markets: The World's Political-Economic Systems,* as have Immanuel Wallerstein and Charles Lindblom.

25. Weber tempered this belief as he matured—evident in the tentativeness of his *Kategorienlehre,* ca. 1914—and of course in response to World War I, which surprised him only in its intensity.

faced in his research. This is what I have called the cognitive re-production of a unique *Weltanschauung*, whether representing a person, collectivity, or era. This issue is as easy to raise as it is worrisome to resolve; it has long been known for its thickets of contradictions, unidentifiables, and lapses of logic. But in order to proceed, this problem of *Weltanschauung* must be addressed, even if superficially.

Since Schleiermacher gave his lectures on hermeneutics (ca. 1815), most scholars have accepted that an optimal appreciation of classic writings hinges on the reader's "re-creation" of the worldview and intellectual goals that underlie the works in question. Yet German social science has futilely committed untold scholarly resources to the question of how, in what form, even whether contrasting and contradictory *Weltanschauungen* can be compared across cultural epochs separated by time, space, and language.[26] So much ink has flowed over this question probably because it is interdisciplinary in nature, thus irresolvable by standard intradisciplinary consensus. Analysis of worldviews calls upon aesthetics, psychology, phenomenology, history, and sociology. Practitioners of each feel equally qualified to speak to the problem, or to ignore it. But the angles of approach vary so widely, the domain assumptions are so at odds, that mutual disregard or enmity has become the norm. For help out of this quandary, two very different thinkers present themselves, Karl Mannheim and Alfred North Whitehead.

In 1920, at twenty-six, Mannheim published "On the Interpretation of Weltanschauung" in a yearbook on the history of art.[27] His intimacy with Lukács put such questions in a Weberian context,[28] and his remarks throughout the fifty-page essay on the identifica-

26. Jacob Burckhardt introduced this issue into Weber's milieu. See Reinhard Bendix, "Jacob Burckhardt," in Bendix and Guenther Roth, *Scholarship and Partisanship*, pp. 266–281. See also Karl Weintraub, *Visions of Culture*, pp. 115–160; and Arnaldo Momigliano, *Essays in Ancient and Modern Historiography*, pp. 295–305.

27. Published in English for the first time after Mannheim's death in *Essays on the Sociology of Knowledge*, pp. 33–83. The quotations below are taken from this edition. In the Introduction to *From Karl Mannheim*, Kurt Wolff fixes the article within Mannheim's professional biography (pp. xviii–xxi).

28. Mannheim had emigrated from Budapest to Germany in 1920, one of the extraordinary group of Hungarian Jews who so much influenced European intellectual life. He was related by blood to Lukács. See Joseph Gabel, "Hungarian Marxism." I have spoken with Ernest Manheim, cousin of Karl, who reported that Lukács and Mannheim were frequently in each other's company while Lukács knew Weber in Heidelberg.

tion of "meaning" in works of art as expressing "global outlooks" reflect a developing dependence on Weber. Mannheim hoped to establish a scientific method for comparative analyses of eras and their artistic productions by ascertaining the meaning of various artforms. He was influenced in this by Husserl—thus the "intentional act" and "intentional object" appear—but at the same time was gravitating toward Weber's sociological perspective. (Weber's recent death had left Heidelberg, where Mannheim first taught, in shadow.)[29] His paper, then, might reasonably be taken as an appendix to *Wirtschaft und Gesellschaft* proposing a theory of interpretation, about which Weber had preached little and practiced much. Mannheim in fact cites Weber's masterwork, published the year before.

Mannheim distinguishes three types of artistic meaning: "objective" (simple, formal, or literal meaning conveyed by form), "expressive" (the aesthetic content intentionally transmitted by the artist), and "documentary" (art as reflecting the artist's consciousness, thus serving as an "indicator" of an epoch). A detailed defense of this typology takes up the bulk of the essay. Much of Mannheim's attention is given to the sociologically richest category, "documentary" meaning, from which he expected potent sociocultural and aesthetic analyses. Mannheim did not establish a method for comprehending global outlooks that positivism would accept. But this hardly means he failed. Like so many of his youthful essays, this one wells over with observations, epistemological and ontological, that illuminate theorizing in social science. Because of Mannheim's surroundings and his link to Weber's students, these notions reflect views which the master may well have encouraged among his protégés.[30] For this reason, among others, it is worthwhile to present some of Mannheim's major points.

The following excerpts apply to three matters germane to my

29. Weber's death shocked Heidelberg. Leo Lowenthal recalls that the town became still upon learning of his death, not unlike what happened in American cities when Roosevelt died. If this kind of homage to an intellectual seems uncanny today, it serves to remind us of the cultural distance between Weber's milieu and ours.

30. It is well known, for instance, that Weber read and greatly admired Lukács's early books, *Soul and Form*, and *The Theory of the Novel* (both trans. Anna Bostock) and was impressed by the early Budapest school of philosophy and social science which produced Mannheim and Lukács. The two were intimates and Mannheim cites Lukács in the essay under discussion.

study: the first, to the nature of theorizing; the second, to "reconstituting" *Weltanschauungen* as a necessary preliminary to fruitful hermeneutics; and the third, to the encompassing problem of irrationality, meaning, and their interrelation.

> Many things are given of which no clear theoretical account can be rendered. . . . Criteria of exactness cannot be transferred from one field to another. . . . It would be a fundamental misconception of the function of theory if we assigned to it the sole task of reproducing on the conceptual level the full wealth of what has already been grasped in immediate experience. . . . Man is a citizen of several worlds at the same time. . . . The paradoxical nature of theoretical thought, distinguishing it from the other forms, consists in this, that it seeks to superimpose a logical, theoretical pattern upon experiences already patterned under other—for example aesthetic or religious—categories. But if this is so, we cannot accept that extreme form of irrationalism which holds that certain cultural facts are not merely a-theoretical but are radically removed from any rational analysis [a point made many times by Weber]. Aesthetic or religious experiences are not wholly devoid of form; it is only that their forms are *sui generis* and radically different from that of theory as such. To reflect these forms and what is in-formed by them, without violating their individual character, to "translate" them into theory, or at any rate to "encompass" them by logical forms, that is the purpose of theoretical inquiry, a process which points back to pre-theoretical initial stages, at the level of everyday experience; and we cannot help feeling uncomfortable while translating the nontheoretical experience into the language of theory, since we cannot avoid the impression that the theoretical categories are inadequate and distort the authenticity of direct experience upon which they are superimposed.
>
> There must be something to theory, something positive and fruitful; it must achieve something else besides chilling the authentic experience with the cold blast of reflection—a repatterning of the original experience, by which light is thrown upon it from an entirely new side. Otherwise it would be incomprehensible why the ethical, aesthetic, and religious realm (that is, the realm of the a-theoretical) is shot through with elements of theory even in its original, unreflected state. . . . Theorizing, then, does not start with science; pre-scientific everyday experience is shot through with bits of theory. The life of mind is a constant flux, oscillating between the theoretical and a-theoretical pole, involving a constant intermingling and re-arranging of the most disparate categories of many different origins. And thus theory has its proper place. (pp. 33, 71, 72, 39–40)

There was a time, at least thirty years ago, when this essay and its remarkable commentary upon theorizing were better known, but the volume in which it appears has long been out of print. Mannheim's stipulations about the correct approach for social theory were inspired and informed by an apprenticeship in art history and aesthetics. He shared this avenue to abstraction with Weber, Lukács, Jaspers, and many others crucial to theorizing in Germany between 1900 and 1933. These paragraphs show his high regard for the empirically given, and a delicate concern for the dialectics of seeing and knowing, that is, the strain between honest perception on the one hand and the desires of theoretical subsumption on the other. His is not bold abstraction in the mode of natural science— which tells us, for instance, that the light we plainly see comes from a star long dead—but an almost tender wish to embrace what is manifest with theoretical arms that contain but do not harm the original. This very important viewpoint has been lost in much subsequent social theorizing, as has much of the Schleiermacher-Dilthey impetus in social science. Mannheim helps recover that unique message.

> The theory of Weltanschauung is an interpretive rather than explanatory one. . . . What it does is to take some meaningful object already understood in the framework of objective meaning and place it within a different frame of reference—that of Weltanschauung. By being considered as "document" of the latter, the object will be illuminated from a new side. . . . The difficult and paradoxical nature of the concept of Weltanschauung stems from the fact that the entity it denotes lies outside the province of theory. Dilthey was one of the first to recognize this; cf. his remark, "Weltanschauungen are not produced by thinking." . . . In so far as that indefinite something, Weltanschauung, is concerned, however, it belongs to the realm of the a-theoretical in a still more radical sense. Not only that it is in no way to be conceived of as a matter of logic and theory; not only that it cannot be integrally expressed through philosophical theses or, indeed, theoretical communications of any kind—in fact, compared to it, even all non-theoretical realizations, such as works of art, codes of ethics, systems of religion, are still in a way endowed with rationality, with explicitly interpretable meaning, whereas Weltanschauung as a global unit is something deeper, a still unformed and wholly germinal entity. . . . The question is whether structural analysis [Mannheim's term for his own procedure] is irreconcilable with psychological simultaneity . . . of this immediately given structure. . . . Documentary meaning is a matter, not of a temporal process in which certain experiences become actualized, but of the character, the essential nature, the "ethos" of the subject which manifests itself in artistic creation. . . . To understand the "spirit" of an age, we have to fall back on the "spirit" of our own—it is only substance which comprehends substance. (pp. 81, 38, 40–41, 64, 55)

Without belaboring the obvious, it may be worth noting that Mannheim is silently invoking the phenomenological path of Brentano, Husserl, and Scheler, plus of course that of their major inspiration,

Dilthey. "The" theory of *Weltanschauung* is thus an amalgam, distinctly at odds with the more positivistic understandings of personality then in vogue, and much more encompassing. The major theoretical point is, recalling Dilthey, that *Weltanschauungen* are representations of the major category *Leben* (life), which "lies outside the province of theory . . . a still unformed and wholly germinal entity." Today's perspective, less modest, freely calls for ordering and reformulating at will whatever lies at hand, to fit research or analytical schemes. Mannheim's cautionary tone once again acts as an important corrective, mainly because it takes worldviews under theoretical auspices as preestablished empirical units. This is what I hope to do in examining Weber.

> Once again we find ourselves confronted by the problem of rationalism and irrationalism, or better, the question whether and how the a-theoretical can be "translated" into theory. . . . We must recognize this sphere of non-theoretical meaning as something intermediate between theory and intuition, if we do not want to consider everything non-theoretical as intuitive and irrational. . . . The wholly irrational . . . the opaque region of the unorganized . . . may even be the most vital part of our existence. (pp. 39, 66, 67)

The sentiments expressed here implicitly and explicitly are doubly useful. Not only do they still apply to the interpreter's dilemma, but they reveal a good deal about an important style of European theorizing just after Weber's death, a style he helped shape. Also noteworthy is Mannheim's unembarrassed use of "fuzzy" formulations such as "non-theoretical meaning [is] something intermediate between theory and intuition." Viewed from our period, so much less speculatively inventive, Mannheim's daring is enviable, especially given the subject at hand.

The Aesthetic Dimension to Social Theory:
Whitehead, Simmel, and Others

Even without exegesis of the preceding quotations—which, done correctly, could occupy many pages—two points are manifest that require emphasis regarding Weber (also Pareto) and *Weltanschauungen* as interpretable in scholarly works. One, to be taken up below, concerns Weber's worldview. First, however, comes the question of aesthetics: why is Mannheim's theory of interpretation, saturated with the vernacular of art criticism, appropriated here, when

Weber's theories and research are not art? Because classical social theory shared intellectual space with the properly "artful." Important art critics and aestheticians such as Dilthey, Wölfflin, and Max Dvorak were read by theorists, and some, like Simmel, published aesthetic interpretations themselves.[31] For them theorizing was as much the aesthetic management of ideas as it was logical deduction or mechanical construction. Discoveries in natural science have for some time been seen as uncertain mixtures of systematic investigation and "intuitive leaps." Such a perspective has not hitherto been allowed, except incidentally, to explain developments in social thought, but there is good reason to assess social theory, and the action it represents, partly by way of such an aesthetic.

The best-known statement on the nature and utility of "aesthetic apprehension" (or "prehension") of reality and ideas, and which complements Mannheim, comes in the last pages of Whitehead's *Science and the Modern World:*

> There is no substitute for the direct perception of the concrete achievement of a thing in its actuality. We want concrete fact with a high light thrown on what is relevant to its preciousness.
>
> What I mean is art and aesthetic education. It is, however, art in such a general sense of the term that I hardly like to call it by that name. Art is a special example. What we want is to draw out habits of aesthetic apprehension. According to the metaphysical doctrine which I have been developing to do so is to increase the depth of individuality. The analysis of reality indicates the two factors, activity emerging into individualized aesthetic value. Also the emergent value is the measure of the individualization of the activity. We must foster the creative initiative towards the maintenance of objective values. You will not obtain the apprehension without the initiative. Or the initiative without the apprehension. As soon as you get towards the concrete, you cannot exclude action. Sensitiveness without impulse spells decadence, and impulse without sensitiveness spells brutality. I am using the word "sensitiveness" in its most general signification, so as to include apprehension of what lies beyond oneself; that is to say, sensitiveness to all the facts of the case. Thus "art" in the general sense which I require is any selection by which the concrete facts are so arranged as to elicit attention to particular

31. Among many relevant works, see Dilthey, *Poetry and Experience,* which includes "Imagination of the Poet" (1887), "Three Epochs of Modern Aesthetics and Its Present Task" (1892), and long interpretations of Goethe (1910) and Hölderlin (1910). Also Max Dvorak (quoted by Mannheim), *History of Art as the History of Ideas,* trans. J. Hardy; Georg Simmel, *Rembrandt* and *Goethe;* Heinrich Wölfflin, *Principles of Art History.*

values which are realizable by them. For example, the mere disposing of the human body and the eyesight so as to get a good view of a
sunset is a simple form of artistic selection. The *habit of art* is the
habit of enjoying vivid values. . . . A self-satisfied rationalism is in
effect a form of anti-rationalism. (pp. 199–200; emphasis added)

Eleven years after this was written, Whitehead defended his philosophy at a symposium where he offered another fruitful observation on the relation between perceptual and cognitive aesthetics:

Philosophic thought has to start from some limited section of our experience—from epistemology, natural science, theology, or from
mathematics. Also, the investigation always retains the taint of its
starting point. Every starting point has its merits and its selection
must depend upon the individual philosopher.

My own belief is that at present the most fruitful, because the
most neglected, starting point is that section of value-theory which
we term aesthetics. Our enjoyment of the values of human art, or of
natural beauty, our horror at the obvious vulgarities and deface-
ments which force themselves upon us—all these modes of experience are sufficiently abstracted to be relatively obvious. And yet evidently they disclose the very meaning of things.

Habits of thought and sociological habits survive because in some
broad sense they promote aesthetic enjoyment. There is an ultimate
satisfaction to be derived from them. Thus when the pragmatist asks
whether "it works," he is asking whether it issues an aesthetic satisfaction. The judge of the Supreme Court is giving his decision on the
basis of the aesthetic satisfaction of the harmonization of the American Constitution with the activities of modern America.

Now there are two sides to aesthetic experience. In the first place, it
involves a subjective sense of individuality. It is *my* enjoyment. . . .
Aesthetic enjoyment demands an individualized universe.

In the second place, there is the aesthetic object which is identified in experience as the source of subjective feeling. In so far as
such abstraction can be made, so that there is a definite object correlated to a definite subjective reaction, there is a singular exclusive
unity in this aesthetic object. There is a peculiar unity in a good
pattern.[32]

Of myriad reflections on the epistemological meaning of artistic
perception, Whitehead's, as given here and elaborated in later
work,[33] most nearly matches my own. He argues for perception
grounded in a "habit of art," which is precisely what suffused
Weber's writings, though it was there carefully sublimated and disciplined.[34] Also, Whitehead's thoughts on unity, holism, and the

32. Whitehead, *Interpretation of Science*, pp. 211–212.
33. *Process and Reality*, pp. 251–326; corrected edition, pp. 219–280.
34. The same habit of aesthetic intellection was given much looser rein in the
work of Alfred Weber, who seems to have been more willing to allow properly aes-

cognitive validity of subjective response as a correlate to aesthetic perception are substantially at one with Dilthey's precepts for hermeneutics, an approach of great appeal to Weber. Whitehead seemed sympathetic to the intellectual-emotive response Dilthey held up as the hallmark of correctly rendered *Weltanschauungen*.[35] This artistic view of interpretation in many ways surpasses better-known interpretative schemas (e.g., the more causality-seeking theory of Cassirer, which puts to use "aesthetic intuition").[36] It is still amazing that Whitehead published these sentiments in 1925, long before science became reflectively self-critical. Some of the tenets central to Whitehead's philosophy of science cannot be "operationalized." But an effort to include something of his sensitivity to perceivable reality *and* the process of interpretation that makes it humanly significant would strengthen numerous analytic procedures and lend pliability to the attitudes behind them. In short, I applaud Whitehead's view of cognitive process, and Weber, with his "vivid values," may well have felt the same.

A rare book that considers these delicate matters is John Cuddihy's *The Ordeal of Civility: Freud, Marx, Lévi-Strauss and the Jewish Struggle with Modernity*. It unintentionally exposes blind spots in discursive theory analogous to those Feyerabend identified in schemes formally more deductive. Cuddihy needed "an

---

thetic factors to enter his cultural analyses than was his brother. This difference—reflected in their contrary views of Burckhardt's approach—further troubled their relationship.

35. I can find no evidence that Whitehead was familiar with Dilthey, but Whitehead's parallel ideas could be read as intellectual endorsement of Dilthey's hermeneutic theory. In the final sentence of the last extract above, Whitehead resorts to a word, *peculiar*, that has some aesthetic appeal. Quite often when a writer struggles to document an unusual experience, perceptual or intellectual, the phrase "a peculiar . . ." or "a certain . . ." crops up. The probability of finding these phrases in difficult passages helps in defining the contemporary aesthetics of scholarship. Language in this century has been so overpowered by positivist, nomothetic, technocratic thought and expression that phenomena not immediately accessible suffer in analysis. The "rise and influence of rationalism" (as Lecky put it) and the "decline of magic" and the irrational have conspired to rid the language of words and phrases most suited for describing the idiosyncratic or intuitive. It is assumed that precision was gained as "flowery" phrases were banished to figurative writing. There is some truth to this, but not enough to redeem all that was lost. And in this transformation Weber clearly struggled to be "modern," while Pareto carried forward the belles-lettres style—another reason for Weber's triumph and Pareto's lack of followers. This issue, and the larger one of which it is part—how form and content interact in theory—requires elaboration that to date it has not gotten.

36. Ernst Cassirer, *The Logic of the Humanities*, esp. pp. 6, 117ff.

hermeneutic" (p. vii) of an unusual sort for interpreting theory composed by Jews. He focused upon the interactional gruffness of Jews, in marked confrontation with straight-laced Gentile culture, and submerged qualities of "Jewish theory" became apparent. The personal style ("aesthetics of self-presentation," perhaps) that marked the dominant bourgeoisie, orchestrated by "the Protestant Esthetic or Protestant Etiquette," found the bluntness of the Jews repugnant, intellectuals included. According to Cuddihy, this friction crucially affected theorizing, because its authors "subconsciously" vented their displeasure at the censorious Victorians.

As might be expected, Cuddihy, himself half-Jewish, has endured severe critique. Yet his overriding idea remains plausible as still another interpretation of the commonplace that accepts nonrational factors in behavior and thought. The same phenomena Cuddihy studied are normally explained through impartial, "objective" hermeneutics or with scientific theories of personality that stress the nonunique, that is, the "rationalizable." But this underplays that aspect of Jewish intellectualism which Cuddihy uncovered while rereading the classics. Even more intriguing are his quotations from Weber. Some of these—for instance, his remarks to friends about the social-psychological, irrational factors behind the anti-Semitism rampant in the academy of imperial Germany— do not often appear in studies of his work.

Cuddihy is not slandering Marx, Freud, and others, of course, nor questioning their theories on racial grounds. Instead he is making the novel point that our civilization, reeling from multiple genocides, insists on an ideal of cultural homogeneity that violates fact. Thus theoretically potent distinctions among groups or individuals (Mannheim's divergent "global outlooks") are lost.

George Holton's essays illustrate his conviction that science is neither "meter reading" nor "tautologies" masquerading as propositions.[37] "Science in the making" is best visualized by "themata." These guiding threads are highly generalized, and not expressible in the logic of method caricatured in textbooks. They are composed of tacit aesthetic preferences, of positive feelings for particular methods or perspectives. Holton shows what themata are not ("paradigms," "myths," "archetypes," "visions," "folklore," etc.),

---

37. George Holton, *Thematic Origins of Scientific Thought*, pp. 28ff.

but gives less definition to what they are. Yet his main premise is congruent with those of writers from other fields: simplifications of cognitive processes into rationalized, mechanistic models do not capture what happens in the scientist's mind. Nor do they explain, I would argue, what occurred in Weber's *before* he converted stupendous reading and ordering into scholastic prose.

As might be expected, the phrase "aesthetic preferences," denoting key decisions in theoretical activity (e.g., conceptions of light and space in early Greek astronomy), figures centrally in Holton's book as he generalizes about scientific progress and changes of "themata." The same can be said of Feyerabend's *Against Method.* He believes all important methodological and substantive choices spring from decisions essentially aesthetic, and that versions of complex methods, particularly when proffered by those in the hard sciences, often mystify less easily defended, personal preferences attached to ordinary intellectual experience, far removed from the logic of inquiry. (A work much ahead of its time that explicitly confronted these matters is Ludwik Fleck's *Genesis and Development of a Scientific Fact.*)[38]

Not only natural scientists such as Whitehead, Holton, or Feyerabend have recognized the unrationalized underbelly of science, but social scientists as well. Arthur Stinchcombe has remarked, "If the kernel of esthetic experience in sociological theory is the unity of sociological and psychological statements, the outer covering is irony."[39] Derek Phillips's *Abandoning Method*, named after an essay by Feyerabend, revels in the suddenly familiar notion that methods operate with small regard for rational procedure and are largely an outgrowth of subjective values not unlike those informing art. Phillips, too, thinks methods must be surveyed aesthetically.

Years ago Robert Nisbet published "Sociology as an Art Form."[40] It contains little with which to disagree, except that Nisbet's understanding of "sociological" art is almost too literal ("portraits," "landscapes," and so on). He says little about a phenomenology of aesthetic perception of the kind that inspired nineteenth-century

38. Ludwik Fleck, *Genesis and Development of a Scientific Fact*, esp. pp. 95ff. Also of interest is Deane Curtin, ed., *The Aesthetics of Science*, a symposium on the topic by Nobel Laureates.
39. In Lewis Coser, ed., *The Idea of Social Structure*, p. 28.
40. See the enlarged version, Robert Nisbet, *Sociology as an Art Form.*

theorists. With different intentions, Peter Clecak excoriates Marcuse for "confusing aesthetic and political categories" in his "Marxist utopianism."[41] Clecak prefers "plain" Marxism, failing to recognize the cogency of Marcuse's arguments against Western culture (which are patterned after Horkheimer and Adorno's *Dialektik der Aufklärung*). Marcuse intentionally confused the aesthetic and political, since only this amalgam could open up "administered culture" to the critical gaze—or so the Left's cultural critics believed. A comparison of Baran and Sweezy's political economy with Marcuse's work such as *Negations* demonstrates Clecak's underestimate of this technique.

And the literati have not been silent about the foolishness of those who deny the importance of aesthetic perception in life and thought. For instance, Thomas Mann: "The pleasure we take in a metaphysical system, the gratification purveyed by the intellectual organization of the world into a closely reasoned, complete, and balanced structure of thought, is always of a preeminently aesthetic kind."[42] More colloquially, Robert Pirsig has written, in the celebrated *Zen and the Art of Motorcycle Maintenance* (pp. 317ff.), a lengthy sequence of thoughts about the comfort taken in "the esthetics of doing things" that are familiar. The methodical sameness of mechanical actions, often mundane chores, helped Pirsig survive schizophrenia. It is likely that social researchers feel similar security when repeatedly using shopworn methods. The place of habit in intellectual work, an important element in these special aesthetics, has not been examined.

Having established, then, that theory-building has something to do with aesthetic perception and organization of data, I must repeat that insights into this condition are as numerous as sustained discourse is scarce. Essayists (as far back as Pascal) and book reviewers often toss out lines that indicate their awareness of this situation, but systematic investigation, a rationalization of insight, is hard to come by.

I am hardly alone in having noticed all this. As was noted above, Robert Friedrichs claims that "aesthetic predilections" help shape paradigmatic shifts within academic fields, "where persuasion, not

41. Peter Clecak, *Radical Paradoxes*, p. 229.
42. In "Schopenhauer," *Last Essays*, p. 255.

proof is king."[43] In a book that redefined the field, Feyerabend offers an antithetical theory of scientific growth, in debate with Lakatos, Popper, and Kuhn. He proposes that decisions scientists make in "choosing" their paradigms are *mostly* the product of aesthetic choices, that is, after standard logical processes have "explained all the variance they can." He calls his theory "anarchistic," though not in a political sense. Of particular interest is one section that deals with irrationality in scientific developments, as in the cases of Galileo and Copernicus.[44] By elaborating his "anarchistic epistemology," Feyerabend demonstrates that he is not only original but also a well-trained methodologist. But although, as was mentioned above, many contemporary writers have added their voices to this discussion, in no case has a systematic analytic or descriptive framework been constructed that would help in unraveling threads of "aesthetic predilection" from those of resolute, scientific induction.

Yet some effort was put toward this goal many years ago. Numerous indicators point to Weber's developed sense of aesthetics and correlative tolerance for tensions and ambiguity.[45] We can now see, in view of current thinking about creativity,[46] that he probably wrote and thought via an aesthetically attuned and directed ana-

---

43. Friedrichs, *Sociology of Sociology*, p. 2. Werner Stark has said much about the "aesthetico-artistic world-view" and its relation to the sociology of knowledge. In his best-known work, Stark supports Whitehead's view of epistemology but writes more sociologically: "The naive epistemology which was classically expounded by the philosophers of the Enlightenment and which has become the implied metaphysic of the common man of our day, regards art as the absolute antithesis of science in that science is supposedly bound to the facts and art is not; in that science must show the truth of what is, whereas art may explore the beauty of what might be. In scholarship the mind is supposed to be essentially receptive, i.e. passive; in music, for instance, or painting, essentially imaginative, creative, active. This dichotomy is very ill conceived. . . . However reluctant our rationalists-in-the-street may be to acknowledge the kinship between scientific and artistic thought, the historian of ideas knows very well that it exists in fact and in truth, for he discovers in every age a prevailing common style of thought . . . which informs all characteristic thinking of the period" (*Sociology of Knowledge*, pp. 123, 125). Stark documents and refines these claims in passages ignored by contemporary social theorists.

44. Paul Feyerabend, *Against Method*, pp. 145–162, 171–189. A laudatory review by Ian Mitroff appeared in *Contemporary Sociology*.

45. For example, and as previously noted, Weber esteemed Lukács's early book, *Die Seele und die Formen* (1911) (translated as *Soul and Form*), a volume saturated with idealistic aesthetics.

46. From the copious literature, see Albert Rothenberg, *The Emerging Goddess*, esp. pp. 125–137, and Howard Gardner, *Frames of Mind*.

lytic apparatus. Weber's unbroadcast but deep indebtedness to Nietzsche can be detected in Nietzsche's striking sentiment "Nur als aesthetisches Phänomen das Dasein der Welt gerechtfertigt ist" (the existence of the world is justified only as an aesthetic phenomenon).[47]

Too much can be made of Weber's reliance on aesthetics, but so also can too little. Insufficient attention has been paid to the artfulness of Weber's arguments. His inclusions and exclusions can only be penetrated if understood as affected by a unique aesthetic orientation, his intellectual aesthetics. This faculty worked in tandem with immense induction, and it should not be obscured by the formalist precision of his theorizing, especially in *Wirtschaft und Gesellschaft*. At work is a scarcely disclosed set of idiosyncratic compositional rules,[48] subtly arranged and constructed, which regulated Weber's writing. In itself this might hold little importance, had not Weber's undisclosed tastes tacitly infiltrated current theorizing. Perhaps this is not more often brought up because readers take Weber too much at his word, to their interpretative disadvantage. His obsessive reliance on the words *logical* and *rational*, lending an air of sternest science to texts which do not qualify as such, has gone unquestioned. (*Rational* and its cognates, for instance, appear more than fifty times in the first fifteen pages of *The Protestant Ethic*.) Marcuse has been one of the few to notice this and to find in it a "deep structure" trying to surface.[49]

This general line has been freshly pursued by Richard Kuhns. With an eye to the crossroads of philosophy, ethics, and art, he writes, "philosophers and literary artists suggest the possibility that literary values—indeed perhaps all values—are ultimately aesthetic."[50] Kuhns's analysis corresponds to Weber's category of

47. Friedrich Nietzsche, *The Birth of Tragedy*, in *Basic Writings of Nietzsche*, trans. and ed. Walter Kaufman, p. 22.

48. Weber's intellectual works indisputably bear the stamp of his age, but I still believe his self-imposed guidelines were *relatively* idiosyncratic.

49. It is not my primary task to bring up "structures" which avoid the light. Few structuralist analyses of Weber exist, and of them, I have found of interest only Jameson's "The Vanishing Mediator."

50. Richard Kuhns, *Structures of Experience*, p. viii. The stimulating quality of this remark, reminiscent of Schiller and subsequent idealist aestheticians such as Croce, depends on a definition of *aesthetic* much broader than current usage allows. More than art, formally understood, is intended, as had been suggested by Whitehead.

wertrational motives and action, which, he stipulated, could not be fully analyzed or understood, since such "ultimate values" are irrationally grounded. What Weber was not willing to admit was the irrational component of scientific, logical thought. Kuhns's comment is compatible with the Kant-Schiller-Hegel-Schlegel tradition of philosophical aesthetics regarding the art/truth relationship, which Weber took in "as with his mother's milk." This irresistible influence certainly figures in Weber's finished theories with regard to irrationality and thought, as it did in his theorizing as a process unto itself. But he refused to acknowledge this influence publicly.[51]

Unfortunately, speculation like Kuhns's is usually lost to mere *aperçus* when applied to social theory, even by a master like Adorno. Or if shoved toward systematic development, it slips into personalized, difficult-to-communicate metaphysics, expressed as aesthetic/moral axiology. (Horkheimer's late work—e.g., *Dawn and Decline*—or E. M. Cioran's books suffer from this.) Such works today are merely provocative, lying permanently at the border of social thought. Nietzsche, Bergson, and Scheler wrote works that deal persuasively with these problems, but with still unacknowledged import for social science. Let us begin with Nietzsche:

> I attributed a purely esthetic meaning—whether implied or overt—to all process: a kind of divinity if you like, God as the supreme artist, amoral, recklessly creating and destroying, realizing himself indifferently in whatever he does or undoes, ridding himself by his acts of the embarrassment of his riches and the strain of his *internal contradictions*. Thus the world was made to appear, at every instant, as a successful *solution* [italics in original] of God's own *tensions*, as an ever new vision projected by that grand sufferer for whom illusion is the only possible mode of redemption. That whole *esthetic metaphysics* might be rejected out of hand as so much prattle or rant. Yet in its essential traits it already prefigured that spirit of deep distrust and defiance which, later on, was to resist to the bitter end any moral interpretation of existence whatsoever.[52]

The final sentence speaks for many thoughtful Germans of this period, including Weber. The intelligentsia were fascinated by "para-

---

51. He was more candid in private. He once admitted to his wife, "It could be even that I *am* a mystic"—hardly the stereotypic Weberian persona (Eduard Baumgarten, ed., *Max Weber*, p. 677; cited in Bendix and Roth, *Scholarship and Partisanship*, p. 279).

52. From the 1886 introduction to *The Birth of Tragedy*, pp. 9–10; cited in Kuhns, *Structures of Experience*, p. 51 (emphasis added).

dox" and "tension." In addition to the many examples in Weber's writing, others appear in Marianne's biography: "It is at this point that the tension of the paradox reaches its climax" vis-à-vis Puritans and salvation (p. 340); "in our souls the artistic gospel coexists quite amicably with social concerns. It is certainly inconsistent to give space to two such dissimilar forces, but it is beautiful to feel the wealth of life in the tension between the two," referring to unlike friends of the Webers, Stefan George and Friedrich Naumann (p. 464). Thus another aspect of Weber's intellectual aesthetics is partially disclosed.

Bergson attained cult status during his life,[53] but he has slipped into oblivion for most Anglo-Americans. Exciting, "literary," and speculative is the third chapter, "On the Meaning of Life," of his most popular, though not most important, book, *Creative Evolution* (1907). His division of mind into "intuition" and "intelligence" is historically important because William James valued it. James praised this book in the same year Weber agonized over methodological essays *against* just such an epistemological position.

Scheler's place in the history of phenomenology has prompted translations of his works. Less attention is being given his sociological work than his axiology, even though the former has broadly affected European and South American *Wissenssoziologie.*[54] It remains to be seen whether Scheler's nonrelativistic value schema and the attempt to locate moral norms within common emotions (developed in *Formalism in Ethics and Non-Formal Ethics of Values*) will regain support. *Formalism,* which reached English sixty years after the fact and included the important essay "Ordo Amoris,"[55] made him "the greatest figure in the axiological school of ethics."[56] Scheler's just fame derived from his theorizing about matters Weber chose not to develop. As Herbert Spiegelberg says of Scheler, he was "a star of the first magnitude whose dazzling light revealed more than a prominent member of a new school: a philosopher of the age. . . . there can be little question that in the early 20's Max

53. See H. Stuart Hughes, *Consciousness and Society,* pp. 113–125.

54. Only the first third of *Die Wissensformen und die Gesellschaft* has come into English, as *Problems of a Sociology of Knowledge,* trans. M. Frings; see my review in the *Journal of the History of Sociology.*

55. See the bibliography for other translations of Scheler.

56. Vernon Bourke, *History of Ethics* 2: 108.

Scheler was in the eyes of the German public the number two phe-
nomenologist" (behind the much older Husserl).[57] Finally, Scheler's
theory of love bears directly upon my interest in the relatedness of
meaning and irrationality.[58]

The pressing issue of the place of aesthetic factors in works not
typically subject to aesthetic interpretation, or themselves partially
the product of nonexplicit, aesthetically defined norms, has been
broached here because it is necessary to a new reading of the classics. There is theoretical utility to elaborating an aesthetics of intellectual creation in a way that protects it from premature dismissal
by social scientists committed, as I am, to genuinely cumulative social knowledge. Simmel made a theoretical practice of using the
concept of aesthetics, in what has been called "the aesthetic dimension of sociality."[59] His perspective on the "aesthetic management"
of ideas and actions is similar to those discussed above. Simmel's
good friend Weber viewed his social psychology as too subjec-
tivistic,[60] an opinion that has clouded Simmel's reputation. His
ideas seem dangerously remote from mediating social structure,
through which individual consciousness and action develop, and
by contrast to which they are comprehensible.

Nevertheless, Simmel's essays (on "the nature of the psychic
process and of communications," on dyads, and so forth)[61] stand
closer to the avenue I wish to follow than do the works of any other
classic theorist. For instance:

> Our actual psychological processes are governed by logic in a much
> slighter degree than their *expressions* make us believe. If we look
> closely at our conceptions as they pass our consciousness in a con-
> tinuous temporal sequence, we find that there is a very great dis-
> tance between any regulation by rational norms and the characteris-
> tics of these conceptions: namely, their flaring up, their zig-zag
> motions, the chaotic whirling of images and ideas which objectively
> are entirely unrelated to one another, and their logically unjustifi-
> able, only so-to-speak probative, connections. But we are only rarely
> conscious of this, because the accents of our interests lie merely on
> the "usable" portion of our imaginative life. Usually we quickly pass

57. Herbert Spiegelberg, *The Phenomenological Movement*, 2: 228.
58. For details, see Manfred Frings, *Max Scheler*, pp. 49–80, 176–193; and John
Staude, *Max Scheler*, pp. 137–201.
59. Georg Simmel, *Georg Simmel on Individuality and Social Forms*, p. lxi.
60. Weber 1972, p. 156; also *Economy and Society* 1: 4.
61. Kurt Wolff, ed., *The Sociology of Georg Simmel*, e.g., pp. 122ff., 311–312.

over, or "overhear," its leaps, its non-rationality, its chaos, in spite
of their psychological factualness, in favor of what is logical or otherwise useful, at least to some extent.[62]

With that delicacy of expression for which Simmel is known, this
paragraph concisely covers the dual concern before us: (1) nonrationality as a feature of meaning-seeking activity, and (2) the
need for a theory of interpretation—of texts *and* action—using aesthetic concepts. Had Simmel concerned himself at length with irrationality per se, he would have played a larger role in this study.
His epigrammatic essays are more insightful than Weber's but less
systematic in treating social action, rational or otherwise.

Among current writers, some are beginning to venture into this
region of metatheory: for example, Alvin Gouldner's essay on
"metaphoricality" and, even more pertinent, Alan Blum's *Theorizing*. Relevant as well is the work of Blum's associate Derek Phillips,
whose contribution to "reflective" theory is *Abandoning Method*.[63]
As was already mentioned, Feyerabend's *Against Method* is the
most important of all these works. In it he touches many of my
interests: irrationality and meaning, the aesthetic dimension of
theory-building and choice of methodology, and the socialization
of scientists that encourages them to delete irrationality and nonrationality from their vocabulary of motives and explanation.

Although no systematic rendering of aesthetics and intellection
has appeared, then, writers from many disciplines are intrigued by
the effect of artfulness and the irrationality it represents, in works

62. Ibid., p. 311.

63. Alvin Gouldner's essay is titled "The Metaphoricality of Marxism and the
Context-Freeing Grammar of Socialism." Blum (*Theorizing*) discusses the underside
of theorizing in a style that emulates the complexity of the phenomena themselves.
It seems a new form of sympathetic magic. (See Marvin Israel's review in *Contemporary Sociology*; he is overwhelmed by the euphony of Blum's words.) Yet Blum has
attacked difficulties most would not risk attacking, and the precognitive nature of
these problems may give rise to nebulous writing. Richard Harvey Brown has contributed the most sustained analysis by an American in *A Poetic for Sociology* and in
essays (one on Dilthey) in *Structure, Consciousness, and History*, ed. Brown and Stanford Lyman. Brown calls his intervention a "cognitive aesthetics" or "critical poet-
ics," and opens his book thus: "Our thesis is that an aesthetical view of sociological
knowledge—a poetic for sociology—can contribute greatly to resolving methodological (and, implicitly, praxiological) contradictions confronting the human studies
today." Written ten years ago or more, Brown's innovative approach to theorizing
has not been so much evaluated and discarded as simply ignored. It was probably
published in advance of its rightful time. Perhaps his latest statement, *Society as
Text*, will be more warmly received.

that since the eighteenth century were thought to be free of such influences.

Retrieving Weltanschauungen

At the beginning of the preceding section I stated that two points requiring attention stemmed from Mannheim's interpretation of *Weltanschauungen*. The second point, concerning Weber's world-view, is twofold and more basic than the first. (1) Why should it be assumed that a scholar's worldview is specifiable, reclaimable, known by its substantial intimacy ("elective affinity") with a cultural epoch? (2) Is attempted reconstruction of a scholar's *Weltanschauung* needless methodological or scholastic purism?

Mannheim thinks "global outlooks" are indeed specifiable, but only indirectly and in fragments. They can be known by juxtaposing cultural artifacts, taken as data without being denatured, so that a cohesive, "intellectually-artistically" coherent gestalt or set of images emerges. This construction would plausibly describe a sociocultural milieu. (Carl Schorske's *Fin de Siècle Vienna* is a celebrated example of this technique.) Mannheim is less confident about the method's scientific status when analysis shifts from *Zeitgeists*—even if richly variegated—to the miniature confines of a single worldview. This is odd, since Mannheim hoped to differentiate and characterize entire artistic periods, but this would seem to demand returning to individual artists. Perhaps he was tilting against a view that ignored sociological dimensions in explaining art, so he pointedly limited attention to "great men." His organizing assumption has become axiomatic in the sociology of knowledge: character, habitual patterns, beliefs, and even capacity for synthesizing information are determined, restricted, and motivated by the peculiarities of the historical constellation into which the individual falls.

Such sociological determinism has been softened somewhat since Marx, following the philosophes, drew its outline in the early manuscripts and *German Ideology*. Its resistance to absolute ruin is surprising, since the key terms of its major propositions (i.e., "reflect," "determined," "conditioned," "historical moment," and so on) have never been fully expanded or, so to speak, tested against cultural reality. Obvious slippage occurs between sociocultural constraint and the individual or collective drive to alter social or conceptual arrangements. The precise nature of that slippage remains elusive, as does the functioning over time of this conceptual and practical dialectic between coercion and flux.

Nevertheless, the guiding tenet of cultural and intellectual history, that people are bonded to their time such that innovation calls for a true Hercules, has become an unquestioned part of sociological thought. Should this, albeit imperfect, conceptual shorthand be accepted, one must ask: was Weber a man and a mind of his time (determined by it), and if so—assuming that the determinate features of his environment can be named—how does this affect current interpretations of his work? More important, do the peculiarities of his epoch mean anything for today's readers who wish to use his concepts and his example of how theorizing should be done? (We momentarily avoid determining the extent of his involvement in affairs around him.) These questions need only be asked to have impact. Rather than reciting the litany of insightful paradoxes about Weber,[64] in an effort to find answers it might be wiser to consider some related notions that can serve as a prolegomenon.

Weber was attuned to the tones of his era in every way that is important to a scholar. His achievements were unlike Einstein's or Leonardo's, who saw the ordinary in new ways. Weber was more a Michelangelo, working reasonably well with existing techniques and satisfied to perfect accepted aesthetic, or scholarly, goals; his genius lay in elaboration and refinement, not trailblazing. From his socialization and the extraordinary models for emulation that were part of it,[65] he gained obsessively methodical habits, an unshakable private morality (which seems from today's perspective a *slightly* diluted Puritanism of the ideal type), and a rigid belief in his duty as scholar, along with the muted conviction that men of knowledge—a group to which Weber felt privileged to belong—existed, finally, to inform men of action when given the chance.

64. For example, he was politically of his time, but ahead of it; a passionate participant yet objective observer of his society; personally volcanic but publicly olympian.

65. E.g., the senior historian of the age, Theodor Mommsen, who publicly said, "But when I have to go to my grave, there is no one to whom I would rather say, 'Son, here is my spear . . .' than the highly esteemed Max Weber." Mommsen was seventy-two, Weber twenty-five. (Marianne Weber, *Max Weber*, p. 114.)

Specifically related to my interests is Weber's typically northern German "aesthetic pantheism,"[66] which his scientific self strained to suppress. From his youth it weakened Weber's ability to appreciate, and allowed him to understate theoretically, the private, irrational responses of social actors to social structure, no matter how patently rationalized structure alone might seem. (Consider, for example, the influence Peter Gay's history of Victorian sexuality, *The Bourgeois Experience*, might have had on Weber's ideas had it been available to him.) The individual's lifelong search for meaning (interpersonally or autonomously framed) Weber accepted as a prime ingredient of social life, which, given his position vis-à-vis Dilthey, is hardly surprising. Against political economy, he allowed that irrationality often informed this search. Yet he would not build irrationality into his formal sociology, seeing the dilemma it would create for logical analysis. Thus he squeezed from human behavior—by weighting each type of social action in terms of its utility to science—the bulk of meaning-seeking activity, since irrational and nonrational motives remain, by their nature, largely unrationalizable. Although Weber decried the "de-magicalization" of modern life and accepted the importance of the most irrational political force, charisma, his guidelines for social and political-economic analyses assert the paramount nature of *zweckrational* action. This attitude handicaps our understanding of current social structure.

Notes Toward a Hermeneutic of Weber

The preceding pages have reintroduced hermeneutic arguments known to Mannheim and his peers sixty years ago, but not seriously pursued by American sociologists until quite recently. Mannheim is worth recalling since he reminds us that classics cannot be made ours unless unusual care is taken when interpreting them. If studied observations like Mannheim's on the problems facing competent interpretations teach anything, it is that a "scholar's worldview should *not* be assumed either to be specifiable . . . or known

---

66. This mixture of thought and feeling was best captured by another student of the period, Thomas Mann, also subject to this *Weltanschauung*, in an early short story, "Little Herr Friedemann" (*Stories of Three Decades*, pp. 3–22). Revelatory too are Mann's *Buddenbrooks*, "Tonio Kröger," and "Disorder and Early Sorrow." *Doctor Faustus* clarifies Weber's metaphysics.

by its substantial intimacy with a cultural period." This much at least phenomenology has shown, even with its preeminent interest in singular consciousness, untrammeled by structure. Husserl's axiom that consciousness, "everyday" or theorized, can be known and reported convincingly only by its "possessor" has become bedrock for his sociological followers. The contents of mind are not reflections of external objects but the product of concatenations that defy photographic description owing to their self-generative, "intentional" complexity. Thus, ontology during this century, unlike that of the past, claims that it cannot be confidently assumed that we are equipped to imagine another's mental terrain, even approximately. For the moment we can conform to recent sociological prejudice and evade ontology proper. For though it is likely that Weber's *Weltanschauung* cannot be reproduced with the ease Mannheim thought possible, it is still feasible to approximate Weber's position in the interest of better discourse. The alternative is to avoid the theorist's person altogether, working exclusively with his (in this case, translated) words. I would label this the New Critical fallacy. Cumulative knowledge must rest, instead, on reflective, self-adjusting interpretative technique. Only recently have American critics adopted highly developed European regimens. Although some Continental interpreters imitate New Criticism, those most useful to this study oppose separation of author and product. Holistic analysis, following Hegel, Schleiermacher, Dilthey, and Gadamer, proves most helpful in this devilish matter.

Interpretation of classic theories and the revival of ideas that come from it succeed if the reader brings the works to life by climbing inside the author's head. This is not needless methodological purism. Disagreement on this point merely registers changes in academic fads. Not long ago *The Meeting of East and West, Eastern Religions and Western Thought,* and *Ways of Thinking of Eastern Peoples*[67]— whose purpose was to reconcile opposed *Weltanschauungen*—were treated with intellectual respect. Present folkways see them as naive in their optimism, reckless in scope. So too the effort to open up "private" aspects of the theorist's life—those idiosyncratic, unruly drags on theorizing, such as personal values—too easily is stig-

---

67. F. S. C. Northrop, pp. 9–14; S. Radhakrishnan, pp. 18–20; Hajime Nakamura.

matized as a hindrance from the nineteenth century. In this case to follow the past is the surer road.

From this come two basic hermeneutic rules. First, classical theory is dead on the page until informed by the reconstructed consciousness, *Weltanschauung*, or, at a minimum, the theoretical goals of its author. (The improbability of imaginatively recreating the writer's worldview in perfect facsimile is taken for granted.) Second, the capacity of this reconstructed consciousness to portray the theorist adequately cannot be judged apodictically. Rough consensus within a community of scholars has become the standard surrogate for interpretative certainty. This compromise (the "perspectival knowledge" Merleau-Ponty commended to sociologists) [68] reflects the pull of philosophical relativism, the loss of absolutes. Yet it seeks to end the uneasiness of the relative in spite of itself. Scholarly consensus is frequently an unreliable sponsor of truth or accuracy. The nature of group dynamics indeed abets cyclical changes in "expert opinion," sometimes simply for the sake of change. Despite attempts by positivists on the one hand, phenomenologists on the other, to overcome this malady, social scientists, having emptied themselves of absolute, a priori values, still take "knowledgeable opinion" as the arbiter of intellectual disputes, especially when interpreting theoretical intentions and realizations fashioned some time ago.

Validity by consensus, then, holds its ground even after Kuhn's demonstration that progress, or simple change, within science occurs when accepted scripts are countered by theoretical and factual anomaly. The ultimate result is paradigmatic shift, necessarily the achievement of scientists trained to disregard at some level the weight of consensually founded truth. Preceding Kuhn's observations by many years were those of the physicist-philosopher Gaston Bachelard, whose comparable notion, "epistemological break" or "rupture," furthers the claim that innovative knowledge expands just as professional norms of reputable work decline and are finally transcended. [69]

68. *The Essential Writings of Merleau-Ponty*, pp. 64–80. Maurice Natanson makes phenomenologically important distinctions between "intersubjectivity" and "consensus"; see his *The Journeying Self*, pp. 1–67.

69. Thomas S. Kuhn, *The Structure of Scientific Revolutions*, pp. 23ff., 52ff. (Also of interest regarding creativity and "tension" is Kuhn's "The Essential Tension: Tra-

Many social scientists have found reflections of this sort compelling (especially practitioners of the "strong program" in the sociology of science). It is probably true, however, that changes within natural science are not precisely imitated by events in social science. Thus the strength of Kuhn's "paradigmatic shifts" falls off in explanatory power when applied to the *Geisteswissenschaften* (a point freely admitted by Kuhn himself). Perhaps this is fortunate, helping to preserve a key fiction in the workings of a social (or human) science seeking significance: that agreement upon an intricate theoretical or interpretative matter, by scholars sensitized to the issues at hand, is justifiably regarded and transmitted as knowledge, not common opinion. (This process connotes an "aestheticization" toward certain information, and the modes of perception and discussion linked to its apprehension.) The assertion is easy to puncture on logical grounds. But, as I will show with reference to Weber's infatuation with "logic,"[70] this illogic is not a crucial failure for interpretative social science, or for hermeneutics, and it means nothing in the realm of human meaning theoretically comprehended.

Weber's lifelong uneasiness over the epistemological and meth-

---

dition and Innovation in Scientific Research," ibid., p. 79n.) Only Bachelard's aesthetic and ontological works have been translated into English. For his philosophy of science, see Dominique Lecourt, *Marxism and Epistemology: Bachelard, Canquilhem, and Foucault*, pp. 7–22 passim.

70. "Logic," for Weber, should be understood as practically pure symbol, viz.: "All interpretation, as does science generally, strives for clarity and verifiable proof. Such proof of understanding will be either of a *rational*, i.e. *logical* or mathematical, or of an emotionally empathetic, artistically appreciative, character" (Weber 1962, trans. H. P. Secher, p. 30, translation slightly changed, emphasis added). Mannheim saw the inadequacy of Weber's declarations about "scientific" interpretation and method and must have wondered at remarks so dogmatically set against the *Kulturwissenschaften* much practiced at the time, preeminently by Weber's esteemed friend Lukács. In a long note in his essay on interpretation of worldviews (*Essays on the Sociology of Knowledge*, p. 63n), Mannheim tried to add sophistication to Weber's lines quoted above. But Mannheim was not, I think, zealous enough in his emendation. He in effect defends his own tripartite typology of meaning against Weber's dichotomy, apparently without considering Weber's duality a genuine threat to his more elaborate breakdown: "This distinction between 'intended' and 'adequate' meaning corresponds to the distinction Max Weber makes between 'actual' and 'correct' meaning. *Wirtschaft und Gesellschaft*, Pt. I, Sect. 1, pp. 1ff" (ibid.). Weber's "distinction" is inadequate on every level of theoretical interest; moreover, it is practically incomprehensible in translation (see Weber 1947/1964, pp. 89–90) and takes up only eleven lines. It is clear that Weber was avoiding the concept of meaning but felt compelled to mention it perfunctorily.

odological concerns that preoccupied Dilthey, Rickert, and their followers reflects a scholarly atmosphere at once paralyzed by veneration of natural science and haltingly emulating it. A vortex of reasons forced the question of which portion of social reality sociology could reasonably apprehend and with what confidence it could be explained.[71] This seems a foundational difficulty preceding substantive analysis. Although Weber became first bored, then irritated, by these matters and the suffocating polemics they occasioned, he did not really transcend or eliminate them in his writings on method. He was wise, however, in withdrawing after a time from the contest—again serving as the role model in this professional stance for American sociologists much later. Yet if his tastes in this were prescient, he formally did little to end quarreling over the nature of proof and validity in social science. Of course, his monographs became exemplars of fine social research, but their methodological approach and empirical lavishness gained few imitators and left little in the way of programmatic guidelines for his followers.

Since Weber ignored the epistemological weakness of relying for judgments of validity upon scholarly opinion, the opinions of Sombart, Troeltsch, Michels, Jellinek, and his other peers must have seemed to him a steady bulwark against errors. His directives on method, chiefly about ideal types, causality, and *Verstehen*, are opaque, incomplete, and debated still. Finally, his knowledge, wide and deep, separates him from scholars today. Considering all this we may ask, did Weber extend the *Geisteswissenschaften* to a distant shore, only to have marked a path impossible to follow?

Some have complained that his astounding substantive work, when set beside the methodological proclamations, has created great confusion about what approach should be taken in social science. This is most true on the question of irrationality. He confirmed the prevailing opinion that certain puzzles are insoluble with positivist tools and thus better left alone. Sociologists had little chance, it was thought, of resolving such questions, which seemed in any case too philosophical or psychoanalytic. What is more, according to Weber's example, energy could best be spent

71. On this point see Ringer, *Decline of the German Mandarins,* pp. 14–80; of particular importance is "Rationality and Culture," pp. 83–90.

gathering and synthesizing "clean" data (e.g., trade documents, vassalage agreements, the full range of economic and legal records) in whatever form was easily communicated to co-researchers. He was skeptical of data from self-reports of the emotional life. This was not one of his more fortunate lessons for sociology. By assuming this posture, and realizing it was just that, he relegated human meaning and its connection with irrationality to the "residual category" where Parsons found them—and was happy to leave them.

It is pointless to wonder whether Weber was justified in his advice that sociology ignore certain avenues to difficult areas of study in order to foster the short-term growth of its scientific stature. When the strident academic rivalries of imperial Germany are remembered, Weber's choices are understandable. But as the world has been transformed along every axis since he made those thematic suggestions, prudence might ask that we jettison some of Weber's strictures, especially those both disruptive of current theoretical aims and also unfaithful to contemporary experience. This is not easily accomplished, for many of Weber's preferences, which set the subliminal tone of his work, lie buried within his desiderata. They await a "hermeneutical motion," as George Steiner puts it,[72] capable of raising into public discourse the latent structure that sponsored his directives for sociological analysis.

Modern hermeneutics has developed over the last two hundred years, first in Germany between 1770 and Weber's time, now in France and Italy as well. An evaluation of this body of interpretative theory and technique as applied to classical social thought is overdue. Paul Ricoeur and Jacques Lacan have produced hermeneutic evaluations of Freud; Jürgen Habermas has sparred at length with the leading hermeneutic theorist, Hans-Georg Gadamer, while trying himself to create a "hermeneutical sociology."[73] Weber and Pareto have not as yet been subjects of a study in English that originates in contemporary hermeneutics. The feasibility of such a study and the promise hermeneutics may hold for students of theory require discussion.

72. George Steiner, *After Babel*, pp. 296ff.
73. Paul Ricoeur, *Freud and Philosophy*; Jacques Lacan, *The Language of the Self*; Jürgen Habermas, "Rhetorik, Hermeneutik, und Ideologiekritik," in *Hermeneutik und Ideologiekritik*, Karl-Otto Apel et al., pp. 57–82. Americans could profit from study of Gadamer's catalogue of interpretative problems. Its neglect in the United

"Pre-Hermeneutical" Concerns:
Scholarship Past and Present

There exist still other barriers to textual understanding, a series of quasi-epistemological, pre-hermeneutical factors that strain exegesis. The professional self-expectations of American social scientists are in some ways more relaxed today than they were around 1885, when G. H. Mead, William James, and Albion Small joined other novitiates in Europe with hopes of becoming learned. They assumed that scholarship that set out with confined aspirations forsook its main chance. Theirs was an age that still saw cultural and societal problems as soluble through the subtle intervention of reason. Sociologists no longer subscribe to this bracing definition of scholarship, partly owing to their education and conditions of employment. Nor do many view themselves as intellectuals, since a person of this faded title was expected to cross many boundaries, to embody a cohesive, widely acknowledged heritage. The intellectual was supposed to see many things through a polished theoretical lens. Lacking much of this—broad learning gained through multilingual apprenticeship, diverse and plentiful sociocultural knowledge, and a confidently applied theory—social scientists tend now, in self-estimation and professional practice, toward the role of technician. They resemble Znaniecki's "technologists," not "sages" or "scholars."[74] Even though they routinely plunder old theories for usable bits, such readers are not prepared to interpret writers whose achievements transcended academic borders and who viewed schematism, of contemporary or historical events, as the most venal scholarly sin. This is important to remember as attempts are made to recapture the classics.[75]

States is reflected in the widespread practice of what Richard Palmer termed "rape theories of interpretation" (*Hermeneutics*, p. 247). Gadamer's sensitivity to linguistically mediated existence, the force of history in altering textual meanings, and the "immersion" that precedes skilled interpretation is germane to the dissection of classical theories.

74. Florian Znaniecki, *The Social Role of the Man of Knowledge*, pp. 31–55, 72ff., 91ff.

75. The vision of what is likely to be fruitful in sociocultural study, the preconditions for intuitive leaps, the manifold undiscussed, perhaps incommunicable private mental facets of theoretical originality which enliven the consciousness of any major thinker all fructified within Weber's intellectual "machinery" (or *Weltanschauung*) in the course of his stupendous compilation of data: legal, eco-

When ambitious works appear today that aspire simultaneously to general intellectual and sociological prominence,[76] many readers within the field react with indifference, hostility, or, given the pace of specialized research, benign neglect. Often specialists produce overweening, inaccurate comparisons between such ambitious books, as uncommonly good as they may be, and those of classic writers, notably Weber, who, so it is claimed, has been surpassed.[77] The superiority of the present is assumed. This kind of temperocentrism demolishes competent hermeneutics before it is begun.

Graduate education consistently leads to misapprehension (or codification)[78] of classic texts, a condition widely known but infrequently countered. The central task of this study—commentary on irrational processes within social life—makes it necessary to avoid the path normally trod, unwittingly perhaps, by many, who follow "the footsteps of Monsieur Pangloss and Dr. Bowdler."[79] As scholars, sociologists have not guarded their legacy jealously enough; they no longer read closely.

Two independent factors have in the last several decades conspired to weaken sociology's hold on its past: (1) quantitative re-

---

nomic, historical, linguistic, religious, philosophical, aesthetic. It is as plain now as it was then that this ardent accumulation of fact is essential for composing persuasive theories, especially macro theories. These homilies are worth rehearsing because hermeneutics stipulates that often the most serious obstacles to successful interpretation, though in plain view, go unnoticed. These superficial reflections about Weber's learning and ours are not often or sincerely enough thought over. This works against thorough exegesis. Since major existential distinctions obtain between scholarly life then and now, they need to be recorded.

76. E.g., Immanuel Wallerstein's *The Modern World-System;* Reinhard Bendix, *Kings or People;* Barrington Moore, *Injustice,* and *Privacy;* and Orlando Patterson, *Slavery and Social Death.*

77. Gerhard Lenski claims that Wallerstein's *Modern World-System* sheds more light on the origins of the world economy than Weber's writing (review in *Social Forces,* p. 701). Similarly, Norbert Wiley believes that Randall Collins's *Conflict Sociology* has beneficially transformed Weber "from a historicist to a variable analyst" (review in *Contemporary Sociology,* p. 237). As uncommonly ambitious as these two books are, one could argue that such evaluations are generous.

78. I do not use the term in Merton's sense, since for him the word carried some positive connotations. For me it is roughly synonymous with *shortcut* or *gloss.* Cf. Robert K. Merton, *Social Theory and Social Structure,* pp. 69–72, 153–155.

79. Andreski, *Social Science as Sorcery,* p. 51. Some interpretations do not deserve Andreski's epithet, e.g., Bryan S. Green, "On the Evaluation of Sociological Theory," and Robert Alun Jones, "On Understanding a Sociological Classic." The former is free of any influence from hermeneutics but arrives at similar conclusions. The latter, though formally about Durkheim, makes general remarks about the difficulties of interpretation.

search techniques, which by their nature are often ahistorical, presupposing and demanding of their user little beyond the mechanical
application of formulae; and (2) the deaths of many older (particularly European) scholars, who were relied upon by their American
students and colleagues to act as storehouses for the history of social thought. The long-term discipline associated with becoming
widely versed in theory and the cultural opportunities open to European scholars born at the turn of the century are no longer readily at hand. This lack is taking its toll in the transfer of theory from
one generation of sociologists to the next.[80] The cost of ignoring
this decline seems high indeed, since trivialization and dilution of
the field are the likely results.

Clearly, then, contemporary usage of past discoveries is not an
easy or automatic process. The effort is plagued by worrisome obstacles, some cognitive, others existential. Yet most of these, to the
degree required for textual integrity, are superable if recognized
early enough in the endless process of rereading and reinterpreta-
tion.[81] This process has always been central to hermeneutics and
continues to figure in much contemporary French thought, but has
not until recently been very evident among Americans. "Hesitating
to forget its founders" is not a fault of sociology in the United
States.

The lessons of hermeneutics will be brought to bear upon Weber's
(and Pareto's) works, in pursuit of a more adequate reading. At
times such an interpretation will consciously oppose standard versions accepted, judging from their citations, at face value by many
sociologists. Hermeneutics can help relocate Pareto theoretically,
forty years after he was last taken seriously by social theorists. He

80. Consider, for instance, the difference in quality, comprehensiveness, and
depth of textbooks used some time ago either for introductory courses (e.g., Robert
MacIver, *Society: Its Structure and Changes*, or Pitirim Sorokin, *Society, Culture and
Personality*) or in theory courses (Sorokin's *Contemporary Sociological Theories* or
Barnes and Becker's *Social Thought from Lore to Science*) with today's pabulum. See
also Robert K. Merton and Matilda White Riley, eds., *Sociological Traditions from Generation to Generation*, and Buford Rhea, ed., *The Future of the Sociological Classics*.

81. The process of rewriting and appropriating intellectual history does have
its limits. A work in which reviewers saw "bad hermeneutics" at work is Herman
Schwendinger and Julia Schwendinger's *Sociologists of the Chair*, a portrayal of early
American sociology from a Marxist-feminist critical viewpoint. Their book does considerable violence to simple facts in order to effect its interpretative aim, thus violating the dicta of hermeneutic theory.

is easier to treat than Weber, since the latter's penchant for rationality is an essential part of the contemporary scene, while Pareto is
more of an undisturbed theoretical corpse.[82]

Lessons of Classical and
Contemporary Hermeneutics

Since theories of textual interpretation are no longer deemed a necessary part of methods for American sociologists, it might be wise
to note their major propositions.[83] The ideal approach to such a
task would be historical, but it is hardly feasible to write a history
of interpretative theory here.[84] A genuine understanding of hermeneutics could only be gained through familiarity with its development, which would include theories of Friedrich Ast, Friedrich
August Wolf, Friedrich Schleiermacher, Wilhelm Dilthey, Martin
Heidegger, Emilio Betti, and Hans-Georg Gadamer. Newer voices

---

82. Pareto is not ignored universally: European use of his work continues. See
John E. Tashjean, "Interest in Pareto's Sociology: Reflections on a Bibliography,"
and Jaroslav Bilous and John H. Quirk, "Interest in Pareto's Sociology: An Essay in
the Quantitative History of Social Science." Two books in English may stimulate
thought about Pareto: Placido Bucolo, ed., *The Other Pareto*, and, more important,
Pareto's *Compendium of General Sociology*, abridged in Italian with the author's ap-
proval by Giulio Farina, English text edited and collated by Elisabeth Abbott.

83. One might ask why an investigation of classical or contemporary theory requires a formalized hermeneutic, especially given today's scholarly environment,
where application rather than commentary—a post-hermeneutic condition—prevails. Study of classical theory can be done differently, perhaps better, than it usually is. Of the dozens of major Weber and Pareto treatments, very few capture the
originals they hope to "re-present." A competent interpretative act is demanding,
elusive, and worthy of pursuit, and can advance social thought. Social science must
either admit to meager knowledge of older work and forge ahead with ab nihilo
theory, or master hermeneutic principles and practice. Classical theory is not
skimmable.

Some literary critics can dissect social theory, regardless of content, with more
grace than most sociologists. For instance, Fredric Jameson's Review Essay on Erving Goffman's *Frame Analysis* (in *Theory and Society*) deserves emulation. Jameson's
neologism, "meta-book," exemplifies the type of critical imagination sociology
needs, especially concerning works such as Goffman's that are valued precisely for
their insightful phraseology. Return to careful study of "the word" is called for if the
power of verbal expression is to regain its potential for theorizing. After aesthetic
production, language is the ablest vehicle for describing and analyzing behavior—a
point undebated until recent intellectual history.

84. For a brief history of hermeneutic doctrine, see the appendix to my dissertation, "The Problem of Irrationality and Meaning in the Work of Max Weber,"
pp. 520–649. See also Richard E. Palmer, *Hermeneutics*, one of the first among now
numerous works in English covering philosophical and grammatical, as opposed to
theological, hermeneutics. See the bibliography (pp. 293–307) in Shapiro and Sica,
eds., *Hermeneutics*; and Alan Sica, "Hermeneutics and Social Theory."

are those of Paul Ricoeur, Jacques Lacan, Louis Althusser, Jürgen Habermas, and Roland Barthes, who share a commitment to close reading of classic texts.[85]

The realization that texts' intrinsic ambiguity over time causes scholarly discord has been a minor part of the Western heritage at least since Aristotle. In the *Organon* (essays on logic) from his "third period" (335–322 B.C.) appears "De Interpretatione," a concise rule book of propositions and judgments. It served as the locus classicus for early and modern hermeneutics, despite its unconcern for intertexuality, the conditioning effects of one text upon another within the same cultural milieu. Aristotle's main interest was in poetry and drama, yet the care he prescribed for textual analysis has been emulated even as the range of problematic materials broadened. Perhaps his lasting contribution lies in being the first to emphasize that sober concern over techniques pertinent to interpretative understanding composes unto itself an entire field of speculative and methodologically vital study.[86]

In the seventeenth and eighteenth centuries, as our desacralized worldview took shape, French rationalists attacked theology and religion on every front. Their attentive students, some of the philosophically energetic Germans, responded in part by defending the Bible with interpretations they judged plausible in an atmosphere unfriendly to mythmaking. They advanced a sympathetic version of the Scriptures as ethically sound, though historically incorrect. This was one aspect of a multifaceted reaction to the collapse of moral-political consensus, and those status relations anchored in this defunct harmony—or coercion, depending on one's view of the ancien régime. The wrenching disharmony of this period registered most shockingly in the Thirty Years' War. Its conclusion (1648) prompted work on ethical theories aimed at restoring, on new terms, a viable moral-theological, then political consensus.

Modern biblical hermeneutics began in the mid-eighteenth century. Only after 1789 did the German exegetes succeed in refurbishing a theological-ethical code, the precursor of which the French had abandoned. Schleiermacher's desire for a general hermeneu-

85. Ricoeur's and Lacan's works were cited earlier; Habermas, *Knowledge and Human Interests;* Barthes, *Writing Degree Zero/Elements of Semiology,* and *S/Z;* Louis Althusser and Etienne Balibar, *Reading Capital.*

86. Heidegger makes extensive use of Aristotle's work, as do writers like Gadamer, who in turn borrow from his version of hermeneutics.

tics, growing from the impulse to "civilize" modernity, resonated throughout German intellectual life for some time. It was then eclipsed and absorbed as a technique, when the human sciences supplanted theology during the half-century following Schleiermacher's death. Dilthey was the greatest hermeneutic theorist following Schleiermacher, but after Dilthey the field hovered near obscurity until it was revived by Heidegger in the 1920s. Since 1945, hermeneutics has blossomed as never before. The following hermeneutical dicta partly summarize propositions from the theories just mentioned. They are modeled to suit classical social theory rather than the sources (biblical, historical, philosophical, or literary) to which they were originally directed.

1. Hermeneutics, most generally, is elucidation, the goal of which is to facilitate scholarly consensus about textual meaning or meanings, whenever the possibility of disagreement arises. It involves careful analysis of "the word," recognizing that numerical notation is not as often subject to the extreme disagreements which stem from discrepant readings of complex verbal statements. (For the moment, we leave aside the special problem of translations and the confusion they sometimes stimulate. It was in search of solid translations, from sacred texts, that modern hermeneutics was created in the eighteenth century.) [87]

2. The sine qua non of credible interpretation is intensive and extensive knowledge of the text (or, to change focus, the action) [88] and its author so that all key aspects, the grammatical (semantic), historical (contextual), and *geistige* (the author's creative psychology and the cultural value of the work), may become known.

3. This mandatory accretion of broad knowledge, preceding interrogation of a work, assures that the inner unity of the text will not be violated, that its basic idea or basic concept will not remain obscure.

4. The creative process of the author is reexperienced in order to approximate his worldview and to define the spirit of the work (locked as it is in history, a document of an era and a testament to

87. Theories of translating abound. The most readable is Steiner's *After Babel;* see esp. chapters 4 and 5, "The Claims of Theory" and "The Hermeneutic Motion." Steiner's authority in this field stems from the fact that he has from youth been equally literate in three languages, and thus his sensitivity to the problems of translation exceeds that of normal readers.
88. Cf. Paul Ricoeur, "The Model of the Text." A good study is John B. Thompson's *Critical Hermeneutics,* pp. 36–70, 123–130, 139–149, 216–218.

its own historicality and temporality). Not all readers possess this ability to reexperience—perhaps the most important and difficult step in the process of interpretation—in equal degree. It has been suggested more than once that a certain "lightness of soul," the easy partaking of another's creative and cognitive reality, benefits the most skilled hermeneuticists.

5. Roughly speaking, explanation is the duty of natural science and formal logic, while understanding, specially defined, is the objective of hermeneutics and of the human (or cultural) sciences generally. This division is due to the nature of the data to be explained or analyzed and the ways they are approached and interacted with during analyses.

6. Interpretation of difficult classical texts, whether sacred, ancient, or contemporary, results in an anarchy of views among scholars and prevents or hinders the advance of knowledge; traditionally, impasses are ignored more often than overcome. This is considerably less true for the natural sciences, since scholarly consensus there is more definitively, quickly, and solidly won than in the human sciences. This partly explains the natural sciences' impatience with convoluted discussions of methodology and epistemology. A prime purpose of hermeneutics in social science, then, is to make generally acceptable explanations of key thinkers and their traditions a more regular feature of intellectual life. These explanations (or understandings) must, of course, be faithful to the texts. Scholars would then be free to proceed with their original work without personally having to reconstruct the history of the discipline beforehand. A conciseness and cleanness of theoretical line might justifiably be called for, one that parallels those often found in the natural sciences, if this cleanness were prevented from displacing completeness of detail and breadth of application.

7. Hermeneutics is more an art than a science in the common senses of the words. Not only must interpretation be quasi-artistic, but culturally significant texts often concentrate upon irrationality in human life, which traditionally is represented aesthetically, not through logically or rationally constructed documents. This tradition, rightly or wrongly, sees pure rationality as isolated from the ambiguity of pre-cognitive experience.[89]

89. See Donald Levine, *The Flight from Ambiguity,* for unusual observations on this notion.

8. Interpretation is made possible via the "hermeneutic circle." This recognizes the totality of a work regarding its constituent parts, and also its contiguity with a cultural milieu. Only by thinking dialogically can the interpreter, moving between part and whole, gain a considered understanding of the text. Initial entrance into this circle is by definition *logically* impossible (a fact often pointed out contra Dilthey). But the interpreting consciousness can "leap" into the hermeneutic circle before specifying the parameters of the entire work (or, following Ricoeur, of the total set of social relationships). It then constructs the entirety piecemeal, from whatever starting point has been selected. The faculty that permits this leap, which obviously violates pure logic, derives from pre-knowledge or pre-reflective consciousness, an artifact of the linguisticality of culture.

9. Reexperiencing and other hermeneutical procedures are divinatory in nature. Therefore, the discipline of interpretation can never be completely systematized, for it requires an intuitive understanding. As such it contradicts the demand for demonstrability that is central to positivist method and proof. But this demand is not relevant to the practice of interpretation, since its goals are not those of inductive science.

10. Interpretation concerns itself with an author's style and what might be called the aesthetics of individuality or genius. An important school of hermeneutics believes that fathoming a text's content is symbiotically joined with understanding its form, that is, the style in which it is presented. In fact, much hermeneutic theory refuses to recognize the hoary divide naturalistic or realist theories of literature see between form and content, since it violates the spirit of holistic analysis.

11. There is no absolute and general set of rules for interpretation. To some extent each interpretative act must be matched uniquely with the text (or action) under consideration. Therefore, the Kantian rigidity of method, which strongly encouraged strict separation of *Natur-* and *Geisteswissenschaften,* is detrimental to the study of culture. (Hegelianism in one form or another has by default become the preferred guide.)

12. In line with the objection to Kantian epistemology, emphasis is given to the fact that the categories which make interpretation possible do not originate in objective structural considerations ei-

ther of Mind or of ideal method but, rather, from the very categories in which *Leben* is known to human consciousness—thus, from categories internal to the works themselves. These categories, originating in life or in the text (which ideally, but not necessarily, overlap to some extent), are invariably subsumed under the broader notion of meaning. Through exposing the finest shades of meaning, interpretation proves its utility to the human sciences. For, as Weber and others have agreed, scientific method can assess only means, not values or ends determined by different varieties and levels of human meaning.

13. Hermeneutics does not dismantle or attack its object of study; rather, it places itself in dialogue with the author and work, meeting in the commonalities of human meaning, experience, and linguisticality, not in the object-over-against-observer posture of the natural sciences. The inner life of humanity becomes examinable, and as public as it is wont to be, only through expressions (texts, actions, or artworks) possessed of *geistig* content. Hermeneutic theory recognizes these as the only objective referents of cultural continuity and change. As such they must be deciphered using tools which are not initially and irrevocably alien to their nature; some methodological homology must obtain between the *interpretandum* and hermeneutic tools.

14. Instead of expecting a scientific epistemology (positivist, nominalist, coherence theory of truth) to serve as the basis of interpretative theory and practice, hermeneutics requires a self-reflexive theory of interpretation to facilitate a critique of historical reason.[90] (This counters the *Critique of Pure Reason*, which is more suitable for physical science.)

15. According to one classical hermeneutic approach (as well as Hannah Arendt's last work),[91] the human psyche, especially as it creates various expressions of consciousness, can be conceived as operating through three major faculties: knowing, feeling, and willing. Since a major goal of hermeneutics is to identify distinct worldviews, it is worth recalling that these faculties of the psyche have historically been associated with religious, artistic, and philosophic *Weltanschauungen*, respectively.

90. This is related only incidentally to Sartre's *Critique de la raison dialectique*.
91. Hannah Arendt, *The Life of the Mind*, 2 vols.

16. The finest interpretation, according to hermeneutics, requires acts of genius not dissimilar in type and magnitude to the original artistic or intellectual performance that produced the text in question. (Of all the principles and guidelines put forth by major theorists, this is perhaps the least convincing, if the most intriguing.)

17. The divinatory act of interpretation may effect a transposition of selves. In this way another window onto a given socio-historical world may be opened.

18. History as known to hermeneutics is a succession of *Weltan-schauungen* among which exists an anarchy of values. Relativism, therefore, is the theology or axiology of hermeneutics.

19. One suggested formula for hermeneutic practice claims that (a) the subject and the object of study are reciprocally related, since the interpreter questions and is questioned by the text and its author, that is, he stands in its presence; and (b) experience, expressions (i.e., ideas, actions, and expressions of lived experience), and understanding make up the entirety of the interpretative event. All must be used and examined simultaneously in order that complete hermeneutical analysis can be achieved, for a totalistic ontological relationship exists among the three.

20. Interpretation is not fighting, overpowering, or dominating an object; it is subtly persuading the cultural expression to yield its fullest meaning. Attempts to bludgeon it, as are made with objects of naturalistic analysis, create distortions and counterfeit results.

Addendum: A Note on the
Gadamer-Habermas Debate

Sociologists who have been influenced by Habermas may have concluded that he had the last and best word when he accused his senior colleague of conservatism and a debilitating fixation on texts isolated from their sociopolitical environments. Habermas's reading of Gadamer was not itself an adequate example of hermeneutics, however, and those who have rejected the latter's hermeneutic theory and practice because of the former's critique may reconsider when the facts of their debate are brought forward.

The first edition of *Wahrheit und Methode* appeared in 1960, the culmination of "hermeneutic praxis during a quarter century of academic activity," as Gadamer turned sixty.[92] His student days with Heidegger had left him with a virtuoso concern for adequate interpretation of artistic and philosophic texts. The Diltheyan task of creating for social science a battery of hermeneutic methods has been, not Gadamer's, but that of his theoretical opponent, Emilio Betti. Gadamer's magnum opus, which reached English readers in 1975, opposes Betti's search for analytic or interpretative tools and concerns itself instead with an ontology of language—the *Sprachlichkeit* (linguisticality) of human existence. In 1967 Habermas charged Gadamer's theory with presupposing an idealized (as opposed to ideal) speech situation, promulgating a specious claim for the universal place of hermeneutics in all understanding, thus all social science, and otherwise falling short of what Habermas demanded from the reputable hermeneutics he agreed was necessary.[93]

Habermas was thirty-one, about half Gadamer's age, when *Truth and Method* was published. Perhaps in this slight fact lies a hint of an explanation for Habermas's unfair and unfairly influential critique of Gadamer's version of hermeneutics. Habermas's theoretical ambition has appropriated for its own purposes Kant, Fichte, Hegel, Wittgenstein, Popper, Pierce, Marx, Dilthey, Freud, Dewey, Mead, and Parsons.[94] Beginning with a volume of the *Philosophische Rundschau* in 1967, Gadamer became another ingredient in the Habermas synthesis.

Reaction to Habermas's work, and particularly to *Knowledge and Human Interests*, has been awe at his bridging of traditions. Given that within the first two decades of academic life he produced a dozen books, at least four of them major, is it not conceivable, if not immediately obvious, that his critique of Gadamer originates in extra-intellectual sources? The entire legacy of hermeneutics dating from Aristotle, which Gadamer has mastered, agrees upon at least one dictum: legitimate interpretation of texts demands extraordi-

---

92. Hans-Georg Gadamer, "The Problem of Historical Consciousness," p. 2.

93. Jürgen Habermas, "Zur Logik der Sozialwissenschaften," *Philosophische Rundschau* 5: 149–176; reprinted as "Der hermeneutische Ansatz," *Zur Logik der Sozialwissenschaften*, pp. 251–290; translated as "A Review of Gadamer's *Truth and Method*," in Fred Dallmayr and Thomas McCarthy, eds., *Understanding and Social Inquiry*, pp. 335–363.

94. Thomas McCarthy, "Translator's Introduction," in Habermas, *Legitimation Crisis*, p. vii.

nary care, even virtuosity, something for which sheer brilliance is
no substitute. Exegesis that does not distort requires pedantic attention to detail and nuance. Can it be that Habermas (and his admirers who have spoken to the point) rejects Gadamer's principal
tenets because of his own style of theorizing?[95] It is not unthinkable
that this protracted debate simply reflects two contrary hermeneutical dispositions, one dedicated to the careful *Überlieferung* ("passing over") of cultural knowledge from one generation to the next,
the other attached to the desire for practical, applicable theory that
can bind (or puncture, depending upon one's reading) late capitalist social structure.

There is also the matter of political obligations. During the 1960s,
when Habermas began dissecting contemporary hermeneutics to
supplement his Dilthey critique, he was locked in battle with the
radical student left. Perhaps his repeated objection to Gadamer's
"rehabilitation of authority and tradition" is partly a result of
Habermas's lack of an "ideal speech situation" vis-à-vis the militant
left, and his strategic need to distance himself from any apparently
conservative position. Gadamer had also been for many years
on close theoretical terms with influential (Bultmannian) German
theologians. A Marxist of the Frankfurt type could hardly ally himself with any theory that had already won acclaim among the
clergy.

An indication that these nonimmanent factors do illuminate the
peculiar relationship between critical theory and hermeneutics lies
in the fact that Gadamer has frequently rebutted Habermas's ac-
cusations about his political conservatism, but to no avail.[96] In this
case "communicative incompetence" due to a lack of "general sym-
metry" will surely not "dissolve barriers to communication" in the
interest of consensual truth, in the way Habermas had hoped
when devising his "universal pragmatics."[97] This impasse between

95. Thomas McCarthy, "A Theory of Communicative Competence"; Anthony
Giddens, *New Rules of Sociological Method,* pp. 54–71; R. Keat and J. Urry, *Social Theory as Science,* pp. 222–227; Albrecht Wellmer, *Critical Theory of Society,* pp. 41–51,
and "Communications and Emancipation," in John O'Neill, ed., *On Critical Theory,*
pp. 231–263; Karl-Otto Apel et al., *Hermeneutik und Ideologiekritik.*

96. Preface to the 2d edition, *Truth and Method,* pp. xvi–xxvi and 495–498; also
"Introduction (1975)" to "The Problem of Historical Consciousness."

97. McCarthy, "Theory of Communicative Competence," passim, esp. pp. 484,
486.

critical theory and hermeneutics is ironic since the very art of lower-
ing transtemporal barriers to understanding is blocked from the
temple of critical theory, except in denatured form, because of selective and incomplete interpretations of key texts.

The major Gadamer commentary by Habermas occurs in *Zur
Logik der Wissenschaften*, "Der hermeneutische Ansatz." This "review of *Truth and Method*," plus Habermas's other comments on
Gadamer and/or contemporary hermeneutics, reveals features of
his critique which, as in most similar instances, seem elusive as a
result of the unavoidable drawbacks of printed, nondialogical debate.[98] In his review Habermas liberally quotes from *Truth and
Method*. These quotations considered in relation to the entire text
show that the "book" Habermas reviewed is but one of several
within the covers of Gadamer's volume. Defining the book Habermas elected to evaluate, a pedestrian but vital task, helps explain
why Gadamer, when defending himself from the left, seems genuinely bewildered. A study of the relevant documents reveals interesting discoveries. With the exception of a few incidental citations,
Habermas comments only on eighteen pages (258–276) of this 540-
page work. This selection falls between "Second Part: II, 1, b, iii"
and "Second Part: II, 2, b" of the book, a minuscule portion of the
whole, both literally and in terms of Gadamer's overall project. In
fact the volume contains three distinct "books," which Gadamer
calls the First, the Second, and the Third Part. Habermas has little
to say about the First or Third and in dealing with the Second limits
himself to three small sub-subsections, "The Hermeneutic Significance of Temporal Distance," "The Principle of Effective History
[*Wirkungsgeschichte*]," and "The Hermeneutic Problem of Application."

At work here is that textual aggression and assimilation which
typifies Habermas's writing. His appropriation of hermeneutics
and Gadamer turns around the problem of application. It is this
merciless hunt for the usable meat of an argument, regardless of
the source's character, that shows both Habermas's strength and

98. Habermas, "Der hermeneutische Ansatz," *Zur Logik der Sozialwissenschaften*,
translated as "A Review of Gadamer's *Truth and Method*," in Dallmayr and McCarthy, eds., *Understanding and Social Inquiry*, pp. 251–290; also "Die Universalität-
sanspruch der Hermeneutik," in Apel et al., *Hermeneutik und Ideologiekritik*, pp.
139–158.

his weakness. While it is true that under these three headings he has identified parts of Gadamer's hermeneutics which are *among* the most important, it is also the case that within *Truth and Method* one can find much more. So if, strictly speaking, it is unfair to chide Habermas for attending to those few elements that suit his project, it is equally wrong that many have adopted his assessment of hermeneutics, which has become what might be called sub-stitutively definitive. Without being facetious, one could designate Gadamer-H as that portion of Gadamer's ideas transmitted by Habermas and his commentators, who seldom reject his Gadamer critique.[99] If there is reason to question Habermas's use of lin-guistics or his modernizing of Marx, there is more to wonder at in his critique of hermeneutics, for he has thought more seriously about the former two subjects than the latter. How strange that Habermas abuses the very discipline designed to eliminate textual misinterpretation and mishandling, particularly that type produced by the blind pace and common rashness of today's scholarship.

An intriguing postscript to the Gadamer-Habermas debate of twenty years ago is the younger man's *laudatio* for his elder on the occasion of Gadamer's winning the Hegel Prize from Stuttgart in 1979.[100] Habermas at fifty is full of praise for Gadamer's achieve-ments and seems less inclined to draw hard lines between his ver-sion of critical theory, its emancipatory potential, and Gadamer's liberating hermeneutics of *Dasein*.

99. Dieter Misgeld, "Critical Theory and Hermeneutics," in O'Neill, ed., *On Critical Theory*, pp. 164–183. Misgeld studied with Gadamer.
100. "Urbanizing the Heideggerian Province," in Jürgen Habermas, *Philosoph-ical-Political Profiles*, pp. 191–199.

3

Weber's Aporia:
Irrationality and Social Action

Bibliographical Prologue

Hermeneutics requests that comprehensive knowledge of a theorist's work precede exegesis, which in turn anticipates reapplication to contemporary interests. When done properly, interpretation ought not to occur so much *during* critical reading of the collected works in question as *after*. That interpretation in the less formal sense begins at the very outset goes without saying, but this sort of ongoing examination is actually pre-hermeneutical. Hermeneutic practice concerns itself so seriously with conceptual totalities because of the belief that until the *Lebenswerk* comes into full view, a merely fragmentary understanding will occur. This is the *ideal* prescription provided by virtuoso interpreters, and it probably does no harm that contemporary scholarship seldom lives up to it.

In Weber's case, this strategy is problematic for reasons other than the magnitude of his lifework. First, his writing falls into distinct, often mutually exclusive substantive categories. Each of these bears varyingly on general theory, and especially on the problem of irrationality. It roughly divides into categories represented by each volume in the *Gesammelte Aufsätze*, including, in order of appearance, the sociology of religion (3 volumes, 1920–1921), political writings (1922), the methodology of science (1922), sociology and economic history (1924), and sociology and social policy (1924). To this substantial collection must be added two other titles. First, *Wirtschaft und Gesellschaft* (1922), known fragmentarily to Americans prior to 1968 as a combination of Part II, "Power," of *From Max Weber* (1946); *The Theory of Social and Economic Organization* (1947); *On Law in Economy and Society* (1954); *The City* (1958); *Basic Concepts of Sociology* (1962); *The Sociology of Religion* (1963); and, from the second German edition, *The Rational and Social Foundations of Music*

(1958). Second are Weber's Munich lectures on economic history (1923), the first to be translated into English (1927). Altogether these comprise over 4,850 printed pages in German. Unlike Pareto's sociological writing, though comparable in bulk, the entirety is not aimed at a unified theoretical and substantive end. Thus, despite our hermeneutical scruples, judicious selection must take place before interpretation can begin.

For the first forty years or so after Weber's death, the most complete and frequently cited bibliography of his works appeared at the end of the first German edition of Marianne Weber's *Ein Lebensbild*.[1] She lists 88 items, including most of Weber's best-known, most significant works. Dirk Käsler has since assembled what may be the definitive bibliography. Because of its relatively late appearance, in *Kölner Zeitschrift für Soziologie und Sozialpsychologie* of December 1975, it has had little influence on American historians of social thought, and, since it is in German, it may not affect Weber studies here for some time. This is unfortunate since Käsler has outdone Marianne considerably by locating 231 items (including some repetition). Of special interest are 5 composed between 1898 and 1900 which Marianne did not note, written when Weber was emotionally at his worst.

Naturally, most of Käsler's items, and many of Marianne's, need not be considered for my purposes. Probably least directly relevant are the political essays and newspaper articles. Yet here we face another problem. The *Gesammelte politische Schriften* (3d edition, 1958), by no means exhaustive of Weber's politically oriented writing, includes thirty-one essays, among them "Politics as a Vocation" and "Parliament and Government in a Reconstructed Germany." (Also present are the famous articles on revolutionary pre-Bolshevik Russia, "Zur Lage der bürgerlichen Demokratie in Russland" and "Russlands Übergang zum Scheinkonstitutionalismus," the writing of which prompted Weber to master journalistic Russian in fourteen days.) Of the thirty-one essays, English readers have access only to the two mentioned above; 395 pages (67 percent) are

---

1. Pp. 715–719. See Reinhard Bendix, *Max Weber*, p. xi. Two other pre-definitive bibliographies were assembled: by J. Winckelmann in 1956 (*Soziologie/Weltgeschichtliche Analysen/Politik*); and by Eduard Baumgarten in 1964, which integrates a chronology of the events of Weber's life along with his works (*Max Weber*, pp. 680–720). Both of these were based largely on Marianne Weber's list.

still untranslated. Much of the untranslated material concerns Germany and World War I and lies beyond the bounds of theorizing proper. But given Weber's characteristic thoughtfulness in composing even minor pieces, they cannot be categorically judged to be irrelevant to our purposes. Several excellent books exist on Weber and politics, yet with the exception of Mommsen's they focus more on his theory of politics as expressed in documents which have been translated than on Weber as political analyst of contemporary events.[2] And given Weber's meticulous theorizing in the long essay "Parliament and Government in a Reconstructed Germany" (appended to *Economy and Society*), where he demonstrates the utility of macro theory in analyzing political disintegration and reconstitution, certain of the other political essays may well contain important formulations about irrationality. This is especially likely since nationalism, along with ethnicity and eroticism, represents for Weber one of the most irrational elements of social life. Most of the material of theoretical interest that Weber introduced into what were primarily journalistic statements is, however, also a part of other, more formal works, and there in more cogent form.

An identical situation exists regarding accessibility of the other volumes in the collected works. From *Sozial- und Wirtschaftsgeschichte* only three out of six selections are translated, and two of these have been in English a fairly short time (*The Agrarian Sociology of Ancient Civilizations* and "Developmental Tendencies in the Situation of East Elbian Rural Labourers").[3] Weber's dissertation on medieval Italian and Spanish trading companies (1889, 131 pages) and

2. The classic commentary is J. P. Mayer, *Max Weber and German Politics*. Later contributions are David Beetham, *Max Weber and the Theory of Modern Politics*; Ilse Dronberger, *The Political Thought of Max Weber*; and Wolfgang J. Mommsen, *The Age of Bureaucracy*, an updated slice from his much longer *Max Weber und die deutsche Politik 1890–1920*, published when its author was twenty-nine. Stephen Turner has called Mommsen's "certainly the best book ever written on Weber." Turner's review of the new English translation, "Weber Agonistes," appears in *Contemporary Sociology*.

3. Arnaldo Momigliano, one of very few scholars capable of evaluating such things, has reservations about the English translation of *Agrarian Sociology*: "Professor Frank's introduction is not analytical enough to help us to understand the book he translates. . . . The translation is certainly useful. Those who do not feel like wrestling with Weber's notorious German here have an *Ersatz*. But at a price. The translation is not always correct and very often insensitive to the tone of the original" ("Max Weber and Edward Meyer," pp. 292–293). The other important new translation is by Keith Tribe (Weber 1979).

his work on Roman law—for some reason omitted from the collected works and now a rare book even in German—have both
eluded translators. Because the towering historian of the day, Theodor Mommsen, was impressed enough with these early works to
laud Weber publicly,[4] it is especially unfortunate that they have
lacked an English readership. Thus English readers miss 208 pages
from this one volume on social and economic history, including a
report on an "empirical" research project which Weber directed,
one of the first of its kind.[5] The contents have, however, been summarized by Anthony Oberschall and others,[6] but few scholars make
use of the originals. Perhaps now that sociohistorical study has once
again come into vogue among American sociologists, these "lost"
Weberian works will one day enter English-language scholarship.

Weber's *Wissenschaftslehre* has fared far better. With new translations of *Roscher and Knies* and *The Critique of Stammler* finally published, the important "Kategorienlehre" article having already for
some time been available as a thesis, and the last small essay having just been translated, the entire 613 pages are accounted for.[7] Of
all the essay volumes edited by Winckelmann and his predeces-
sors, this has enjoyed the most scholarly attention. In fact, more
has been written about some of Weber's methodological essays,
which he openly disparaged, than about his *Hauptwerk* (*Wirtschaft*

---

4. Marianne Weber, *Max Weber*, p. 114. On the continuing importance of Weber's
work in this area, see M. I. Finley, *The Ancient Economy*, pp. 26, 117, 122, 125. The
eminent Roman historian Momigliano (in speaking of the "new school of research
on Hellenistic and Roman History that developed in Germany towards the end of
the last century") writes that "Max Weber . . . was behind the new interest in agrarian history" and that "Roman agrarian history has of course been made fashionable
by Max Weber," no mean feat for a man under thirty (A. D. Momigliano, *Studies in
Historiography*, pp. 94, 96).

5. Anthony Oberschall, *Empirical Social Research in Germany 1848–1914*, pp. 111–
136. Also see Paul Lazarsfeld and Anthony Oberschall, "Max Weber and Empirical
Social Research."

6. See J. E. T. Eldridge, "Weber's Approach to the Sociological Study of Indus-
trial Workers," in *Max Weber and Modern Sociology*, ed. Arun Sahay. Also important
is Gert Schmidt, "Max Weber and Modern Industrial Sociology: A Comment on
Some Recent Anglo-Saxon Interpretations," *Sociological Analysis and Theory* 6, no. 1
(February 1976): 47–73; and Sven Eliaeson, "Some Recent Interpretations of Max
Weber's Methodology. Part 3: Lazarsfeld's and Oberschall's Conception of Empirical
Weberian Methodology," pp. 54–60.

7. Weber 1970; condensed into an article, Edith Graber, "Translator's Introduction to Max Weber," *Sociological Quarterly* 22, no. 2 (Spring 1981): 145–150
and Weber 1981b. The last essay is Weber 1984. See also Alan Sica, "The Unknown
Max Weber."

und Gesellschaft) itself.[8] Entire books have been published that dwell exclusively on three of the methodological essays, which total less than 300 pages in German, or roughly 4 percent of Weber's output.[9] Perhaps this marked preference for the *Wissenschaftslehre* over Weber's more substantive works reflects the fact that confronting the former requires no special knowledge outside of logic, while competent critique of his nonmethodological essays calls for a quantity and breadth of knowledge not easily amassed.

One final note about the essays on method: inasmuch as they are extremely difficult to bring into English from Weber's "improvisations" in German—particularly in the articles on Roscher, Knies, and irrationality, where sentences often continue for pages— and since no fewer than ten translators over the years have presented their versions, we cannot hope for stylistic congruence or continuity. Accuracy itself is sometimes lost. (It is well known that certain widely used Weber translations have been poor. One has, indeed, been completely supplanted, but only after it held the field for a decade.) It is not just that Weber's major works have been translated over a fifty-year span by so many hands (at least thirty); Dante has been translated by dozens with no fatal effect. But when English-language students refer to Weber, the question is, whose?[10] Although other factors come into play, an important reason for the discrepant readings (or understandings) is that translations are

8. Though it should be mentioned that Winckelmann, in his fifth revised edition of *Wirtschaft und Gesellschaft*, has outdone everyone in producing a truly definitive one. His 303-page appended volume of notes and explanatory apparatus will surely add a dimension to Weber's major achievement which his other works do not at this point possess. See Guenther Roth's two reviews.

9. For example, Thomas Burger, *Max Weber's Theory of Concept Formation*.

10. A classic problem arising from this situation lies in Parsons's translation of *Handeln* as "action," with others sticking to the more literal "conduct"—an important distinction, as Parsons's own works make plain. Guenther Roth also speaks to the broader issue: "In drawing on a given passage, the choice of terms in translating it often depends upon the issue with which the researcher tried to deal. A straight translation of a whole work is more concerned with general readability and consistency than with multiple meanings and nuances, which may become visible or relevant only in a particular context" ("History and Sociology in the Work of Max Weber," pp. 316–317). This kind of intentional distortion, necessary as it may be to smooth translation, handicaps the hermeneutical process. Similar problems were noted quite some time ago by Bendix, in *Max Weber*, pp. 272n–273n. Instances could be multiplied endlessly. These differences of opinion have surfaced among only four translators, Parsons, Roth, Mommsen, and Bendix, but with seven times that many associated with Weber translations, the possibilities for error, disagreement, and distortion are formidable.

characteristically unsystematized, even regarding pivotal terms or master categories. The unfortunate, perhaps by now hopeless career of *Verstehen* and "ideal types" as methodological concepts makes the case. At least in the establishment of a consensually sponsored lexicon of key terms in translation, Dante, as well as others of importance to the history of social thought, such as Marx and Engels, has indeed been better served than Weber.[11]

Considering all this, how can a study of Weber and Pareto seeking thoroughness and precision rely on translations? Several notable studies have not, and this, as in the case of Julien Freund's introduction to Weber, sometimes sets them apart in quality from others not so executed. Like most Americans, I often use translations because Weber's writing is difficult even for native Germans. But there is a better reason. I am concerned with Weber and Pareto not only as social theorists and researchers but also, even more important, in the impact they have had on today's conceptions of the discipline's methods and goals. And since very few postwar American sociologists read the originals, close inspection of the translations becomes not only justified but necessary. (Other, related problems, arising from the fact that entire traditions of scholarship rest on translations, cannot be pursued at the moment.)

This once again brings up the shocking contrast between the linguistic facility of current academics and those in Weber's period. He himself mastered Greek, Latin, Spanish, Italian (both medieval and modern), Russian, Hebrew, French, and English, besides his own academic German. Nearly all these he learned for the express purpose of carrying out a single piece of research: Italian and Spanish for his dissertation, Hebrew for the study of ancient Judaism, Russian for the events of 1905 and to converse with the Russian revolutionaries who flocked to Heidelberg,[12] English to facilitate his trip to the United States in 1904 and for work on the *Protestant Ethic,* and French to have access to important anthropological writings which figured in his work on ancient and Oriental civiliza-

---

11. The projected fifty-volume Marx/Engels *Collected Works,* a joint project of translators and editors in New York, London, and Moscow, shows in its first twenty-three volumes what excellent results can come from such agreement beforehand. Such an edition of Weber seems but a dream, even though Allen and Unwin has plans for partial translations from the *Gesamtausgabe* just begun by J. C. B. Mohr.

12. See Alexander Vucinich, *Social Thought in Tsarist Russia,* pp. 128ff.

tions. He bemoaned the fact that Sanskrit and Pali were beyond him, as was Mandarin, and therefore for his studies of India and China he had to rely on English, French, and German monographs and translations of ancient documents. He paid a high scholarly price for doing so, for it is clear that whenever he did use originals (as in *Ancient Judaism*) his contributions to a given debate (for instance, ancient Roman versus German law) were striking and not in the least derivative. It is also true that specialists have most frequently faulted his sociohistorical judgments when he leaned heavily on secondary sources. He would surely have paid even more dearly had translation (as in the still unrivaled series edited by Max Mueller, *The Sacred Books of the East*) and comparative monographs (e.g., Paul Deussen's *Philosophy of the Upanishads*) not reached such fantastic heights in the latter part of the nineteenth century.[13] His originality soared thanks to a thorough knowledge of Latin and Greek (which he studied for nine years in the gymnasium) and his consequent ability to interpret vital documents of ancient political economy and law. His precocious scholarship in these areas won him chairs both in Roman and in German law, and then in economics, at a time when to gain a chair in a single field was considered admirable. Weber's linguistic skill certainly contributed to his innovative analyses of ancient data and to his making interconnections using a truly comparative method to which specialists had no access.[14] It is strange, considering the recent enthusiasm for comparative sociology, that the dire need for multilinguistic training, long the basis of comparative study in fields such as law, literature, and ethnology, is ignored.[15]

It should not be thought that Weber's languages came easily to him. Marianne notes that he detested learning medieval Spanish

13. "Without overlooking what was accomplished elsewhere . . . it can be fairly said that the era of scholarship beginning with Ranke's historical seminar and culminating in the new physics of Einstein, Planck, and Heisenberg was an age of genius" (Thomas E. Willey, *Back to Kant*, p. 13). See also Nirad C. Chaudhuri, *Scholar Extraordinary*, for details on the heights of Teutonic scholarship.

14. For the most detailed discussion of Weber's borrowing from specialists in the field of ancient agrarian history and his effect, in turn, upon them, see Paul Honigsheim, "Max Weber as Historian of Agriculture and Rural Life." Companion pieces by the same author are "Max Weber as Applied Anthropologist"; "Max Weber as Rural Sociologist"; and "Max Weber: His Religious and Ethical Background and Development," all excellent and underutilized.

15. See, for example, Neil Smelser, *Comparative Methods in the Social Sciences*.

and Italian—both obscured in peculiar dialects—in order to complete his dissertation.[16] But having decided to pursue the problem and finding the essential materials in their archival resting places, undisturbed by previous scholars, he had no choice but to learn languages he apparently never used again for academic work. The intellectual investment and self-discipline evidenced by this sort of feat is impossible to grasp nowadays, just as is the setting of bourgeois intellectualism Weber entered at birth and in which he evidently thrived, albeit at high personal cost.

To return to the collected essays: we find that the volume on *Soziologie und Sozialpolitik* has yielded little to American scholars. Out of 518 pages, comprising seven essays, not a word had reached English until J. E. T. Eldridge published a selection of Weber's writings in 1971 that included two of the shorter essays, one on socialism, the other the "Methodological Introduction for the Survey of the Verein für Sozialpolitik [Society for Social Policy] Concerning Selection and Adaptation (Choice and Course of Occupation) for the Workers of Major Industrial Enterprises."[17] Good as it is to have at least this much translated, we are yet deprived of two essays which have long been valued by German experts on Weber, "Die Börse" (The Market, 66 pages) and "Zur Psychophysik der industriellen Arbeit" (On the Psychophysics of Industrial Work, 194 pages). Three other long essays dealing with social policy, mostly concerning Prussia, make up the collection.

The article on psychophysics was a preliminary part of the Verein's massive survey of industrial workers between 1909 and 1911. In preparing it, Weber spent a summer in a relative's textile mill at Örlinghausen, observing the workers firsthand and

> studying the wage records and loom records of the factory and assiduously preparing graphs for the hourly, daily, and weekly output of the weavers in order to find the psychophysical causes of fluctuations in performance. But these laborious investigations were not an end in themselves; they were to have only "illustrative" signifi-

16. *Max Weber*, p. 113. Marianne Weber reports that he himself said the dissertation gave him "an inordinate amount of trouble" and complained that the documents were "written in disgusting ancient dialects, and one is surprised people understood that gibberish."

17. Weber 1971b, pp. 191–219, 103–155. In addition to the methodological essay (the first sixty pages of the German volume) and a 1918 lecture on socialism (pp. 492–518), several fragments have reached English. Eric Matthews (in Runciman's *Weber: Selections in Translation*) rendered the last four pages of Weber's long article on the

cance. . . . His main endeavor, then, was the clarification of the *methodological* problem, particularly of the question of whether the sciences of heredity on the one hand and psychophysical experiments on the other could be of service to sociological analysis.[18]

The overall project was characterized by Weber in a letter to his brother Alfred, who proposed the survey, in this way:

> I intend to suggest that the *Verein für Sozialpolitik* start a series of investigations which, in order to have a popular label, one could perhaps call *Lage der geistigen Arbeit in der modernen Grossindustrie* (The Situation of Intellectual Work in Modern Heavy Industry). I thought of including the inner structure of the various industries in regard to the extent and type of the *skilled* work, the continuity of the work force, *professional opportunities, change of occupation,* etc. From this "morphological" side we might get at the question of the psychological selection industry makes, its tendency in the individual industries, and conversely its being conditioned by the psychophysical qualities of the population, be they hereditary or instilled.[19]

This begins to reveal a subterranean Weber who is omitted from the history of social thought and social research—the very kind of loss that hermeneutics seeks to remedy and to explain. Again, antiquarianism is not at issue. It is clear that this neglected facet, if viewed in its true form, would benefit the study of Weber's work per se, while also correcting the prevalent notion of who Weber was and what he now, as intellectual symbol for social science, might represent. Incidentally, Oberschall rates the Verein survey, which Weber unofficially directed (the second immense, cooperative empirical research effort he had overseen in a sixteen-year period), as "the most carefully thought through piece of empirical research of the pre-war period."[20]

Early Works (1889–1897)

Thus far, then, we have "unearthed" more than 1,100 printed pages of Weber's untranslated, and for the most part, undigested

---

stock exchange, and Jerome Gittleman published two portions of the proceedings of the first German Sociological Society meeting at Frankfurt in 1910, in one of which Weber responds to Tönnies and Troeltsch—and Simmel gets in a single word: "Reason!" ("Max Weber on Church, Sect, and Mysticism," *Sociological Analysis* 34, no. 2 [Summer 1973]: 140–149); and Weber's debate with Ploetz on race (*Social Research* 38, no. 1 [Spring 1971]: 30–41.)

18. Marianne Weber, *Max Weber,* p. 330.
19. Ibid., p. 367.
20. Oberschall, *Empirical Social Research in Germany,* p. 8.

work within the collected works alone,[21] a corpus unto itself which outstrips the total lifework of most scholars.[22] Luckily, though, we do have full translations of the other J. C. B. Mohr–Paul Siebeck volumes, including the *Religionssoziologie, Wirtschaftsgeschichte,* and, as was mentioned above, *Wirtschaft und Gesellschaft,* in much improved editions over those which prevailed in Germany itself until the late 1950s. So although a comprehensive, hermeneutically perfect picture of Weber's thought is not yet available, either in translation of primary sources or in studies of his work (on a scale of, for instance, Ernest Jones's *Freud,* based on limitless use of the subject's papers), it is probably true that irrationality as an organizing concept in this thought *can* be studied fairly.

In the earlier works (which constitute the bulk of the untranslated material),[23] Weber was not yet *formally* interested in irrationality to the degree he later became. He was, though, privately well aware of it, as we know from a variety of sources, especially his *Jugendbriefe,* where at times little else is being dealt with, particularly where Weber discusses such youthful topics as honor, loyalty, and love. A representative sampling of these enliven the earlier chapters of Marianne's biography. It also puzzled Weber why the eastern German peasants so vigorously resisted—in opposition to their own rational economic interests—attempts by the Prussian

21. Additional material that may never surface in English includes Weber 1936, 375 pp.; portions of Weber 1956, 564 pp.; some of Weber 1956b, 129 pp.; the monstrous field study Weber directed and wrote up, Weber 1892, 892 pp.; "private" material from Eduard Baumgarten's important compilation, *Max Weber,* 720 pp., about 143 pp. of which appears nowhere else and originates in various Weber archives; and Weber 1895–1896, 325 pp.

22. More broadly and accurately, we can calculate (using Käsler's bibliography and other sources) that out of 7,300 pp. of German text—Weber's total output minus certain fragments on Islamic civilization thus far unpublished, 300 pp. of archival mss., and 143 pp. of new material in Baumgarten's book—2,143 pp. (29.4 percent) have been translated into English. Thus it is quite an illusion to believe, as I think most American sociologists do, that Weber "is available" in translation. (And if we subtract *recent* translations, which account for 516 pages of the originals, only 22.3 percent of Weber's work was available to Americans before 1975.) For a tabular breakdown and other details, see Sica, "The Unknown Max Weber."

23. Of 2,063 pp. of material published by Weber in the first decade of academic life (1889–1897), plus those few (47 pp.) which came out during his five years of incapacitation, English translations have accounted for only 47 pp. thus far, or about 2.2 percent. Weber's first fifteen years of productivity are virtually unknown to us except by way of later work which capitalized to some extent on the earlier material. A great deal, though, like the first empirical study (892 pp.) and the four articles in "Goldschmidt's *Zeitschrift*" on the "*Börsenquete*" (375 pp.) are scarcely mentioned even by some of our finest Weber scholars such as Roth and Bendix.

Junkers to alter semi-feudal arrangements in order to begin modernization of their gigantic agricultural holdings. This curiosity lay behind much of Weber's early empirical work. In fact, Weber's observations of peasant tenacity in the face of encroaching rationalization of agricultural practices seem to have constituted a good portion of his first intimations of both traditional and *affektuell* behavior, that is, irrational, economically incomprehensible social action.

Marianne Weber relates that as a young man Weber was embroiled in family disputes and misunderstandings which had their bases primarily in issues that became central to his mature work. We need not take certain events, particularly concerning his father, Max, and his mother's religiosity, quite so far as Arthur Mitzman in order to recognize Weber's dread fascination with the role played in some bourgeois personalities by ultimate, absolutistic values and otherwise irrational vectors.[24] This fascination, often linked with Nietzsche's *Genealogy of Morals*, pervades all Weber's mature works. Perhaps because he needed psychological relief from the sensitive spiritual condition of his family, his two early academic works, the dissertation and habilitation, spoke very little to those elements of social life that are of interest here and became paramount in his later work: the interrelations of the sacred and secular, charisma and the bureaucratized state, irrational (e.g., erotic and aesthetic) and rational (e.g., legal and economic) processes and social institutions. By his own account, these two weighty achievements typify the tediously careful, even plodding rite de passage then demanded of junior academics. They simply demonstrated Weber's competence in both Roman and medieval law. Very shortly before being called to Berlin for his first academic post, Weber was interviewed in Bremen for a job as the city's attorney, so he was then uncertain over the choice between an academic and a more conventional career. His dissertation and habilitation do not evidence the least philistinism; he prepared them with enough meticulousness that their instrumental function—to get him a job—is fully masked. Yet his agonizing letters of the period document how degraded he felt by living in his father's house at the age of nearly

24. Arthur Mitzman, *The Iron Cage*, pp. 39–74. For a spirited description of the patriarchal crisis of Bismarck's Germany, see Martin Green, *The von Richthofen Sisters*, pp. 3–11.

thirty and how desperately he wanted to gain his manhood by establishing a "roof of his own." Before he could explore irrationality
to the extent he later would, escape from the psychosexual, political, and moral suffocation of his father's domain and from the lasting quarrel between the patriarch's *vita activa* and the mother's con-
templative pietism became absolutely necessary.

The bibliography to this study lists about two hundred articles
and books in English on Weber and is not comprehensive. One
subgroup deals with Weber's treatment of *rationality* and *rationalization*, related but not synonymous terms.[25] Oddly, although some
of these authors number among the most astute Weberians, none
provides an answer to a simple question: when did Weber first
come upon the idea of rationalization and begin writing about the
differences in rational, irrational, and nonrational types of social
action? They make several points repeatedly: for instance, that
Weber's Kantianism connected freedom with rationality, science
with rational procedure, the death of absolute values and value
judgments with advancing rationality, and so on. But the origin in
Weber's work of the concept that has become synonymous with his
name has thus far, to my knowledge, remained buried. Since I do
not have access to all of his work,[26] locating this origin is provisional. But, as it turns out, since Weber's awareness of cultural ra-

25. See Karl Löwith, "Weber's Interpretation of the Bourgeois-Capitalistic World
in Terms of the Guiding Principle of 'Rationalization'" (in *Max Weber*, ed. Dennis
Wrong, pp. 101–122). For an informed account of why this partial translation of
Löwith's essay created a peculiarly overrated reputation for the author and his
ideas, see Gerd Schroeter, "Exploring the Marx-Weber Nexus," a review essay
covering four books, one of which is the new, complete translation of Löwith's *Max
Weber and Karl Marx*, trans. H. Fantel and first published in 1932. Other useful stud-
ies include Ferdinand Kolegar, "The Concept of 'Rationalization' and Cultural Pes-
simism in Max Weber's Sociology"; John Torrance, "Max Weber: Methods and the
Man"; J. E. T. Eldridge, "The Rationalization Theme in Weber's Sociology," in his
Max Weber: The Interpretation of Social Reality; Julien Freund, *The Sociology of Max
Weber*, esp. pp. 1–11, 17–32, 142–148; Bendix, *Max Weber*, p. 278n; Michael Landmann, "Critiques of Reason from Max Weber to Ernst Bloch"; and Honigsheim,
"Max Weber: His Religious and Ethical Background and Development."
26. I have made efforts to examine all of Weber's work from his early period,
99 percent of which, as mentioned before, is still in German. His dissertation occupies pp. 312–443 of Weber 1924a. The habilitation is not included in the collected
works and is somewhat scarce; I did finally obtain a copy, however. The other two
massive works of the first period are the Verein study and four articles on the market (translated by Bendix as "stock exchange," but also including grain futures in
the commodity exchange) which appeared in "Goldschmidt's" *Zeitschrift für das
Gesammte Handelsrecht* (1895–1896). Other work of the period is incidental.

tionalization paralleled certain developments in his psychic *and* professional life, a relatively firm date can be established. That is, Weber's first work *in form* is much the kind that filled academic journals of the period. It has already been pointed out how unusually excellent his work was from the point of view of content, but it is nonetheless true that Weber's explicit goal—the fruit of his *zweckrational* behavior—was to impress other academics and thus find employment. (Though his *wertrational* pattern of behavior reflected his belief in the "duty" of being a scholar and remaining true to his primary sources, it did not carry enough weight with him at this point to sway him from using standard modes of scholarly expression. Much later, in fact, he did dispense with *all* the apparatus of academic prose, such as footnotes, paragraphs, headings, subheads, and bibliographies.)[27]

It is not surprising, then, that the dissertation contains very little in the way of social-psychological theory. Instead tidy, quantitatively descriptive chapters discuss medieval trade activity in the cities of Pisa and Florence and the different legal agreements merchant parties made to minimize risk and loss. As has been recorded by many intellectual historians, German social science was in crisis around 1890, torn between the blandishments of political economy, economic history, social philosophy, and a more amorphous type of belles lettres which tried to pass for "advanced thought," especially appealing to the middle class. Battle lines were being drawn over appropriate method, what constituted worthwhile knowledge, and, most ominously—in tune with Bismarck's *Realpolitik*—what use academic knowledge was to the state. Weber trod carefully through this minefield and survived by restricting himself to a circumscribed, delimited version of political economy, one that depended largely upon quantitative historical data for its results, gingerly mixed with "softer" analyses of contracts and other legal documents. Bendix claims that these early

27. John Torrance interestingly observes that Mitzman's hypotheses about Weber's severe oedipal conflicts are needlessly unsociological, that in fact what should be kept in mind regarding Weber's early scholarly activity is *not* so much the part played by his nuclear family but, rather, the peer pressure under which he operated. This would be more plausible were it not for Marianne Weber's reports of the importance Weber's family held for him, and the *relative* casualness with which he treated academic affairs and contacts until his associations with Sombart and Simmel after the turn of the century. See Torrance, "Max Weber," pp. 157–158.

studies "defined the problems which were to occupy [Weber] during a lifetime of scholarly work."[28] I think this is true only in a general sense, for nowhere do we find even a hint that this same man, fifteen years hence, would be writing treatises on religion and music and be planning a comprehensive sociology of the arts as his final achievement.

The habilitation follows in much the same stylistic vein, though in only two years Weber had mastered an entirely different set of data, moving from fourteenth-century Italy to the late Roman empire. Honigsheim succinctly describes his accomplishments in the "field" (for such it surely was at the time) of Roman agrarian history:

> The basic developments that he either elaborated for the first time or, had they been asserted hypothetically elsewhere, empirically supported are these eight: (1) Upward social mobility of the plebians as a result of their integration into the Hoplite army; (2) the interest of the plebians in the conquest of non-Roman lands; (3) increasing consideration of the plebians in the distribution of the *ager publicus;* (4) the unimportance of provincial grain deliveries to the capital city in the total process of the genesis of the *latifundia;* (5) the life of the slaves under military discipline on the *latifundia,* investigated by consulting the Latin writings in the field of agronomy as a source; (6) movement, in later Roman times, from coastal cities to inland *latifundia,* proved by evidence and analysis in contrast to the corresponding and rather vague assertions by Seebohm; (7) the development of *coloni,* in late Roman times, from the former free tenants who voluntarily chose dependence in order to avoid the load of taxes; (8) uninterrupted continuity of the late-Roman *latifundia* with their natural economy to the early medieval, Christian-Germanic type of landownership, a theory that was based upon sources and analyses, in contrast to Roth's unproved hypothesis.[29]

Examination of the habilitation supports the assumption—clearly indicated by Honigsheim's summary—that Weber to this point had not yet emancipated himself from the scholarly pose which insists that data be allowed to speak for themselves, that they be presented conservatively. And conservative presentation of political-economic data excluded social-psychological theorizing. Therefore

28. Bendix, *Max Weber,* p. 10.
29. Honigsheim, *On Max Weber,* p. 139, originally published as *Max Weber in Amerikanischen Geistesleben* (1950–1951). This is not only admirably dense but also one of the only descriptive analyses we have of Weber's habilitation. In completely omitting it from his "intellectual portrait," Bendix was at once reflecting past practice and setting policy for future Weber study in the United States.

Weber again gave wide berth to reflections and typological reductions depending to some degree upon *Verstehen* of one kind or another, such as are strewn throughout his mature works.

The staggering research report Weber assembled on behalf of the Verein für Sozialpolitik in 1892 is likewise quite straightforward. Its 900 pages are choked with tables of data from the various regions of eastern German agricultural production. His own remarks about the final report indicate that he was looking, not for theoretical synthesis, but for flexible and revealing statistical techniques by which to display the mass of data, all in the interest of influencing social policy. The volume presents detailed descriptions of changes experienced by agricultural laborers in seven major "provinces" of eastern Germany, all of which reflected a basic rearrangement of social structure (displacement of semi-feudal peasants by wage laborers from Poland) that aggravated Weber and his colleagues in the Verein.[30] I found no explicit reference to rationalization at the macro level or to either rational or irrational behavior at the micro level. As noted before, however, during this study Weber for the first time makes explicit reference to what he would later label *wertrationalisches Handeln*. In recognizing that day laborers did not live "by bread alone" and that against their own best economic interests they increasingly sought out what he called the "grandiose illusion . . . of liberty," he was admitting into formal economic discussion the "subjective attitude" and the "sharp individualistic tendency" of the workers. He gently mocked these wage laborers, who chose in ever greater numbers the instant gratification and autonomy won for them through wages over the security and *gemeinschaftlich* qualities of peasant life, and their ineluctable drift toward the "purely psychological magic of 'freedom.'" In this early analysis lie the beginnings of his fourfold typology, composed about two decades later. In one place at least, he even adumbrates his own later phraseology by referring to the "unconscious purposiveness" of the workers.[31]

30. The source of this aggravation—the belief in the need to defend Germanic civilization from the Slavic menace—is recounted by Bendix in what is still the best description, brief as it is, of Weber's part in the first Verein study: *Max Weber*, pp. 14–41.

31. Bendix, *Max Weber*, pp. 22, 43. Selections and translations above are mine; Bendix pointed out the seminal pages in the study: Weber 1892, 55: 796–797.

Weber at this point in his career was no less emotionally charged than later on, when his temperamental outbursts and litigious nature became well known. As early as 1894, in a public speech, he lays himself bare by announcing to the academic and government public the precise program of legislation he believes they should follow in reshaping Germany: "I believe we must forgo the creation of a positive feeling of happiness in the course of any social legislation. . . . We want to cultivate and support what appears to us as *valuable* in man: his personal responsibility, his basic drive toward higher things, toward the intellectual and moral values of mankind, even where this drive confronts us in its most primitive form."[32] Weber must have forced himself to sublimate emotional responses to the agrarian survey data at every turn in order to write the final report in its even, balanced style. Not until the last few pages does he give vent to some of his anxieties concerning the Junkers and the changing work force.

Most of Weber's next important work, on the stock and commodity exchanges in Germany (compared to those in Glasgow, London, and elsewhere), is difficult to find. A shortened version, published about the same time (1894–1896) and skillfully summarized by Bendix (*Max Weber*, pp. 23–30), occupies pages 256–322 in the *Gesammelte Aufsätze zur Soziologie und Sozialpolitik*. This is an interesting transitional piece in Weber's approach to the sociologically and economically irrational. The social actors involved in various, often contradictory, economically irrational performances included Prussian landholders of the old school vying with nouveau riche, bourgeois (urban) capitalists in status competition, the latter buying their way into the nobility and unintentionally destroying the very aristocracy they wished to join; stock and commodity brokers in the "free markets" of the Hanseatic league competing with guild-like brokers from other cities and also with untrustworthy speculators who were infiltrating and corrupting the entire market system; Jewish participants in the market at different junctures, subject increasingly to governmentally sanctioned anti-Semitism, often propagated by ultra-nationalists worshipping Bismarck; and so on. It is a reflection of Weber's robust analytic abilities that he

---

32. Marianne Weber, *Max Weber*, p. 136.

could reduce—without "reductionism"—this cacophony of cultural, political-economic, and racial voices to a relatively simple argument: "The accent of Weber's analysis is thus on the stock and commodity exchanges as an efficient means for the expansion of trade and for the *predictability* of economic transactions—positive results that stood in marked contrast to the negative consequences of commercialization of agriculture in eastern Germany."[33] While there is no doubt that he is completely aware of the emotionally explosive character of *Die Börse,* he manages to reduce this frightening complexity to an issue of economic rationality ("predictability"), a ploy repeatedly turned to by political economists since Adam Smith. And in so doing Weber again adumbrates his own category of *zweckrationalisches Handeln.* (The word *Zweck* [purpose] crops up repeatedly in the text of *Die Börse* but he does not elaborate it at this point.)

Even early in his professional development, Weber chose, albeit with abundant reservations, rational rather than irrational behavior as the proper grounds for analysis and political opinion. He "sympathized" with any number of participants in the given drama, but unequivocally decided, quite rationally and in terms of the nation's welfare, to support government protection of the Junker aristocracy, since they alone could protect Germany from external threat, and they alone embodied a set of values that produced functionaries vital to Germany's survival. Yet he made no secret of the fact that *personally* his favorites in all the bickering and jockeying for position were the farm laborers who refused peasant status and lived the risky but free life of the agrarian proletariat. This was not the last time Weber would voice support, on rational grounds, for one group or person while privately exulting over the opponent's "irrational" behavior. This contradictory—and at times politically schizophrenic—behavior culminated much later, in Weber's excitement when charisma burst the bounds of bureaucratic domination.

It is important, then, to note how early he began embracing what soon became a psychologically untenable position, something approaching the role of grand mediator or counselor of the middle way. In assuming this position, he often undercut his own

33. Bendix, *Max Weber,* p. 29 (emphasis added).

most cherished beliefs and hopes. The "resignation" he spoke of in 1893 when considering Germany's future, and his inability to summon up the "naive enthusiasm" of his father's generation in the face of national problems,[34] might have served as a warning of his breakdown four years later. At the same time it signals the theoretical tension residing in his most elemental cognitive processes, mostly a product of his absolutist dedication to the separation of fact (e.g., Germany's political needs) from value (his high regard for the unwillingness of free agrarian workers to accept patriarchal domination).[35] If we add to this his unreserved admiration for individualism and autonomous action,[36] plus his less elevated affection for the contrary in its own right, for taking the side of the underdog (a characteristic frequently reported by his students), we begin to understand his lifelong struggle to control the irrational—politically, theoretically, and personally. Therefore, I can only half agree with Karl Loewenstein: "What Freud did for the individual, Max Weber did for the collective. He afforded us insights into the na-

34. Ibid., pp. 30–31.

35. Weber's flight from any apodictic positing of values or absolutes is illustrated by Löwith's comment: "Max Weber 'breathes freely as soon as once again . . . the impossibility of pronouncing objectively valid value judgments had been proved' (Honigsheim), it being in keeping with his idea of 'freedom of man.' . . . Weber's concern is with what is no longer merely a specialized sociological task, but a philosophical one: to reveal expressly the 'a priori' of the determining value ideas in all and in each specific individual inquiry" ("Weber's Interpretation of the Bourgeois-Capitalist World," p. 105). This relentless debunking of value claims, which Weber carried out in reaction to his colleagues *and* opponents who tossed about absolutes without empirical bases, limited his appreciation and analysis of irrational process, since, by unhappy accident, the targets of his attacks were often themselves pontificating about the irrational. And because Weber had connected irrationality with bondage, rationality with freedom ("'in spite of it all,' rationality, for Weber himself, is the site of freedom," ibid., p. 110), he became his own worst theoretical enemy for the sake of consistency. Or perhaps it was owing to some form of theoretical, messianic Puritanism: "The real and positive aim of Weber's scientifico-theoretical treatises is the radical demolition of 'illusions.' . . . Weber's methodological considerations arise from his consciousness . . . that 'our eyes have been blinded for a thousand years, blinded by the allegedly or presumably exclusive orientation towards the grandiose moral fervor of Christian ethics'" (ibid., p. 106).

36. "The notion of the autonomous individual was one of Weber's deepest convictions. The question is nothing less than the decision as to whether one ought to follow a radical ethic without regard to the consequences, an ethic stated in its purest form in the Sermon on the Mount; or whether one ought to follow an ethic of responsibility, in which case one can be no saint. . . . It was therefore unavoidable that Max Weber would be preoccupied with Dostoyevsky . . . even more pressing . . . was the necessity of coming to grips with Tolstoy" (Honigsheim, *On Max Weber*, p. 81).

ture, the functioning, and the conduct of those collectivities we call state, city, party, class, and status-group." [37] In his own way, in the subterranean material of his life and work, Weber told us about the individual quite as insightfully as did Freud. But whereas Freud's theory is public, Weber's remained—particularly in his earliest years as scholar—remarkably private. Consider this: Freud was said to have no interest or competence in music; Weber, a pianist in youth, "could not live without it," according to Honigsheim and others. How can one who seeks understanding of subconscious, irrational or nonrational disturbances and processes remain oblivious to the deepest reservoir of irrationality—now used, in fact, to communicate with catatonics, words being useless? This is but one of many instances which suggest that Weber has more to offer in the realm of personality, or social-psychological theory, even if obliquely, than is usually thought. [38] He knew much more about *individual* behavior than he let on in his formal sociology. His carefully managed addiction to Nietzsche could produce no other result. And since sociology has not yet accepted the aid of psychoanalysis, despite repeated urging, [39] it is of some interest to isolate Weber's ideas. If they are not made explicit, the danger is run that they will be "assumed," perhaps incorrectly.

Our task becomes simplified at this point: the next important selection from Weber's works has been in English for quite some time. In 1896 Weber delivered another of his many speeches, this one, before the Akademischen Gesellschaft in Freiburg, entitled "The Social Causes of the Decay of Ancient Civilization." [40] It was

37. Karl Loewenstein, *Max Weber's Political Ideas in the Perspective of Our Time*, p. 104.
38. "With regard to . . . Max Weber's position on Lukács, one should not forget one thing: Weber's *ability to empathize* with, and to *interpret*, the *meaning* of human action was, in a manner of speaking, unlimited; he was therefore able to understand Lukacs' position or, more exactly, his turning from modern occidental individualism to a notion of collectivism" (Honigsheim, *On Max Weber*, p. 27; emphasis added).
39. Fred Weinstein and Gerald Platt, *The Wish to Be Free*, and *Psychoanalytic Sociology*. Other books less programmatic but equally relevant include Peter Leonard, *Personality and Ideology;* Richard Lichtman, *The Production of Desire;* Robert Endleman, *Psyche and Society;* Ira H. Cohen, *Ideology and Unconsciousness;* Jennifer Radden, *Madness and Reason;* C. R. Badcock, *The Psychoanalysis of Culture*, and *Madness and Modernity*. Certainly the most original of all such syntheses is Joseph Gabel's *False Consciousness*, a mixture of clinical psychiatric data with theoretical guidance from Mannheim, Marx, Lukács, Freud, Binswanger, Minkowski, and others.
40. First translated into English by Christian Mackauer in *Journal of General Education* 5 (1950): 75–88; reprinted unchanged in Eldridge, ed., *Max Weber*, pp. 254–

obviously derived from his habilitation, and Weber could presume to speak on this fashionable topic because by then he had established himself as an expert in three disparate fields: German law, Roman law, and contemporary agrarian conditions.

After having written at some length about the panoply of irrational sentiments surrounding markets and exchanges, Weber speaks in this essay from the antithetical position. He sets out to demonstrate that rigorous economic history—expunged of psychological and philosophical elements—delivers excellent explanatory power. He selects the Roman example not only because he knows it, but also because of the stream of psychologistic theories proposed during the nineteenth century, which he believed counted for their plausibility upon the "Roman temperament" and its alleged degeneration.[41] Against such claims he offers his own, which derives from unvarnished historical data and is utterly free of any psychological hypotheses. Weber's argument, contra the spiritualistic explanations of Lamprecht and, later on, of Spengler, recognizes that imperial Rome had come to require slaves in untold numbers in order for its economy to operate correctly. It had failed to perceive early enough the importance of "tenant farmers" or

---

275, from which the quotes herein are taken. I refer to this brief essay as "the next important work" since it has had some impact upon Weber scholarship in English and is the only fragment of his early period accessible to scholars in this country. It should be understood, however, that in Käsler's bibliography it is numbered item 43. The present exegesis is highly selective, not only on theoretical or hermeneutical grounds, but for practical reasons. Thus far I have dealt with items 2, 5, 8, 32, and 47.

41. Among the explanations for Rome's collapse which Weber thought unfounded are these: (1) the numerical superiority of Rome's opponents; (2) the inadequacy of its political leaders; (3) that despotism by its nature "strangled the soul of the ancient Romans"; (4) the moral decline of the ruling elite; (5) the emancipation of Roman women, the loosening of marriage ties, and the comparative superiority of the "German" women of the barbarian tribes; (6) Pliny's belief that the "*latifundia* ruined Italy," an argument quickly transposed to imperial Germany, the Junkers being substituted for the rich landowners of the *latifundia*; (7) the "Darwinistic hypothesis" that the strongest men were drafted into the army and decimated or "condemned to celibacy" (pp. 255–256). It is interesting that Weber begins the article (p. 255) with a *cultural*, not economic, argument: "But most important: the decay of ancient *civilization* was not caused by the destruction of the Roman *Empire*. The Empire as a political structure survived by centuries the acme of Roman culture. This culture had vanished much earlier." But he rapidly shifts from this task toward what might be construed as a quasi-Marxist position, emphasizing changes in substructure preceding those in the superstructure. Weber uses these terms, but not in the traditional way. He speaks at one point of "the superstructure of the exchange economy" resting upon "a ceaselessly expanding substructure of an economy without exchange (a 'natural economy')" (pp. 259–260).

slaves who could reproduce in their own households, choosing the short-term efficiency and productivity of single male slaves over the long-term guarantee of workers who, while costing more per unit, could stabilize the work force indefinitely. When external sources of slaves dried up, the Roman economy followed suit. In addition, the deliberate policy shift in empire-building, from coastal to inland development, worked a tremendous strain on the empire's fiscal health, there being little regularized internal commodity exchange. This de-urbanization founded, quite unintentionally, the self-sufficient provincial manor, whose ties with the cultural and economic centers became increasingly tenuous and in which was located the origin of feudal Europe. Weber's answer to the riddle of the fall is this:

> The fall of the empire was the necessary political result of the gradual disappearance of commerce and the spread of "natural economy." This fall meant essentially the abolition of that state administration and, hence, of the political super-structure with its money economy character which was no longer adapted to its changed economic basis. . . . We can hardly suppress a feeling of sadness when we witness a culture that seems to aim at perfection lose its material foundation and collapse. But what is it actually that we are witnessing in this gigantic process? In the depth of society organic structural changes occur (and had to occur) which, if we look at them as a whole, must be interpreted as an immense process of recovery. Individual family life and private property were restored to the masses of unfree people; they themselves were raised again, from the position of "speaking inventory" up to the circle of human beings. The rise of Christianity surrounded their family life with firm moral guarantees. (pp. 273–274)

Although Weber manages to include in the short space of the essay discussions of wheat trade in the empire, the growth of the *oikoi*, the place of the *villici* and *coloni* in agricultural production, the role of Tiberius in terminating expansion, the strange function of *ergastula* on large estates, sexuality among slaves, constrictions upon the accumulation of venture capital, and so on, he perpetrates upon his reader the same ill manners accorded him when he gathered data for his dissertation: "Well, I had plenty to do, and if the results are meager rather than copious, it is less my fault than that of the Italian and Spanish city councillors who failed to put in the statutes precisely those things that I was looking for."[42] Though as

42. Marianne Weber, *Max Weber*, p. 113.

usual he makes substantive remarks indicating that the theme of rationalization was lying just beneath the surface, again he "fails" to use the word or any of its cognates and other terminological relatives (such as rational, irrational, nonrational, or legal-rational). For that initial moment of illumination we must continue our search.

Recovery, and Early Methodological Essays

We emerge from Weber's early period, of which his speech on the decline of Rome constitutes a late segment, only to find him completely submerged in his long night of psychopathological distress. He developed the typical symptoms of advanced neuroses, including insomnia, the inability to concentrate or read, paralysis of limbs and chronic back problems, and so on, all of which came upon him gradually after his father's death on 10 August 1897. By the next summer he was institutionalized in the sanatorium on Lake Constance. For the next four years he spent most of his time away from Germany, in Corsica, Rome, Florence, Holland, the Riviera; finally, at the invitation of Harvard philosopher Hugo Münsterberg, he traveled to the United States in 1904, his recovery nearly complete.

This brings us to 1903–1907, an unbelievably fertile segment of Weber's career. Those many months spent staring out the window of his study onto the Neckar finally bore fruit. As usual, we must interpolate among a half-dozen English translations in order to reproduce the chronology as reported in Käsler's list. The first essay, "Roscher's 'historische Methode,'" was published in *Schmoller's Jahrbuch* in 1903, the only important statement of any length (42 pages) Weber had made in over five years. Along with its two sister essays in the *Jahrbuch für Gesetzgebung* (1905 and 1906),[43] these constitute perhaps the most ambitious, ambiguous, and—for my pur-

---

43. According to the translator, Guy Oakes, Weber began this set of essays in Rome during the spring of 1902, having been asked to prepare an article for a Festschrift honoring Weber's last place of employment, the University of Heidelberg. Oakes speculates whether Weber chose the devilishly complex task of subjecting Roscher's and Knies's works to rigorous logical analysis in order to test his faculties, the frailty of which had been frustrating him for so long. Oakes designates these as "metatheoretical" works and rates them very high beside the five hundred other pages Weber gave to similar topics. The three essays Oakes has brought together within one book (Weber 1975b, 281 pages) represent items 60, 68, and 75 in the definitive bibliography.

poses—relevant methodological (or metatheoretical) essays he ever wrote.

Without warning, we find ourselves confronting textual material saturated with the notions of rationality and irrationality, terms quite unexpected after Weber's early work. The immediate question arises whether Weber's terminological innovations merely reflect the newness of the books he is dissecting, if the books under examination appeared while he was incapacitated. This is impossible, for Weber begins his essay on Roscher with the frank admission that he is addressing vintage texts indeed: *The Life, Work, and Era of Thucydides* (1842), *Outline of Lectures on Political Economy According to the Historical Method* (1843), and "the essays he wrote during the 1840s" (p. 54). Although Oakes believes that Weber's interest in the problems of historical logic and method is traceable to his juvenile essay on "*Volk* Character, *Volk* Development, and *Volk* History" of 1879 (pp. 6–7), it is probably more likely that he was responding to a debate among his peers which he had been forced to ignore during his convalescence. Judging from the ferocity of his eventual response, he must have been seething over the polemics swirling through learned journals throughout the 1890s. During the preceding period, too, his youth may well have prevented him from challenging such aged luminaries as Roscher and his own instructor at Heidelberg, Knies, whose lectures he found insufferable, and whose chair he had assumed in 1896.[44] But Roscher died in 1894 and Knies four years later, so this problem dissolved. Another possible motivation for carrying out these highly technical, mentally strenuous essays,[45] and for referring in them repeatedly

---

44. Marianne Weber, *Max Weber*, p. 65.

45. H. Stuart Hughes: "These essays make extremely heavy reading" (*Consciousness and Society*, p. 301). Oakes concurs: "Redundant, serpentine, bewildering, occasionally even mysterious, by no relaxation of the tenets of style could Weber's prose be called 'clear and distinct.' . . . His main theses are often concealed within a labyrinth of dependent clauses, different styles of typefacing, subordinately numbered paragraphs, and notes of fatiguing length, all of which the reader must unravel for himself. Subtle points are amended by still more subtle qualifications, until comprehension of the main point is effectively barred for all but the most patient and diligent student." He goes on, no less, to quote Marianne Weber's "explanation" for this horrid opacity: "Weber gave no attention to the systematic presentation of the results of his thought. He had no desire to be an academic logician. The form in which the wealth of his ideas appeared was quite without importance to him" (Weber 1975b, pp. 8–9; from the German edition of Marianne Weber's biography,

to "intuition" and other "irrationalities" of cognition, may lie in his own undeniable outbreak of gross irrationality and psychopathology. By 1904 Freud's work was becoming known, and by 1907 Otto Gross, the notorious popularizer of Freudianism at its most literal, had taken Heidelberg by storm, spreading a congeries of views which mixed free love with rituals of intense personal introspection. It has been documented beyond any doubt that Weber (and many of his students and friends) were affected by Gross's irrepressible magnetism, which was of such power that at one point he fathered a child by Weber's star female pupil, Else Jaffé, and around the same time impregnated her sister Frieda, later D. H. Lawrence's wife.[46] Thus notions of the unconscious, the repressed, and the irrational were very much on intellectual minds about the time Weber composed these essays.

There is little point in searching further for a definitive answer to the riddle of why Weber suddenly permitted the concept of irrationality into his scholarly work. But of this we can be sure: by 1904 at the latest, he had accepted the *basic* conceit (though not most ramifications) both of Freudianism and of the more established and diffuse *Lebensphilosophie*, not to mention Nietzsche's seductive work. In his own words, "das Leben in seiner irrationalen Wirklichkeit und sein Gehalt an möglichen Bedeutungen sind unausschöpfbar" (variously translated as "Human life, in its irrational reality, contains an inexhaustible variety of possible meanings," or the earlier rendition, "Life with its irrational reality and its store of possible meanings is inexhaustible"; the latter more literal, the former more interesting).[47] Oakes makes a good deal of this: "The complexity of Weber's academic prose was a consequence of his

---

p. 322). She also makes this psychologically arresting remark: "A convalescent like Weber, who recovered only very slowly and whose capacity for work continued to waver for years, required, in his own opinion, *increasingly novel motivations* in order to overcome the impediments of his illness. What he did and the manner in which he presented it were all the same to him, if he was simply able to work" (*Max Weber*, p. 319; emphasis added). Perhaps Weber truly "burned himself out" in his twenties and thereafter eschewed the drudgery of straight political economy. The *Irrationalitätsproblem* would certainly have qualified as a spicy item.

46. For details see Green, *The von Richthofen Sisters*, esp. pp. 32–72. See Weber's "Freudianism" (part of a letter to Edgar Jaffé of 13 September 1907), which Eduard Baumgarten calls "Weber's Polemic against a Freudian" in *Max Weber*, pp. 644–648, contra Otto Gross's writing.

47. Weber 1922a, p. 213; Weber 1975b, p. 10; Weber 1949, p. 111.

disposition to distrust any theory which was or pretended to be 'systematic': that is, any theory which presumed to deduce exhaustive solutions to any domain of problems from a single set of self-consistent premises. In Weber's view, systematic thought distorts reality."[48] Were this absolutely the case, we could dispense with most of Kant, Hegel, Marx, Schopenhauer, and others who influenced Weber's style of thought. But Weber's remark does signal his acceptance of a motif central to Nietzsche's anti-systemic philosophy as well as of the very systematic presentation in Schopenhauer's *Die Welt als Wille und Vorstellung,* an acceptance which acceded not only to Weber's private store of existential assumptions but, much more important, to his public philosophy of scientific method. This, it seems evident, is a turning point in his overall intellectual development virtually without parallel. It opened up to him entire sociocultural and psychological worlds of knowledge and experience which, had he remained tied to the limited definitions then prevalent of the "legal scholar" or "political economist," he would never have subjected to his special variety of global scholarship. While it is reasonably clear, for instance, that Rudolf Otto's idea of the nonrational "numina" of religious experience (in *Das Heilige,* 1917)[49] did not directly influence Weber's understanding of religion, a comparison of Otto's work with Weber's in the 1890s highlights the importance of the latter's alteration of mindset before writing his *Religionssoziologie.* Otto, an important theologian and academic contemporary, criticized "this bias to rationalization . . . not only in theology but in the science of comparative religion in general, and from top to bottom of it."[50] Weber finally escaped such reductionism when he admitted irrationality into social-scientific dialogue.

Yet this is not all of the story, to be sure. More than once he rebuked those whose intellectual scruples allowed them to invoke "intuition," "spirit," or other forms of pseudo-idealist obfuscation, surrendering before the difficulties of determining causality. Our point of interest, however—though involving some of the same words—is different. As we shall see, Weber's extraordinary cau-

48. Weber 1975b, pp. 9–10.
49. Translated by John W. Harvey as *The Idea of the Holy: An Inquiry into the Non-rational Factor in the Idea of the Divine and Its Relation to the Rational.*
50. Ibid., p. 3.

tion when writing of the nonrational in general, and specifically of those intrapsychic forces which resist cultural rationalization,[51] mirrors his heartfelt yet ambivalent antagonism for the literati and salon dilettantes who enjoyed a strong following among some of central Europe's bourgeoisie. He realized that their inspiration was rooted in reasonably defensible observations about the relation between what Bergson called "intuition" and "intellect." Weber's anger arose when these sorts of perceptions, especially when used by certain historians and philosophers of culture, were applied haphazardly to whatever objective referent came to hand.

His demands for what was and was not acceptable when interjecting irrationality into explanations of behavioral phenomena were most severe and led him at times into the impossible position of calling for the practice of *Verstehen*, yet recoiling from those very features of life most analytically susceptible to its use. He wrote of his good friend Simmel (the champion of *verstehende Soziologie* up to this period, and its most successful practitioner), "crucial aspects of his methodology are unacceptable. His substantive results must with unusual frequency be regarded with reservations, and not seldom they must be rejected outright."[52] Yet, after more battering prose, the dialectic forces a retraction: "On the other hand, one finds oneself absolutely compelled to affirm that this mode of exposition is simply brilliant and, what is more important, attains results that are intrinsic to it and not to be attained by an imitator."[53] A most perceptive and charitable characterization, espe-

---

51. His awareness of these forces stemmed not only from reading and his own experiences but also from the events surrounding the tragic life (and death) of Otto, one of Weber's young cousins. He and Marianne watched over the young man in Heidelberg, Corsica, and Rome, even as Weber himself was struggling to repair his injured psyche, but to no avail. Otto's suicide, as might be imagined, depressed Weber considerably. See Marianne Weber, *Max Weber*, pp. 245–248.

52. Weber 1972, p. 155. According to the translator, Donald N. Levine, "Simmel's pioneering forays into the philosophy of history, notably his *Problem der Geschichtsphilosophie*, provided a persuasive argument for a methodology based on the procedures of empathic understanding (*Verstehen*)" (p. 155). Simmel's book has been translated by Guy Oakes as *The Problems of the Philosophy of History*. For the relation between Simmel and Weber, a peculiar and somehow "unresolved" friendship, see Levine's introduction to *Georg Simmel on Individuality and Social Forms*, pp. xliii–lxi.

53. Weber 1972, p. 156. This fragment, recently discovered by Winckelmann at the Max Weber Institut of the University of Munich, was probably written in 1908 but was left unpublished "because Weber felt it might jeopardize Simmel's chances of obtaining a professorial appointment" (ibid., p. 157). The full title of the fragment

cially when we remember that by the time of *Wirtschaft und Gesellschaft*, Weber's originally warm regard for Simmel's work had cooled: "The present work departs from Simmel's method (in his *Soziologie* and his *Philosophie des Geldes*) in drawing a sharp distinction between subjectively intended and objectively valid 'meanings'; two different things which Simmel not only fails to distinguish but often deliberately treats as belonging together."[54] A strange irony resides in the fact that although Simmel's portraits of interpersonal as well as intrapsychic life have won deserved plaudits from generations of American sociologists (his work appeared in Park and Burgess's "green Bible" as well as other places long before Weber became known here),[55] Weber's incidental, hesitant, unfinished analyses of similar phenomena seem arguably both more incisive and more sociologically tenable. Put another way, either Weber's thoughts and observations are truly more timeless than Simmel's, or we have all become so imbued with the former's idea of what sociology ought to be that formalist sociology becomes by contrast less convincing. In any event, Weber's ambivalent response to Simmel's work, embodying as it does the requisite amount of *Spannung* ("tension"), documents his inability either to abandon the pursuit of the irrational altogether or to take on the challenge with the same thoroughness and zeal that typifies his more complete analyses of *zweckrationalisches Handeln*, especially in *Wirtschaft und Gesellschaft*.

Of the selection of "metatheoretical" essays presently under consideration, "Roscher's 'Historical Method'" comes first. Into its 67 pages (pp. 53–91, and notes on pp. 209–236) Weber poured a phenomenal amount and variety of material, as might be expected

---

is "Georg Simmel als Soziolog und Theoretiker der Geldwirtschaft." Levine, in describing the difference between Simmel's and Weber's positions on the analysis of meaning (subjective versus objective), notes that the two theorists operated with opposed forms of "sociological musicality," Simmel attuned to the "*mezzo piano*" of life, Weber to the "*fortissimos*," an apt and most unusual distinction (Weber 1972, p. 156).

54. Weber 1968a, 1: 4.

55. As early as 1895 Simmel published "The Problem of Sociology" in the *Annals of the American Academy of Political and Social Science* 6: 412–423. And his first piece in the *American Journal of Sociology*, "Superiority and Subordination as Subject-Matter for Sociology," appeared in 1896–1897: trans. Albion Small, 2: 167–189, 392–415. See further bibliographical details in Nicholas J. Spykman, *The Social Theory of Georg Simmel*, pp. 274–286.

when we recall the psychotherapeutic significance it must have had for him.[56] In general terms, he sought to reach three ends: first, to repudiate the positivist resolution of the *Methodenstreit*, proposed by followers of Carl Menger; second, to perform a related dissection of intuitionist epistemologies (in consideration of which Weber first deals with versions of irrationality), then as rampant among certain social scientists as was their opposite, mechanistic positivism; and, third, to offer solutions to limitations inherent in epistemological positions discussed earlier in the essay.[57] Although it would be inappropriate here to summarize Weber's vigorous pursuit of these matters, we should take note of several unusual aspects of the essay. For instance, Weber's two early mammoth reports of copious empirical data, the Verein study of agricultural workers and the companion examination of the stock and commodity markets, acquainted him sufficiently with statistical technique that he felt called upon to point out to his less numerically skilled colleagues the insuperable limits to correlation and its uncertain connection with cause (pp. 63–66). His keen insight into the very core of positivist or empirical method, written, it must be remembered, during what is thought of today as the prehistory of advanced quantitative technique, must be read (at least in part) to be appreciated:

> The philosophical [nomothetic] sciences have the following aim: to order an extensively and intensively infinite multiplicity of phenomena by employing a system of concepts and laws. In the ideal case, these concepts and laws are unconditionally and universally valid. The concrete "contingent" properties of the "things" and events perceptually given to us, the properties which make them objects of

56. Joseph Schumpeter, who knew Weber and enjoyed the rare distinction of having published in 1914 the first volume in Weber's series *Grundriss der Sozialökonomik* (*Epochen der Dogmen-und Methodengeschichte*, 1914), has written of this essay, "'Roscher and Knies . . .' is the most important of his many 'methodological' studies" (*History of Economic Analysis*, p. 817n). In the same passage Schumpeter characterizes Weber in a way that reflects his own Austrian background, somewhat removed from the hero-worshipping that went on in the "Weber-Kreis": "Max Weber was one of the most powerful personalities that ever entered the scene of academic science. The profound influence of his leadership—in large measure due to a chivalrous ardor for doing the right thing that sometimes verged upon the quixotic—upon colleagues and students was something quite outside of his performance as a scholar, yet was a vitalizing force." (More information about this important but neglected relationship is supplied in Gerd Schroeter, "A Conversation Between Joseph Schumpeter and Max Weber.")
57. Oakes's summary, p. 25, slightly altered.

perception, are progressively stripped away. This project is a consequence of the logical ideal of these disciplines, which pure mechan-
ics approximates most closely. . . . Their uncompromising logical
commitment to systematic hierarchies of general concepts under
other concepts still more general and their standards of precision
and unambiguity commit the philosophical sciences to the most
radical reduction possible: the qualitative differences of concrete reality are reduced to precisely measurable quantities. (pp. 55–56)

Thus far we have a succinct and competent rendering of differences Windelband, in his famous inaugural lecture, had already
pointed out, but free of example. Suddenly, though, Weber's prose
style and substantive content leap eerily into our own time: "If
these disciplines are ever to transcend a mere classification of appearances finally and fundamentally, then it must be possible to
employ their concepts in order to formulate propositions of general
validity. If these propositions are to be absolutely *strict* and mathe-
matically self-evident, then they must be formulated as equations
which describe *causal* relations" (p. 56). And just when Weber appears to be championing nomological epistemology and method,
he diabolically attacks:

> In consequence, the results of these sciences become increasingly re-
> mote from the properties of empirical reality. Empirical reality is in-
> variably *perceptual* and accessible to our experience only in its con-
> cretely and individually qualitative peculiarities. In the last analysis,
> the product of these sciences is a set of absolutely nonqualitative—
> and therefore absolutely imaginary—conceptual entities which un-
> dergo changes that can only be described quantitatively, changes the
> laws of which can be formulated in equations that express causal re-
> lations. The definitive logical *instrument* of these disciplines is the
> use of concepts of an increasingly universal *extension*. For just this
> reason, these concepts become increasingly empty in *content*. The
> definitive logical *products* of these disciplines are abstract *relations* of
> *general validity* (laws). Their *domain* is that set of problems in which
> the *central features* of phenomena—the properties of phenomena
> which are worth knowing—are identical with their *generic features*.
> A problem, therefore, lies within this domain only if our theoretical
> interest in the empirically given individual case is satisfied as soon
> as this case can be classified as falling under an abstract concept.
> (pp. 56–57)

On the heels of this prescient attack on "naive empiricism," quite
compatible with those of today, Weber discusses "the kind of
knowledge which is necessarily unattainable if we accept the perspective of the nomological sciences: knowledge of *concrete reality*,

knowledge of its invariably qualitative properties, those properties responsible for its peculiarities and its uniqueness" (p. 57).

Although he has not yet brought up the *Irrationalitätsproblem* itself, it is clear that his repeated use of the word *peculiarities* serves to recommend for practitioners of the *Geisteswissenschaften* a distancing from the rational, regularized, and predictable sorts of phenomena suitable to nomothetic cognition. For the "sciences of concrete reality" (*Wirklichkeitswissenschaften*),[58] Weber has in mind a precise program and set of expectations:

> The logical ideal of these disciplines is to differentiate the *essential properties* of the concrete phenomenon subjected to analysis from its "accidental" or meaningless properties, and thereby to establish intuitive knowledge of these essential features. The attempt to order phenomena into a universal system of concrete "causes" and "effects" which are immediately and intuitively understandable commits these disciplines to an increasingly sophisticated explication of concepts. These concepts are meant to *approximate* a representation of the concrete actuality of reality by selecting and unifying those properties which we regard as "*characteristic*."
>
> Therefore, the definitive logical instrument of these disciplines is the formation of relational concepts which are increasingly rich in *content*. In consequence, they are of increasingly limited *extension*. Their definitive products—if they may be said to have any conceptual character at all—are concrete *substantive concepts* of universal— or, as we may say, "historical"—*significance*. Their domain is found wherever the essential features of phenomena—that is, those which we regard as worth knowing—are not exhaustively described by a classification of phenomena under some generic concept: that is to say, wherever concrete reality *as such* is the object of our interest. (pp. 57–58)

He concludes these opening paragraphs of the essay with a synthetic statement that is uncharacteristically nonpartisan. In essence he argues that no sciences, of physical *or* social phenomena, "can develop their concepts exclusively from only one of these two metatheoretical[59] points of view" (p. 58). Weber adopts an olym-

---

58. Oakes at times translates *Wissenschaften* (literally, "sciences") as "sciences of concrete reality," where there is no obvious textual justification, thus introducing a needless complication of phrase and thought. See for instance in the original (1922a), p. 5, paragraph 2; and Weber 1975b, p. 57.

59. The German is *Zweckgeschichtspunkt* (1922a, p. 6). *Geschichtspunkt* means "point of view," and *zweck* is an all-purpose term which in this case probably connotes the heuristic nature of the two epistemologies. Thus Oakes is taking considerable liberties by inserting "metatheoretical," a word Weber did not use, but which Oakes values for his own reasons. (Oakes's translation is not as a rule very literal.)

pian stance, giving each side its due and refraining from joining the passionate fray as, by this time, many of his colleagues had. Yet, olympianism aside, the seeds of theoretical disruption concerning the particular "peculiarity" and "uniqueness" of nonrationalizable qualities of life were sown in this early methodological essay. In fact, to jump ahead considerably: an essay of analogous import and motive, "Science as a Vocation" (1919), in its frank admission, even humbleness, before the fact of irrationality in human personality (both in the object of social research and as part of the *Weltanschauung* of the researcher as subject) catches Weber not only at his most olympian but at his most honest. For obvious psychological reasons, if for no others, he was unable to invest in these earlier metatheoretical works the kind of stunning frankness about scientific method that continues to draw readers to his last writings on the subject.

Another surprising and otherwise little-known side of Weber's methodological consciousness appears somewhat later in "Roscher's 'Historical Methods'" when he mocks those who mystify, while glorifying, the process of empathy or empathic understanding as a tool of social and historical analysis. (This attack is taken up more strongly later in the book.) And finally, at one unorthodox juncture Weber cites a passage from *Paradise Lost* to illustrate "the inversion of Puritanical modes of thought" (p. 229). If the author had not intended, then, to write a tour de force in this first essay on Roscher, he did so in spite of himself. The range of example and the strength of the logic both indicate a superior work. But our search for the beginnings of the concept *rationalization* does not permit us to pause to admire the full measure of Weber's inventiveness and the marked superiority, both in example and in organization, of his work over other, better-known contributions to the *Methodenstreit*.[60]

After making observations about positivist and antipositivist methodologies in general, Weber incisively points to the *apparent* contradiction between Roscher's goals and those of classical political economy: "Its exclusive project [Roscherian economics] must be the intuitive reproduction of the total reality of economic life." The

60. For example, Heinrich Rickert, *Science and History;* Carl Menger, *Problems of Economics and Sociology.*

classical economist seeks other ends, "to discover in the multiplicity of events the lawlike and uniform rule of simple forces" (p. 58). Roscher's objections to this approach include what Weber also thought of as the unfortunate elimination of the "historically contingent," producing a body of knowledge "in which concrete 'contingencies' have been, as much as possible, stripped away" (p. 59). And yet, according to Weber's interpretation of what Roscher left only to speculation, Roscher's special form of idiographic method is actually more in keeping with Menger's nomothetic model than with that of his opponent, Schmoller (in whose camp Roscher "should" have fallen). For Weber, Roscher's objections to Austrian economics are other than what might be expected. They involve not so much the style of data collection as its search for static, ahistorical laws. Weber's reading of Roscher indicates that he opposed two special points of doctrine among the marginalists:

> (1) the deduction of absolutely valid practical *norms* from abstract analytical axioms (this is what Roscher calls the "philosophical" method); and (2) the principle according to which economics has heretofore *selected* the *subject matter* of its investigations. . . . As Roscher sees it, the task of science is not only to discover the laws of simultaneously occurring phenomena, but also to discover the laws of the succession of phenomena. Scientific research should establish nomological regularities in the relations between simultaneously occurring phenomena. But, above all, its task is to establish evolutionary laws of *historical* change. (pp. 59–60)

Weber could well have been writing about Pareto (had he known of him, a point we shall pursue later).

Via this paragraph we finally arrive at what I take to be Weber's first mention of irrationality in all his scholarly work, appearing on page 9 of the German edition, and also on the ninth page in the translation (p. 61). In locating Roscher in the tradition of German social science, he had this to say: "Roscher's methodological model was the methodology of the German historical school of jurisprudence. He explicitly draws attention to their method as analogous to his own. But in fact—and in its essentials this point has already been made by Menger—his methodological model is a peculiar *novel interpretation* of this method" (p. 61). This contradiction internal to Roscher's method, which was to some extent opposed to his larger purpose, seems to have struck a sympathetic chord in Weber, for he too was indebted to both camps in his economic and sociological approach. Naturally, his close personal attachment to Schmoller and Rickert (in some ways little more than an accident of birth, Rickert being a family friend in Berlin—not unlike Schumpeter's "geographically necessary" connection with Austrian marginalism) forced Weber to weigh very carefully his public pronouncements about the virtues of historical versus scientific social science. He gets to the heart of the matter:

> Savigny and his school, in their struggle against the legislative *rationalism* of the Enlightenment, found evidence of the *fundamentally irrational character* [*das prinzipiell irrationalen*] of law. Laws develop and obtain within a cultural community. They cannot be deduced from general maxims. Emphasizing the inseparable connection between law and all other aspects of cultural life, they hypostatized the concept of an *essentially* [emphasis in original] *irrational* and unique "*Volkgeist:* as the source of law, language, and the entire cultural capital of a people." (p. 61; emphasis added)

Weber immediately makes clear his objections to this hypostatization, though he is still not operating at full polemic force, perhaps owing to his own perplexity about the subject:

> This concept "*Volkgeist*" does not function as a provisional heuristic device for the preliminary description of a large number of concrete perceptual phenomena the logical status of which remains unclarified. On the contrary, it is treated as a real, uniform entity which has a metaphysical status. It is not the *result* of countless cultural influences. Just to the contrary, it is viewed as the *actual ground* of all the individual cultural manifestations of a *Volk*, the source from which they all *emanate*.
>
> Roscher stands squarely within this intellectual tradition, a tradition which may be traced back to certain views of Fichte. As we shall see, Roscher, too, believes in the metaphysical homogeneity of the "*Volk* character." (p. 61)

This passage brings up a multitude of items for discussion. In the first place, it might serve some purpose to determine what in this gentle polemic is based on scholarly understanding and what on other, less standard grounds. Weber never portrayed himself as a Fichte scholar or even as a very serious student of philosophy at all, with the special exception of the antiphilosopher Nietzsche. He more than likely picked up this characterization of Fichte from his wife, for she had recently published a lengthy and weighty study in a series edited by Weber, Carl Fuchs, and Gerhard Schulze-Gävernit (*Volkswirtschaftliche Abhandlungen der Bad-*

ischen Hochschulen), entitled *Fichte's Sozialismus und sein Verhältnis zur Marx'schen Doktrin.* It is extremely unlikely that Weber around this time possessed the intellectual discipline to examine Fichte and the related intellectual tradition in which he thought Roscher belonged. A much more important point stems from his disdain for the "concept '*Volkgeist*.'" This may well have been the root of his lifelong aversion to various manifestations of irrationality, which he struggled to master in the interests of his typological expansion and of intellectual honesty as well.

The imperialist propagandist and historian Heinrich von Treitschke spoke frequently at Weber's childhood home (along with many other "stars in the academic firmament"),[61] and it is common knowledge that nationalist themes were a mainstay of these seminar-like discussions. At this time, and also later as a college student, Weber heard and became (as he matured) more and more repulsed by Treitschke's Germanophile chauvinism. "*Volkgeist*" was perhaps the central category of the propagandist's thought. It also figured in the Wagner cult, as well as in many of the more offensive ideological statements of Bismarck's government. It was, then, in essence the hallmark of anti-intellectualism, anachronistic Romanticism, and what Weber believed to be degenerate nationalism—as opposed to his own, more "rational" type. In reading Treitschke today,[62] one can readily second Weber's distaste for the term and for the disorganized, unorganically related congeries of notions, prejudices, ideas, and fetishes behind it. But, having said that, it is necessary to admit that Weber's protean cognitive abilities *could* well have been stymied by his own intemperate irrationality in the face of the term and, by "logical" extension, by his strong feelings about conceptual portrayals of irrationality in general. Obviously, as is reflected in his *Rechtssoziologie* (sociology of law, in *Wirtschaft und Gesellschaft*), he owed a significant intellectual debt to "Savigny and his school." This being so, it must also follow that *their* anti-*Aufklärung* (Enlightenment), antirationalist impulse and the related conviction that rationalist theories of law shortchanged actual historical development became part of his scholarly *Weltanschauung* or domain assumptions. So far as I know this connection,

---

61. Marianne Weber, *Max Weber*, p. 39.
62. E.g., Heinrich von Treitschke, *Politics*, ed. Hans Kohn.

tenuous as it may seem, has not been made before, perhaps because, as in so much of Weber scholarship, many of his pivotal decisions, preliminary to actual concept formation, have not been examined. Even critics who assiduously pummel Weber's more famous
methodological ideas do not as a rule concern themselves with his
instant, relatively unthinking repulsion at various forms of irrationality (especially vis-à-vis political action and bourgeois religiosity).[63] Yet time and again the "ambiguity" and "tension" so frequently claimed for Weber's theories in general lead nowhere in
particular. His only response to the problem is a throwing up of
hands. These early "convalescing" essays can, I believe, beam light
into the "impermeable" darkness and inexplicable remoteness of
Weber's intellectual "ambiguity" and "tension."

Weber continues deflating Roscher's epistemology by attacking
"*Volkgeist*" and infers the difference between his own brand of conceptual nominalism and Roscher's freewheeling realism. He accuses Roscher of using the term as a catchall and a substitute for
true analysis, investing it with reified characteristics at once representative of the individual development of single individuals and,
by some sort of quasi-magical infusion, also of the national culture
at large. Weber subtly points out the proper use of concepts by illus-
trating with quotations that Roscher "does not conceive it [*Volkgeist*]
as an abstract generic concept, relatively empty of content. . . . He
uses arguments . . . against the 'atomistic' conception of the nation
as a 'mass of individuals'" (p. 62), naturally Weber's choice.

> Roscher is careful in placing restrictions upon his use of the concept
> of an "organism." He does not employ this concept unreservedly as
> an *explanation* of the essence of the "*Volk*" or the "*Volk* economy."
> On the contrary, he emphasizes that he uses the concept only as
> "the most economical way of referring to a large number of prob-
> lems." However, one conclusion can be drawn from these remarks:
> the purely rationalistic concept of the "*Volk*" as the coincidental col-
> lectivity of politically associated citizens does not satisfy him. In

63. During the last fifteen years, Marxists like Marcuse and others like Mommsen
have all but destroyed key aspects of Weber's methodology, as well as several related components of his politics, for those in their audiences. Yet they are especially
blind to Weber's peculiar treatment of irrationality, largely a result, I believe, of
Marx's very similar blindness. Important statements appear in Otto Stammer, ed.,
Max Weber and Sociology Today, esp. pp. 83–151. Recall Weber's words, quoted by
Löwith and cited above in part, about the "demolition of 'illusions'" and the need
for "scientific impartiality" to open eyes "blinded for a thousand years . . . by the
. . . grandiose moral fervor of Christian ethics."

> place of this generic concept, which is a product of abstraction, he employs the following conception of the *"Volk"*: it is an *intuitable* totality, the bearer of a *meaningful* total essence. (p. 62)

Although I have written above that some commentators (Gerth and Mills, for instance) have overdrawn Weber's disdain for Hegel and Hegelianism, in this quotation we do find a clear delineation of the classical Kant-versus-Hegel feud. Roscher's organicism, whether derived from Hegel or Darwin, would find Weber's extreme Kantian nominalism (*Volk* as "coincidental collectivity") laughable for its very "emptiness," the same emptiness Weber considers its principal asset. Perhaps it is not only Hegelianism in Roscher's "intuitable totality" that irks Weber, but also its strange admixture with the organic analogy:

> This theory leads Roscher—like so many modern "sociologists"—to believe that generic features and features which are essential from an historical standpoint are necessarily identical. Therefore, only the recurrent historical event can be of any significance. For this reason, Roscher believes that he can employ the unanalyzed concept of an *intuitable multiplicity* of *"Volk"* in the same way that a biologist works with the unanalyzed concept of the perceptual manifold "elephant." . . . The individual peculiarities of nations do not prevent the historical theorist from treating nations as members of a class and comparing their development in order to establish *correlations*. (p. 63)

There is far too much going on in these dense paragraphs to unpack in proper hermeneutic form within the available space, but we must take note of several points before moving on. Again Weber writes in a schizoid style. His sentiments, when appraised from within the *Methodenstreit* we have been experiencing for the last several decades,[64] seem to labor under a forced dialectic, rushing from one pole to the other, always on the verge of joining a camp but refraining at the last possible moment. This quality Marxists have found particularly irritating about Weber's writing, interpreting it as an outgrowth of his relentless categorizations and at-

---

64. A convenient date for the beginning of the latest round would be 1959, when Mills publicly attacked Parsons and the empiricists as well. But this choice probably holds more biographical than historical legitimacy, for an equally plausible date is 1939, when Lynd published *Knowledge for What?* and MacIver reviewed it harshly, creating an intellectual rift which has since been recreated many times.

tendant "value-*Freiheit.*" They are not alone in feeling this way, for surely Weber writes as a divided man, and his loyalties—equally attached to science and lucid conceptual formulation on the one hand, historical richness and fidelity on the other—have left many in our own *Methodenstreit* as hamstrung as he was. For my purposes, though, it is always his displeasure over certain specific conceptual problems, which he indicates time and again with the same phrases and words ("the purely *rationalistic* concept," "an *intuitable* totality," "an *intuitable* multiplicity," "the individual *peculiarities* of . . . ," "the *fundamentally irrational* character of . . . ," and so on [emphasis added]), that reveals what is most theoretically intriguing. Whether or not he successfully takes Roscher to task over purely logical faults, the organic analogy, or even particular historical judgments, the truly vital qualities of the essay originate elsewhere, in Weber's inability to separate his latent psychological metatheories about motivation and human values from the more formalist issues over method proper. In other words, his personal distress over the nature and place of irrationality in his own life contaminated these putatively logical exercises, in spite of his struggle to maintain purity. This condition persisted for most of his intellectual career, or so I shall try to demonstrate. (Pareto's relatively serene theoretical posture regarding irrational elements of private and social life highlights Weber's round of troubles with them.)

Weber's perception of what makes up proper methods continues to be paradoxical and inconsistent. He takes on the issue of whether or not, "with the progressive completeness of observation," the resulting collection of "correlations" will culminate in complete knowledge. He admits that the "*heuristic* value" of this sort of approach, producing a "complex of regularities," would be high, but as the "ultimate *goal*" of science they will not do: "Neither a 'nomological' nor an 'historical' science, neither a 'natural' science nor a 'sociocultural' science" could be satisfied merely with "regularities" in great profusion (p. 63; emphasis in original). At this point in the text (pp. 63, 216–218) an immense footnote is introduced which needs examination for its bearing on Weber's "ultimate values" regarding method. In it he is his most candid.

The note does no less than to establish Weber's position on all the major points of the *Methodenstreit:* the nature of concepts, the problem of "other minds," natural versus social-science epistemology, and so on. (He relegates all this to a note probably to register his opinion of what he once publicly labeled the "methodological pestilence [that] prevails in our discipline.")[65] He begins by crediting Dilthey for devising one dichotomy of the sciences, Windelband and Rickert for the other, and then, as he often did, turns to Rickert's specific arguments for comparison with Roscher's.[66]

The first item of business is Rickert's "basic thesis," that "the manner in which mental entities are 'given' to us is *not* essential to any difference of concept formation between the natural and historical sciences" (p. 216). Friedrich Gottl, a figure apparently central to this debate but seldom mentioned in Anglo-American commentary, is introduced so that Weber can argue against his major contention, in *Der Herrschaft des Wortes* (The Power of Words), that "inner experience" and "external phenomena" constitute an "ontological dichotomy." Weber's response is interesting, for it is clear that in order to maintain his desired distance from the private self, that center of irrationality and potential psychopathology, he must somehow undercut Gottl's contention.

> The point of view fundamental to the present study is close to Rickert's in the following respect: we both claim that "mental" or "intellectual" phenomena—regardless of how these ambiguous terms might be defined—are just as susceptible as "dead" nature to an analysis in terms of abstract concepts and laws. The modest degree to which strictness can be attained and the limitations upon quantifiability are not a consequence of properties peculiar to the "mental" or "intellectual" objects of the concepts and laws in question. (pp. 216–217)

65. "Gutachten zur Werturteilsdiskussion im Ausschuss des Vereins für Sozialpolitik" in Baumgarten, *Max Weber*, p. 139 (cited in Weber 1975b, p. 13). The occasion was the 1913 meeting of the Verein.

66. The issue of Rickert's influence on Weber has been a live one since Weber's death, whereupon Rickert announced to the Heidelberg circle that Weber had been an exponent of his philosophy, something Weber himself occasionally said, but as reflecting his modesty more than actual fact. Jaspers, in a famous interchange with Rickert around 1922, made it clear that if Rickert were remembered, it would be because of some footnote in one of Weber's books—a precisely accurate prediction. The magnum opus from which Weber took most of his Rickert material was *Die Grenzen der naturwissenschaftlichen Begriffsbildung*, which has been revised many times. Burger goes into the actual relationship between Rickert's and Weber's ideas on method in some detail (*Max Weber's Theory of Concept Formation*, pp. 94–153), as does H. H. Bruun (*Science, Values and Politics in Max Weber's Methodology*, esp.

Although this lacks absolute clarity, at least in today's terms, the drift does seem amenable to current prejudices and "unspoken" epistemological assumptions in the social sciences. What follows is more direct and more revealing, which probably helps explain why it is more often quoted: "On the contrary, the real question is *whether* the generally valid laws which may eventually be discovered make any contribution to the *understanding* of those aspects of cultural reality which we regard as *worth knowing*. . . . Naturalistic causal reasoning is often useless in attaining knowledge of what we regard as essential" (p. 217). Here again we become aware of Weber's sensitivity to, first, the nature of subjective experience and, second, the needs of social science searching for its elusive quarry—that juncture where subjectivity, or organized experience, enters the rigidity of social structure and struggles to overcome, transcend, or alter it in pursuit of its own goals. Thus Weber sees in Gottl's "ontological dichotomy" the genuinely valuable recognition that inner experience does indeed have qualities that vitiate modes of intellectual attack suitable to—even prompted by—external phenomena. Again Weber is too honest not to give Gottl credit, indirectly, for this awareness, but at the same time he sticks to Rickert's general program, all the while protecting his own fragile inner experience from examination. (Of course the question of what is worth knowing can only be decided on *wertrationalische* terms, the point usually made when this passage is recalled. But this is less interesting than Weber's associated sentiments, also displayed in the paragraph, since value relativism was not new with Weber. The new twist was his steadfast decision to eliminate the subjectively unpredictable, whimsical, pathological, or rebellious from his model of social action. It is to discover the origin of his decision that we investigate these sections of the essay.)

In concluding the bulky note, Weber affirms his conviction that in spite of the "fundamental inaccessibility of other minds" (Rickert's concern), "the course of human conduct and also human expressions of every sort are susceptible to a *meaningful interpretation*" (pp. 217–218). (The precise content of a meaningful interpretation

---

pp. 81–101, 124–134). The consensus on this point holds that Rickert greatly overestimated his impact upon Weber and that Weber's self-effacement cannot conceal his independence and originality of mind.

he leaves unanalyzed, in a way not unlike Roscher's in using "*Volk-geist*," except to say that what is worth knowing is meaningful—a naked tautology.) The note, read between the lines, seems to reveal Weber's earnest, though still to this point unsuccessful, effort to rid himself of certain demons—products of the "methodological pesti-lence." He had inherited a *Methodenstreit* (from Rickert and Windel-band, Roscher, Knies, Gottl, and others, which had begun when Weber was nineteen, with Schmoller's attack upon Menger in 1883), the central dispute of which did not interest him or in any serious way impinge upon the course of his work. His substantive research up to this point (1903) gives no evidence of having been constrained by undue allegiance either to a "*naturwissenschaftlicher*" or "*geistes-wissenschaftlicher*" methodology. Perhaps what in the last analysis these lines tell us is that Weber, the consummate artist of scholar-ship, made up much of his method and analytical apparatus as he went along, as do all creative workers. He paused from time to time and reflected on what he had done, then codified it as best he could for collegial consumption. That the codification never matches or adequately portrays the substantive work which pre-ceded it probably speaks for Weber's limited patience with meth-odological discourse. But the numerous ambiguities he failed to resolve add to the difficulties of our task—and that of all those who try to civilize, rationalize, or systematize Weber's unwieldy achievements.

At this point in the essay, discussion again turns to the logical status of correlations, which once more are shown to be devoid of causal properties. Weber begins to wonder what sort of knowledge correlations could provide. He comes up with the unusual thought that general concepts derived from correlations of events and con-ditions, (as a result of their tendency toward being "increasingly empty of content and alienated from empirically intelligible real-ity" [p. 64]), even if they could approach the "logical ideal"—"a system of *formulae* of absolutely general validity"—could not rep-resent historical reality. The internal logic of such a system would generate, at its extreme of perfection, "purely quantitative catego-ries of some sort" to which all "cultural phenomena" would inten-tionally be reduced.

Now he asks, of course rhetorically, "Suppose, on the other hand, these disciplines attempt to *understand* reality," rather than

simply to correlate and categorize it?[67] This is the first time he uses
Verstehen in a way that has since become synonymous with his
name. He initiates his commitment to the term by pointing out that
in using it we "become aware of the characteristic *meaning* of single,
concrete cultural elements together with their concrete causes and
effects, all of which is intelligible from the point of view of our
'inner experience.'" In a footnote he qualifies this statement: "If we
may use this expression at this point without further clarification"
(pp. 65, 219). What is literally being said is clear enough, but what
is involved sub rosa, or subtextually, relates to Weber's psychological *and* intellectual need to appear "hard-boiled" in his methodology (Parsons's description of Schmoller), while simultaneously remaining true to his own superior analytic perception of social life.
But he remains in awe of the "limitless—and therefore insuffi-
ciently intelligible—concrete manifold of the perceptually given,"
which "correlations" (a symbol at this point for inductive science)
must convert to "a limited and therefore *intelligible*—although no
less concrete—representation of certain elements of the manifold:
those placed in relief by the analysis because we see them as significant" (p. 65).

Again we meet this strange mixing of solid inductive procedure
culminating in correlations (to this day the hallmark of advanced
technique in many quarters) with the purely subjective, in Kuhn-
ian terms irrational, demand for significance, for what is worth

67. In 1922a, p. 14; Weber 1975b, p. 64. Up to this point I have purposely not
followed the path of many previous writers when analyzing Weber's methodological work—that is, to rely heavily upon chapter 16, "Max Weber, III: Methodology,"
pp. 579–639 in Talcott Parsons's *The Structure of Social Action*. In spite of its unusual
and admirable clarity in places, particularly in trying to unravel the positivist-
empiricist-idealist tangle, its weaknesses outweigh its strengths. Parsons's interpretation illustrates a typical shortcoming. On p. 538 he claims that *Verstehen* first
appears in Weber's work in his article on Knies, on p. 67 of 1922a, but in fact, in the
article we are now examining and to which Parsons gives almost no attention, the
notion of understanding as a special mode of inquiry is first mentioned on p. 14 of
1922a, p. 64 of the translation. The main reason I have foregone the temptation to
carry on a running debate with Parsons's reading of Weber is that his book, now
fifty years old, cannot be expected to measure up to expectations engendered by a
half-century of intense Weber scholarship. He was a pioneer and as such an excellent one. But that does not alter the fact that most of Parsons's citations are very
highly concentrated in only a few sections of the work; the rest he leaves unanalyzed and unincluded. What he gained in clarity and facile expression, he may
have lost in accuracy. Perhaps this is a trait endemic to works of commentary, but
for our purposes his omissions and selective interpretations are critical.

knowing. Weber realizes he is on thin ice and admits, "The question of whether and under what conditions they [concrete concepts, derived empirically] can constitute an adequate technique for this purpose is quite problematical," as it still is. He registers his strong suspicion of nominalist tendencies: "Obviously, there is a priori not the slightest reason to believe that the *meaningful* and essential aspects of concrete patterns would be identified by the abstract concepts of the correlations. If this is not kept in mind, then the use of correlations may commit historical research to the most vexatious errors" (ibid.).

Weber next briefly summarizes the preceding discussion. He reminds the reader that two possible goals of historical research have been presented, one that favors *"generic* features" and leads to *"generally* valid *formulae,"* the other speaking to the "concretely *meaningful* features [arranged] in universal—but concrete—*patterns."* Never content with simplicity, Weber now introduces a complication which bears on our topic:

> However, there appears to be a third possibility. . . . Suppose one accepts the Hegelian theory of concepts and attempts to surmount the *"hiatus irrationalis"* between concept and reality by the use of "general" concepts—concepts which as metaphysical realities, comprehend and imply individual things and events as their instances of *realization*. Given this *"emanatist"* conception of the nature and validity of the "ultimate" concepts, the view of the relation between concept and reality as strictly *rational* is logically unobjectionable. On the one hand, reality can be deduced from the general concepts. On the other hand, reality is comprehended in a thoroughly perceptual fashion: with the *ascent* to the concepts, reality loses none of its perceptual content. The maximization of the content and the maximization of the extension of concepts are, therefore, not mutually unsatisfiable conditions. In fact, they are mutually inclusive. (p. 66)

Weber put himself through this tortuous exercise for the purpose of addressing the question of the extent to which Roscher's historiography was determined by Hegelianism. What interests us, however, is his unprecedented use of the term *hiatus irrationalis* (literally, "irrational opening" or "gap"). The phrase appears only one other time in his work (in *Roscher and Knies*, p. 85) and there too lacks any kind of documentation or elaboration other than what can be gathered from the context. I have searched through sources Weber used, as well as others, and can find no standard or technical use of the term (although the phrase does crop up in

Hegelian commentary from time to time). Perhaps, then, it is what Max Rheinstein (in his lengthy introduction to *Max Weber On Law in Economy and Society*) calls "a term of art," one of the phrases Weber introduces for a specific use when none in the conventional lexicon suits him. Whatever its origin, the term points to an important (if not unalloyed) aspect of Weber's attitude toward irrationality in general: that it blocked the growth of knowledge or, to expand somewhat, retarded the movement of rationalization. And in this usage we could as easily be speaking of Hegel—for whom, it is often reported, Weber had no use—as of Weber.

The meaning of "emanatist" conception is less obscure. Parsons writes repeatedly of "naive emanationist" or "idealistic emanationist" views,[68] signifying the Hegelian notion of structure reflecting or arising from "Ideas." Weber, allowing the emanatist position, finds "logically unobjectionable" its practice of equating "concept" and "reality" in terms of what is "strictly *rational*" (emphasis in original). And to the amazement of those trained to believe in Weber as another neo-Kantian, he does *not* take this obvious opportunity to demolish the radical idealist epistemology. It could conceivably be inferred from his allowing the opportunity to pass that his heart was not in the Kantian *Weltanschauung* and that Hegelianism, even of Roscher's historiographic type with its totalitarian conceptual aggression upon the irrational, held a certain appeal for him. What is happening here, in philosophical terms, is this: whereas Kantians had reconciled themselves to the fact of phenomenal (rational) and noumenal (irrational) realities remaining eternally separate, and the latter quite impervious to examination, Hegelians trounced this distinction and coaxed the irrational back into the scientific arena. I contend that the ambiguity which pervades so much of Weber's methodological writings stems, at least in part, from his unwillingness to choose sides between the latent Hegelianism of Roscher (and Knies) and the outspoken Kantianism of his personal friends, Rickert among them. The former deserved appreciation for their boldness and unwillingness to abide by the bifurcated world Kant had bequeathed to German thought,

68. Parsons, *Structure of Social Action*, pp. 478, 536, 572, and so on. Parsons relates "emanationism" to Fichte and Hegel, in opposition to the "subjectivism" of Kant on p. 478, and he enriches the discussion with the help of Freyer, Troeltsch, and Meinecke.

and in the noumenal portion of which they had found some of the most compelling qualities of historical event. The more conservative, scientific Kantians accepted the dichotomy, then worked at humanizing it. This they did through the "ideal-type," "hermeneutics" (Dilthey), and *Verstehen;* but all within a circumference of investigation which in 1903 did not satisfy Weber. Academic-philosophic boundaries being what they were at the time, Weber could only somehow mitigate the weaknesses and blind spots of the predominant (Kantian) persuasion by introducing into it carefully selected fragments from the opposition. In such a highly charged atmosphere, this required no little courage. But he apparently mustered the nerve to speak out since he objected to reductionism on one hand, reification on the other.

This basic refusal to "denude concrete reality of its full actuality through abstraction" (p. 67) led him down substantive and methodological pathways unheard of at the time and, as I have argued, still only half understood. It is, for instance, definitely out of keeping with Weber's imagined demeanor today, but completely consistent with the scholar trying to mediate between competing definitions of social science, for him to have written:

> It is not a *concept* of maximum abstraction and generality which lends coherence to the work of the historian—and to the work of the poet—but rather a "comprehensive intuition." However, a formula or a definitional concept cannot articulate this "comprehensive idea" in a satisfactory way. History and poetry attempt to comprehend the fullness of life. The discovery of analogies is a technique for this sort of comprehension. . . . Regardless of how we evaluate the details of Roscher's formulation of these claims, it seems obvious that at this point he has correctly identified the essence of historical irrationality. However, many of the claims which he makes in this . . . work show that he was not aware of its significance. (p. 68)

It seems that Weber suffered similarly, for though he was probably unaware "of its significance," these words read almost identically with many of Dilthey's, and by 1903 he was considered hopelessly fond of the unique, biographical, irrational, and strange in social life, and to be pitied for this unsophistication. Though it is seldom described in these terms, is it not reasonable to picture Dilthey's voice as that of "pre-rationalized" social science, one ear attuned to poetry, the other to history, with later contributors of a nonhermeneutical frame of mind (whether of Schmoller's or Menger's camp) as spokesmen for the expanding, bureaucratizing, "professionalizing" *Geisteswissenschaften* under Bismarck's spell? Spokesmen, in other words, for rationalized social knowledge, free of the "comprehensive intuition" Weber obviously feared to relax his grip upon although he was conscious all the while of its anachronistic, Romantic, *weiche* (mushy) reputation.

Interlude: Practical Limits to
Adequate Hermeneutics

Roland Barthes's *S/Z*, as is well known, amounts to a line-by-line analysis—via Barthes's idiosyncratic structuralist aesthetic—of a short story by Balzac. It has met with mixed response in this country,[69] but perhaps the single most noticeable and alarming feature of the book is its lack of what Americans would call pace. Barthes isolates 561 "lexias" divided into five "codes," and he does so with such a leisurely (but also dogged) style that the 33-page short story receives (or is accosted by) 238 pages of commentary and apparatus. Barthes is not unique in this regard. Derrida does much the same thing—making an entire study of Nietzsche's marginalia—as do Ricoeur and Lacan, and their interests are precisely focused upon social theory rather than literature. While there are those (mostly Anglo-American critics) who see all this as pure scholasticism and intellectual degeneracy, it is nevertheless a fact that hermeneutics of an important kind has been taking this direction for the last twenty years or so, at times procuring unprecedented and illuminating results.

In the present hermeneutic exercise, many pages have been committed to the exegesis of fourteen pages in Weber's essay on Roscher. This sort of "progress" may be variously interpreted and could even be taken as a justification for Parsons's reliance upon secondary analyses. But several goals are being pursued simultaneously: discovery of Weber's initial reaction to the problem of irrationality in social analysis; ascertaining Weber's existential and

---

69. One reviewer wrote, "It will afford profit and pleasure to that numerous class of persons who have no instinctive enjoyment of literature" (cited in Roland Barthes, *S/Z*, p. ix). On the other hand, Susan Sontag has said, "*S/Z* demonstrates once again that Roland Barthes is the most inventive, elegant, and intelligent of contemporary literary critics."

scholarly motives, if any, for coming to his conclusions; incidental comparison with Pareto's position or other possible positions; and so on. None of these is usually given very close treatment in Weber commentaries, so it is at least possible to summon up sympathy for the lack of pace. I am in no position to argue whether this style of analysis is justified, fruitful, wise, or even responsible. It is at least consistent with current hermeneutical precepts and practices, and increasingly exegeses of this kind—for better or worse—have replaced the much looser, more "stratospheric" exegetical strategies sociologists have come to recognize as typical, through books like *The Structure of Social Action*. If I may use an old argument in a new way: these newer close readings are perhaps part of the discipline's maturation, when the fruits of pioneer genius are dissected and delivered in palatable bits to the congregation. If we reflect even momentarily upon those gifted theorists and researchers whose *total* accomplishments have simply been lost to current discourse (e.g., Sorokin, Mannheim, Mead, MacIver, Znaniecki, Schutz, and many from earlier years), then the utility of "unpacking" texts—even at great length—may stand revealed.

It has become a platitude that sociology is going through a crisis of some kind, and its theories seem to be especially hard hit, much more so than its rather self-confident methods.[70] This development often turns on Merton's shaping of sociology's self-conception, especially with regard to one of its younger sacred texts, his *Social Theory and Social Structure*. Like most long, difficult, holy books, this one has been much more often cited than carefully read. Those who have read the work, particularly his essays on what to do with sociology's theoretical classics, are well served in appropriating for themselves past masters. But as the book went through several editions between 1949 and 1968, many writers with only slight understanding of Merton's actual position—and no knowledge at all of his humanist classic, *On the Shoulders of Giants*—used Merton as a figurehead for their own attacks on classical theorizing. "His" message, then, has become a vital and inescapable part of the sociolo-

---

70. Richard J. Bernstein documents a good deal of this malaise, which he believes began in earnest around 1960 or so; see *The Restructuring of Social and Political Theory*. See also Mark Wardell and Stephen Turner, eds., *Sociological Theory in Transition*.

gist's professionalization since the early 1950s. In its coarsest and most popular form, the message mis-taken from Merton is as follows: theory "for its own sake" (itself an asinine notion, but widely "understood" among the atheoretical) is degenerate;[71] large-scale theory of old is to be *used*, not venerated, in "theories of the middle range" in order to "test" hypotheses expressed parsimoniously, which at their most advanced means in mathematical or graphic forms. Thus, the history of social thought should preferably become a graveyard for the "untestable" notion or the grandiose conjecture which, under modern rigor, has either been proved or rejected.

Many sociologists are more comfortable in the same pew with natural science and its methods than with the humanities and arts. This prevalent version of what sociology should be vis-à-vis its theoretical past has grabbed legitimation from wherever it could.[72] Unfortunately for Merton, who does not share in these gross simplifications, his name has been chosen as an insignia for would-be scientists. Merton has never concealed either his affection for the natural sciences or his knowledge of their history. And from his acclamation of natural science and its procedures, careless readers have supposed that he wished the same for sociology, regardless of its peculiar development and current condition. Merton's writing is a legend in sociology because it is literary in the best sense and therefore widely, if not deeply, read. But he was not and never intended to be primarily a historian of social thought, and later generations of scholars have argued against some of his famous interpretations of the classics, for instance, Durkheim's suicide rates.[73] Because of Merton's misuse at the hands of those who want sociology to sever itself from all humanistic impulses, the argument has arisen that it is time not only for a post-Parsons understanding of

71. I will not discuss the inherent absurdity of this formulation (and I am not attributing it to Merton himself), but it does reflect, I believe, an attitude prevalent in the field, especially among those most distant from the history of social thought, and it can easily be taken from a shallow reading of Merton's essays.

72. It is analyzed somewhat in Robert Friedrich's *A Sociology of Sociology*, esp. pp. xxi, 68.

73. Among others, see Steven Lukes, *Emile Durkheim*, pp. 191–225; and Dominick La Capra, *Emile Durkheim*, p. 165n; recent work that attempts to achieve hermeneutic completeness, even exhaustiveness. Merton's goal, the shaping of postwar sociology, was different.

classical thought—which some would hold has already been accomplished—but for a post-Mertonian conception as well.[74] Perhaps *post-mertonian* is the better term, since the distance between Merton's actual beliefs and the scientistic distortions made in his name has become undeniable.

In simplest terms, the pertinent issue is this: now that definitive editions of many classical works are becoming available in English, sociology might well take a new tack. My preference would be a shift from cannibalizing classical statements in search of testable fragments to a comprehensive hermeneutical effort to "learn the codes" unique to each thinker (I use Barthes's idiom only metaphorically)—that is, to come to a *contextual* or holistic understanding of the theorist's "project" and, through this completed lens, to become capable of *legitimately* isolating ideas or hypotheses of interest when the text gives itself to this sort of operation. This would mean that "rape theories of interpretation," as Richard Palmer labeled them,[75] be retired and henceforth regarded as artifacts of an earlier, rougher day in the history of the discipline. The work involved in this sort of endeavor would be prodigious, of course, but with manpower no longer the problem it was in the days of Barnes and Becker, Parsons, and Sorokin, suitable studies could well be forthcoming. Wholesale distortion of the past (willful or not) could diminish and future research be grounded in a less superficial, fanciful, or "instrumental" re-creation of what has come before.[76]

74. This is the substance of a recent symposium on the aging issue of presentism and historicism in the history of theory, with contributions by Steven Seidman, Robert Alun Jones, and Merton himself, in *History of Sociology* 6, no. 1 (Fall 1985): 121–160.

75. Richard E. Palmer, *Hermeneutics*, p. 247.

76. Cf. Harry Elmer Barnes and Howard Becker, *Social Thought from Lore to Science;* Parsons, *Structure of Social Action;* and Pitirim Sorokin, *Contemporary Sociological Theories.* I am obviously accepting, for the moment, Merton's most general proposition, that good research and good theory are absolutely necessary to one another. I am not completely in accord with this sentiment, however. Surely there are other, "purer" justifications for the existence of "theorizing" (as Alan Blum argues): for instance, because theory qua intellectual product may attain the status of a creation that deserves unmediated study. Lukács's work on reification and the historical role of the proletariat comes to mind. Adorno's *Negative Dialectics* is generally regarded as a masterpiece of quasi-Marxist aesthetic and social theory, but the probability that it will ever contribute to any form of empirical research is slight (just as he would have wished). Another argument for theory's relative autonomy from empirical research (a concept which has gained tremendous ground since around 1970, especially in England and Europe) centers on the contention that only theory (of a spe-

Behind this suggestion for a redefinition of exegesis lies a paramount value which makes the entire project an example of *wertrationalisches Handeln*. The value is intellectual or historical integrity,[77] and it stands in some opposition to others with a firm hold on the discipline, for instance, "empirical demonstrability of hypotheses," "convertability to inductive statement," or "propositional parsimony." And as Weber rightly put it, contrary to Lukács's objections, values are irrational, thus undebatable via rational discourse and the rules of logic.

We return to the immediate issue. I have searched all of Weber's works and most of Pareto's (excluding some economic treatises)[78] in pursuit of a more or less complete understanding of the conceptual role irrationality played in their works. Clearly, based on the preceding exegesis, a hermeneutically *adequate* analysis and interpretation (in Gadamer's terms, for instance) would call for thousands of pages.[79] So having just advanced the idea of a post-

cial kind, as for instance in Weber) can approximate a totality. And as such it can serve, *indirectly*, as a model of *extended* and intensive sociological labor, unlike one-shot research projects. This quality of protracted, continuously modified, "nurtured" theorizing perhaps helps explain why Mills' work continues to be read. His lifelong interest in power, inequality, and the relationship of consciousness to social structure, inspired by the classic tradition, gives life to empirical research which otherwise by now would be collecting dust.

77. I mean by this more the sense of wholeness or completeness than of honesty. I do not in any way mean to impugn the honesty of Merton's (or Sorokin's or Parsons's, etc.) interpretations, nor even the care given to them. The issue comes down to integrity as reflecting its Latin origin, *integritat*, denoting wholeness, "untouched," "entire." That there is, however, the most intimate relation between wholeness and accuracy (hence honesty) cannot be questioned.

A hermeneutical work that embodies virtual completeness is Hal Draper's *Karl Marx's Theory of Revolution* of which volume 1 (which occupies two books totaling 728 pages) out of three projected volumes is published. Should Draper finish his labors, there is a fair chance that *nothing* more new will be able to be added to the subject, one that has certainly stirred great debate over the past century.

78. Pareto's achievements in mathematical economics are of the first order, and his name is a sacrosanct part of every text in elementary economics or income distribution (e.g., Jan Pen, *Income Distribution*, pp. 234–241). His *Cours* (1896) was the first text of political economy to make statistics a centerpiece of the presentation; in *Manuel* (1906) he became the first economist to use simultaneous equations, in demonstrating and refining Walras's "equilibrium theory"; finally, he developed the famous Pareto ophelimity (or optimality) principle, plus "Pareto's law" of income distribution, $N = A/x^a$.

79. I have been prompted to study hermeneutics because of the conviction that students of thought within my field do not generally fare well when compared with historians, philosophers, or literary critics, whose interests are similar. (Martin Jay's *The Dialectical Imagination* and Mark Poster's *Existential Marxism in Postwar France*

Mertonian reading of the classics, I must add the obvious note that such a reading is hardly a one-person task. A heuristic alternative must be devised, one that maintains intellectual integrity along with that of the material under study (the original purpose of hermeneutics), while at the same time expediting the project.

Henceforth I will deal adequately only with those passages which, based on close reading of broad scale, exhibit most clearly Weber's point of view as it pertains to my special interest. In adopting this editorial procedure, I am blocked from creating the comprehensive portrait that should serve as the ultimate hermeneutic goal in research of this type. It is not pure casuistry, however, to distinguish between this approach and more standard instrumental interpretations. For example, an author of an article on Weber's methodology (of which there are hundreds)[80] is not currently expected to pursue the topic *throughout* Weber. As noted above, entire monographs are published dealing exclusively with small portions of Weber's work which *he* may well not have recognized as separable from the larger fabric. In this essential the present study is distinct, for it is predicated upon a complete reading.[81]

This effort is unconventional in still another way. Since nothing of the kind has been done before, except for the *Religionssoziologie*, and there with different ends,[82] I will list those places where Weber

---

demonstrate how dependent students of social thought in sociology proper have become upon professional historians.)

80. Seyfarth and Schmidt, in their 2,348-item bibliography (*Max Weber Bibliographie*, pp. 193–195), list (counting conservatively) 307 items relating to the methodology.

81. Again, this is a purely quantitative evaluation, holding no absolute qualitative meaning.

82. In a footnote, the contents of which I have seen nowhere else, Ferdinand Kolegar reports, "A useful inventory of passages pertaining to the concept of rationalization in Weber's sociology of religion has been made by Ernst Graf zu Solms [Max Ernst Graf zu Solms-Roedelheim] in the appendix to his selections from Max Weber, *Aus den Schriften zur Religionssoziologie* (Frankfurt: Schauer, 1948), pp. 318–323." Kolegar at this point in his essay is discussing the terminological problem inherent in *rational, rationality, rationalization*, etc., and goes on to say, "Weber himself was fully aware of this unavoidable ambiguity and commented on it several times" ("The Concept of 'Rationalization' and Cultural Pessimism in Max Weber's Sociology," p. 361). It is unfortunate that so few Weberians seemed to know about Solms-Roedelheim's little compendium when it appeared, nearly forty years ago. The eight passages he selected from Weber's work that bear on "die Begriffe des Rationalen und der Rationalisierung" (p. 318) are as follows in available English translations:

makes use of *irrationality* as an important term. I will also indicate the many passages where, without literally pairing *Bedeutung* (meaning) with *Irrationalität*, Weber clearly connects the two. These lists should help to close the gulf between the ideal treatment I would like to provide and that which necessity dictates. It may also moderate a fiction of scholarship to which we have become too inured. As specialization intensifies, professional audiences accept proffered interpretations less and less critically; they trust their informants for the most part, especially those already well known. This vicarious expertise is unavoidable to a point in our academic setting. In the present case, the fiction that my interpretation is reliable is less farfetched than would be the case were it written without the guidance of hermeneutics. No more than that can be said. This approach of course does not guarantee accuracy or "integrity," which is another issue.

A Note on Scholarly Response
to Weber's Terminology

In addition to the compendium of phrases concerning *rationality* and *rationalization* assembled by Solms-Roedelheim, there are other comments on the problems Weber created by leaving these vital terms partially unanalyzed. Mannheim, Schutz, Marcuse, Bendix, Habermas, Dahrendorf, and Percy Cohen are the major sociologists to have written essays or parts of books which consider *rationality* or its cognates in Weber's work. The first item in this genre was published in 1927 by Hermann J. Grab, *Der Begriff des Rationalen in der Soziologie Max Webers*. Though often cited as a book, its forty-eight pages do not qualify it for that designation. Schutz (in *Phenomenology of the Social World*, p. 239n21), says, "For an analysis of the concept of rational action see Hermann J. Grab's valuable mo-

---

(1) Weber 1930 (Scribner's edition), p. 26; (2) ibid., p. 194n9; (3) ibid., pp. 76–78; (4) Weber 1946, pp. 280–281; (5) ibid., pp. 286–287; (6) ibid., pp. 293–294; (7) Weber 1951, p. 226; (8) Weber 1946, p. 324. Though tiny by comparison with my project, had it been taken seriously it could have helped direct attention to this underside of Weber's thought to which Kolegar alluded in 1964. However, only the first and fourth excerpts discuss *ir*rationality, and not so well as in the methodological essays.

nograph. . . . Needless to say, my agreement with Grab can only be partial, since he presupposes Scheler's concept of objective values." Schutz's objection aside, Grab's little study does provide one of the most direct treatments of Weber's problem with terminology regarding irrationality. Almost as an afterthought to his introductory chapter, and with no elaboration anywhere later in the book, he observes:

> Now something must be said about the use of the words *rational* and *irrational*. Despite the fact that the words are from this representative standpoint given a positive meaning—as everything is generally called rational which is palpably ordered—and not to cause terminological confusion, the words should not be used here in a positive way. In modern philosophy—and also with Max Weber—the use of the words *rational* and *irrational* is symbolic for the two poles of modern metaphysical dualism, the dualism in which is also arranged the contrast between value-engagement and value-freedom. . . . Values appear inaccessible for every rational scientific point of view; they stand in Kant's sense in the irrational sphere of freedom (which is of the individual). This is the assumption that Max Weber also took over from idealism. . . . Science has nothing to do with the primary order of the individual's "ultimate" value-determination; it must be left, surrendered, to irrational life. (p. 13)

Parsons includes Grab in his 1937 bibliography, but it is not clear that he took this passage seriously with regard to Weber's handling of irrationality, the clear connection to Kantian freedom, or, most important, the deeply *symbolisch* phrase *dem irrationalen Leben*, "irrational life." Such attention would have elevated aspects of Weber's word-choice and the theoretical focus that stemmed from it into a legitimate area for inquiry.

Very few more recent works deal directly with rationality/irrationality. Ann Swidler's brief "The Concept of Rationality in the Work of Max Weber" offers nothing substantially new, nor is it very detailed. The most interesting of recent brief treatments is Arnold Eisen's "The Meanings and Confusions of Weberian 'Rationality.'" Eisen identifies six senses Weber gives to *rationality* in some of his major works (presented in tabular form, pp. 62–63): purpose, calculability, control, logical coherence, universality, and system. Once again, brevity undoes the final effect of this unusual effort to comprehend Weber, since only *Economy and Society*, the music book, *Religion in China*, *Ancient Judaism*, and "Science as a

Vocation" are discussed, and those very selectively. Still, Eisen's conclusion, that Weber's attachment to rational behavior reflects his modulated respect for the *Berufsmensch*, is a worthy one and does to some extent soften, as Eisen believes it should, attacks critics such as Marcuse made upon Weber for his apotheosis of "reason." In brief, Weber's own *Irrationalitätsproblem* was markedly irrational in origin—a fact which by now should be fairly clear. Roger Brubaker's *The Limits of Rationality: An Essay on the Social and Moral Thought of Max Weber*, despite its promising title, cannot do more than review this master category in Weber's major works, also due to limited space. Brubaker does not consider the *Irrationalitätsproblem* in the way I have; that is, it remains tangential to his enterprise. The most interesting effort is Toby Huff's set of review essays on *Roscher and Knies, Critique of Stammler*, and other works by Simmel and Dilthey, inspired by his having been introduced to "the hermeneutic tradition" by Robert Bellah. The essays, originally published in *Philosophy of the Social Sciences*, were reissued with an introduction in book form as *Max Weber and the Methodology of the Social Sciences*. It is in the book (pp. 43–49) that Huff follows Weber's arguments with Roscher and Stammler on "The Problem of the 'Irrationality' of Human Action." As far as it goes, Huff's study is competent and unusually sensitive to the concerns I have about interpreting Weber's larger theoretical goals. Yet once again, the essay is not long enough for the full-scale hermeneutic of the problem that is required.

Unbelievably, *no* major works consider Weber's *Irrationalitätsproblem* other than incidentally. I believe this proves, more than anything else, how potent Weber's own predilections and methodological directions have been for the 1,400 or more authors who have sponsored his continuing importance through their writings. If, as Kolegar reports, Weber recognized the intrinsically problematic character of his *zweckrational* category and his more encompassing *Rationalisierung*, this omission becomes difficult to explain.

As an example of how perplexing scholars—even those who otherwise write with supreme confidence—seem to find the *Irrationalitätsproblem* in Weber's work, we might record Percy Cohen's error when he wrote, "Almost everything Weber has to say about the types of rational and nonrational conduct is contained in

Weber, M. (1968), pp. 22–6."[83] This could hardly be more wrong, but it does reflect a widespread belief, especially among sociologists who fail to examine any of Weber's statements on the subject except those that appear in the first few pages of *Wirtschaft und Gesellschaft*, or, in Henderson's and Parsons's translation, *Theory of Social and Economic Organizations* (pp. 112–123).

83. Designating, of course, *Economy and Society*, Vol. 1. See *Rationality and the Social Sciences*, ed. S. I. Benn and G. W. Mortimore, p. 153.

4

The Middle Period

Roscher and "Objectivity"

Having moved from the hermeneutically desirable to the manage-
able, we may return to "Roscher's 'Historical Method.'" Once
Weber has established Roscher's ambivalent relation to Hegelian
historiography, he pursues several themes simultaneously through
the rest of the essay. First he accuses Roscher of "recognizing no
distinction between discursive knowledge and intuitive knowledge" (pp. 69–70), a result of Roscher's relying upon "Hegelian em-
anatism" while rejecting the general philosophical position. Here is
another instance of Weber turning the tables on those who have
long held that he subscribed methodologically to an "intuitionistic"
Verstehen and little else.[1] Thus Weber takes Roscher to task precisely
for thinking sloppily and overdoing the intuitionist perspective.

   Some other interesting observations are introduced at this point,
bearing upon Roscher's firm but muted belief in God, which he
throws against "Hegel's panlogism." Weber exposes himself along

---

1. Some of the common fallacies of this position (many of them resulting, as
usual, from unfortunate choices made by translators over the years) are forcefully
pointed out by Peter Munch, "'Sense' and 'Intention' in Max Weber's Theory of Social Action." He accuses Henderson and Parsons of having given "a definite psychological twist to Weber's concept of social action, particularly in terms of the 'imputation of motive' in a psychological sense" (p. 61). He goes on to note that a root
of the problem lies in Weber's term *gemeinter Sinn*, which Munch translates literally
as "intended sense." The Parsonian slight alteration, "intended meaning," psychol-
ogizes Weber's approach to the interpretation of meaning (hence *Verstehen*) and
wrongfully provides "evidence" for those who over the years have repeatedly accused Weber of undue interest in motives. (Munch locates the beginning of this mistake in Abel's article "The Operation Called *Verstehen*.") Munch's ideas gain their
utility almost exclusively from his uncommon and assiduous attention to problems
of translation. In fact, he claims that much of Marcello Truzzi's symposium on the
subject, *Verstehen*, is an outgrowth of a tradition of misreadings based upon poor or
debatable translations. The translator of the crucial *Logos* article, Edith E. Graber,
has appended to Munch's a short piece clarifying some other points germane to the
discussion, with the provocative title "Interpretive Sociology Is Not Part of a Psychology," actually a quote from Weber's article.

another line of interest by chiding Roscher (in a footnote) thus: "Roscher's section on Kant in his *History of Economics* is quite superficial. Kant is disposed of merely as a representative of 'subjectivism.' This illustrates Roscher's profound antipathy—the antipathy of the historian as well as the antipathy of the religious man—against any truth that is purely *formal*" (p. 222). This says two important things. First, Kant for Weber was not (as we still read today) the exponent of a subjectivist epistemology that Hegelians accused him of being. And, second, here we see for the first time the theoretical foundation of the *Kategorienlehre*, made public in 1913 (a decade after the Roscher essay was written), then incorporated in much abbreviated form into *Wirtschaft und Gesellschaft*. Although Weber later realized that "the most precise formulation cannot always be reconciled with a form which can be readily popularized" (*Economy and Society*, p. 3) and made some effort (at the request of colleagues) to simplify his typologies, rarefied formalism remained a stock feature of his prose. This is taken to its most extreme in chapter 2, "Sociological Categories of Economic Action," of part 1 of *Economy and Society*, an almost unreadable accretion of definition piled upon definition—as dry, lifeless, and free of example in many cases as his *Religionssoziologie* is rich, almost entertaining, in its illustrative material. Weber had clearly decided rather early in his most productive period to use a formalist and, relative to those like Roscher, nonintuitionist mode of expression. This reveals his own nascent antipathy (not unlike Roscher's in its nonrational origin) to aspects of socioeconomic reality more easily dealt with by the techniques of "emanatist" writers than by his own abstract reductions and ideal-typifications. Most of these items (nationalism, the *Volk*, art, race differences, and so on) of course contain the irrational in abundance.

At this point in the essay the English translator, Oakes, inserts a promising subhead, "Roscher's Concept of Evolution and the Irrationality of Reality," which is pure fabrication on his part, there being neither the subhead itself in Weber's text nor even any explicit comments about irrationality in the section he designates (pp. 73–80). What we do find is a timely, sensible attack upon some of Roscher's more resolutely Romantic, even reactionary, articles of faith. Weber destroys Roscher's contentions surrounding his overarching concept, *Volk*, which he not only mystifies and personifies à la Treitschke but also integrates into a denatured version of Spencer's social evolutionism. All of this Weber finds impossible to consider seriously.

The most interesting feature of Weber's refutation is his summoning up of Spinoza, Marx, Thucydides, Otto Hintze, Du Bois-Reymond, and others to combat this religico-mystical version of historiography. And as in many other instances, he turns Roscher's faulty thought to advantage by contrasting it with his own conception of appropriate goals and methods for *die Wissenschaften:*

> Before as well as after Roscher, the fundamental substantive and methodological problem of economics is constituted by the question: how are the origins and persistence of the institutions of economic life to be explained, institutions which were *not* purposefully created by collective means, but which nevertheless—from our point of view—function purposefully. This is the basic problem of economics for the same reason that the problem of the explanation of the "purposefulness" of organisms dominates biology. (p. 80)

He goes on to criticize Roscher's approach to a related problem, "In what conceptual form is the relation between individual economic institutions and the broader contexts in which they are implicated to be scientifically construed?" (ibid.). The fact that he chides Roscher's answer is by this time expected, but the similarity between the position he denounces here and the one he himself eventually took up points to internal inconsistencies in his own thought, the sort of thing we have seen before:

> In Roscher's view . . . this question can be answered only on the basis of certain assumptions concerning the psychological basis of the *action of individuals.* At this point, we find the same contradictions in Roscher's methodological reasoning which we noted earlier in his philosophy of history. Roscher's intention is to conceive the processes of life historically: that is to say, in their full actuality. Therefore we should expect that . . . he should focus his investigation on the constant influence of *non*economic factors on economic action. That is to say, we should expect him to focus upon the *causal heteronomy of the human economy.* (p. 80)

Without distorting Weber's intentions unduly we can interpret some of these sentiments (about institutions that "function purposefully" without conscious direction, or the search for "*non*economic factors" in economic action, for instance) as Weber's still repressed awareness that the rational model of classical economics could not hope to explain very much of economic history or everyday action. Hence this should be remembered: his objections to Roscher are those of one who *approves* of the latter's general intentions (in combatting Enlightenment rationalism, as had the "historical school of jurisprudence") but takes the offensive in order to save his chosen strategy from incapacitation at the hands of a well-meaning but fumbling spokesman. The characteristics of social life which have captured Weber's attention—undirected purposefulness, atomistic individual actions, the "heteronomy of the human economy"—all correspond to highly unsystematized and unrationalizable elements of social life. His (and Pareto's) enormously ambitious goal is to provide social science with a model that tames and regularizes these gross quotidian irregularities, the likes of which had found no place in Ricardo's theory of the market but had been too handily embraced (and disfigured) by the historicists. The latter naturally appealed to Weber, but, in a sense, he had to protect himself (and his "project") from his own "best friends" even more than from mechanistic theorists beyond the pale.

The next important passage occurs several pages later. In rounding out the essay, Weber advances critiques of Roscher's terminological shortcomings, especially with regard to "his concept of the 'organic'" (p. 84). Some familiar notions are repeated and amplified:

> According to Roscher, the fundamental limitation upon the possibility of knowledge in economics is not constituted—or at least not primarily constituted—by the *"hiatus irrationalis"* between concretely and individually given reality, on the one hand, and abstract, general laws and concepts, on the other. Roscher has no doubt . . . that the concrete actuality of economic life is *in principle* analytically comprehensible in the form of laws. Of course, "innumerable" natural laws . . . are necessary for an exhaustive analysis of economic life. It is not the irrationality of reality which resists subordination under "laws," but rather the "organic" *uniformity* of sociohistorical complexes. . . . [According to Roscher] the limits of rational knowledge are constituted by the following consideration: because of their dignity as "organisms," these universal sociohistorical complexes and their objective products cannot be explained as *causal* consequences of individual phenomena. . . . They are structured according to a (metaphysical) causal nexus of a higher order. (p. 85)

Part of the difficulty in interpreting this is the strange mixture of plausible—even compelling—speculation (whether Roscher's, or Weber's in response to it) with noticeably antiquated philosophizing. But beneath this surface confusion Weber's activity is visible, correcting with one hand Roscher's quasi-religious excesses and with the other buttressing those claims and observations which fit into his own developing philosophy of method. The passage just quoted (which, it should be pointed out, is Weber's interpretation of Roscher's beliefs, not a presentation of his own) again illustrates that "the irrationality of reality which resists subordination under 'laws'" was an important concern for Weber, and one he clearly believed Roscher had slighted by resorting to the "dignity" of "universal sociohistorical complexes" and their "'organic'" interrelation. However, it could be argued that in the end Weber's superior analytic ability did not save him from likewise constructing a subterfuge to conceal the difficulty associated with "the irrationality of reality."

The merciless dissection of Roscher's method comes to an abrupt close with several other significant points. First Weber demonstrates his own modernity compared to Roscher's confused *Weltanschauung* (part true believer, part dedicated scientist) by noting, "Roscher's relativism reaches its limits at this point: he never goes so far as to admit that the value judgments which constitute the basis of practical economic maxims are of only *subjective* significance" (p. 87). Weber seems to take some pleasure in distancing himself from normative absolutes, a theme which he pushed to its logical limit in "Science as a Vocation" many years later. He mocks Roscher further: "He has renounced in principle the attempt to rationally justify general *ideas.* He conceives himself 'not as a guide, but rather as a map'" (ibid.). A few pages later, becoming bolder, he punctures Roscher's most cherished beliefs (e.g., "the 'real needs' of a *Volk* will prevail spontaneously" through economic development):

> The autonomous selection of his ultimate goals is not a possibility for the individual. For this reason, Roscher could retain his relativistic standpoint without committing himself to ethical evolutionism. In fact, he explicitly rejected evolutionism in its *naturalistic* form. Consider the idea [Weber's inevitable lead into a particularly destructive comment] that the concept of *historical* evolution could produce a similar depletion of the *normative* content of moral imperatives. It was inevitable that Roscher would fail to take this idea into account. *He* was convinced of its impossibility. (p. 89)

This illustrates beautifully Weber's temperamental affinity with Nietzsche at this point in his life. The essay is finalized with Weber's portrait in miniature of Roscher's "rather primitive form of homely religious faith," the obstacle to historiographic theory which could match that of its intended victim, Hegel; for Roscher, "unlike Hegel, . . . failed to grasp the methodological importance of the *logical* problem concerning the relationship between a concept and its object" (p. 91).

Other essays of equal importance written almost simultaneously by Weber indicate similar concerns. The first is the very well known article of 1904, " 'Objectivity' in Social Science and Social Policy,"[2] in which Weber, as co-editor of the new *Archiv für Sozialwissenschaft und Sozialpolitik,* delivered a brilliant statement stipulating, among other things, which scholarly values the *Archiv* should in his opinion support. Because it has inspired voluminous commentary ever since its translation, I will keep my remarks to a minimum.

The tone of his essay is much "improved," one might say, over that of the Roscher polemic. In it Weber assumed an olympian posture dispensing various desiderata to prospective contributors to his journal, while simultaneously constructing his own private epistemology and working out the relationship between values and "scientific" knowledge. This was essential, given the *Archiv*'s ultimate goal of publishing scholarly articles which might serve as background to legislation. Thus the improvement in tone arises from Weber's opportunity in this work to address a wide variety of problems directly, without having to reach them by way of Roscher's often uncongenial formulations. As might be imagined, this change advanced the level of argument substantially, and, because of the very public nature of the editorial statement, Weber worked hard at producing a seamless surface to his thought.

He immediately points to the chasm between "existential knowledge" and "normative knowledge" but opposes other writers in attaching the dilemma of social science only indirectly to this dichotomy:

> The formulation of this distinction was hampered, first, by the view that immutably invariant natural laws,—later, by the view that an unambiguous evolutionary principle—governed economic life and

---

2. Weber 1949, trans. Edward Shils and Henry Finch, pp. 50–112; in 1922a, pp. 146–214; item 62 in Käsler's list.

that accordingly, *what was normatively right* was identical—in the former case—with the immutably *existent*—in the latter—with the inevitably *emergent*. With the awakening of the historical sense, a combination of ethical evolutionism and historical relativism became the predominant attitude in our science. This attitude . . . tried to give a *substantive content* to ethical norms. (pp. 51–52)

With this syntactically burdened beginning, Weber pursues what for him is the key problem (which, incidentally, is *not* the old refrain about "values" being "subjective" and therefore somehow problematic, a truism he easily accepts): "What is the meaning and purpose of the scientific criticism of ideals and value-judgments? This requires a somewhat more detailed analysis" (p. 52). This seems at first glance removed from our concern, but is not, for in solving this riddle Weber for the first time introduces the rudiments of what would serve as his *Gattungsbegriffe* (generic concepts) in *Economy and Society*:

All serious reflection about the ultimate elements of meaningful [*sinnvollen*] human conduct is oriented primarily in terms of the categories "end" and "means." We desire something concretely either "for its own sake" or as a means of achieving something else which is more highly desired. The question of the appropriateness of the means for achieving a given end is undoubtedly accessible to scientific analysis. . . . We can . . . estimate the chances of attaining a certain end by certain available means. In this way we can indirectly criticize the setting of the end itself as practically meaningful (on the basis of the existing historical situation) or as meaningless with reference to existing conditions. (pp. 52–53)

Of all the material examined thus far, this holds, in one way at least, the most promise for understanding Weber's conception of meaning and of the means-ends relation, around which all his categories of social action revolve.[3] By extension, then, it also speaks forcefully to the problem of irrationality as it works upon (or, to use Weber's bias, "deflects") meaningful (*sinnvoll*) action. I have already made very clear the weaknesses endemic to this conceptual apparatus (taken, strangely enough, from the same classical economic model Weber—under *other* circumstances—rebukes for its "unrealistic" nature). But note that already in 1904 Weber fastened

---

3. It should be noted that he treats meaning in more elaborate form in another selection, "Knies and the Problem of Irrationality," written at almost the same time.

upon this attitude and held to it for the rest of his life whenever he felt called upon to lay out his most basic ideal (*Grundideen*) in purely formal terms. We have already established that he placed some stock in formalist categorization, for he classified Roscher's discontent with formalism as a theoretical defeat. All this illustrates the correct and frequently heard designation of Weber as a "voluntarist nominalist," but does nothing to dispel perplexity regarding his earlier remark in the Roscher essay: "The autonomous selection of his ultimate goals is not a possibility for the individual" (p. 89). Throughout his writings Weber makes reference to one form or another of constraint (usually in conscious dialogue with Marxism) upon actual "voluntarism," what we have called in a slightly different context "the constraining immediacy of life."

Why did Weber, fully aware of the *lack* of real choice for practically every social actor in industrial society, insist upon building into his system this undependable, unquestionably heuristic plank? If the answer could be teased from the subterranean Weber, it might well bear the mark of his ultimate, nonrational scholarly (and political) values as a German *Bürger*. For this reason the contemporary student must read his prescriptions for defensible method warily. They probably have more to do with his existential and collegial needs at the time (as is clearly the case in the *Archiv* statement) than with what he privately valued for study and which he found most intriguing. An indication that this might be true lies in the fact that, by and large (except for one final empirical study), his policy-oriented scholarship had come to an end and he had turned exclusively to analyses of religion, music, and the various developments of "spirit" he found interesting (e.g., those of the Protestants, or of medieval legalists who began the rationalization of law). But the fact remains, and bears repeating, that for *public*, prescriptive purposes, Weber clung to the rationalist model of action—and its facile definition of *meaninglessness*—with the same sort of dogmatic tenacity he found so detestable in Roscher's commingling of religiosity and confidence in "evolution."

In a proximate sentence ("It is self-evident that one of the most important tasks of every science of cultural life is to arrive at a rational understanding of these 'ideas' for which men either really or allegedly struggle," pp. 53–54), *rational* is used in a way that has since joined common parlance in the social sciences (and beyond), but with a connotation (correct, accurate, modern, sensible, apparent, obviously so, self-evident, scientifically perceived, cognitively legitimate—ad infinitum) that is foreign to Weber's serious writing to this point. Almost in spite of himself (and against the philosophical suggestion of Nietzsche), he begins to equate "rational" qua "cost/benefit calculation" with "rational" qua "good" or "decent."[4] This lessening of terminological subtlety continued to infect his *Kategorienlehre* but, luckily, stayed wide of his sociology of religion and other, less self-consciously formal analyses. Nevertheless, its presence reveals in Weber the quality of mind he most wished to extinguish in those around him: the confounding of (irrational) values with (rational) scientific procedure and outcomes. This schizoid, Faustian dimension to Weber's personality is often enough mentioned but is less often connected with his "ascetic" drive to rid *Geisteswissenschaften* of its shadow.

In the midst of fighting off the truth-claims of political ideologies on one hand, naive positivism on the other, Weber gives us a version of his understanding of *meaning* and its relation to knowledge that has become famous: "The fate of an epoch which has eaten of the tree of knowledge is that it must know that we cannot learn the *meaning* of the world from the results of its analysis, be it ever so perfect; it must rather be in a position to create this meaning itself" (p. 57). How strange that he could arrive at this juncture in epistemology (advanced for the time and alien even now to many in its pronounced relativism), yet stop himself from analyzing this creation of meaning he demands from secular humanity. His olympianism discloses its existential frailty. He assigns himself and his co-editors the bold task of preventing readers from "deceiving themselves in the conflict of ideals by a value mélange of values of the most different orders and types" (p. 59), yet his role as gatekeeper of objectivity excludes him from examining exactly that which typifies human life and gives it its intrinsic interest, the "value mélange of values." But then, having obliterated several

---

4. Somewhat amazingly, Weber uses terms very much in keeping with those of today: "What will the attainment of a desired end 'cost' in terms of the predictable loss of other values?" (p. 53).

noxious value-positions and pseudo-scientific "schools," eight pages further on he takes a new turn, more sophisticated and intense, and not unlike Dilthey. It appears within a defense of the view that takes seriously the search for "economically *conditioned* phenomena":

> The influence of social relations, institutions and groups governed by "material interests" extends (often unconsciously) into all spheres of culture without exception, even into the *finest nuances of aesthetic and religious feeling*. The events of everyday life no less than the "historical" events of the higher reaches of political life, collective and mass phenomena as well as the "individuated" conduct of statesmen and individual literary and artistic achievements are influenced by it. (p. 65; emphasis added)

This is Weber at his least pretentious and defensive, when he stopped settling border disputes among competing disciplines, silenced his phobic reaction to the possible contamination of "science" by "values," and reviewed the world around him with an open, humanistic temper.

Little else in this essay adds to our subject. A few characteristics of Weber's thinking, reflected in certain mannerisms of expression, ought to be noted since they do relate, perhaps at the pre-cognitive level, to Weber's war with irrationality. For instance, in no fewer than six passages (on pp. 72, 78, 82, 84, 96, 111), he argues that the "finite human mind" (as it struggles to "reflect about the way in which life confronts us in immediate concrete situations, presenting an infinite multiplicity of successively and coexistently emerging and disappearing events, both 'within' and 'outside' ourselves," p. 72) cannot hope to understand the "characteristic uniqueness of the reality in which we move." He uses *infinite* whenever he means to convey the sentiment that human cognition is faulty before empirical reality and thus requires the aid of strict rules of observation and analysis. Weber refers to historical individuals who "naturally constitute a chaos of infinitely differentiated and highly contradictory complexes of ideas and feelings" (p. 96) and whose *Weltanschauungen* the unfortunate historian must somehow represent. I label this a mannerism since almost everywhere else Weber writes with great analytic confidence, even with disdain for "mystifiers," yet these passages concerning "infinite complexity" are quite unduly mystifying in themselves. Were Weber not usually such a champion of theoretical clarity, even when his own theory is clouded, these phrases would not stand out so. My suspicion is that once again he is hiding from the issue, this time not by reduction but by mystification, and the issue is the same: the interlocking, inevitable relation between the "infinite complexity" of personality and social structure. And he knew that "personality," an unruly combination of rational and irrational components, could reduce the firmest "action" typology to ruin. Even the concept he proposed as substitution for "laws" (in the natural-sciences sense), "objective possibility" (*objektiven Möglichkeit*), was threatened when confronted with too much fluctuation in the "regularities of social and economic life" (pp. 8off.). This section threatens to destroy his conceptualization through sheer lack of form: " 'Culture' is a finite segment of the meaningless infinity of the world process, a segment on which *human beings* confer meaning and significance" (p. 81). In his effort to defuse teleologies of right and left, with their entelechies and organic relations, he very nearly empties the social world of any *telos* whatever, of any functional relations. He is left with a social ontology so bereft of order that it resembles more than anything else what one might imagine the interior perceptions of a psychotic to be.

Following this labyrinthine journey through his partly public, partly private epistemological inferno, Weber suddenly, as is his wont, reverts to marvelous lucidity. This time his subject is the nature of economics as it developed, first as mere technique, then as a serious intellectual undertaking:

> It was on the other hand, from the very beginning, more than a "technique" since it was integrated into the great scheme of the natural law and rationalistic Weltanschauung of the eighteenth century. The nature of that Weltanschauung with its optimistic faith in the theoretical and practical rationalizability of reality had an important consequence insofar as it *obstructed* the discovery of the *problematic* character of that standpoint which had been assumed as self-evident. As the rational analysis of society arose in close connection with the modern development of natural science, so it remained related to it in its whole method of approach. (p. 85)

This is one of the few times in the "Objectivity" essay that he uses *rational* as a term, and one of the few instances in any of the methodological essays in which *rationalizability* appears. He was, then, near to formulating the processual concept of rationalization, the cornerstone of his comparative sociology, while he was perfectly aware of his own rationalist roots. Though he was intimately bound to Schmoller, Dilthey, Rickert, and other antirationalist, antipositivist descendants of historical jurisprudence, there is a distinctly Gallic quality to his categories and typologies. The case can fairly be made, I think, that more of the optimistic faith of the Enlightenment undergirded his general approach to method than he admitted, and more than his admirers have conceded.

Another interesting aspect of Weber's sensibility begins to manifest itself. Weber evidences concern over the development "of a— still to be created—systematic science of 'social psychology' as the future foundation of the cultural sciences" (p. 88). He sets high goals for the field yet to be born:

> In concrete cases, psychological analysis can contribute then an extremely valuable deepening of the knowledge of the historical cultural *conditioning* and cultural *significance* of institutions. The interesting aspect of the psychic attitude of a person in a social situation is specifically particularized in each case, according to the special cultural significance of the situation in question. It is a question of an extremely heterogeneous and highly concrete structure of psychic motives and influences. Social-psychological research involves the study of various very disparate *individual* types of cultural elements with reference to their interpretability by our empathic understanding. (pp. 88–89)

It is often, and correctly, pointed out that Weber lacks a social-psychological theory, but this quotation documents his belief that he needed one. And surely his "types of action," among other features of his *Hauptwerk*, would have benefited from such a theory. In fact, had he spent more time working on a theory of his own in this direction, he might well have rearranged his categories of behavior to fit life as lived, rather than "abstract economic theory . . . an ideal picture of events . . . organized on the principles of an exchange economy, free competition, and rigorously rational conduct" (pp. 89–90). While the "analytical accentuation of certain elements of reality" is no doubt necessary to the construction of theory, where "accentuation" ends and outright distortion begins Weber did not say.

He concludes his essay with several unusually graceful references to the "aesthetic satisfaction" gained when the "adequacy of our imagination" proves itself in apt conceptualization. And, finally, he quotes one "F. Th. Vischer" to the effect that

> there are . . . "subject matter specialists" and "interpretive specialists." The fact-greedy gullet of the former can be filled only with legal documents, statistical worksheets and questionnaires, but he is insensitive to the refinement of a new idea. The gourmandise of the latter dulls his taste for facts by ever new intellectual subtleties. That genuine artistry which, among the historians, Ranke possessed in such a grand measure, manifests itself through its ability to produce new knowledge by interpreting already *known* facts according to new viewpoints. (p. 112)

And he concludes with remarkable prescience, almost as if he were speaking to an audience today:

> All research in the cultural sciences in an age of specialization, once it is oriented towards a given subject matter through particular settings of problems and has established its methodological principles, will consider the analysis of the data as an end in itself. It will discontinue assessing the value of the individual facts in terms of their relationships to ultimate value-ideas. . . . The significance of the unreflectively utilized viewpoints becomes uncertain and the road is lost in the twilight. The light of the great cultural problems moves on. (p. 112)

With this, and the ritualized quotation from *Faust*, the essay ends. We are for the moment left with his disquieting (but altogether typical) mélange of great insight, incredible terminological subtlety, plus confusion, and still no clear position on the social psychology—of character and social structure—that he would very soon thereafter confront directly, in *The Protestant Ethic*.[5]

The Protestant Ethic

Weber's two lengthy essays on the Protestant ethic (brought together by Parsons in one volume) have elicited more comment than any of his other writings.[6] Yet we still do not have a study which, in

---

5. The two lengthy articles which intervene chronologically between "Objectivity" and *The Protestant Ethic* (one on the problem of Prussian deeds in trust, the other a review of the literature concerning the origins of ancient German social structure) need not be considered here. They are the fruits of research and his state of mind in the 1890s and bear no immediate link with the set of essays now under consideration. Käsler lists them as items 63 and 64, *The Protestant Ethic* as 65.

6. Seyfarth and Schmidt list 339 items in their bibliography of the secondary literature (pp. 193–194).

my opinion, meets them on their own terms. The majority are either theoretical discussions concerning the "validity" of Weber's
association of the Protestant belief system with capital accumulation, or "applications" to other points in history or other countries
undergoing development. The historical data and the underlying
social-psychological theory have not—as a unit—won an adequate
response.[7] This may reflect the difficulty in determining exactly
what his theory (or, at the least, his hypotheses) of social psychology was. We have just learned that around the time he composed
the two essays he was fully aware that a need for such a theory
existed. But these issues are somewhat tangential to our own, so
we proceed.

Johannes Winckelmann has argued that "the introduction to his
collected essays in the sociology of religion . . . is probably the last
writing from Max Weber's hand."[8] As most (but not all) Weber
scholars have long known, this final piece of work was placed by
Parsons as the "introduction" to the American edition of *The Protestant Ethic* (pp. 13–31), and as such is quite interesting, since its
content is separated by sixteen years of intense scholarship from
that of the body of the book. It is especially significant in the context of the present study, since in it Weber makes extraordinary use
of *rational, irrational,* and their cognates. As was pointed out earlier, the first fifteen pages (pp. 13–27) contain fifty-six instances of
their usage. On one amazing page (p. 26), Weber depends upon
the terms a full dozen times, in what seems a parody of himself at

7. The two well-known historical monographs often cited as "corrections" to
Weber primarily consider the proper use of specific data and not his theory, thus
leaving half the job undone. This is in keeping with standard historiographic procedure in the United States and England (where history is often thought of as the antithesis of theory), but it does not fill the need for a comprehensive study. See
Michael Walzer, *The Revolution of the Saints,* and David Little, *Religion, Order, and
Law.* I have omitted from the discussion the first book-length treatment of Weber's
thesis, H. M. Robertson's *Aspects of the Rise of Economic Individualism,* since it has received such harsh and apparently justified treatment from various critics and is
often reproached as a severe misreading of Weber. See Ephraim Fischoff, "The Protestant Ethic and the Spirit of Capitalism"; and for an update of the controversy see
Benjamin Nelson, "Max Weber's *The Protestant Ethic.*" Also interesting is Herbert
Lüthy, *From Calvin to Rousseau,* pp. 3–101, "Variations on a Theme by Max Weber."
Recent additions to the literature are Hisao Otsuka, *The Spirit of Capitalism;* Gianfranco Poggi, *Calvinism and the Capitalist Spirit;* and the most useful single volume to
date in English, Gordon Marshall, *In Search of the Spirit of Capitalism.*

8. Translated by Benjamin Nelson in "Max Weber's 'Author's Introduction'
(1920)," p. 270. Taken from Winckelmann, ed., *Max Weber,* p. 534.

his worst. We know that this brief preface was composed very rapidly (completed 7 June 1920, only seven days before his death) and was designed to serve as Weber's announcement to the academic world of the perimeters of his comparative religion. Its significance should not be underestimated (Benjamin Nelson called it one "of the most revealing and seminal essays that Weber ever did"),[9] for volume 1 of the *Religionssoziologie* was the first of Weber's mature works ever published, and his first book in nineteen years. However, since the introduction falls out of chronological sequence, we should postpone its analysis for the time being.

Chapter 1 offers us nothing important, having only one direct reference to "rational action" (p. 40) (where Weber first proposes the definitive difference between Protestant and Catholic commercial behavior and describes the former's tendency toward "economic rationalism"). He does, in footnote 19 (p. 191), deal with a form of "irrational action" when he rather strangely writes of the "traditional laziness" of the "Polish girl" and the "migratory Italian laborer" in their native lands, transformed as if by miracle into virtuous workers when placed in an industrial setting in a capitalist country. He marvels that the Polish girl,

> who at home was not to be shaken loose from her traditional laziness by any chance of earning money, however tempting, seems to change her entire nature and become capable of unlimited accomplishment when she is a migratory worker in a foreign country. . . . That this is by no means entirely explicable in terms of the educative influence of the entrance into a higher cultural environment, although this naturally plays a part, is shown by the fact that the same thing happens where the type of occupation, as in agricultural labour, is exactly the same as at home. . . . The simple fact of working in quite different surroundings from those to which one is accustomed breaks through the tradition and is the educative force. (p. 191)

This unseemly bit of chauvinism is atypical in Weber's work. That aside, the passage does signal one of his strongest beliefs, and one that figured prominently in his action typology as well as elsewhere: that industrialization and modernization inevitably broke through tradition and liberated those held in bondage to the dead weight of the past. The realization that their reward for this liberation was often little else than gaining entrance into the "iron cage" of modernity—another of his famous insights—did not stop Weber

9. Nelson, "Max Weber's 'Author's Introduction,'" p. 271.

from extolling the virtues of the rational present against the irrational, stultifying bonds of tradition. Once again a Weberian contradiction crops up, probably as a result of theoretical tension he could not escape, given his wish to haul traditional behavior into both his typology and his comparative sociology just long enough to eject it as intrinsically uninteresting (or unmanageable) when compared with *zweckrationalisches Handeln*.

Seven pages into chapter 2 ("The Spirit of Capitalism") rests one of the most unembroidered of all the earlier conceptualizations Weber made of irrationality. Attached to it is a fascinating footnote about Lujo Brentano, author of *Die Anfänge des modernen Kapitalismus*, upon whom Weber counted heavily in these essays. It needs little explication:

> In fact the *summum bonum* of this ethic, the earning of more and more money, combined with the strict avoidance of all spontaneous enjoyment of life, is above all completely devoid of any eudaemonistic, not to say hedonistic, admixture. It is thought of so purely as an end in itself, that from the point of view of the happiness of, or utility to, the single individual, it appears entirely transcendental and absolutely irrational. (p. 53)

Here Weber inserts the following note:

> Brentano . . . takes this remark as an occasion to criticize the later discussion of "that rationalization and discipline" to which worldly asceticism [*innerweltliche Askese*] has subjected men. That, he says, is a rationalization toward an irrational mode of life. He is, in fact, quite correct. A thing is never irrational in itself, but only from a particular rational point of view. For the unbeliever every religious way of life is irrational, for the hedonist every ascetic standard, no matter whether, measured with respect to its particular basic values, that opposing asceticism is a rationalization. If this essay makes any contribution at all, may it be to bring out the complexity of the only superficially simple concept of the rational. (pp. 193–194)

There is to my knowledge no more forthright characterization than this of precisely what Weber intended by "irrationality of action" in any of his early works. He rounds out his description:

> Man is dominated by the making of money, by acquisition as the ultimate purpose of his life. Economic acquisition is no longer subordinated to man as the means for the satisfaction of his material needs. This reversal of what we should call the natural relationship, so irrational from the naive point of view, is evidently as definitely a leading principle of capitalism as it is foreign to all peoples not under capitalistic influence. (p. 53)

These statements allow for some interpretation. First, there is generally no disagreement with Weber's claim that the "*summum bonum*" of Protestant mercantile behavior (limitless capital accumulation unleavened by pleasure of any kind extrinsic to the process itself) is indeed—as are all "ultimate values"—"absolutely irrational." The modern sociologist would substitute for *irrational* a term such as *status competition* or *role achievement*, probably to Weber's disapproval, because of the this-worldly quality of *status* and the secular peer relations with which it is by definition associated. His reading of the historical data persuaded him that the ethic was not at base of social origin so much as sacred, and accumulation as an activity was not designed, if that is the right word, so much to impress fellow parishioners as to impress an ultimate sacred arbiter of ontological worth. But, this disagreement aside, contemporary sociology would agree completely, almost automatically, with Weber in labeling this sort of behavior and its underlying value system as technically irrational. With this I have no particular disagreement, since Weber is addressing precisely the individual Calvinist merchant's *fear*, itself a product of some sort of ontological anxiety (*Angst*) in the face of his own mortality. The proper examination of these kinds of predominantly private dilemmas falls within the province of other disciplines, and sociology can only speak to them superficially.

My disagreement lies with the footnote. Weber claims (apparently with Brentano's help) that "a thing is never irrational in itself, but only from a particular rational point of view." This sentiment has found nearly unanimous support among contemporary American sociologists. Though on its surface it seems sound, more careful examination discloses a problem. Weber was deeply enough imbued with scientistic fervor to place high value upon rigorous conceptualization and measurement. Because of his interest (especially around this time, as he took over the reins of the *Archiv*) in promoting a nonideological, nonsectarian, nonpropagandistic social science, he was inclined to overemphasize the possibility of objectivity and rational perception, even for those most desirous of achieving the comfort of this intellectual haven. Parsons and others carried his optimism over intact into sociology in the United States. But what if "a particular rational point of view" is something gained only rarely, and then only by mandarins whose (nonrational) self-conceptions demand that they outdo Voltaire himself in purging their theorizing of the "merely" subjective? A social theory of action is supposed to describe the behavior of ordinary mortals, not only that of professional thinkers whose powers of sublimation and emotional self-denial are expected to be extraordinary. (Recall Gadamer's opinion of Weber's "deep irrationalism" and "quixotic magnificence" on behalf of his "scientific asceticism and methodical integrity.") Compared to the moments of ordinary life in which the fiction "pure rationality" can be seen at work (in determining critical choices and behavior pursuant to them), the residue (all the habitual, emotionally based, physically demanded, whimsically pursued, purely arbitrary actions) overwhelms in bulk and *significance* (*Bedeutung*) that portion preferred by those theorists following Weber's lead.[10] And "Weber's lead" in these matters can be thought of as beginning in this footnote. His obvious belief—qualified, to be sure ("to bring out the complexity of the only superficially simple concept of the rational")—is that one can attain a rational point of view, at least for the purpose of analyzing someone else's behavior, if not one's own. Since he does not define what the dimensions of this *Standpunkt* would be, I can only argue with him in general terms, as above, and conclude that he overestimates normal cognitive abilities. Put another way, he subscribes in essence to a mind/body dualism not much in keeping with the more sophisticated epistemologies developed since then.

On a less abstract plane I see an additional fault, more pressing for sociology as it is usually practiced. When Weber wrote, "A thing is never irrational in itself," I feel sure his *emotional* spur was to free analytically all human activity from the condescending rank chauvinism prevalent in the German academy at the time, particularly regarding the "native" behavior widely reported from Germany's new African colonies. This connection has not previously been made in Weber scholarship, but I believe it influenced Weber's firm declaration of cultural relativism. (He extended this point of view to American Indians, whose tribal behavior fascinated him— as it did many educated Germans—and the observation of which gave special meaning to his American tour in 1904.)[11] Most Weber

10. I restate my basic hypothesis contra Weber, spelled out in Chapter 1, for narrative purposes, not as if introducing something novel.
11. "There were many other things of burning interest to Weber—above all, those which Europe could not offer him: the conquest of the wilderness by civiliza-

The Middle Period 163

students probably sense his latent values and approve of his wish
to temper his colleagues' patronizing attitude toward "primitive"
cultures. And because his prejudices are so consistent with today's,
his claims are not challenged on the *theoretical* level, having passed
muster on moral-ethical grounds.

Weber, then, committed a theoretical error on behalf of intellectual morality. For by now it seems evident, in view of developments in psychology, psychiatry, social psychology, and psychoanalysis (the *specific* tenets of which I do not invoke), that the
assertion "A thing is never irrational in itself" is untenable, and not
only for minds clinically judged abnormal. Let us resort to a handy
example. Long before it was formally documented,[12] "impulsive"
(hence irrational) behavior was known to play an essential role in
consumerist economies; that is, without the incessant activity of an
entire industry (and various subindustries) whose sole function is
to invent marketable fantasies and attach these to objects to which
they bear slight intrinsic or "organic" relations, advanced industrial societies would collapse. It has become routine to observe that
the mechanisms of the market economy produce irrationalities of
production, distribution, and consumption and that its backbone,
built-in obsolescence, is itself irrational in terms of ecology, equality of consumption opportunity, and so on. How remarkable, then,
that the behavior which undergirds the entire system (including
breathless zealousness in the pursuit of money, oftentimes involving two and three different jobs for workers out of reach of professional occupations, plus the complementary zealousness in spending
more money than is earned for items—*not* experiences—rapidly
cast aside for still others), has not more often in the sociological orbit been properly labeled as irrational. Even more startling, it must
be noted, is the ease with which Pareto *accepted* irrationality of this

---

tion, a developing city and the developing state of Oklahoma in an area that had
until recently been reserved for the Indians. Here it was still possible to observe the
unarmed subjugation and absorption of an 'inferior' race by a 'superior'. . . .one. . . .
Weber stayed with a halfbreed near McAlester [in southeast Oklahoma]. He watched,
listened, transformed himself into his surroundings, and thus everywhere penetrated to the heart of things." A lengthy letter follows in which Weber describes in
loving detail the "Leatherstocking romanticism," as he called it, of Indian life as it
confronted relentless pioneer capitalism. (Marianne Weber, *Max Weber*, pp. 291ff.)
   12. See Stuart Ewen, *Captains of Consciousness;* Stuart Ewen and Elizabeth Ewen,
Channels of Desire; Tibor Scitovsky, *The Joyless Economy.*

kind, plus so many others, then perfected his analyses accordingly. Yet, as if Pareto had never existed, many accept Weber's preposterous claim at face value, without remembering that a theoretical antidote for his shortsightedness is available.

Though we have hardly exhausted these paragraphs, other important sections in *The Protestant Ethic* beckon in which several essential matters repeatedly surface. Weber's use of *rational*, for instance, is rather consistent throughout the essay, though it does appear within a certain range of regular usages. One of the most typical is the meaning of "rigorously calculated," "bookkeeping," or, in our terms, "efficiency-oriented." Weber describes how the "spirit of capitalism . . . had to fight its way to supremacy against a whole world of hostile forces" (p. 56), which included the "stone wall of habit," "the exploitation of political opportunities and irrational speculation," and the "immensely stubborn resistance" of "traditionalism."[13] One of many passages in which he uses *rational* conventionally:

> This [contra "capitalistic acquisition"] has not only been the normal attitude of all ethical teachings, but, what is more important, also that expressed in the practical action of the average man of pre-capitalistic times, pre-capitalistic in the sense that the rational utilization of capital in a permanent enterprise and the rational capitalistic organization of labor had not yet become dominant forces in the determination of economic activity. (p. 58)

And for the first time we find extensive use of the master term *rationalization* as a general process: "At the same time he [the early entrepreneur] began to introduce the principle of low prices and large turnover, there was repeated what everywhere and always is the result of such a process of rationalization: those who would not follow suit had to go out of business" (p. 68).

While these quotations, and many others that convey similar information, consistently portray "rational" activity as something to be lauded, and not the "pudendum" (p. 73) medieval theologians

---

13. Pp. 56, 62, 76, 60. In one of his virtuoso footnotes Weber provides an unusually intriguing analysis of early religious resistance to capitalist activity: "The decisive factors were: on the one hand, a traditional, mostly inarticulate hostility towards the growing power of capital which was impersonal, and hence not readily amenable to ethical control (as it is still reflected in Luther's pronouncements about the Fuggers and about the banking business); on the other hand, the necessity of accommodation to practical needs" (p. 202).

thought it to be, just as regularly "irrational" behavior received Weber's most caustic remarks. Rationality produced "innovators" (p. 69) rather than the bumbling traditionalist businessmen of before, embalmed, as it were, in the "traditional manner of life, the traditional rate of profit, the traditional amount of work, the traditional manner of regulating the relationships with labour, and the essentially traditional circle of customers and the manner of attracting new ones" (p. 67). For Weber this is clearly an inferior modus vivendi, and from this we may conclude that "traditional" behavior, as presented in his action typology some years later, is an inferior way to act, one to be disdained when compared to the hallmark of Occidental achievement, the *zweckrational* type: aggressive, acquisitive, "temperate and reliable, shrewd and completely devoted to . . . business" (p. 69). Once more we find Weber in gross self-contradiction. In "Objectivity" he tilts on behalf of the exclusion of value judgment from the *Wissenschaften*. Then, in complete violation of his own standards, he berates Polish girls, Italian migratory workers, Prussian peasants, and the French in general, in addition to "the middle-class groups in the Romance Catholic countries" (p. 77), for being "peoples" who "practice the doctrine of undisciplined *liberum arbitrium*" (p. 57); therefore "capitalism cannot make use of their labour," and they block the progress of civilization itself. We see, then, how readily the "scientific" veneer peels from Weber's typology of *soziales Handeln*. However, hermeneutic principles demand that we recognize Weber's genuine ambivalence about capitalist rationalization, in the *final* analysis. But we find a needed counterbalance to the ritual status of his "iron cage" metaphor (p. 181) in identifying Weber's paramount values and how they affected his historical and sociological interpretations.

Another regular use Weber makes of the term *irrational* is in association with what he calls the "eudaemonistic" perspective. In addition to the instance quoted above, he writes on page 70 that Protestant asceticism always appears "so irrational" if "seen from the viewpoint of personal happiness" or "from the standpoint of purely eudaemonistic self-interest." He is clearly imputing a necessary relation between enjoyment or momentary happiness and irrationality, an equation he frequently made, beginning as early as his *Jugendbriefe*, where he often contrasted "duty" with "mere" happiness. It is peculiar, therefore, that he describes Benjamin Franklin's "manner of life" as one out of which "he gets nothing . . . for himself, except the irrational sense of having done his job well" (p. 71). Perhaps Weber wanted to highlight the dilution of dogma that had occurred between the time of Calvin and that of Franklin, when certain behavior persisted after the inspiring ideology had long been forgotten. Yet this "irrational" seems contrary to previous usage, since the feeling "of having done his job well" verges on eudaemonism in its purest form, but a type linked *with* occupational zeal and not opposed to it, as before.

The concluding paragraph of the chapter provides a still more accurate picture of Weber's attitude toward the irrational:

> It might thus seem that the development of the spirit of capitalism is best understood as part of the development of rationalism as a whole, and could be deduced from the fundamental position of rationalism on the basic problems of life. . . . A simple way of putting the question will not work, simply because of the fact that the history of rationalism shows a development which by no means follows parallel lines in the various departments of life. . . . If under practical rationalism is understood the type of attitude which sees and judges the world consciously in terms of the worldly interests of the individual ego then this view of life was and is the special peculiarity of the peoples of the *liberum arbitrium,* such as the Italians and the French. . . . But we have already convinced ourselves that this is by no means the soil in which that relationship of a man to his calling as a task . . . has pre-eminently grown. In fact, one may—this simple proposition, which is often forgotten, should be placed at the beginning of every study which essays to deal with rationalism—rationalize life from fundamentally different basic points of view and in very different directions. Rationalism is an historical concept which covers a whole world of different things. It will be our task to find out whose intellectual child the particular concrete form of rational thought was, from which the idea of a calling and the devotion to labour in the calling has grown, which is, as we have seen, so irrational . . . but which has been and still is one of the most characteristic elements of our capitalistic culture. We are particularly interested in the origin of precisely the *irrational element* which lies in this, as in every conception of a calling. (pp. 76–68; emphasis added)

Abundant conjecture and theoretical speculation lie in this passage. Two items stand out. First is the fact that Weber's belief (in 1904) that "devotion to labour in the calling" was still "one of the most characteristic elements of our capitalistic culture" was almost certainly justified. But, in nearly perfect historical recapitulation, as Franklin's behavior externally mimicked that of early Protestants without possessing the same internal moorings, so the rapacious businessman today may resemble the *Bürgers* of Weber's acquaintance, in terms of calculated social action, but without the sustenance of their quasi-Kantian moral apparatus. One of my main goals is to demonstrate the time-boundedness of Weber's categories, and certainly here, in his characterization of advanced capitalist culture and its human subjects, the dated quality of his thought is evident.

Look also to the last sentence of Weber's paragraph, where he refers to the "irrational element" of the calling. He is probably right in this particular observation, that the "calling" (*Beruf*) and its tremendous meaning for Protestant merchants are best thought of as "irrational" (i.e., beyond their conscious control). What is bothersome is Weber's inconsistent *attitude* and resulting theoretical posture. Earlier he lambasts an ensemble of social actors whose traditionalism he sees as patently irrational and hindering modernization. Against this traditional obstinacy struggle Protestant capitalists as heroes. But in the final scenes of this confrontation, the heroes themselves become fatigued with "irrationality." Granted, this presages "traditional" versus "value-rational" action, but at this early stage of their theoretical elaboration, the categories seem to escape Weber, and are frequently confounded.

Chapter 3, "Luther's Conception of the Calling," adds little, except for a display of special scholarship which up to this point Weber had not found necessary in his research. In following his own dicta—"One should really only criticize things which one has read, or the argument of which, if read, one has not already forgotten" (p. 201), and, in critique of Sombart's and Brentano's haphazard use of Baxter's writings, "one must know this whole literature thoroughly in order to use it correctly" (p. 259)—he wrote material the like of which is seldom seen. For instance, the first three footnotes (pp. 204–211) amount to a treatise on the origin of a "calling," in pursuit of which Weber surveys etymology in Hebrew, Greek, Latin, Spanish, Italian, Dutch, Swedish, Old English, Middle High German, Middle Low German, and English. Beyond the spectacle of Weber's own obsessive scholarship, however, "irrationality" as a concept receives no brighter light in this chapter.

We now enter part 2, "The Practical Ethics of the Ascetic Branches of Protestantism," a rapid but concise study of religious ethical dogma as promulgated by four major denominations. (In the interest of expediency, I will summarize, reserving only a few passages for extended comment.) In the first chapter of the section (p. 105) Weber introduces the phrase *Entzauberung der Welt,* translated by Parsons as "the elimination of magic from the world,"[14] and otherwise known to English readers as the "disenchantment of the world." "Magic" in the religious realm is for Weber the quintessence of irrationality (just as "kahdi justice" in Islamic culture is the most irrational form of law, an example Weber uses often in his *Rechtssoziologie*). So a new motif begins to enliven the text again and again, built around Weber's firm conviction that the "rational calculation" of business, societal rationalization, and the diminution of "tradition" all combined to destroy *formal* magical practices and beliefs. Weber wisely left aside the question of whether or not a rationalized social world retained within it—in opposition to its formal nature—fragmented but still powerful magical elements. Yet indirectly he leads readers to believe that extirpation of all magic, especially that represented in the fine arts, was an important goal for many Puritan and Protestant sects: "But the situation is quite different when one looks at . . . the fine arts. Here asceticism descended like a frost on the life of 'Merrie old England.' . . . The Puritan's ferocious hatred of everything which smacked of superstition, of all survivals of magical or sacramental salvation applied . . . to all spontaneous religious art" (p. 168). In the corresponding footnote, Weber pursues the subject with tongue in cheek, having already noted the "decline in lyric poetry," drama, pictorial art, and novels among the Puritans: "But very striking is the decline from what seemed to be a promising musical beginning . . . to that absolute vacuum which we find typical of the Anglo-Saxon peoples later, and even to-day. Except for negro churches, and the professional singers . . . in America one also hears as community singing in general only a noise which is intol-

14. Parsons's choices are not always this fortunate. Reinhard Bendix (*Max Weber,* p. 273n) points out what seems an inexplicable confusion of terms. Earlier in this chapter (p. 97), Parsons translated *Antrieb* (impulse) as "sanction," a distortion of the first magnitude, but typically in keeping with Parsons's own interests. Thus the sentence reads in Parsons's edition, "We are interested in ascertaining those psychological impulses." Since an "impulse" is by definition "irrational" and a "sanction" is something altogether different, one might suspect that Parsons has inadvertently purified Weber's text of grist for our mill but has in fact "rationalized" the text to some extent.

erable to German ears" (p. 272). Given Weber's ambition to write as his final work a comprehensive sociology of culture, it is reasonable to suppose that this resolute destruction of the arts (at the hands of the same bold entrepreneurial innovators whose "heroism" was cheered earlier in the book) added to Weber's ambivalence about rationalization and its inevitable complement, "disenchantment" through "philistine" aesthetics. How disturbing it must have been for him to applaud the agents of rationalization when they managed to shake peasants from their medieval torpor, while detesting the same mentality as it stripped Western culture of its rich cultural irrationality, formally expressed.

In performing his exegesis of religious texts, Weber uses *irrationality* and *irrational* in ever broader constructions. He speaks of the irrational Lutheran need for the *"unio mystica* with the deity" (p. 112), of "Christian asceticism" in its many forms as having "become emancipated from planless otherworldliness and irrational self-torture" as it achieved its increasingly "rational character" (p. 118), to which he adds: "It has developed a systematic method of rational conduct with the purpose of overcoming the *status naturae,* to free man from the power of irrational impulses and his dependence on the world and on nature. It attempted to subject man to the supremacy of a purposeful will, to bring his actions under constant self-control with a careful consideration of their ethical consequences" (pp. 118–119). This eventually culminated in the "quiet self-control which still distinguishes the best type of English or American gentleman today." Apparently Weber had allowed himself momentarily to forget that these men of "quiet self-control," whom he openly admired, are the ideological and ethical descendants of those Puritans who "ferociously" destroyed the arts. He makes explicit the tie between the two groups, separated by three centuries:

> The Puritan, like every rational type of asceticism, tried to enable a man to maintain and act upon his constant motives, especially those which it taught him itself, against the emotions. . . . The end of this asceticism was to be able to lead an alert, intelligent life: the most urgent task the destruction of spontaneous, impulsive enjoyment, the most important means was to bring order into the conduct of its adherents. (p. 119)

Weber's supposition here is that pre-rationalized "personalities," wrapped in "the power of irrational impulses and . . . dependence on the world and nature," cannot, by definition, lead "an alert, intelligent life." Weber's anthropology clearly suffers from a surprising Eurocentrism. One wonders how "intelligent" a man could be whose "absolutely dominant" goal in life (to the end of "getting rid of the fear of damnation") was to achieve *certitudo salutis* through *poenitentia quotidiana*, in search of the *fides efficax*—in sum, a gross manifestation of irrational frenetics, as Weber knew (see pp. 110, 113, 114).

On page 126 of the Parsons translation, a novel term is introduced, *nonrational*, in this phrase: "a purely utilitarian doctrine of good works . . . which would never have been capable of motivating such tremendous sacrifices for non-rational ideal ends." But the original German (volume 1, p. 125, of the *Religionssoziologie*) "*um irrationaler und idealer Ziele,*" does not justify Parsons's sudden change from his usual *irrational*. This is unfortunate from our point of view, since it would have indicated a broadening of Weber's conceptualization. Parsons is more accurate on page 136 when he translates *antirationalen* (p. 140 in the German) as "anti-rational," yet even here Weber is not registering a refinement of his previous idea, judging from its context.

Among the handful of other interesting remarks Weber makes in this section regarding irrationality is one in still another footnote, bearing upon the use various historians have made of the "expression individualism [which] includes the most heterogeneous things imaginable" (p. 22). Weber refers to Dietrich Schafer, who believed that "irrational factors then [in the Middle Ages] had a significance which they do not possess today." Weber immediately adds, "He is right," a fantastically ill-timed remark in view of European history between 1914 and 1918. Nearby Weber quotes from Richard Baxter's *Christian Directory,* further defining his own conception of the issue: "It [friendship] is an irrational act and not fit for a rational creature to love any one farther than reason will allow us. . . . It very often taketh up men's minds so as to hinder their love of God" (p. 224). Weber elaborates Baxter's prescriptions for the rational (hence holy) life by commenting, "The Calvinist was fascinated by the idea that God . . . must have willed things to be objectively purposeful as a means of adding to His glory. . . . The active energies of the elect . . . thus flowed into the struggle to rationalize the world." Weber also for the first time explores the relation among sexuality, irrationality, and Puritan ethics (in note 22, pp. 263–264) and covers more ground than can be presented here. He does not, however, augment his theoretical argument. It is also worth mentioning that on page 178 he first uses *charisma*, a concept intimately keyed to irrationality (and which Parsons mistakenly believed Weber had invented; p. 281n105; see *Economy and Society,* p. 216n1).

As a conclusion to our inspection of *The Protestant Ethic,* I must make plain that *rationality, rational, irrational, impulsive, emotional,* and other analogous concepts are strewn throughout the essay, and I have made no attempt to discuss even each important instance. My goal, as in previous exegeses, has been, rather, to illustrate the lack of consistency, the ambiguity, the philosophically questionable and otherwise curious qualities of Weber's usages.[15] (Perhaps it is forgivable to mention again that Weber was, in my opinion, *essentially* correct in analytically disposing of "experience" [historical and modern] in the way he did; the motive of my "corrective" analysis is to highlight some of his exaggerations, and those of his students and admirers.)

One item in *The Protestant Ethic* is unique in Weber literature: in it he tilts against the leading American student of religious behavior, William James. Weber sets about deflating James's "pragmatic" view (e.g., in *The Varieties of Religious Experience,* pp. 444ff.) that the "content of ideas of a religion" is relatively unimportant, by performing a brief but pointed display of *Wissenssoziologie.* This statement is important not only for its documentation of the Weber-James split but because it gave Weber a chance to write with unusual candor about irrationality and religious experience:

> James' pragmatic valuation of the significance of religious ideas according to their influence on life is incidentally a true child of the world of ideas of the Puritan home of that eminent scholar. The religious experience as such is of course irrational, like every experience. In its highest, mystical form it is . . . distinguished by its absolute incommunicability. It . . . cannot be adequately reproduced by means of our lingual and conceptual apparatus. . . . Every religious experience loses some of its content in the attempt of rational for-

15. Those pages on which appear significant allusions to *irrationality* are 17, 20, 21, 26, 53, 194, 70, 71, 78, 222, 224, 233, 118–119, 126, 136, 256, 148, 269, 167, 171, 276, and 281. (Lack of sequence is due to the position of endnotes relative to their correlated pages in the text.)

mulation, the further the conceptual formulation goes, the more so. . . . But that irrational element, which is by no means peculiar to religious experience, but applies (in different senses and to different degrees) to every experience, does not prevent its being of the greatest practical importance. . . . How unbelievably intense, measured by present standards, the dogmatic interests even of the layman were [of the early Baptist sects], everyone knows who is familiar with the historical sources. (pp. 232–233)

This paragraph includes one of the rare moments where Weber (presumably under pressure from James's then recent, important book) admits that the "irrational element . . . applies . . . to every experience," a point he never lost sight of completely but quite often sidestepped while theorizing.

Knies and Irrationality

Items 68 and 75 on Käsler's list are the two parts of "Knies and the Problem of Irrationality (I: The Irrationality of Action)," published in 1905 and 1906. "Part II" was never written. As is mentioned from time to time by various commentators, Weber usually entitled his essays very modestly. "Knies" is not only humbly but misleadingly titled. Weber has included critiques of Knies, Wundt, Münsterberg, Simmel, Gottl, Lipps, and Croce, all to the end of airing his own methodological opinions concerning "empathetic understanding," "adequate interpretation," "interpretive causal theories," "the logical structure of knowledge," and, most important here, "the concept of irrationality" and "the concept of the 'personality'" (for instance, on p. 131). And with rare exceptions, his opinion differed substantially from those of the theorists listed, plus Husserl's, Lamprecht's, Mach's, and Eduard Meyer's concerning the relation between perception and knowledge.

Yet, for our purposes only a few passages require study.[16] Beginning early in the essay (pp. 96ff.), Weber defines "human action" ("the subject matter of economics") as "a product of both natural and historical conditions" and as a mixture of *"freedom of the will"* on the one hand, "elements of *necessity*" on the other. He does this

---

16. References to *irrationality* in the English translation occur on pp. 96ff., 100, 159, 191ff., 237, 272. Other noteworthy topics not indexed are *hermeneutics* (pp. 250–251, 253), *rationality* (pp. 26, 71), and *sociologists* (pp. 63, 100, 240, 251).

because for Knies freedom and irrationality are necessarily inter-
twined, and Weber immediately sets out to disable Knies's theory.
He does not find this terribly difficult. First, Knies's book (*Die Politische Ökonomie vom Standpunkte der geschichtlichen Methode*) was already fifty years old when Weber attacked it, and its methodological logic showed its age. But, beyond that, Knies's nomological
knowledge took a most peculiar form:

> In place of the distinction between purposeful human action, on the
> one hand, and the natural and historical conditions for this action,
> on the other, we therefore find an *entirely different* distinction. The
> "free," *and therefore irrational-concrete*, action of persons, on the one
> hand. Nomological determination of the naturally given conditions
> for action, on the other. . . . In Knies' view, this is because the free-
> dom of the human *will*—in the form of "personal" action—is em-
> bedded in the economy.
> We shall see that this "fundamental" ground of the irrationality
> of economic phenomena is inconsistent with what Knies says in
> other passages about the effects of natural conditions on the econ-
> omy. In these passages, the geographically and historically "con-
> crete" structure of the conditions for the existence of the economy is
> identified as the element which *excludes* the discovery of general
> laws of rational economic action. (pp. 96–97)

If this representation of Knies's argument is accurate, Weber's disdain seems valid. But what is really at issue is not so much Knies's
confused epistemology as his domain assumption, which Weber
introduces thus:

> Further, they [historians] see this problem in quite the same sense as
> Knies sees it. In these discussions, we repeatedly find reference—
> explicit or implicit—to the "unpredictability" of personal conduct.
> This is alleged to be a consequence of "freedom," the definitive
> source of human *dignity* and therefore the proper subject matter of
> history. At the same time, a distinction is drawn between the "crea-
> tive" significance of the acting personality and the "mechanical"
> causality of natural events. (pp. 97–98)

For reasons he never makes clear, Weber is entirely opposed to
this "mystification" of personality and the irrationality of action
that historians and political economists of the period counterposed
to nascent positivist attempts to define action. In a footnote to the
section just quoted, Weber lampoons Hinneberg, Stieve, Meinecke,
and Treitschke for their use of "this 'unknown quantity'—the irrational 'residue' of the personality—as the 'inner sanctuary' of the
personality" (p. 238). And though Weber concedes to them the dis-

tinction they all have in mind, between physical and social data, he muses, rhetorically: "However, they are all based on the same curious idea: the idea that the dignity of a science or its object is due to those features of the object about which we *can know nothing* at all. In which case, the peculiar significance of human action lies in the fact that it is *inexplicable,* and therefore *unintelligible"* (p. 238). This tells us that Weber found it theoretically unpalatable, untenable in fact, to conceive of human freedom as in any way related to irrationality, hence to unpredictability. One wonders whether his consistent charges to this effect were mainly a reaction to certain nineteenth-century German prejudices among scholars that he found distasteful, or whether a more basic element of his own philosophical anthropology was at work. Weber was on the verge of recovering from the most humiliating, intellectually painful and irritating "neuro-pathological" [17] condition conceivable for a scholar: the inability to read, write, or concentrate. It is at least plausible that Weber's violent reaction to Knies's apotheosis of the irrational (particularly given Knies's clumsy formulation) was grounded in his own herculean efforts to regain control of himself. For him, irrationality was not something to be celebrated. He believed freedom, in the most genuine sense, lay elsewhere.

Weber never tires of pointing out the shortcomings of Knies's action theory. Probably the most accessible example occupies the first

17. He uses this word, but very rarely: for instance, on p. 130 in Weber 1930, in describing "religious ecstasy." Without overblowing its significance, we might reflect momentarily upon Weber's unprecedented use of the word *residue* in the paragraph just quoted. The German (p. 46 of 1922a) is *dem irrationalen "Rest" der Persönlichkeit,* thus Oakes's translation is literal. I have in mind, of course, Pareto's use of the identical word in almost precisely the same way. It is instructive to consider Weber's reaction to the claim that such a "residue"—impermeable to examination— actually existed in individual personalities. He is incredulous and outraged that true scientists would accept this defeat of their inquisitive faculties. Pareto, by contrast, with far better credentials as a scientist and a more realistic understanding of what science was about, *posits* a residue (actually, residues) within the individual psyche and just as quickly retreats before it, relinquishing any power or rights of explication. He simply thought it too complex and convoluted to explain systematically, so, at least in terms of his own version of scientific method, he left it out of the explanatory portion of his theory (after having admitted that it existed). Pareto's fascination, then, with "derivations" held no appeal for Weber, since "meanings" interpreted "adequately" were for him the target of social science, and not the more epiphenomenal "explanations" (or what we call accounts) of behavior. Perhaps the difference in the German and Italian "minds" of the period proclaims itself in these antithetical strategies.

paragraph of a section Oakes has entitled "The Irrationality of Concrete Actions and the Irrationality of Concrete Natural Events" (pp. 120ff.): "We shall . . . make some remarks germane to the belief in the peculiar *irrationality* of human action or the human 'personality.' For the present, we shall simply render the concept of 'irrationality' in the vulgar sense of 'incalculability.' In the opinion of Knies, and of many others even today, this is the characteristic mark of human 'freedom of the will'" (p. 120). In the "remarks" that follow, Weber dwells upon methodological conundrums not likely to cause much disagreement or wonderment today, the most important being the logical statement that "individual human conduct is in principle intrinsically less 'irrational' than the individual natural event" (p. 125). But he does not actually refute the belief, apparently widespread among his peers and immediate intellectual ancestors, that human dignity—in fact, humanness itself—sprang from a form of incalculability foreign to natural events; foreign, in other words, to phenomena lacking consciousness or will. Without belaboring the point, we should recognize that Weber was quite divided on this issue: his students report (as did Marianne) that *personally* he always favored historical and contemporary characters whose force of will in the face of coercion or conformity—the mechanisms for producing calculable behavior—carried them into heroic action. He unsuccessfully attempts to extricate himself from this confused position by accusing Knies of using *irrational* in the sense of "noninterpretable" (p. 125), something Knies did not intend. Weber contrasts two events ("the splintering of the falling boulder" and "the conduct of Friedrich II during the year 1756"), labeling the former "completely irrational," the latter "teleologically rational" (pp. 126–127). Following this dubious distinction, he finally shows his scholarly hand, and perhaps a good deal more: "Human action manifests the same degree of irrationality found in natural processes only when we encounter a directly pathological reaction . . . that is, only when we encounter a reaction the immoderation and meaninglessness of which *exclude* the *possibility of interpretation*" (p. 127; emphasis added). This tautological dictum suggests that, for Weber, meaning (presumably for the social actor involved in a given performance) necessarily had to be interpretable (by the social analyst). This mistaken relationship is the root weakness in all of Weber's thinking about social action. By this time in the history of social science, we no longer find privatized mean-ing-systems a difficult concept. For Weber, privatized, hence non-interpretable, hence irrational meaning (or expressions of freedom) was the privilege only of the pathological. It is clear, I think, that in his efforts both to advance science (to wrest it away from the dilet-tantes and literati) and to hurl himself out of darkness and back into the light of reason and intellectual power, he felt compelled to overstate his case.[18] (That his reactive apotheosis of rational action has not occasioned more critical comment becomes the truly inter-esting problem for the historian of social thought, one that exceeds in difficulty those being treated here.)

In the section Oakes calls " 'Rational' Interpretation" (pp. 186ff.), the reader discovers material that tacitly serves as the theoretical substructure of both the *Logos* article (1913) and *Wirtschaft und Gesellschaft*, and which is here much more explicit in its ultimate determinants. Weber proposes for adoption "a certain kind of 'in-terpretive' knowledge: 'rational' interpretation which employs the categories of 'ends' and 'means'." Then, in an almost mechanical way, certain "suppositions" are extended: that "we 'understand' human action as determined by clearly conscious and intended 'ends' and a clear knowledge of the 'means' required for those 'ends'" (p. 186). If his prescription thus far for the analysis of social action is accepted, the next step becomes inevitable: "the relation

18. Weber becomes more explicit yet, in his critique of Friedrich Gottl. There he writes, not about the intrinsic nature of human experience, but about "the specific direction of our interest, which is conditioned by *values* and related to the possibility of meaningful interpretation. . . . Historical events can be 'interpreted.' They are possible objects of an understanding in which they are reproduced in immediate experience" (p. 158). This is in brief just the "instrumentalist" epistemology Lukács criticized and which Mannheim tried to overcome by infusing Weber's method with Husserl's psychological theory, in hopes of broadening and deepening social analy-sis. In the same section Weber offers, by example, the very model he would later advance, center stage, as part of his action theory: "Consider an 'inference' of the meaning of an action from a given situation which presupposes the *rational* charac-ter of the motivation of the action. Such an inference is invariably only a hypothesis proposed for the purpose of 'interpretation.' In principle, it always requires verifica-tion. . . . Therefore it must be possible to verify any such hypothesis. We can 'un-derstand' the irrational sway of the most extravagant degree of affect just as well as a rational set of 'calculations.' The same holds for the action and feeling of the crimi-nal and the genius. . . . Conduct can be *reproduced* in immediate experience, in the same way that we can reproduce . . . the conduct of the 'normal human being'" (pp. 158–159). Although in this passage Weber seems the picture of moderation— and completely aware of just how heuristic his inference (presupposing "the ra-tional character of the motivation of the action") would have to be, he was not able to maintain this posture.

between 'means' and 'ends' is intrinsically accessible to a rational *causal account which produces generalizations*, generalizations that have the property of 'nomological regularity'." Finally, "Rational interpretation of action can, therefore, assume the form of a conditional judgment of necessity" (p. 187).

Weber was making a trade: he decided he would rather study behavior subject to this "ideal" description than concern himself with what I have called before life as lived. Those moments of contemporary existence in which a social actor applies "clear knowledge of the 'means'" to "clearly conscious and intended 'ends'" are not so numerous as one would think in view of Weber's ideal-typical formula. Trivial, logic-text examples abound ("In order to cross from my house to the market, it would be 'rational' to follow Pleasant Street") that fall within the Weberian scope. At the opposite pole, ultimate decisions about whether or not to live seem in *some* difficult-to-define measure to follow "cost-benefit" analysis. But the mass of human experience (much of which has nothing to do with decision-making at all) does not operate in accord with classical political-economic notions of exchange, and this is particularly the case, I would argue, for that which is most meaningful for the actor. As numerous quotations have already demonstrated, Weber recognized the limitations of the rational means-ends model, but in opposition to Knies and dozens of others, he chose it for adoption in the social sciences anyhow—even though in most of his substantive works he used it very selectively. His confidence in its utility was so great that in a later part of the essay (p. 190) he claims that "the 'self-evident' rational construct, if it is 'correctly' constituted, can even make possible knowledge of the *non-rational* elements of actual economic action." All of this takes on a puzzling character when we also read this epistemologically and sociologically alert observation: "A teleological scheme of rational action . . . is an interpretation the empirical *validity* of which is problematic. . . . Schemata of this sort, however, are 'ideal-typical conceptual constructs.' The construction of teleological schemata of rational action is possible only *because* the employment of the categories of 'means' and 'ends' requires the rationalization of empirical reality" (p. 191). This is indeed a stunning admission that alone could serve as a decisive critique of the very "ideal-type" Weber had earlier posed.

In concluding this rich, problematic essay, Weber covers what

Oakes labels "The Twofold Meaning of the Category of Causality and the Relations Between Irrationality and Indeterminism" (pp. 191ff.). Weber seeks to "shed some light on the claim that the 'personality' and 'free' action are empirically and intrinsically irrational." This claim has served as his bête noire throughout the essay. It is here that Weber juxtaposes his notion of personality with that of his opponents. For Weber *personality* is a "concept which entails a constant and intrinsic relation to certain ultimate 'values' and 'meanings' in life, 'values' and 'meanings' which are forged into purposes and thereby translated into rational-teleological action" (p. 192). Against this is the "romanticist-naturalistic concept of 'personality'": [it] "seeks the real sanctuary of the personal in the diffuse, undifferentiated, vegetative 'underground' of personal life; i.e., in that 'irrationality' which rests upon the maze of an infinitude of psychophysical conditions for the development of temperament and feeling. This is a sense of 'irrationality' in which *both* the 'person' and the animal are 'irrational'" (p. 192). Once more we catch Weber at his own form of mystification. This time he uses the familiar phrase "the maze of an infinitude," suggesting that the empirical phenomena—if conceived in the "romanticist-naturalistic" mode—threaten to overwhelm the researcher unless drastic theoretical desiccation takes place. In one last blow on behalf of his perspective, he writes:

> From the viewpoint of historical "interpretation," the "personality" is not a "riddle" [as "Treitschke occasionally refers to" it, "a fashionable expression"]. On the contrary, it is the only possible object of interpretive "understanding." Nor is human action and conduct at any point—including the point at which rational interpretation is no longer possible—more "irrational," in the sense of "incalculable" or inaccessible to causal explanation, than *any concrete* event as such. (p. 193)

These few quotes should not be regarded as an adequate representation of Weber's exegesis. Many important items are being omitted (such as his connecting Knies with the "organic theory of natural right" and the "emanatist theory of action from the *substance* of the personality," to which Parsons often refers [pp. 199ff.]). But Weber's obsessively dialectical and intellectually scrupulous turn of mind would not allow him to ignore accuracy, however it might frustrate his own pet aims. In a footnote concerning Simmel's "theory of understanding" he says the following, which seems in absolute contradiction to the last several quoted above, yet obviously did not seem that way to him: "Even Simmel cannot fail to see that the infinitude, which he too admits, and the *absolute irrationality of every concrete manifold* is a conclusive epistemological *proof* [emphasis in original] of the absolute absurdity of the idea of the 'reflection' of reality by any science" (p. 251; emphasis added). We leave "Knies," a pivotal chapter in the development and refinement of Weber's thoughts on irrationality, realizing that its conflicting contents and sentiments reveal that a sediment of contradictions and confusions continued to cloud Weber's analyses of others' writings and weighed down his "original" statements as well.

Logic in the Cultural Sciences

"Cultural Studies in the Logic of the Cultural Sciences" (Käsler item 71), published in 1906, is the next work for consideration. My comments are restricted to a small section of the essay in which Weber, without explicitly meaning to do so, puts his critique of Knies in final form. He is at this point progressing very rapidly in his methodological thinking, for already he refers to "this old error" (of relating freedom to irrationality), only a matter of months after having treated it with much less condescension. And now he freely admits what in the Knies essay he had left to implication: "The error in the assumption that any freedom of the will—however it is understood—is identical with the 'irrationality' of action, or that the latter is conditioned by the former, is quite obvious. The characteristic of 'incalculability,' equally great but not greater than that of 'blind forces of nature,' is the privilege of—the insane" (p. 124). While this claim follows logically enough from everything else Weber wrote about the subject, suddenly he advances the argument a good deal and puts forth a proposition which has become the best known to students of Weber as his "refutation" of the "romanticist-naturalistic" viewpoint:

> We associate the highest measure of empirical "feeling of freedom" with those actions which we are conscious of performing rationally—i.e., *in the absence of physical and psychic "coercion," emotional "affects" and "accidental" disturbances of the clarity of judgment,* in which we pursue a clearly perceived end by "means" which are the most

adequate in accordance with the extent of our knowledge, i.e., in accordance with empirical *rules*. (pp. 124–125; emphasis in original)

If this is read out of context (as it often is, owing to its repeated appearance in discussions of his method), then Weber's entirely negative evaluation of the position urging examination of the irrational seems unequivocal. It offends him, as was pointed out earlier, because for him freedom means control of one's environment and one's self. "Incalculability" in external or internal terms denotes for Weber the "animal" level of existence, insanity, and subjection to "the blind forces of nature." If it even occurred to him that "incalculability" could also denote rebellion against rationalization and habitation of the iron cage, he was not at this point ready to admit it, at least in the passage just quoted.

If we continue to read in the essay, however, a different mindset emerges; moreover, it documents what we must interpret as the most intellectually bifurcated (or schizoid) position Weber has espoused thus far, when compared with his previous statements, all composed within a year of each other: "If history had only to deal with such rational actions which are 'free' in this sense, its task would be immeasurably lightened: the goal, the 'motive,' the 'maxims' of the actor would be unambiguously derivable from the means applied and all the irrationalities which constitute the 'personal' element in *conduct* would be excluded" (p. 125). We should note parenthetically that in this sentence Weber performed an about-face on the question of whether personality is intrinsically irrational, something he refused to concede to Knies, Roscher, and others: "Since all strictly teleologically (purposefully) occurring actions involve applications of empirical rules, which tell what the appropriate 'means' to ends are, history would be nothing but the applications of those rules" (ibid.). A footnote is attached:

Cf. in this connection, the considerations present in "Roscher and Knies"—strictly rational action—one could also put it thus—would be the simple and complete "adaptation" to the given "situation." Menger's theoretical schemata, for example, presuppose the strictly rational "adaptation" to the "market situation" and exhibit the consequences thereof in "ideal-typical" purity. History would in fact be nothing more than a body of practical patterns (pragmatics) of "adaptation" . . . if it were solely an analysis of the emergence and interconnections of the particular "free," i.e., teleologically absolutely rational, actions of single individuals. (ibid.)

The following year (1908) Weber published "Marginal Utility Theory and the Fundamental Law of Psychophysics," translated in 1975 by Louis Schneider. Here Weber goes into some detail on the heuristic value of the rationality assumptions behind marginal utility theory and expands upon his admiration for Menger's formalism. Especially in the last few pages of the essay (pp. 32ff.), he takes quite the opposite position from the one about to be brought up here in "Cultural Studies," chiding critics of the rationalist model, who, he believes, do not understand that it is not meant as a substitute for an "empirical" psychology of behavior. Rather, it merely serves certain kinds of *economic* analysis. What is interesting here is the ease with which Weber transferred properly *economic* tools of analysis to *sociological* data, apparently without much worry over theoretical or epistemological legitimacy.

We return to the text for the paramount section:

> The impossibility of purely pragmatic history is determined by the fact that the action of men is *not* interpretable in such purely rational terms, that not only irrational "prejudices," errors in thinking and factual errors but also "temperament," "moods," and "affects" *disturb his freedom*—in brief, that his action too—to very different degrees—partakes of the empirical "meaninglessness" of "natural change." Action *shares* this kind of "irrationality" with every natural event, and when the historian in the interpretation of historical interconnections speaks of the "irrationality" of human action as a disturbing factor, he is comparing historical-empirical action not with the phenomena of nature but with the ideal of a purely rational, i.e., absolutely purposeful, action which is also absolutely oriented towards the adequate means. (p. 125; emphasis added)

With the exception of one other relevant reference (p. 165),[19] Weber nowhere else in this essay addresses our topic so directly.

This is a vastly more realistic vision of behavior, and a more plausible way of analyzing it, than any Weber has previously presented. But problems still obtain, for instance his dogged insistence that "affects," "moods," "temperament," and other typical attributes of personality "disturb [one's] freedom." This sort of Kantian "freedom," in being so defined, falls beyond the parame-

19. Weber there includes an important qualification which in his mature works he frequently did not, presumably for stylistic reasons. But the effect, of course, has been to mislead some readers, who could not know about the missing qualification: "the acting person weighs, insofar as he acts rationally—*we shall assume this here*—the 'conditions' of the future development which interests him" (emphasis added).

ters of normal existence and bears more upon a truly "idealized"—
as opposed to "ideal-typical"—notion of autonomous, almost mechanical action than is useful to sociology. More important, Weber
has not thought about an obvious and vital dilemma created by the
use of his rational ideal-type. In contemporary statistical jargon,
the error term (unexplained variance) in an equation designating
social action, that is, one constructed around his concept of "undisturbed" rationality, would be enormous in proportion to explained variance. While this does not seem to impede much empirical research today (which often operates under the onus of
error terms five and six times the size of the explained behavior),
on the *theoretical* plane that level of tolerance for error should not
be allowed. For, as we know, the slippage between the content of
theoretical prediction and what is actually explained after the theory is applied through various testing instruments is substantial.
Therefore to build into the theoretical statement, *prior* to any application, the guaranteed inability to explain, predict, or even describe systematically phenomena of interest does not bode well for
the perfecting of theory.

The next work in English is "Capitalism and Rural Society in
Germany," [20] which adds nothing new to the issues at hand. In 1907
Weber published what since 1977 has been known as *Critique of
Stammler* (Käsler item 80), an interesting and important addition to
English Weber materials. Somehow strangely, and quite unexpect-
edly, it does not change or augment in any appreciable way our
understanding of Weber's feelings about irrationality and related
matters, as displayed in earlier methodological work. The German
title of the essay, which can be translated as "R. Stammler's 'Refutation' of the Materialist Conception of History," suggests what
Weber was about, but his previous and subsequent work would
not suggest what extraordinary care he took in dismantling Stammler's theoretical apparatus. This is the only extended work Weber
wrote that truly qualifies as hermeneutical; his standard practice
was to dissect others' works very selectively to highlight his own
preferred theoretical or substantive tack. By contrast, the Stammler

20. Pp. 363–385 in Weber 1946. I am excluding from discussion Weber's two
lengthy articles on Russia, also composed at this time, since they introduce nothing
new, theoretically, in Weber's thought.

critique is marked by meticulous, virtually page-by-page destruction of the argument. It is a tour de force of critical exegesis, and when it becomes better known it will reshape Weber's image in this country, where he is usually thought of as the great collector of comparative data more than a student and critic of texts. That notwithstanding, the book can be bypassed, because for the moment Weber put aside the issue of irrationality.

Recapitulation

It is time for a reckoning. Thus far the results of my Weber survey have been presented, taking in his writings between the dissertation in 1889 and the pivotal methodological essays nineteen years later. I have tried to establish a reasonably clear understanding of his battle along the way with the *Irrationalitätsproblem*. To his wife and students Weber made it no secret that this spate of lengthy essays (nine in all between 1903 and 1909) had convinced him that there were more productive ways to spend his time. Added to these purely logical works was a series of highly polemical articles he wrote in defense and clarification of the Protestant ethic thesis,[21] a debate from which he formally withdrew after 1910. Following this period, with the exception of the *Logos* article he became much more involved in the practice of scholarship (essentially in comparative religion and law) than in what Oakes has correctly designated "meta-theory." In a way this lightens our task spectacularly. Had Weber continued writing methodological, metatheoretical essays at the rate he did during his recuperative period of a dozen years or so, exegesis within a reasonable space might prove impossible. As it is, our hermeneutical exercise upon Weber is much nearer completion than might be expected judging from our present location on Käsler's list, item 80 out of 179 (up to Weber's death).

Let us very briefly review Weber's important works after 1910 in order to demonstrate that his views on the irrationality problem were essentially fixed by 1907 or so, and as such were automatically

---

21. Virtually unknown in this country until quite recently, they were collected and published by Winckelmann in a new edition (Weber 1968b). See also Weber 1978a.

embodied in subsequent works, in a form practically identical to that we have now come to recognize as distinctly Weberian. Put another way, Weber had confronted an exhausting range of methodological problems between 1903 and 1908. The decisions he reached in that period—among them, a very definite attitude toward those theories stressing irrationality in personality and meaningfulness— satisfied him sufficiently so that by and large he stuck to them for the rest of his professional life. Having said that, another significant point must be borne in mind. Were we to explicate *only* works written between 1910 and 1920, we would find within them certain undebatable differences concerning our particular interest. Moreover, an evolution of sorts occurred within Weber's thought, a maturation it might be called, in the direction of bringing ever broader and more diffuse behaviors into his model, as he assembled his monumental collection of data on religious, economic, and legal practices in comparative perspective. My point, though, is that the development of his theoretical position on irrationality between 1889 and 1907, when assessed in terms of intrinsic changes, was far greater (and immensely more troublesome to him personally and professionally) than alterations during the second, later period. Let us proceed, then, with a quick estimation of his later work, isolating where possible a few crucial passages for comparison with those already noted. In the interest of efficiency, I will dispense hereafter with commentary upon *each* of Weber's writings as they appear chronologically, but for the record, they are as follows (Käsler numbers follow each item):

1908   "A Research Strategy for the Study of Occupational Careers and Mobility Patterns" (90)
       Various articles on education, collected in *Max Weber on Universities* (82, 83, 85)
1909   *The Agrarian Sociology of Ancient Civilizations* (95)
1911   More articles on education (103–108)
       "Max Weber on Church, Sect, and Mysticism" (110, 111)
       The Rational and Social Foundations of Music (211)
1913   "On Some Categories of Interpretive Sociology" (116)
1916   *The Religion of China* (127)
       The Religion of India (128)
       "The Social Psychology of the World Religions" (127)

5

Mature Works

Kategorienlehre

Aside from Weber's more or less final formulations in *Economy and Society*, the single most important work from the "second" period is the 1913 *Logos* article, available in English since 1970 in a fine translation but unpublished until more recently in revised form.[1] Between the time of "Knies" and "Cultural Studies" (1905–1906) and the *Logos* piece, Weber apparently found some unstated motivation for tempering several of his less propitious claims just examined. For instance, his unseemly suggestion at one point that so-called pre-modern irrationality is an "inferior" state of mind bordering in fact on the "insane," he retracts: "The 'savage' knows infinitely more of the economic and social conditions of his own existence than the person termed 'civilized' in the usual sense. And it also is not universally true that the action of the 'civilized' is subjectively more rationally purposeful. This varies in the individual sphere of action, a problem in itself" (pp. 106–107/178–179). This important revision of his previous position occurs on the final page of the essay and is augmented by a concise, two-conditional description of rational versus irrational societies. According to Weber, "What gives the state of the 'civilized' its specific 'rational' note . . . in contrast to the 'savage'" is, first, the assumption that "the conditions of his everyday life . . . are principally of rational essence . . . are human artifacts accessible to rational knowledge, creation and control," which Weber relates to the stabilization of "consensus." And, second, "the confidence that they function rationally . . . that, in principle, . . . one can count on them, 'calculate' their be-

---

1. "A Translation of Max Weber's 'Über einige Kategorien der verstehenden Soziologie,' with Introduction and Footnotes," M.A. thesis by Edith E. Graber; published as "Some Categories of Interpretive Sociology," *Sociological Quarterly* 22, no. 2 (Spring 1981): 151–180. I used the thesis translation, which is noted first; pages in the published version are listed second.

havior and can orient his behavior to clear expectations created by them" (p. 107/179). I will not discuss for the moment the question of validity concerning his first premise ("the conditions of everyday life . . . are principally of rational essence"). But the observation might be made that while "savages" bowed to the opaque demands of "magic" and "sorcerers" (at the same time doing their "rational" best to influence outcomes, it should be added), contemporary social actors frequently find themselves subject to various forms of domination. On the one hand, they may culminate in "substantive irrationality" under the guise of formal rationality,[2] or, on the other, they may be so new in the history of culture that their rational versus irrational properties have not yet been analyzed or understood completely. One immediately thinks of the multifarious mechanisms intrinsic to advanced industrial societies concerning status definitions and the necessity of motivating people to "kill themselves" working in pursuit of desirable status; and, appended to this, the equally irrational pursuit of goods thought to be indicative of status achievement. "Consumerist culture" in the American vein had only just begun when Weber wrote these essays. (He was aware of Veblen, of course, but the latter's work on the subject held for only a thin stratum of the affluent.) It is unsurprising, then, that his dichotomy of "savage" and "civilized" societies seems even more naive and empirically suspect—with regard to irrationality, that is—than Weber himself would have thought.

The *Logos* essay demonstrates quite clearly Weber's growing sophistication in all methodological matters. His dialectical capabilities have advanced considerably. This passage is not atypical:

> It naturally does not follow that rational interpretation is to be regarded as the goal of sociological explanation, because of the specific certainty of rationally purposeful behavior. One could as well argue the opposite—citing the role which "irrational" (*zweckirrationale*) emotional states and "feeling states" play in the actions of men. One could also cite the fact that every rational interpretive analysis continually encounters ends which are no longer significant as "means" for other ends, but rather must simply be accepted as goals (*Zielrichtungen*) which are no longer rationally interpretable. (p. 45/152)

2. One of the finest fictional treatments of this condition is Vladimir Nabokov's anti-Stalinist novel *Bend Sinister*, in which the indomitable philosopher Krug wages psychological warfare upon his schoolmate Paduk, Nabokov's version of Stalin.

This precedes by a few pages far and away the most exciting section of the essay, "Relationship to Psychology" (pp. 49–58/154–158).[3] Within this brief compass Weber delivers his clearest, most logically coherent, and, in many ways, most perspicacious analysis of the interaction, conceptual and empirical, between rationality and irrationality. The distinction he struggles to establish between "interpretive sociology" and "empirical psychology" was the fruit of a debate more pressing in 1913 than today but, that aside, his other remarks demand serious thought.

He begins with the blunt declaration, "Interpretive sociology is not a part of a 'psychology'" (p. 49/154). He restates his familiar position, that the "most understandable" types of action are those which are "subjectively rigorously rational" and "oriented to means which are held to be unambiguously adequate for the attainment of unequivocal and clearly grasped ends." (I have alluded earlier to Weber's penchant for qualification. If we strip this sentence of its qualifiers—"unambiguously," "unequivocal," "clearly grasped," and so on—the phrase reads: "rational action oriented to the attainment of ends." This is roughly congruent with the perception many readers have of Weber's intention; thus, it would seem, his qualification went for nought.) He continues in defining the objective of *vertstehende Soziologie:*

> One seeks to make the deduction from subjectively held expectation as to the behavior of objects (subjective purposeful rationality) which were formed after valid experiences (objectively correct rationality) [*Richtigkeitsrationalität*] and only from these. The more clearly an action is oriented to objectively correct rationality, so much the less will its course be meaningfully understandable through any possible psychological consideration. (p. 51/154)

Weber's uncertainty about the progress of his argument shows through. The first sentence is practically impenetrable, the second clearly wrong even if we struggle to recall what *psychology* meant for Weber around that time.[4] But after this inconclusive beginning,

---

3. The only scholarly use of this section that I know of is that of the translator, Edith Graber, "Interpretive Sociology Is Not Part of a Psychology."

4. Karl Jaspers published in 1913 his *Allgemeine Psychopathologie*, and having then recently become a member of the Weber-Kreis, almost certainly made Weber aware of it. This philosophical work, though distant from what we know as psychology, bore more resemblance even then to psychology than to sociology; the English translation is *General Psychopathology*.

he introduces the notion of the limiting case, one that figures in all his subsequent work:

> Conversely, every explanation of "irrational" processes (i.e., those in which either the "objectively" correct conditions of rationally purposeful action had been disregarded or, again, those in which the subjectively rational purposeful deliberations of the actor has been substantially eliminated—a stock market panic, for example), needs to discern above all, what action would have been taken in a rationally ideal-type limiting case of absolute purpose and objectively correct rationality. Only when this is determined . . . can the causal attribution of the course of both objective as well as subjective "irrational" components take place. (p. 50/154)

Weber is so immersed at this point in his special type of formalist construction that he cannot ask himself, "in midstream," whether the "limiting case . . . of objectively correct rationality" carries anything other than nominalist value. That is, he refuses to judge his analytic device in terms of empirical reality and he feels justified in ignoring the issue so long as he restricts himself to "type-constructions." Though it was agreed long ago that in the social sciences the relation between concepts and phenomenal reality need not fit a "realist" definition or ontology, it is nevertheless true that *somewhere* in the analytic process, *some* approximation of concept to substance must be made; it is not enough to create models ad infinitum. This approximation—which would confer a measure of plausibility to the construction in question—Weber did not supply. He assumed that the utility of the rational type outweighed the disutility inherent in its substantial distance from life as lived, an assumption he apparently made due to his admiration for Menger and others of the scientific turn of mind.

Weber cautions, in the interest of "causal attribution," that only after comparison with the rational model can action be said to spring from "interrelationships which rest on motives based on objectively erroneous orientation or on subjective irrationality [*Zweckirrationalität*] and in the latter case are comprehensible only in generalization from experience but not understandable or on motives which are understandable but not rationally purposeful and interpretable" (pp. 50–51/154). Again verging on the incomprehensible, he leads himself to this understatement: "In the middle between the absolute (subjective) rationally oriented action and the absolutely incomprehensive psychic data (although actually bound together in fluid transition) lie the rest of the 'psycho-logically' understandable irrational interrelationships into whose very difficult theoretical differentiation we could not enter here" (p. 51/154). This sentence gives Weber's closest venture toward utter candor about the limitations of his thought, which he knew to be a function of a reliance upon rationality. With the words "actually bound together in fluid transition," Weber lets slip sound perception of motivation, and the necessary interrelation of irrationality and action. But with the complementary phrase, "interrelationships into whose very difficult theoretical differentiation we could not enter here," he admits he has no intention of pursuing this bond. He has shunted aside, by unperplexed fiat, a prime task of the social theorist: to determine as precisely as possible the relation between (irrational) psyche-personality and (rationalized) structure within different societal configurations—a task ably taken up by, for instance, Norbert Elias. This eminently empirical question Weber tossed aside, taking refuge in the rational model and leaving his students either to follow his lead—and the inevitable fetishization of the limiting case which it produces—or to develop their own solutions. A few pages later he restates his unwillingness to enter certain arenas of phenomenal reality: "In such cases, the subjective (though unperceived) rationally purposeful and the objectively correct very easily converge in a not always clear relationship to each other, which shall not occupy us further here" (p. 54/155). He then draws up short, freeing himself of comprehensive analytic responsibilities.[5]

Weber becomes less hesitant as the essay proceeds. He begins to define the scope of sociology in positive rather than merely reactive terms: "Sociology takes notice not only of motives of action made conscious through existence, of 'substitute satisfactions' of instincts and the like [presumably his version of Freudian sublimations], but is especially aware that quite 'uninterpretable' qualitative components of a motivational course co-determine these in the most far-reaching way" (p. 54/156). He hypothesizes that "qualitative states of mind direct the motivation chains . . . into hetero-

---

5. I am not, be it understood, questioning for a moment the comprehensiveness of Weber's actual analyses, particularly of religious phenomena. Rather, his exclusively programmatic, methodological suggestions are at issue.

geneous paths." Then, with an imperious command of the materials, he announces:

> For sociology the following are bound together in completely fluid transitions: (1) the more or less approximately attained objectively correct type; (2) the subjective rationally purposeful type; (3) the only more or less conscious or perceived and more or less clearly rationally motivated behavior; (4) that which is not rationally purposeful but is in a meaningfully understandable interrelationship; (5) the motivated behavior which is in an interrelationship which is more or less meaningfully understandable, more or less strongly obstructed or influenced by incomprehensible elements; and finally, (6) the wholly incomprehensible psychic or physical phenomena "in" and "around" a person.
>
> For sociology, not every course of action which is progressing in an "objectively correct rational" manner was conditioned by subjectively rational purpose; further, it is self-evident that it is not that which is logical and rational but that which is "psychological" which determined the course of the action. (p. 55/156)

Vigorous explication of this paragraph, full to the brim with ambiguity and contradiction, must await another opportunity. The point that needs to be made does not match the complexity of the ideas from which it originates. Very simply, it is that this collection of sentiments, this attempt at a catalogue of behavior, identifies Weber's frustration and dissatisfaction with the rational model. If everything is "bound together in completely fluid transitions" (undefined as they may be), it becomes quite clear how little use can be made of *any* limiting model, particularly one so artificial and contrived as Menger's. In essence, I interpret this pathetically convoluted paragraph as Weber's admission of indecision and defeat. He saw the deficiencies of conventional thought, but at this point he could not develop an alternative.

More than halfway through this portentous section, Weber, in almost visible weariness, makes one last effort to be conclusive:

> Enough; the relationships of interpretive sociology to psychology are formed differently in each individual case. The objectively correct rationality serves interpretive sociology over against the empirical action, the rationally purposeful over against the psychologically understandable, the meaningfully understandable over against the non-understandable motivated action as ideal type. It is through comparison with one another that the causally relevant irrationalities (in the varying meaning of the word) are established for the purpose of causal attribution. (p. 56/156–157)

And no sooner has he put the lid on discussion than he opens it again: "The significant and difficult general ambiguity of the 'rational' in history need not be cleared up at this point" (p. 58/157). To this he appends a tantalizing footnote in which he promises to provide an "illustration" of the "juncture" of the "correct type of a behavior and the empirical behavior." This "juncture" he characterizes in a familiar way: "These relationships are the juncture, at which the tensions between the empirical and the correct type can rupture and they are thus dynamically of the highest importance in development" (p. 115/179). (The promised example turned out to be his sociology of music, which in fact by this time he had already written.) "Junctures rupturing through tensions," a splendid bit of cognitive imagery, does little to dispose of the thicket of problems Weber has up to this point discovered and, simultaneously, created for himself.

One final note about the *Logos* article: appearing near the end is a hint that Weber's patience with certain constraints of Menger's model, especially those having to do with the range of analyzable behavior, had worn thin. In a general discussion of "consensual social relationships," he writes, "This example, and especially also one of the erotic relationship, indicates further that the meaning relationship and 'expectations' constituted through consensus need not in the least have the character of a rationally purposeful calculation and an orientation to rationally constructable rules" (p. 87/170). The example of the erotic relationship is new to Weber's store of illustrative material and suggests the direction he was beginning to take, certainly a more bracing and courageous path than one bound essentially to "economistic" rationality.

Zwischenbetrachtungen *and "Religious Rejections of the World"*

One of the final Weber selections of interest is the Introduction to part 3, volume 1, pages 237–275, of the *Religionssoziologie*. Gerth and Mills entitled this essay "The Social Psychology of World Religions" (in *From Max Weber*, pp. 267–301), and in a footnote date it as having been published in September 1915. Käsler does not agree, but dates the piece sometime in 1916. It complements another essay Gerth and Mills translated (also to be considered), "Religious Rejections of the World and Their Directions" (*From Max Weber*, pp. 323–359), taken from the same volume in German, the section called "Zwischenbetrachtung," (pp. 536–573, not 436, as printed in the English edition). Since they appear to have been written almost simultaneously, I shall consider them in the same order they were printed in the Gerth and Mills reader.

At this stage of his writing, Weber fairly explodes with rationality. Among a multitude of usages, many of them mutually inconsistent, we find the following: "ethical rationalization of life" (p. 270), "a *rational* view of the world" (p. 273), "a rational supplement to magic" (p. 274), "the rational conception of the world" (ibid.), "a rational theodicy of misfortune" (ibid.), "the development of a rational religious ethic" (p. 276), "the rational interest in material and ideal compensations" (p. 277), "a systematic and 'rationalized' image of the world" (p. 280), "the core of genuine religious rationalism" (p. 281), "rational cognition and mastery of nature" (p. 282), "to rationalize the image of the world" (ibid.), "the rationalism of heirocracy" (ibid.), "rational ritualism of the law" (p. 284), "the tendency towards a *practical* rationalism" (ibid.), "the tendency of technological and economic rationalism" (ibid.), "an *ethical* and rational regulation of life" (ibid.), "'psychological' as over against 'rational' connections" (p. 286), "the rational religious pragmatism of salvation" (ibid.), "establishing a rational ethic of everyday life" (p. 289), "rationally raised into a vocation" (p. 291), "the methodical rationalization of conduct" (ibid.), "the particular rationalization of civic life" (p. 293) (at this point there appears what by now can only be construed as a joke: "We have to remind ourselves in advance that 'rationalism' may mean very different things," p. 293), "Confucianism is rationalist" (ibid.), "the Renaissance was 'rational'" (ibid.), "the *substantive* rationalization of administration and of judiciary" (p. 298), "*formalist* juristic rationalism" (p. 299), and "the delivery of political rationalism" (p. 300). As was mentioned above, the Dilthey scholar H. A. Hodges acutely understood that "the word 'reason' or 'rational' itself is often used emotively, as a cheer-word, and a careful examination of the ways in which it is applied might be disconcerting."[6] Within the twenty-eight examples just given, certainly there is a modicum of consis-

---

6. G. H. R. Parkinson, ed., *Georg Lukács*, p. 96.

tency, but not enough to justify Weber's obsessive theoretical use of the word and its cognates.

By comparison, *irrational* shows up about once for every twenty instances of its opposite (though irrational *types* of behavior, not necessarily so defined, are strewn throughout the essay). Some interesting and theoretically legitimate examples are these: "religion has been shifted to the realm of the irrational" (p. 281); "music [has] put irrationality into the service of the richness of tonalities" (ibid.); "The various great ways of leading a rational and methodical life have been characterized by irrational presuppositions" (ibid.); "the irrational elements in the rationalization of reality" (ibid.); probably the most interesting figure in the essay, "the irrepressible quest of intellectualism for the possession of supernatural values has been compelled to retreat . . . the more so the more denuded of irrationality the world appears to be" (pp. 281–282); "the irrationality of 'fate'" (p. 283); and, finally, the most instantly recognizable as mature Weberianism, "charismatic authority is 'irrational'" (p. 296).

This is not a complete or random sampling of Weber's peculiar, almost linguistically ritualistic mobilization of *rationality*—that is, what he conceived the term to mean theoretically—in "The Social Psychology of World Religions." Neither have I presented a close textual analysis to the end of isolating changes in Weber's thinking. The prospect of "rationalizing" the meanings Weber attached to these terms—disentangling, systematizing, and differentiating them—is daunting, which may account for its never having been done. What mere listing does make obvious, I think, is Weber's compulsive dependence on the rationality-irrationality dichotomy, a bipolar conceptualization which apparently held for him some great private meaning, and which became, one might argue, an incantation. I say this hesitantly, since his great analytic power was not appreciably diminished, at least in this essay (which, it should be noted, is truly a virtuoso performance) due to the incantational functions of his pet dichotomy. But he stretched the terms so far beyond what is conventionally viewed as appropriate or terminologically wise that we must conclude they served some sort of supra-normal intellectual function for him. Perhaps his chronic dependence can be put in the perspective of traditional scholarship if we pose this question: had a scholar of less stature (Tönnies would be the logical example, given his interest in rationality) presented articles to the public so laced with a master term or category not as yet definitively explicated and refined, would the response have been as warm? Would the articles still enjoy the readership they do, and would the choice of terminology upon which their theoretical legitimacy rests have been so readily incorporated into tradition?

"Religious Rejections of the World and Their Directions" calls for a different style of commentary. It too is a beautifully dense essay, but, thankfully, purged of gratuitous "rationals." Weber's task is "to clarify briefly, in a schematic and theoretical way, the motives from which religious ethics of world abnegation have originated, and the directions they have taken" (p. 323). He believed this to be the first step in discovering their meaning. This essay is frank in its heuristic limitations: "As will readily be seen, the individual spheres of value are prepared with a rational consistency which is rarely found in reality" (ibid.). Yet for all his humbleness before the empirical actuality of humanity as irrationally bounded, he insists on due respect for the rational model: "For the rationality, in the sense of logical or teleological 'consistency,' of an intellectual-theoretical or practical-ethical attitude has and always has had power over man, however limited and unstable this power is and always has been in the face of other forces of historical life" (p. 324). The "has and always has had" might be contested by some anthropologists, but since Weber skirted hyperbole I assume that he had specific evidence in mind.

Sections Six ("The Esthetic Sphere"), Seven ("The Erotic Sphere"), and Eight ("The Intellectual Sphere") contain comments on the nature of irrationality calling for examination. He addressed the question of how a religious ethic, bent on abnegation of the world, can subdue the "natural" antagonism felt for itself by proponents of aestheticism, eroticism, and intellectualism. Judging from their contextual arrangement, Weber perceived all three realms of experience and thought as sharing important components, particularly as they related to social (or, in this case, "religious") action. He begins with a characterization of the "esthetic sphere" in which many of the phrases he habitually used to convey "difficult" matters, that is, those involving "irrationality," occur:

> The religious ethic of brotherliness stands in dynamic tension with any purpose-rational conduct that follows its own laws. In no less

degree, this tension occurs between the religious ethic and "this-worldly" life-forces, whose character is essentially non-rational or basically anti-rational [*arationalen oder anti-rationalen*, p. 554 in the German]. Above all, there is tension [*Spannung*] between the ethic of religious brotherliness and the spheres of esthetic and erotic life. (pp. 340–341)

He outlines the historical *Spannung* between "magical religiosity" and art on the one hand, the ethics of abnegation on the other. As we have already seen, this special type of tension held more interest for him, notably after 1911 or so when he wrote his essay on the sociology of music, than practically any other: "The relation between a religious ethic and art will remain harmonious as far as art is concerned for so long as the creative artist experiences his work as resulting either from a charisma or 'ability' (originally magic) or from spontaneous play" (p. 341). "Ethical rigorism," then, is by definition the enemy of the "ecstasy" typically induced by ritually orchestrated artistic (especially musical) practices. Succinctly put, "sublimation of the religious ethic and the quest for salvation, on the one hand, and the evolution of the inherent logic of art, on the other hand, tended to form an increasingly tense relation" (p. 341). Furthermore, the "development of intellectualism and the rationalization of life" alters the "original" arrangement, and "art becomes a cosmos" of "consciously grasped independent values which exist in their own right." A conflict that is central to Simmel's analysis of modern life becomes inevitable:

> Art takes over the function of a this-worldly salvation, no matter how this may be interpreted. It provides a *salvation* from the routines of everyday life, and especially from the increasing pressures of theoretical and practical rationalism.
> With this claim to a redemptory function, art begins to compete directly with salvation religion. Every rational religious ethic must turn against this inner-worldly, irrational salvation. For in religion's eyes, such salvation is a realm of irresponsible indulgence and secret lovelessness. (p. 342)

Apparently keen to produce a catalogue of the most ferocious enemies of the "brotherly ethic," Weber writes, "The most irrational form of religious behavior, the mystic experience, is in its innermost being not only alien but hostile to all form." Though he does not say so, "form" is synonymous with "rationalization": "Form is unfortunate and inexpressible to the mystic because he believes precisely in the experience of exploding of all forms" (p. 342). This analysis ties logically into that of "eroticism."

In a sentence structure almost identical to that of the earlier statement, he proposes, "The brotherly ethic of salvation religion is in profound tension with the greatest irrational force of life: sexual love. The more sublimated sexuality is, and the more principled and relentlessly consistent the salvation ethic of brotherhood is, the sharper is the tension between sex and religion" (p. 343). After acknowledging that "originally the relation of sex and religion was very intimate, sexual intercourse [being] very frequently part of magic orgiasticism," he shows that this ended with the onset of the "cultic chastity of priests" (p. 344). From this it is a short step to marriage, about which Weber makes this insightful remark: "The contrast of all rational regulation of life with magical orgiasticism and all sorts of irrational frenzies is expressed in this fact [regulated sexual intercourse in favor of *marriage*]." There follows an intense, revealing section in which Weber writes more convincingly about eroticism ("a gate into the most irrational and thereby real kernel of life, as compared with the mechanisms of rationalization," p. 345) than at any previous point.

This newfound sophistication could have had at least two sources. Either his relations with Otto Gross, Else Jaffé, and others had given him firsthand knowledge, or his research into Hinduism (and its subcults) had brought him face to face with anthropological data of a kind he had not previously studied. Whatever the cause, he seems to have worked out the theoretical relation between irrational eroticism and the rational "brotherly ethic" extremely well by this time. For Weber "the irrational" was expressed at its most extreme in eroticism:

> The tension of religion and sex has been augmented by evolutionary factors on both sides. On the side of sexuality the tension has led through sublimation into "eroticism," and therewith into a con- sciously cultivated, and hence, a non-routinized sphere. Sex has been non-routinized not solely or necessarily in the sense of being estranged from conventions, for eroticism is a contrast to the sober naturalism of the peasant. And it was precisely eroticism which the conventions of knighthood usually made the object of regulation. These conventions, however, characteristically regulated eroticism by veiling the natural and organic basis of sexuality.
>
> The extraordinary quality of eroticism has consisted precisely in a gradual turning away from the naive naturalism of sex. The reason

and significance of this evolution, however, involve the universal rationalization and intellectualization of culture. . . . The total being
of man has now been alienated from the organic cycle of peasant
life. . . . All of this has worked, through the estrangement of life-
value from that which is merely naturally given, toward a further en-
hancement of the special position of eroticism. Eroticism was raised
into the sphere of conscious enjoyment (in the most sublime sense of
the term). Nevertheless, indeed because of this elevation, eroticism
appeared to be like a gate into the most irrational. (pp. 344–345)

And having sketched very incisively a history of this transmogrifi-
cation of "natural organic sexuality" to "eroticism," he crests in
analytic power:

> This tension between an inner-worldly and an other-worldly salva-
> tion from rationality must be sharpest and most unavoidable pre-
> cisely where the sexual sphere is systematically prepared for a highly
> valued erotic sensation. This sensation reinterprets and glorifies
> all the pure animality of the relation, whereas the religion of salva-
> tion assumes the character of a religion of love, brotherhood, and
> neighborly love.
>
> Under these conditions, the erotic relation seems to offer the un-
> surpassable peak of the fulfillment of the request for love in the di-
> rect fusion of the souls of one to the other. This boundless giving of
> oneself is as radical as possible in its opposition to all functionality,
> rationality, and generality. It is displayed here as the unique mean-
> ing which one creature in his irrationality has for another, and only
> for this specific other. (p. 347)

This astounding passage displays Weber at his finest, that is, at the
juncture at which he not only maintains an olympian analytic posture but simultaneously speaks of human life in its full actuality,
not in the shadow world of rationalist models. One might even forgive him his counter-Victorian, Stefan George–like "lyricism" regarding sexuality and its connection with "love," which in fact he
may have learned from Simmel.

The next few sentences reveal Weber in a light unknown to most
American sociologists. In them he reads very much like Dilthey,
Martin Buber, Jaspers, even Spengler, and while this brief flash on
the mammoth Weberian screen of learning cannot support a wholesale revision of the man's thought, neither can it remain forever
in oblivion while Weber as theorist of bureaucracy, domination,
and the capitalist spirit retains false hegemony over Weberian
sociology.

> However, from the point of view of eroticism, this meaning, and
> with it the value-content of the relation itself, rests upon the possi-

bility of a communion which is felt as a complete unification, as a fading of the "thou." It is so overpowering that it is interpreted "symbolically": as a sacrament. The lover realizes himself to be rooted in the kernel of the truly living, which is eternally inaccessible to any rational endeavor. He knows himself to be freed from the cold skeleton hands of rational orders, just as completely as from the banality of everyday routine. This consciousness of the lover rests upon the ineffaceability and inexhaustibleness of his own experience. . . . Knowing "life itself" joined to him, the lover stands opposite what is for him the objectless experiences of the mystic, as if he were facing the fading light of an unreal sphere.

As the knowing love of the mature man stands to the passionate enthusiasm of youth, so stands the deadly earnestness of this eroticism of intellectualism to chivalrous love. (p. 347)

With these reflections, it seems to me, Weber has deepened the claims of *verstehende Soziologie* by a factor of ten. In spite of his own warnings to the contrary, penned only a half-dozen years previously, he has burst analytically into the "irrational and thereby real kernel of life." The beauty and importance of his analysis are, however, of a special nature. Armies of scholars have written perceptively about sexuality, love, and art, and more still on the battle between magical orgiastic eroticism and bureaucratized, rationalized religion. But among them, social theorists of Weber's stature are not well represented. It is difficult to assemble the names of even a small group of modern social theorists who have contributed significantly to the analysis of these conundrums. Weber was stepping out of the mainstream of German political economy, beyond the perimeters of all the *Geisteswissenschaften*, in order to pursue the most elusive quarry of all: natural, phenomenal man, unmediated by externally imposed notions of behavior, thought, or sentiment. One wonders, in fact, if the connection between Husserl and Weber, seldom explored in depth (not even by Alfred Schutz, so far as I can tell),[7] might account for some of Weber's redirection and enriching of the sociological project.

I close this hasty analysis of "Religious Rejections" with some

7. Little has been done about examining Weber's quiet use of phenomenology in his own work. Thomas Burger notes that Johannes Winckelmann claimed more importance for Weber of Husserl than is usually the case, but Burger is not impressed with the data: see Johannes Winckelmann's *Legitimität und Legalität in Max Webers Herrschaftssoziologie*, pp. 12–19, and Burger's *Max Weber's Theory of Concept Formation*, p. 183n38. Weber cited Husserl's *Logical Investigations*, which were published in 1900, just as he was beginning to write his methodological studies, several times in his essay on Knies.

lines from "The Intellectual Sphere." Weber spends several pages outlining all the myriad ways intellectualism confronts religion in a state of tension. As a summing up, he offers the following, which includes the link to our concern, the *Irrationalitätsproblem:*

> Culture becomes ever more senseless as a locus of imperfection, of injustice, of suffering, of sin, of futility. For it is necessarily burdened with guilt, and its deployment and differentiation thus necessarily become ever more meaningless. Viewed from a purely ethical point of view, the world has to appear fragmentary and devalued in all those instances when judged in the light of the religious postulate of a divine "meaning" of existence. This devaluation results from the conflict between the rational claim and reality, between the rational ethic and the partly rational, and partly irrational values. With every construction of the specific nature of each special sphere existing in the world, this conflict has seemed to come to the fore ever more sharply and more insolubly. The need for "salvation" responds to this devaluation by becoming more other-worldly, more alienated from all structured forms of life, and, in exact parallel, by confining itself to the specific religious essence. The reaction is the stronger the more systematic the thinking about the "meaning" of the universe becomes, the more the external organization of the world is rationalized and the more the conscious experience of the world's irrational content is sublimated. And not only theoretical thought, disenchanting the world, led to this course, but also the very attempt of religious ethics practically and ethically to rationalize the world. (p. 357)

This material documents that Weber had quite completely transcended the limitations—intellectual and personal—which earlier he had believed were intrinsic to social science. In large measure, this connotes a reversal in attitude toward the conceptualization and discursive analysis of irrationality and the multitude of social manifestations associated with it.

Economy and Society

Since Weber's *Hauptwerk* encapsulates most of his previous substantive work in one form or another (with the exception of his sociology of music and the policy studies discussed above), we need not treat it as utterly new.[8] As readers of the English edition know,

---

8. The only substantial body of Weber's work I have not discussed are those translated portions of Weber's *Religionssoziologie* known as *Ancient Judaism, The Religion of China,* and *The Religion of India.* The decision to omit discussion of the comparative religions is theoretically defensible, I believe. Religion is by definition a

almost every page holds some slight reference to rationality, rationalization, or irrationality. By the time Weber composed the masterwork (roughly 1910–1914, Part 2, 1918–1919, Part 1), these ideas had become the major organizing concepts around which everything else revolved. He himself publicly described the project as having originated "from the view that the development of the economy must be investigated primarily as a particular phenomenon of the *general rationalization* of life."[9] Even more indicative of the link between works we have already examined and the present one is the fact that the *Logos* article served as the backbone to the "Conceptual Exposition" (Part 1) of *Economy and Society*, the Weber early American readers have come to know best, since Parsons and Henderson's translation was one of the first Weber fragments made available in English.

Certainly the best-known of all Weber's statements or codifications concerning irrationality comes within the first thirty-two pages of the work (pp. 87–118 in *The Theory of Social and Economic Organization*, hereafter *TSEO*). It is familiar not only because of its location in the book but because Parsons dealt with some of its shortcomings quite articulately in his extensive introduction (see pp. 13–14) as part of his influential interpretation of "Weber's Methodology of Social Science" (pp. 8–29). Parsons's remarks in these pages are, I believe, in fact a good deal more on the mark

---

manifestation of irrationality. Thus, in a loose sense, all three books deal, in their entireties, with social irrationality. Moreover, with only minor exceptions, what Weber had to tell us on the general level, and particularly regarding irrationality, he told best in (1) sections of *The Protestant Ethic*, (2) the essays just examined, "The Social Psychology of World Religions" and "Religious Rejections of the World and Their Directions," originally important interstitial material in the *Religionssoziologie* itself, and (3) that portion of *Economy and Society* known to Americans as *The Sociology of Religion*, and not in the massive substantive studies. The single other work that falls beyond my discussion is *General Economic History* (Weber 1981a). The relevant chapters, to the degree they are such, are 29 and 30, pp. 249–270. I do not rank this as a major work since it is, to begin with, the work of hands other than Weber's (a compilation of student notes), and, second, gives a concise history of economic change in the West, nothing more nor less. *Irrationality* as we have approached the concept does not receive much attention, and what there is does not qualify as ground-breaking in Weber's thought.

9. Marianne Weber, *Max Weber*, pp. 419–420 (emphasis in original). For details of the tremendous difficulty Weber had in organizing the series of which *Wirtschaft und Gesellschaft* was to be a part, and the consequences this had for the structure and goals of the work itself, see ibid., pp. 418–420, and Guenther Roth's additional details in his introduction to the English translation, pp. lvi–lxi.

than much of *The Structure of Social Action,* since in the former he sublimates—to some extent—his private theoretical goals on behalf of explicating Weber's. It may be expeditious here to reproduce some of Parsons's reactions to Weber's treatment of irrationality.

Parsons first notes that the rational ideal-type appealed to Weber because of its congruence with cognitive aspects of scientific method, and therefore he "concentrated overwhelmingly" on them (p. 13). Some of Weber's basic contentions are reiterated: that the ideal-type describes, not actual behavior, but a "normatively ideal course"; that Weber was interested in an "'objectively possible' course of action"; and so on. But Parsons preliminarily accuses Weber of having "failed to place [the rational ideal-type] adequately in relation to certain other possibilities, thus neglecting alternative formulations and falling into certain biases" (ibid.). The four types of action are introduced, and the two associated with irrational action are designated as "residual categories" (p. 14). According to Parsons, Weber's determination to use his four ideal types throughout analyses forces him into an epistemologically dangerous "type atomism" and leads to a slighting of "systematic" features of action. More important, since there was "a marked tendency for Weber's thought to move in terms of the dichotomy of rational and irrational," massive simplifications and omissions from empirical reality had to be made. And with irrational actions being treated as "deviations" from the pure rational type, tremendous sacrifices in the perception of behavioral subtleties and certain "mixtures"—of calculating *and* affective action—inevitably had to be made in the analyses. (Schutz had made identical charges in 1932.)[10] Here Parsons makes a most interesting observation, one that to my knowledge is very seldom voiced in studies of social thought: "All the important problems of a system of action which arise in connexion with Pareto's category of that part of *non*-logical action which is not *il*logical, are obscured by Weber's mode of approach" (p. 16). Unfortunately, this is not developed, but it is, I believe, a fruitful alternative to Weber's defective conceptualization. Parsons does pursue the point, albeit without again bringing in Pareto:

> Partly, this is simply an error of omission. Certain elements, the presence of which is logically implied, are ignored [in Weber's the-

10. In Alfred Schutz, *Der sinnhafte Aufbau der sozialen Welt,* translated into English in 1967 as *The Phenomenology of the Social World.*

ory of social action]. But this is not all. Since the basic dichotomy of Weber's analysis is that of the rational and the irrational, and since the latter elements are treated as elements of *deviation*, the tendency is to create a false, theoretically unwarranted antithesis. Elements which may well in some empirical cases be integrated with the rational elements in a system, are pushed into conflict with it. Thus ultimate values tend to be treated as an absolutely "irrational" force. In a closely connected sense affect is also treated as irrational. Weber again and again, in these methodological remarks, refers to it in these terms. (p. 16)

Even with the superfluous reference to "system," this comprises an astute assessment of certain analytic calamities that befell Weber's *Kategorienlehre* when transferred to *Economy and Society*.

After a page of "correcting" Weber in the interest of Parsons's notion of "unit acts," we come again to a valuable bit of exegesis. Parsons notes the clumsiness inherent in ideal-types when analysis is confronted with the ubiquitous case of action (or "value-orientation," as Parsons puts it) that strictly speaking is not rational but cannot be thought of as irrational. Very simply, the criterion of rationality may not apply to every case. Parsons wraps up the brief hermeneutic with this:

Weber falls into what is not so much a naïve "rationalistic bias"—an interpretation against which he justifiably protests [Parsons notes at this point Weber's resistance to this accusation, appearing on p. 92 of *TSEO*, p. 6 of *Economy and Society*]—but rather a question of thinking in terms of a certain kind of abstract dichotomy in a far too limited theoretical context. . . . This difficulty plays an important part in some of Weber's broadest empirical generalizations, notably those touching the "process of rationalization." (p. 17)

Somewhat later in the introduction, Parsons offers the opinion that "Weber . . . got into serious trouble which could have been greatly mitigated had he extended his systematic theory into a more careful analysis in the direction of psychology" (p. 27). Just before, he had made the outright claim that "Weber tended not to be interested in psychology and to repudiate its relevance to his problems" (p. 26), an assertion that I believe is not completely justified. Parsons probably has in mind the section of the *Logos* article to which I gave lengthy attention above, where Weber says, "Interpretive sociology is not part of a psychology." Parsons, writing in 1946, is perhaps not remembering what "psychology" meant in 1913 in German universities. References that Weber made in his very early methodological essays to explicitly psychological works indicate that he was quite sympathetic to a *nonreductionist, noninstinctivist* psychology, as can be seen in his high praise for William James and continued admiration for Simmel. Parsons rounds out this argument thus:

> This [Weber's having ignored psychology] is notably true of his treatment of rationality. . . . The isolation of rationality and the treatment of affect as *only* a factor of deviation from rational norms is clearly incompatible with the findings of modern psychology, which rather point definitely to the integration of affective and rationally cognitive elements in the same action. Much the same is true of Weber's tendency to confine ideal type analysis to the rational case and the related tendency to confine, in his methodological formulations at least, the applicability of subjective categories to consciously intended motives. In questions like these Weber shows a vacillating uncertainty which could largely be cleared up by better psychological analysis. (pp. 27–28)

Having registered Parsons's objections to Weber's handling of irrationality (the weaknesses of which were not, incidentally, overcome completely in his own *The Social System* or *Toward a Theory of Social Action*), we may proceed to the text itself. It is important to keep Parsons's observations in mind, however, since his version of what the texts say has thoroughly permeated the theoretical consciousness of the field.

Weber begins *Economy and Society* by defining *meaning*, a category of analysis that frequently figures in his work but receives serious analytic treatment only rarely. The portion of the lengthy definition relevant to our discussion is this:

> All interpretation of meaning, like all scientific observations, strives for clarity and verifiable accuracy of insight and comprehension. The basis for certainty in understanding can be either rational, which can be further subdivided into logical and mathematical, or it can be of an emotionally empathic or artistically appreciative quality. Action is rationally evident chiefly when we attain a completely clear intellectual grasp of the action-elements in their intended context of meaning. (p. 5)

Weber is here repeating his conviction that what is rational is so defined not from the actor's perspective but from the analyst's. This contradicts and confuses an even more basic element of his thought, that "meaningful action" is that "to which subjective meaning is attached," presumably from the viewpoint of the active agent. The latter claim is also more in keeping with the spirit of

Weber's sociology, yet the former shows up repeatedly in his formal definitions and in their ramifications: "The interpretation of . . . rationally purposeful action possesses, for the understanding of the choice of means, the highest degree of verifiable certainty" (p. 5). Much less stiff and more recognizably Weberian is the quasi-methodological sentence immediately following: "The more we ourselves are susceptible to such emotional reactions as anxiety, anger, ambition, envy, jealousy, love, enthusiasm, pride, vengefulness, loyalty, devotion, and appetites of all sorts, and to the 'irrational' conduct which grows out of them, the more readily can we empathize with them" (p. 6). In this we have the sole location in Weber's writing that provides the rudiments of an operational definition of irrationality. It is curious that Weber never saw fit, even in passing or in one of his magisterial footnotes, to elaborate this list of synonyms into something approaching a social-psychological theory or inventory. His awareness that "understandable and non-understandable components of a process are often intermingled and bound up together" for some reason did not spur him toward theoretical clarification.

What might be called the master premise of the entire work is forthrightly stated: "For the purposes of a typological scientific analysis it is convenient to treat all irrational, affectually determined elements of behavior as factors of deviation from a conceptually pure type of rational action" (p. 6). He denies that this strategy commits him to a "rationalistic bias": "It certainly does not involve a belief in the actual predominance of rational elements in human life, for on the question of how far this predominance does or does not exist, nothing whatever has been said. That there is, however, a danger of rationalistic interpretations where they are out of place cannot be denied. All experience unfortunately confirms the existence of this danger" (pp. 7–8). Since Parsons has already commented upon the entirely unsatisfactory nature of this position, I will refrain for the moment, other than to say that Weber was apparently much more cognizant of his vulnerability—and the need for a complementary psychological theory—than Parsons believes. Witness this sentence somewhat further on: "it is precisely on the basis of such rational assumptions that most of the laws of sociology . . . are built up. On the other hand, in explaining the irrationalities of action sociologically, that form of psychology

which employs the method of subjective understanding undoubtedly can make decisively important contributions" (p. 19). Qualifications, all of them, I think, wisely conceived, continue to modify
the program of sociology:

> Precision is obtained by striving for the highest possible degree of
> adequacy on the level of meaning. It has already been . . . stressed
> that this aim can be realized in a particularly high degree in the case
> of concepts and generalizations which formulate rational processes.
> But sociological investigation attempts to include in its scope vari-
> ous irrational phenomena, such as prophetic, mystic, and affectual
> modes of action, formulated in terms of theoretical concepts which
> are adequate on the level of meaning. In *all* cases, rational or irra-
> tional, sociological analysis both abstracts from reality and at the
> same time helps us to understand it. (p. 20)

Finally, still from the preliminary section of the work, Weber introduces another important empirical generalization, one that gives
substance to Parsons's claim that Weber's intuitive perception of
psychological factors in social life embodied more good sense than
some of his formalizations:

> In the great majority of cases actual action goes on in a state of inar-
> ticulate half-consciousness or actual unconsciousness of its subjec-
> tive meaning. The actor is more likely to "be aware" of it in a vague
> sense than he is to "know" what he is doing or be explicitly self-
> conscious about it. In most cases his action is governed by impulse
> or habit. Only occasionally and in the uniform action of large num-
> bers . . . is the subjective meaning of the action, whether rational or
> irrational, brought clearly into consciousness. The ideal type of
> meaningful action where the meaning is fully conscious and explicit
> is a marginal case. (pp. 21–22)

These constitute the most important metatheoretical propositions for our interests in the first part of the book. Following this is
"Section B. Social Action" and then "Types of Social Action," together the core of Weber's formal theory. His definition of social
action is well enough known that I will not repeat it here. Likewise,
I went into some detail earlier (Chapter 1) about the limitations and
mistaken assumptions which can grow out of his fourfold typology
of action. Reiterated in its briefest form: whereas Weber selects
zweckrationalisches Handeln as the leading category for sociological
analysis, I am interested in revising both *affektuell* and traditional
action as loci of research and theoretical speculation, given critical

changes in relative institutional importance since Weber's day and the resultant widening of opportunity (even need) for noninstrumental action.

Parsons is correct in chiding Weber for unwarranted and therefore constraining reliance upon the rational-irrational dichotomy. The first example of theoretical weakness resulting from this syndrome occurs when Weber distinguishes between "communal" and "associative" relationships:

> A social relationship will be called "communal" [*Vergemeinschaftung*] if and so far as the orientation of social action—whether in the individual case, on the average, or in the pure type—is based on a subjective feeling of the parties, whether affectual or traditional, that they belong together.
> A social relationship will be called "associative" [*Vergesellschaftung*] if and insofar as the orientation of social action within it rests on a rationally motivated adjustment of interests. (pp. 40–41)

Although not a crucial blunder (especially since Weber admits he was merely elaborating upon Tönnies's well-established terminology), this absolute disjuncture between the rationality of one and the irrationality of the other form of sociation contradicts contemporary thought. That "associative" relationships (Weber suggests as examples "rational free market exchange," "the pure voluntary association," and so on) are frequently pervaded with nonrational motivation and behavior has become stock sociological wisdom. Weber would argue—as he did in response to all such attacks upon his master dichotomy—that since his ideal-types do not describe empirical behavior, they cannot be held accountable for internal aberrations at the phenomenal level but, rather, should be examined in terms of the *proportion* of behavior actually transpiring. If the proportion leans significantly toward one or the other pole (he uses the phrase "action . . . at the pole of rationality"), then use of the ideal-type is analytically justified. While his modern descendants would chafe at his confidence, in fact they regularly join in similar analytic fictions. They seem merely to be more self-conscious about the heuristic nature of the practice.

Analytically and theoretically Weber is on safest terrain when writing about "Modes of Economic Orientation of Action" and "Typical Measures of Rational Economic Action" (pp. 69–74). Since his primary inspiration for using the rational-irrational continuum stemmed from marginalist economic theory, he had little to fear from the analysis of what might relatively be termed pure economic action. He writes:

> The following are typical measures of rational economic action:
>
> (1) The systematic allocation as between present and future of utilities, on the control of which the actor for whatever reason feels able to count. (These are the essential features of saving.)
> (2) The systematic allocation of available utilities to various potential uses . . . ranked according to the principle of marginal utility.
> (3) The systematic procurement . . . of such utilities for which all the necessary means of production are controlled by the actor himself. Where action is rational. (p. 71)

He continues in this mode, moving with irresistible logic—almost Aristotelianism—from one variety of "rational" economic behavior to the next, until he exhausts the possible universe of action (in, of course, a capitalist market). It is the very ease, strength, and confidence of his analysis, formal and removed from ordinary social reality as it is, that produces the remarkable contrast between Weber as analyst of economic behavior and Weber the sociologist proper. Qualification, backtracking, and equivocation usually indicate scholarly anxiety. The absence of these symptoms assures us of Weber's supreme confidence in his store of knowledge in the fields of law, economics, and agrarian reform and his ability to break it down into conceptual units. He writes here in a smooth discursive tone noticeable by its absence in other sociological sections of the work. Only very occasionally in the course of the lengthy and highly technical chapter 2, "Sociological Categories of Economic Action" (pp. 63–211), does Weber feel the need to introduce a social-psychological observation to bolster his pristine market analysis. A typical instance:

> But all manner of personal considerations may in such a case ["the administration of budgetary 'wealth'"] cause the entrepreneur to enter upon business policies which, in terms of the rationality of the conduct of enterprise, are irrational . . . Such factors as personal indebtedness of the proprietor, his personal demand for a higher present income . . . and the like, often exert what is, in terms of business considerations, a highly irrational influence on the business. . . . The interest in maintaining the private wealth of the owner is often irrational. (p. 98)

While it is undeniable that most of the time Weber presents his confident, scientific face, descriptively accurate reflections such as these do surface frequently enough to cause wonder at his unsystematic response to them. It is almost as if he believed he could block irrationality—pervasive, unavoidable, basic to human life—from impeding the serious business of theorizing if he simply incorporated caveats here and there, like seasoning in a stew otherwise rather bland. This explanation might pass muster were it not for Weber's tremendously incisive intellect, which could hardly have been lulled into witlessness by marginalist patter about rational action.

Continuing in *Economy and Society*, we find other, new uses of the term *irrationality*. On page 102, for instance, Weber uses it to mean "unprofitable." And, in proper dialectical form, as he widens the scope of what *irrationality* is to denote, he subtracts from *rationality* much of its explanatory power and descriptive utility. For instance:

> In combination with the complete indifference of even the formally most perfect rationality of capital accounting towards all substantive postulates, an indifference which is absolute if the market is perfectly free, the above statement permits us to see the ultimate limitation, inherent in its very structure, of the rationality of monetary economic calculation. It is, after all, of a purely formal character. . . . For the formal rationality of money accounting does not reveal anything about the actual distribution of goods. . . . It nevertheless holds true under all circumstances that formal rationality itself does not tell us anything about real want satisfaction unless it is combined with an analysis of the distribution of income. (pp. 108–109)

Almost in spite of himself, he forces the reader to begin viewing irrationality and substantive rationality (related in some instances) as considerably more interesting than their conceptual opposites: "Substantive and formal . . . rationality are, it should be stated again, after all largely distinct problems. This fundamental and, in the last analysis, unavoidable element of irrationality in economic systems is one of the important sources of all 'social' problems, and above all, of the problem of socialism" (p. 111).

It was in delineating this crucial relation between substantive and formal rationality (most thoroughly worked out in Weber's *Rechtssoziologie*), that Karl Mannheim dedicated several of his most memorable essays and books. It is often written, in this connection, that the two brilliant Jewish leftists from Budapest, Mannheim and Lukács, each, in their antithetical modes, took important Weberian themes to their conclusion. But what is not added is helpful speculation about Weber's hesitation to work out these conceptual problems himself. It is difficult to credit this omission simply to the element of time, since most of the gaps in rationalist analytic doctrine—probably the most telling one specifically pursued by Mannheim—Weber had discovered, and written about, a dozen years before his death.

In other ways he was every bit the courageous scholar, for instance, in his brief but illuminating treatment of "The Expropriation of Workers from the Means of Production" (pp. 137–140), where he finds still another use for *irrationality*. It was by no means de rigueur at the time this was written for respectable, bourgeois social scientists to incorporate explicitly Marxist terms into their analyses of capitalism and then to extend the range. This bespeaks a dauntlessness which somehow did not carry over into analysis of other pertinent social phenomena. He writes:

> The expropriation of workers *in general . . . from possession of the means of production has its economic* reasons above all in the following factors: (a) The fact that . . . it is generally possible to achieve a higher level of economic rationality if the management has extensive control over the selection and modes of use of workers, as compared with the situation created by the appropriation of jobs or the existence of rights to participate in management. These latter conditions produce technically irrational obstacles as well as economic irrationalities.
>
> The fact that the maximum of *formal* rationality in capital accounting is possible only where the workers are subjected to domination by entrepreneurs, is a further specific element of *substantive* irrationality in the modern economic order. (pp. 137–138)

Though Marx's passion and rhetorical fire are notably absent here (itself Weber's ploy to distance himself from radical dilettantism while maintaining a quasi-Marxist focus), his analytic view of capitalist domination is done a substantial service. Why, we might ask, if Weber was willing to champion a Marxist economic analysis, was he not also willing to put William James, Henri Bergson, or, much closer to home and entirely accessible, Max Scheler to work in supplementing his underdeveloped social psychological theory? (His refusal to do so is especially odd when we recall that he comments continually upon "empathy" and "sympathetic" understanding, plus various forms of "affectual" action—all of which Scheler had already written about at great length by 1912 or 1913.) This is not easily answered, particularly since it is seldom asked, and as a consequence there is not yet a backlog of scholarship upon which to build, as there is when dealing, for example, with Weber's posture regarding Marxism.[11]

Weber's fearlessness in applying his favorite dichotomy to virtually any substantive issue is displayed in this passage in "Methods and Aims of Monetary Policy" (pp. 180–184):

> Any lytric policy oriented to the *substantive* rationality of a planned economy, which it would seem to be far easier to develop with administrative and especially paper money, is at the same time far more likely to come to serve interests which, from the point of view of exchange rate stabilization, are irrational. For *formal* rationality (of the market-economy type) of lytric policy, and hence of the monetary system, can, in conformity with the definition of "rationality" consistently held to here, only mean: the exclusion of all interests which are . . . not market-oriented. (p. 183)

The tautological quality did not, I believe, so much escape Weber as befuddle him. That is, he recognized the circularity inherent in applying the dichotomy in this way, but he could not fix on an adequate solution to the dilemma. In fact, he compounds the logical ailments of his approach by including within the analysis matters of great substantive complexity and subtlety:

> Thus the use of administrative money, especially paper money, which can be cheaply produced in any desired form and quantity is, from the point of view of a *substantive* rationality, whatever its goals, the only correct way to handle the monetary question. This argument is conclusive in formal logical terms. Its value, however, is naturally limited in view of the fact that in the future as in the past it will be the "interests" of the individuals rather than the "ideas" of an economic administration which will rule the world. Thus, the possibility of conflict between *formal* rationality in the present sense and the *substantive* rationality which could theoretically be constructed for a lytric authority entirely free of any obligation to maintain hylodromy of a metal, has been demonstrated also for this point. (pp. 183–184)

Among other economic phenomena he classified as irrational were (1) the "danger" that a paper-money economy would suffer as a

---

11. See, for example, Robert J. Antonio and Ronald Glassman, eds., *A Weber-Marx Dialogue.*

result of inflationary government spending, something the "rational" metallic-standard economy does not face (p. 192); (2) the "intermittent" financing of enterprise through criminal organizations such as (to use Weber's example) the Neapolitan Camorra and the Sicilian Mafia (p. 195); (3) tax "lending" and "pledging," forms of "tax farming" (p. 196); and (4) "appropriation of benefices, status advantages," and bankers' commissions (p. 202).

In most of these examples, of course, the emphasis is upon "efficiency" and "predictability," those features of "rationality" most students of Weber have come to know, though not through the economic analysis per se. In fact, very little use is generally made by sociologists of this lengthy section in *Economy and Society*. Sociologists' understanding of "rational" as "efficient" comes for the most part from chapter 11, "Bureaucracy." The actual theoretical distance, however, between rationality as portrayed in the earlier (and in some ways more basic) chapter on "Categories of Economic Action" and the way it is used in the famous bureaucracy chapter principally reflects Weber's conformity to intellectual style and conceptualization in the former and his marked innovations in the latter. The fact, though, that rationality as used in the earlier chapter also makes more intrinsic sense has perhaps accounted for the myriad critiques of Weber's bureaucracy theory the field has endured for the past several decades. The earlier market chapter, by comparison, goes untouched and uncorrected.

> Though by no means alone, the capitalistic system has undeniably played a major role in the development of bureaucracy. Indeed, without it capitalistic production could not continue and any rational type of socialism would have simply to take it over and increase its importance. Its development, largely under capitalistic auspices, has created an urgent need for stable, strict, intensive, and calculable administration. . . . Conversely, capitalism is the most rational economic basis for bureaucratic administration and enables it to develop in the most rational form, especially because, from a fiscal point of view, it supplies the necessary money resources. (p. 224)

Currently a great deal of sociohistorical work is being done toward pinpointing the origin of what is generally called worker discipline, along with other victimizing aspects of capitalist development and the destruction of pre-capitalist Europe. Weber's remarks frequently make an appearance, but this particular connection—of bureaucratic domination linked to the supply of "necessary money re-

sources"—has somehow been missed. Historians critical of capitalist disciplining and the additional rationalizing of human activities
are inclined to conceive of Weber as the champion of capitalist bureaucratic efficiency and of the conquest of irrational pre-industrial
society. This is not quite accurate: "Socialism would . . . require a
still higher degree of formal bureaucratization than capitalism. If
this should prove not to be possible, it would demonstrate the existence of another of those fundamental elements of irrationality—a
conflict between formal and substantive rationality of the sort which
sociology so often encounters" (p. 225). Thus we see that for Weber
the "spirit of formalistic impersonality: '*Sine ira et studio*,' without
hatred or passion" (ibid.), is even more likely to infect and de-
humanize socialist than capitalist bureaucracy, such that intended
substantive rationality again falls before the inexorable power of
the merely formal.

The only form of authority that refuses, by its very nature, to be
neutralized and tamed is, of course, "charismatic," probably the favorite among Weber scholars due to Weber's own obvious predilections. He writes of this completely irrational ideal-type in glowing
terms:

> Since it is "extra-ordinary," charismatic authority is sharply opposed
> to rational, and particularly bureaucratic, authority, and to tradi-
> tional authority, whether in its patriarchal, patrimonial, or estate
> variants, all of which are everyday forms of domination; while the
> charismatic type is the direct antithesis of this. Bureaucratic au-
> thority is specifically rational in the sense of being bound to *intellec-
> tually analysable* rules. (p. 244; emphasis added)

This is among the clearest of Weber's many admissions that we, as
social analysts, are to equate behavior we can understand ("logical") with that which is—ontologically, as it were—"rational." I
have pointed out above the fallacy of this assumption, an objection that has gained its clearest expression in discussions among
British theorists (notably anthropologists), who must interpret pre-
rationalized behavior patterns. They worry, of course, that attri-
butions of rationality or irrationality may be inaccurate, to use
Weber's own terms, "on the level of meaning."[12] Apparently untroubled by this epistemological difficulty, Weber continues:

12. This debate received its single biggest push when Peter Winch published
The Idea of a Social Science and Its Relation to Philosophy and was extended considerably

> Charismatic authority is specifically irrational in the sense of being
> foreign to all rules. Traditional authority is bound to the precedents
> handed down from the past and to this extent is also oriented to
> rules. Within the sphere of its claims, charismatic authority repudi-
> ates the past, and is in this sense a specifically revolutionary force.
> . . . The only basis of legitimacy for it is personal charisma so long
> as it is proved; that is, as long as it receives recognition. (ibid.)

And moving to a more psychological level, less abstracted from
historical experience:

> In traditionalist periods, charisma is *the* great revolutionary force.
> The likewise revolutionary force of "reason" works from *without:* by
> altering the situations of life and hence its problems, finally in this
> way changing men's attitudes toward them; or it intellectualizes the
> individual. Charisma, on the other hand, *may* effect a subjective or
> *internal* reorientation born out of suffering, conflicts, or enthusiasm.
> It may then result in a radical alteration of the central attitudes and
> directions of action with a completely new orientation of all attitudes
> toward the different problems of the "world." In prerationalistic pe-
> riods, tradition and charisma between them have almost exhausted
> the whole of the orientation of action. (p. 245)

This is a very strong statement, one that announces a virtual philosophy of history. For to argue, as Weber does, that there were
"prerationalistic periods" (a new phrase) in which a type or types
of cognition and resultant action "exhausted the whole of the orientation of action" is to claim a good deal more than historical data
are likely to support. It is certainly a more drastic, culturally holistic assertion than Weber has previously made, and one from which
contemporary sociology retreats. The level of analysis has shifted
abruptly, as a result, one might imagine, of Weber's unconcealed
excitement over certain specific charismatic leaders (especially the
Hebrew prophets). He casts aside, for the most part, the "mannered" reservations and qualifications which usually dominate his
discourse built around ideal-types, particularly the rational type.
Tempered Weberian caution seems for the moment transcended.

Nothing remarkable occurs again in the text regarding Weber's
treatment of irrationality until "Part 2," written a good deal earlier
than "Part 1" and bearing the inscrutable (but semi-relevant) title

---

by contributors to Bryan R. Wilson's collection *Rationality,* the most relevant articles
of which are those by I. C. Jarvi and Joseph Agassi, Martin Hollis, and J. H. M.
Beatie.

"The Economy and the Arena of Normative and De Facto Powers."
In an excursus written to rebut Stammler, Weber details the attitude suitable to social science when viewing habituation, routini-
zation, the pressure of convention, and other factors bearing upon
the effectiveness of law:

> For the sociologists, the legal, and particularly the rationally en-
> acted, regulation of conduct is empirically only one of the factors mo-
> tivating social action; moreover, it is a factor which usually appears
> late in history and whose effectiveness varies greatly. The beginnings
> of actual regularity and "usage," shrouded in darkness everywhere,
> are attributed by the sociologist, as we have seen, to the instinctive
> habituation of a pattern of conduct which was "adapted" to given
> necessities. . . . The increasing intervention of enacted norms is . . .
> only one of the components, however characteristic, of that process
> of rationalization and association whose growing penetration into all
> spheres of social action we shall have to trace as a most essential dy-
> namic factor in development. (p. 333)

In his concern simultaneously to categorize and analyze all the
possible groups common to pre-rational and rational societies,
Weber introduces still more varied inventories of attitudes and behaviors that can be characterized as irrational. One of the more interesting is Weber's linking of irrationality with "enthusiasm," as
opposed to personally unexciting "systematic rational 'enterprise'":

> If a group pays somebody to act as a continuous and deliberate
> "organ" of their common interests . . . an association comes into
> being. . . . Henceforth, some persons are professionally interested
> in the retention of the existing, and the recruitment of new mem-
> bers. It does not matter here whether they are paid to represent (hid-
> den or naked) sexual interests [a veiled reference to Otto Gross and
> also to one of Weber's lawsuits involving unsavory references to his
> wife] or other "non-material" or, finally, economic interests . . .
> whether they are public speakers paid by the piece or salaried secre-
> taries. The pattern of intermittent and irrational action is replaced by
> a systematic rational "enterprise," which continues to function long
> after the original enthusiasm of the participants for their ideals has
> vanished. (p. 345)

As we might expect by this time, Weber withholds his opinion
about the net effect of enthusiasm's passing and being replaced by
the activity of salaried functionaries. While from one point of view
he is impressed with this contemporary development (for instance,
in huge American political parties: pp. 344–345), from another
he clearly sees the long-term danger: as irrationally unreliable as

"ideals" undoubtedly are, they do produce in their bearers tremendous capability for sacrifice and energetic activity, and without this component any organization risks torpor under hardened bureaucrats. For this condition (already in evidence in certain government agencies when Weber wrote), he proposed no palliative, perhaps believing none existed.

One of the persistent irrationalities of contemporary European life fascinated Weber, yet he wrote of it only sparsely. The first mention, with a concrete example, appears on pages 377–378, where he contrasts the "quite disparate systems, affected especially by different ethnic composition, e.g., Poles and Germans." Weber saw ethnic associations, proclivities, and traits as combining to produce "factors that could be regarded as economically 'irrational' from the very beginning, or that became irrational as a consequence of changes in economic conditions" (p. 378). Whether in discussing the "poor white trash" in the United States or the recurrent myth of "the chosen people" (p. 391), Weber's perspective on ethnic beliefs and behavior foreshadows almost exactly that of contemporary social science. Yet in place of today's essentially political or stratificational emphasis, Weber substitutes cultural or mythical factors. His definition of ethnicity involves "the subjective belief in . . . common descent," "presumed [group] identity," and "overarching communal consciousness" (p. 389), all of which culminate in a "rather low degree of rationalization." But after having presented what even by today's standards would be regarded as a lucid, penetrating, and balanced account of ethnicity (and its difference from kinship), he writes:

> All in all, the notion of "ethnically" determined social action subsumes phenomena that a rigorous sociological analysis—as we do not attempt it here—would have to distinguish carefully: the actual subjective effect of those customs conditioned by heredity and those determined by tradition; the differential impact of the varying content of custom; the influence of common language, religion and political action, past and present, upon the formation of customs; the extent to which such factors create attraction and repulsion, and especially the belief in affinity or disaffinity of blood; the consequences of this belief for social action in general, and specifically for action on the basis of shared custom or blood relationship, for diverse sexual relations, etc.—all of this would have to be studied in detail. (pp. 394–395)

Even though he modestly admits not having accomplished a solid analysis of the phenomena himself (and suggests, furthermore, that "we do not pursue sociology for its own sake and therefore limit ourselves to showing briefly the diverse factors that are hidden behind this seemingly uniform phenomenon," p. 395), this unwillingness to pursue "ethnicity" sufficiently may be in fact another example of Weber's trepidation when facing irrationality at its barest. This distinctive trait of Weber's own work does not bode well for Weberian sociology as it is conceived today, since so many recent and ongoing manifestations of gross irrationality erupt precisely from ethnic and nationalist attachments (which frequently are related, as in Africa). Whereas bureaucracy and the market (analyzed for two hundred pages in *Economy and Society*) no longer pose theoretical or substantive problems for sociology in the way they did for Weber, ethnicity and nationalism (receiving less than twenty pages of attention) seem as irrationally resistant to scrutiny now as then. Perhaps to this extent the ideal-typical method, predicated upon rational models, does indeed include a bit of conceptual realism, in that those items most easily laid open to examination are also those furthest along the continuum toward the rational end. Certainly this occurred to Weber, but only infrequently (and parenthetically) did he admit it.

Volume 2 of *Economy and Society* encompasses two of Weber's most stunning synthetic achievements, his sociologies of religion and of law. Perhaps it is already clear from some of the above that religion and law (following the "apprentice" decade of the 1890s) were the dearest substantive areas for Weber; his contributions via sweeping nomothetic statements about each, augmented by mountainous documentation, deserve books of commentary unto themselves. The few pages which follow represent nothing more than scholarly instrumentalism in search of a conclusion, but they are offered without apology. There may be only a slim theoretical justification for truncated exegesis of this material. But while one of my goals has been to elucidate Weber's understanding of irrationality in all its manifestations and as it affects all aspects of social life, in fact I have been throughout far more interested in his conceptualizations as they apply to modern industrial society than to any of the other dozen (essentially historical) societies he analyzed. A very close reading of the sociologies of both religion and law reveals that quite nearly all the data Weber presents originate in ancient, medieval, or early modern Europe, ancient Islam, and the pre-modern Orient. As a consequence, the substance of the first volume, as well as some of the earlier studies, more readily lends itself to contemporary usages than that making up volume 2. Paradoxically, perhaps, study of volume 2 turns out to be on the whole far more rewarding than of volume 1, since Weber treads more lightly, paying less attention to formalist analysis and more to historical and anthropological description. But for this very reason the modern theoretical temperament looks more favorably upon elements of the testable formalism and seems less enchanted with, for instance, Weber's brilliant analysis of ritual magic or arcane aspects of Islamic law.

An overview of the entire *Religionssoziologie* (pp. 399–634) discloses a single unmistakable tendency that can be obscured somewhat by intense reading of random sections: coercion, however skillful, of even the most constitutionally irrational religious beliefs and practices into some form of rational explanation. This reaches ludicrous extremes at times, though for the most part Weber saves himself from clumsy rationalism with his usual arrangement of qualifications coupled with linguistic craftiness. An excellent example of this occurs in two sections the purpose of which is to summarize the effects of religion upon the "non-privileged strata" and at the same time to consider the related Nietzschean concept of *ressentiment*. The reader is first met with this blunt, overwhelming simplification and reduction concerning "the specific importance of salvation religion for politically and economically disprivileged social groups": "This psychological condition, when turned outward toward the other social strata, produces certain characteristic contrasts in what religion must provide for the various social strata. Since every need for salvation is an expression of some distress, social or economic oppression is an effective source of salvation beliefs, though by no means the exclusive source" (p. 491). The retraction and correction, though not at all complete, comes several pages further on, in the last paragraph of the section.[13]

---

13. Throughout this section, Weber carefully puts his most ambitious and exciting notions to work in genuine "closing paragraphs," a technique he did not bother

Precisely this example . . . demonstrates that the need for salvation and ethical religion has yet another source besides the social condition of the disprivileged and the rationalism of the bourgeoisie, which is shaped by its way of life. This additional factor is intellectualism as such, more particularly the metaphysical needs of the human mind as it is driven to reflect on ethical and religious questions, driven not by material need but by an inner compulsion to understand the world as a meaningful cosmos and to take up a position toward it. (p. 499)

Weber sidesteps the dangers of a Marxist explanation for religious life—which, it appears, gives life to the first passage—by adopting a mitigated "idealist" interpretation that he labels intellectualism but which would be better termed spiritualism. Certainly his remarks in these paragraphs do not hold up well when compared to more recent work by psychologists of religion such as Gordon Allport. There is no longer any doubt that extra-sociological or extra-economic factors—originating, in other words, in internal events of individualized consciousness—must be part of any comprehensive "explanation" of religious behavior.

Weber begins his rationalist onslaught on the bastion of irrationalism with the observation that "religiously or magically motivated behavior is relatively rational behavior especially in its earliest manifestations" (p. 400). Since it "follows rules of experience, though it is not necessarily action in accordance with a means-end schema," this generalization logically follows: "Thus, religious or magical behavior or thinking must not be set apart from the range of everyday purposive conduct, particularly since even the ends of the religious and magical actions are predominantly economic" (p. 400). Clearly this gets discussion off on a particular tack, but one Weber modifies a good deal as he progresses.

In the introductory paragraphs of "Magic and Religion" Weber proposes an evolutionary dialectic of religious development during

---

with in much of the other materials. As a consequence, it is frequently the case that his most important comments about irrationality are included in the final lines of each section, which makes perfect sense, since the *Irrationalitätsproblem* was obviously one of his most pressing and complicated themes. Weber makes reference either directly or by implication to some aspect of irrationality on the following pages of this section: 400, 417, 424, 425, 431, 433, 438, 446, 470, 471, 472, 476, 479, 482, 505, 506, 523, 535, 538, 539, 542, 544, 548, 550, 551, 552, 554, 567, 569, 571, 572, 573, 584, 601, 602–610, 619, 626. *Rationality* and its cognates appear on virtually every page, in dozens of constructions.

which the "original, practical, and calculating rationalism" which, he believes, initiated religion gives way to "successively 'irrationalized' . . . otherworldly, non-economic goals" (p. 424). Put another way, people begin to take religion seriously, and at the same time put aside its "original" instrumental functions. Weber presents sparse evidence for these claims. In pursuit of generalizations about religion as a social force rather than a phenomenon sui generis, he investigates the "rationalization of taboo" and speculates that through the "incredible irrationality of its painfully onerous norms" (p. 433) taboos that separated status groups, protected scarce commodities, and so on should be thought of as "the first and most general instance of the direct harnessing of religion to extra-religious purposes." This sort of facile functional analysis typifies most of what follows. At points, however, he gives himself over to a softer approach, for instance in discussing prophecy. There he notes that the "important religious conception of the world as a cosmos . . . is challenged to produce somehow a 'meaningful,' ordered totality," and with genuine perception writes:

> The conflict between empirical reality and this conception of the world as a meaningful totality, which is based on the religious postulate, produces the strongest tensions in man's inner life as well as in his external relationship to the world. . . . The ultimate question of all metaphysics has always been something like this: if the world as a whole and life in particular were to have a meaning, what might it be, and how would the world have to look in order to correspond to it? (p. 451)

Here, of course, without saying so directly, Weber is addressing the most absolutely irrational of all human cognitive propensities: the need, nay, demand, to know unknowables. Since this need lies so close to the surface of all religious systems and since it does emanate from a splendidly irrational substrate, Weber subdued it whenever he could and turned attention to matters more susceptible to intellectual rationalization.

This brings up Weber's fascinating, nearly inspired treatment of "Intellectualism, Intellectuals, and Salvation Religion" (pp. 500–518). He begins, logically enough, by discussing the "devaluation" of sensuality that always precedes "a disposition toward an 'illuminative' mysticism . . . associated with a distinctively intellectual qualification for salvation" (p. 505). Then this remarkable and very unordinary analysis appears:

The exaggeration and fastidious refinement of sexuality, along with the simultaneous suppression of normal sexuality in favor of substitute abreactions, were determined by the life patterns of those who might be termed "nothing-but-intellectuals"; and these exaggerations and suppressions of sexuality occasionally played a role for which modern psychopathology has not yet formulated uniformly applicable rules. These phenomena are strongly reminiscent of certain phenomena, especially in the Gnostic mysteries, which clearly appear to have been sublimated masturbatory surrogates for the orgies of the peasantry. These purely psychological preconditions of the process whereby religion is irrationalized are intersected by the natural rationalistic needs for intellectualism to conceive the world as a meaningful cosmos. (p. 505)

Analysis of this kind (which may, according to Mitzman and others, have had some autobiographical basis) does not often find its way into Weber's work. It becomes particularly interesting when viewed against the background of his more stolid, formal prose and assumes an even stranger place in *Economy and Society* generally when followed, as it is, by this:

The salvation sought by the intellectual is always based on inner need, and hence it is at once more remote from life, more theoretical and more systematic than salvation from external distress, the quest for which is characteristic of nonprivileged strata. The intellectual seeks in various ways, the casuistry of which extends into infinity, to endow his life with a pervasive meaning, and thus to find unity with himself, with his fellow men, and with the cosmos. It is the intellectual who conceives of the "world" as a problem of meaning. As intellectualism suppresses belief in magic, the world's processes become disenchanted, lose their magical significance, and henceforth simply "are" and "happen" but no longer signify anything. As a consequence, there is a growing demand that the world and the total patterns of life be subject to an order that is significant and meaningful. (p. 506)

If the platitude is true that writers, even social theorists, are at their best when considering topics closest to their hearts, surely the power, precision, and credibility of these passages allow the reader a rare glimpse into Weber's inmost metaphysical concerns. His mother's uncritical religiosity and his own zealous skepticism, slammed together by a son's confused love for an unbending mother and his simultaneous admiration of his father's unreflective pragmatism, caused no end of personal problems. Some of these are expressed here in highly sublimated but nonetheless obvious form. This subject presented Weber with one of the few opportunities in his work to solve a substantive problem of research while "speaking from the heart." And as I said, whenever he allowed himself to do this the results were inevitably excellent.

In sharp contrast to his analysis of irrationality and the intellectual's "religion" is his examination of techniques which aim at "salvation through self-perfection": "Ecstasy as an instrument of salvation or self-deification, our exclusive interest here, may have the essential character of an acute mental aberration or possession, or else the character of a chronically heightened idiosyncratic religious mood, tending either toward great intensity of life or toward alienation from life" (p. 535). Again he verges on a blunder by labeling religious ecstasy as "acute mental aberration," a phrase which for him was probably synonymous with "insanity." In his addition that "these acute ecstasies are transitory in their nature and apt to leave but few positive traces on everyday behavior," we sense even more his lack of empathy, even antipathy, for the phenomenon. Consider the complementary portrait: "The person who lives as a worldly ascetic is a rationalist, not only in the sense that he rationally systematized his own conduct, but also in his rejection of everything that is ethically irrational, esthetic, or dependent upon his own emotional reactions to the world and its institutions. The distinctive goal always remains the alert, methodical control of one's own pattern of life and behavior" (p. 544). How thoroughly incompatible with the "ethically irrational . . . sensual pleasures" of ecstasy, brought on by "acute toxic states, by music and dance; by sexuality . . . in short by orgy" (p. 535). This agrees with another dictum: "Rational ascetic alertness, self-control, and methodical planning of life are threatened the most by the peculiar irrationality of the sexual act, which is ultimately and uniquely unsusceptible to rational organization" (p. 604). It may not be too much to suppose that Weber's very circumscribed sensual life and that of his friends and acquaintances for the most part, plus his mother's advanced state of pietist sexual repression, blunted somewhat his ability to understand "ecstatic" or otherwise irrational states. (It has only been recently, in fact, that sociologists have shown much aptitude in analyzing such conditions, for previously they imitated practices of the founding fathers, among them Weber.)

In my opinion the most penetrating analysis within the *Religionssoziologie* takes place within part 3 of section 14, "The Tension

Between Ethical Religion and Art" (pp. 607–610). Some of the comments are familiar from earlier work: "Just as ethical religion . . . enters into the deepest inner tensions with the strongest irrational power of personal life, namely sexuality, so also does ethical religion enter into a strong polarity with the sphere of art" (p. 607). We will not pause to examine this material, since its theoretical drift was already presented in "The Social Psychology of the World Religions" and "Religious Rejections of the World and Their Directions." Instead I will close this curt interpretation of this part of *Economy and Society* with another quote, one that again, I believe, reveals more about Weber's analytic bias than perhaps even he realized: "The alert self-control of the Puritan flowed from the necessity of his subjugating all creaturely impulses to a rational and methodical plan of conduct. . . . Self-control appeared to the Confucian as a personal necessity which followed from his disesteem for plebeian irrationality, the disesteem of an educated gentleman . . . bred along lines of propriety and dignity" (p. 619).

Weber's sociology of law is a monument of learning which I cannot deal with adequately here. Irrationality is pitted against its opposite in this work in a more thoroughgoing way than in any of the previous works. In them, irrationality meant a great many things, but all those meanings shared a basic anti-predictability or participation in the realm of the nonrepressed. In the sociology of law, the situation is much more complicated. As Rheinstein points out in the splendid introduction to his edition,[14] the reader must deal not merely with rational versus irrational law but with the following categories, each very technically defined: "irrational law," under which are the subcategories "formal irrationality" and "substantive irrationality"; and "rational law," under which fall "substantive rationality" and "formal rationality," itself further subdivided into "extrinsically formal" and "logically formal." Each of these types is illustrated with a multitude of cross-cultural examples. English common law, for example, is a perfect instance of "substantively irrational" law. In any case, I cannot interpret this opus here,[15] both

14. *Max Weber On Law in Economy and Society*, ed. and annotation by Max Rheinstein; trans. Edward Shils and Max Rheinstein, p. xlii. The best guide to Weber's sociology of law is Anthony T. Kronman, *Max Weber*, esp. pp. 75–83, 119–125.
15. One last time for the record: those pages in Rheinstein's edition on which important reference is made to irrationality of one form or another (remember that

because of its extraordinary divergence, in form and content, from any of Weber's other works and because it redefines the terms of interest here to such an extent that little said so far would apply. It is truly a task for another occasion.

---

these instances do not necessarily parallel those in other editions) are as follows: xl, xlii, xlvii (pp. 1–40 are reprinted from portions of *Wirtschaft und Gesellschaft*, already discussed), 59, 63, 73, 75, 78, 79, 80, 86, 87, 89, 90, 131, 136, 145, 210, 214, 224, 227, 228, 229, 232, 237, 241, 243, 260, 261, 263, 264, 265, 267, 278, 282, 297, 303, 307, 309, 311, 313, 315, 317–319, 351, 354, 356. It will be noted that I am leaving aside as well volume 3 of *Economy and Society*, which includes *The City* as well as the "Bureaucracy" chapter. This omission is primarily because of its limited theoretical interest regarding our focus here, and also for reasons of space.

6

Irrationality in Social Life Reconsidered

The Unacknowledged Dialogue of Weber and Pareto

Early in this effort to view Weber's achievement in a somewhat different light from the usual, I called upon the Dilthey expert H. A. Hodges for a corrective statement about irrationality in human action. I then noted that his "position harmonizes with that of Vilfredo Pareto, who will serve hereafter as theoretical foil to Weber concerning irrationality in social life." This raises several issues. First, why a "foil" rather than a more directly compared referent? The word connotes a lesser character in a narrative which, when contrasted to or juxtaposed with the protagonist, illuminates characteristics of the latter that the author wishes known, and not just *any* characteristics, but "good" ones often brought out by maligning or trivializing the foil. Though I have not belabored Pareto to profit Weber, my study agrees with contemporary prejudice by working harder at understanding Weber's textual and subtextual meaning than it will in ascertaining and explicating Pareto's. The reasons for this are several. First, it would be deemed quixotic, even indefensible, at this stage in the history of the discipline to write an extended essay based on the premise that Pareto is the greater sociologist. Judging from publications of the last several decades in the United States, Great Britain, and Germany, this contention would be impossible even to bring up; in France it might receive a polite hearing; and in Italy, serious arguments could be made on its behalf.[1] But even in Italy, senior sociologists such as

---

1. See Piet Tommissen's definitive bibliography, both of Pareto's own works (numbering in the hundreds) and studies of him, in Pareto's *Oeuvres Complètes*, vol. 20, pp. 71–110 for Pareto's works, pp. 111–249 for the secondary works, which lists 1,823 items in English, French, German, and Italian. Note should also be taken of two articles from the main organ for Pareto studies, *Cahiers Vilfredo Pareto*, a multilingual quarterly: John E. Tashjean, "Interest in Pareto's Sociology: Reflections on a Bibliography," and the companion piece, Jaroslav Bilous and John H. Quirk, "Interest in Pareto's Sociology: An Essay in the Quantitative History of Social Science." Both articles document a high level of scholarly productivity associated with Pareto,

Franco Ferrarotti have declared themselves Weberians or Marxists, and while they are far more appreciative of Pareto's contributions than their colleagues who lack Italian or French, they content themselves with a sub-Weberian Pareto.

Strong features of Pareto's decline in sociological reputation, since the 1930s, are extra-intellectual. His antidemocratic political philosophy, its unfortunate and counterfeit coupling in the academic imagination with Mussolini's political crimes, and even his extremely peculiar, resolutely obdurate, and hermetic life as *du savant de Céligny* (as he is known to the faithful) have turned away droves of potential students and emulators. By contrast, Weber's institutionalized Sunday afternoon seminars in Heidelberg, facilitated by a charming and brilliant wife (which Pareto lacked), his own *gemütlich* treatment of students and colleagues, plus his continuous association with important journals and professional groups, all promoted his apotheosis. These sorts of contrasts between the "accessible" Weber and the "vitriolic" Pareto (images which naturally evade reality by a sizable margin),[2] and all the contiguous aspects of their private lives as dedicated scholars could be extended into a study itself: a "sociology of forefathers' imagery," it might be called. But in fact, this particular strategy of comparison—hermeneutically important, in an accessory role, as it could be—is for present purposes quite irrelevant.[3]

---

though, of course, most of it comes from Europe. The only two immediately recognizable Pareto enthusiasts and scholars in American social science are Joseph Lopreato in sociology and Vincent Tarascio in economics. Together their Pareto publications number more than a score. But even so recently as November 1976, the non-Paretian Raymond Aron published "Interpreting Pareto: The Marx of the Bourgeoisie?" seemingly out of the blue, so Lopreato and Tarascio are not completely idiosyncratic in their Paretian interests.

2. For a portrait of Pareto as a polite, gentle, solicitous, and gentlemanly host and friend, see the classic remarks by an Italian socialist who, among many others, found refuge in Pareto's home during "Bloody '98": Vittorio Racca, "Working with Pareto." Along the same lines, the most recent, reliable, and accessible essay in English which punctures an entire array of myths concerning Pareto's personality, his politics, and his work is Joseph Lopreato, "Notes on the Work of Vilfredo Pareto." It serves as a general introduction to a five-article symposium on Pareto, an unusual undertaking in American journals.

3. I disagree with Lopreato's entirely negative evaluation of interest in these matters, particularly regarding Pareto (which he describes as "gossip and contumely," "Notes," p. 459). He seems to have forgotten that the "true" Pareto, like the "true" Weber, is not likely to be established in any given intellectual epoch, and in place of this desirable but unlikely goal, the image of a theorist and his achievement serves as reality for most students devoid of detailed knowledge.

I am not going to argue, then, that were it not for Pareto's supposedly unappealing extra-intellectual qualities he would now be
embraced as the preeminent forefather of the discipline and that,
conversely, had Weber been less politic in German academe his
work might today be less honored. I am willing to admit for present purposes—not having sufficient space to prove otherwise—
that Weber's *Wirtschaft und Gesellschaft* and *Religionssoziologie*, qua
sociology and sociological theory, are "better" (that is, for contemporary uses) than Pareto's sociology and sociological theory represented in his *Trattato di Sociologia Generale* and *The Rise and Fall of the
Elites*, "the two major texts to which the non-economist is generally
referred when he makes inquiry about the non-economic—or more
properly, the other than economic—contributions of Pareto."[4]
Even more to the point, Weber's approach to irrationality also
seems "better" (this time in a larger, not necessarily utilitarian
sense), more subtle and perceptive at points than Pareto's, particularly in the former's discussions of art and religion—two human activities for which Pareto had no talent or sympathy. His intellectual
aesthetics regarding these manifestations of irrationality (this time
in Weber's sense) were deficient, and his analysis overall paid
dearly for this lack. Why, then, bother with Pareto at all? Before the
answer is supplied, a dual codification is necessary, one to explain
Weber's position on irrationality, the other to counterpose Pareto's.

If Chapter 2 reveals nothing else, it displays the inordinate tension Weber felt when faced with irrationality, in his life as well as
when theorizing. As we have seen, he virtually ignored the problem during his first decade of mountainous scholarship. But privately (as expressed in his letters), from adolescence into manhood, behavior and thought foreign to the *zweckrational* model
popularly personified by Bismarck's *Realpolitik* both appalled and
fascinated Weber. And yet, when all the relevant documents have
been examined no crystalline, axiomatic, definitive, or systematic
body of propositions or even of internally consistent observations
emerges. Rather, the rudiments of an inventory of attitudes and
correlated behaviors to which Weber haphazardly attached the
word *irrational* (or *emotional, affective*, and so on) begin to appear.

<hr />

4. Marion J. Levy, Jr., "A Sociologist Who Knew Science," p. 469. Although these
two items do comprise most of what is available in English, there are other translations, and a few pieces Pareto wrote originally in English for British publications.

This is hardly a propitious foundation either for a sociological theory of irrationality or for a complete theory of rationality. Perhaps while writing the unfinished sociology of art, Weber could have forced himself to look these inscrutables in the eye and propose a coherent body of theory not in form unlike his systematized reflections on the historical rationalization of law. (Certainly his young friend Lukács was pushing him in this direction, as were others.) But as it stands we have little more than series of constantly repeated adjectives and adverbs, which, over time, took on for Weber the duties of theory proper, a burden for which they were not suited.

What, then, can we say about Weber's understanding of irrationality, given that he was unable (and I believe that is the correct word) to offer his audience a matured, developed theory? First, like most political economists (especially, of course, Pareto), he was perfectly aware that the (Menger) model of rational action around which he built his ideal-types, including the four types of *Handeln*, had little to do with the bulk of human life or even with most action per se. Naturally, this discounted all the theoretically "uninteresting" components of life as lived such as fantasy, contemplation, reverie, sleep, dreams, isolated quiet, individual work or play, and all the thousand other daily mental and physical events which according to Weber's special definitions did not qualify as "social." (This vast store of humanness phenomenology has claimed for itself by noting, as did Husserl, that positivist and reductionist epistemologies or even, as Schutz noted, *verstehende Soziologie* were uninterested and incompetent to handle the data.) Thus Weber realized that the "real kernel" of life rested in the other than rational. This he admitted freely and even documented over and over again. Why he did not, therefore, do more in the way of including this realization in his *Hauptwerk* (excluding the significant sections on the sociologies of religion and law) remains something of a mystery, though sheer lack of time may be partly accountable.

Weber made dozens of particular uses of the term *irrationality*, either as part of a given explanation for behavior or as his own explanation in foreswearing examination of certain phenomena, as if to say that the irrational was ipso facto impenetrable. But he was not consistent in this or in other important ways in his treatment of the problem, except of course in his lifelong resistance to demands (by Knies, Roscher, Meyer, and others) that irrationality be formally admitted into theoretical reflection, which to him seemed the ultimate contradiction in terms. For Weber, to theorize about social action was to bring it within rational reflection, and through ideal-typification to identify anomalies either as explainable minor deviations from the pure type or as irrationalities and therefore irrelevant. This absolutism in serving the highest epistemological premises put his formal analytic procedures in a straitjacket from which even his splendid capacities could not extricate them. Exegesis of Weber's writings brings out a confused and confounded, though at the same time perceptively brilliant, posture toward irrationality. There can be no *conclusive* rendering of Weber's position, for he never created one. In its place, we can only speculate.

We have come upon the first of several motives for citing Pareto as Weber's foil. Whereas Weber's search for a universal model of action ended in frustration and only partial completion, Pareto completed his project exhaustively. And while *Wirtschaft und Gesellschaft* was published under the auspices of hands other than Weber's, Pareto enjoyed the good fortune of seeing all his major works, including the *Trattato*, through the press long before his death and adjusting them meticulously to reflect his developing notions. Thus there is definite closure to Pareto's sociological project that Weber's chronically lacks, and the tentative nature of the latter's action theory (especially regarding its distance from actual application to contemporary and historical materials) is well reflected in the *Irrationalitätsproblem*. Not only did Pareto have the time and energy to delineate all fifty-two types of "sentiments," lavishly illustrated, but his prose style speaks confidently, without the epistemological qualms that inhibit the nonengineer. Pareto, the pioneer econometrician, railroad executive, and iron-mine superintendent and engineer, stands utterly opposed in his redoubtable self-confidence and discursive aggressiveness to Weber the pure scholar, alienated psychically from much of the mundanity around him, alien at times even to his own consciousness. If they shared any personal characteristic, it was in a rabid dedication to hard work and a mutual curiosity about the limits of rational behavior. Beyond that, they make excellent and equal foils to one another.

Let us return momentarily to the question of theoretical coherence. I have written above that Weber's remarks about behavioral irrationality are in many ways superior to Pareto's, yet it is undebatable that Weber's fragmentary edifice seems paltry compared to Pareto's finished system. The paradox is apparent, not real. Beginning in 1870, at twenty-two, Pareto's fascination with systemic equilibrium states was established (as reflected in his dissertation). This orientation, clearly an artifact of Pareto's knowledge of natural science coupled with advanced mathematics, inspired his lifelong accumulation of data with which to illustrate his master—and minor—arguments, whether in the early *Cours d'économie politique* (1896), the encyclopedic *Les Systèmes socialistes* (1902), the groundbreaking *Manuale di Economia Politica* (1906), or the *Trattato* (1916). We have seen that Weber did not locate until relatively late a master concept, and even when he did settle on *rationalization,* around 1913, he did not allow himself to be coerced by his own pet notion into corralling data, willy-nilly, from unrelated sources. Pareto scoured newspapers from all over Europe in search of examples of his various "sentiments" and their "derivations," but this mode of discovery was totally outside Weber's conception of science and interpretative thought.

So we discover the first of many paradoxes surrounding the two men. Pareto's champions inevitably make claims that he was above all an excellent scientist, zealously dedicated to the logico-experimental method of inquiry and an implacable enemy of mystification, idealism, and ontological quandaries of all kinds. Weber is not so regarded. In spite of his call for "objectivity," it is generally agreed that Weber worked in the epistemological shadow of Dilthey, Rickert, Windelband, even Simmel to some extent, and therefore carried into his sociology a self-consciously reflective, unmistakably philosophical, relativist element. Nevertheless, it is my contention that, at least with regard to irrationality, Weber was the better scientist. This is difficult to explain briefly.

To say he was a superior observer is unfair on two counts: (1) he observed, in the strict sense, relatively little except in the way of historical data, whereas Pareto's sociological work revolves principally around contemporary events and those from antiquity, so that he had to look sharply to current happenings in a way Weber seldom did except when writing his wartime essays; (2) if to observe social life means to keep an exhaustive account of events while attributing supposed causes and effects, Pareto is virtually unrivaled. Is Weber then the finer analyst? This too is problematic, for Pareto's analytic techniques bore the pristine seal of pure science. Obviously, the usual categories for assessing scientific skill do not fit the case. Weber's dissection of and commentary upon irrationality surpassed Pareto's for psychological reasons alone: he could empathize with types of human experience which escaped Pareto as surely as Pareto's simultaneous equations would have stunned and bypassed Weber. As psychologistic as this may appear, it is nevertheless true that Pareto's mindset could not accommodate, without reduction, certain behavior patterns, among them those most irrational: artistic or aesthetic predilections, religious fervor, sexual or orgiastic frenzy, and genuine insanity. Of course the *Trattato* is packed with examples of just these items, but their presence, it will be noted, only serves to sharpen Pareto's vitriolic prose, his debunking, as it were. Whereas Weber interpreted social reality (past and present) with extraordinary attention to "objective possibility" and "adequacy on the level of meaning," Pareto's razor-like intellect was far more closely attuned (in typical Italian style, one might add) to carving away the embroidered explanations and illusions surrounding social action than to comprehending its meaning for the actors themselves. This methodological decision greatly simplified his task, and he could progress rapidly and voluminously in documenting the fifty-two "sentiments." Where Weber hedged, qualified, vacillated, Pareto boldly pushed ahead, brilliantly sizing up, then cutting down whatever data fit his theoretical needs.

And yet, Weber's superior interpretative ability and sensitivity—in short, his better science—notwithstanding, Pareto's perspective must be given the final accolade, and not that of his German contemporary, if we choose to pursue irrationality in the most comprehensive manner. So that I may not be accused of sophistry or gratuitous paradox, let me reiterate. Weber's *verstehende Soziologie* surpassed, I believe, Pareto's logico-experimental method in terms of *general* observational and analytic validity. Therefore it should not be surprising that Weber's specific treatments and comments about irrationality—when he chose to include them, as he did more and more toward the end of his career—very frequently verge on the brilliant, at least by our own standards. More important, they seem adequate, since they do not indulge in obsessive debunking and the distortion that inevitably accompanies it. The unfortunate fact is this, however: Weber very early on, largely in response to sectarian arguments among German social scientists, decided to exclude the irrational *for certain formal analytic purposes.* This central, preeminent, inviolable choice stands in perfect opposition to Pareto's. As is ritually pointed out in overviews of the latter's work, by the time he had composed two lengthy and much lauded treatises on political economy he realized how deficient the rational model was for the scientist who strove for holistic sociological analysis. This lesson Weber had in fact learned several years prior to Pareto's awakening. But he could not take the requisite theoretical steps (again, mostly as a result of German epistemological battles) to transcend this grievous barrier to more complete analysis. And the progression he could have made, from the iron cage of Menger's scientism to the more advanced reaches of social scientific knowledge, he resisted—with the same sort of stubbornness, in fact, that carried Pareto into a completely new mode of sociological research. (Hypotheses have already been proposed above in explanation for Weber's refusal to change his general program; they need not be brought up again here. Pareto's antithetical choice requires no hermeneutic since he spells it out quite clearly himself in the first pages of the *Trattato.*)

We return again to the tactic of using Pareto as a foil. It has been established that Weber offered us no definitive or empirically applicable body of propositions concerning the nonrational but, instead, a multitude of insights, asides, and adjunct material, hinged somewhat incidentally to his central work. It has been claimed (though not hermeneutically demonstrated, for lack of space) that Pareto did create a coherent theory of the nonrational (or "nonlogical," to use his term), one consciously cast in testable propositions,[5] and surrounded with abundant documentation. It has additionally been argued that the virtue of Pareto's system does not so much lie

5. Sally Cook Lopreato is one of remarkably few to have extracted hypotheses from Pareto's work and subjected them to empirical testing, using today's methodology (which, it should be added, on the *mathematical* level is *less* sophisticated than that in Pareto's writings of the 1890s). See her "Toward a Formal Restatement of Vilfredo Pareto's Theory of the Circulation of Elites." Most of the empirical attention English-speaking scholars have given to Pareto's work centers either around his law of income distribution or the circulation of elites. "Nonlogical" action per se has received much philosophical and epistemological comment, particularly around the time of L. J. Henderson's seminars at Harvard, but very little testing.

in his analytic or observational skills and their fruits as in the simple fact that he confronted the nonrational directly (something Weber, for personal and epistemological reasons, could not bring himself to do). To repeat, Weber was better, it seems to me, at analyzing irrationality than Pareto *when* he chose to do so.

The possibility must be considered that they wrote in *conscious* opposition to one another, in which case Pareto would indeed be the ideal foil. This brings up an aspect of the history of social thought which, judging from the dozens of secondary treatments now available (and beginning with Parsons's unequivocal opinion offered forty years ago in the *Structure of Social Action*, p. 535: "Weber, being unacquainted with Pareto's work . . .") is commonly thought to be settled. Weber and Pareto, it has been believed for years, knew nothing of each other. Again, we may cite Parsons:

> Another point strongly in favor of this choice [to use Marshall, Pareto, Durkheim, and Weber as contributors to the development of Parsons's "voluntaristic theory of action"] is that although all four of these men were approximately contemporary, there is with one exception not a trace of direct influence of any one on any other. Pareto was certainly influenced by Marshall in the formulation of his technical economic theory, but with equal certainty not in any respect relevant to this discussion. And this is the *only possibility of any direct influence.* (ibid., pp. 13–14; emphasis added)

As was pointed out above, according to a student of Alfred Weber, Max was fully aware of Durkheim's work and in fact kept in his library in Heidelberg a complete set of Durkheim's journal, the *Année Sociologique*. This was reported to Raymond Aron by Marcel Mauss, who visited Weber, and was in turn made public by Edward A. Tiryakian in a unique article, "A Problem for the Sociology of Knowledge: The Mutual Unawareness of Emile Durkheim and Max Weber." (Aron also claimed that Weber had "borrowed many ideas" from Durkheim.) It is also known, incidentally, that Durkheim knew of Pareto, having published a negative review of his *I Problemi della Sociologia* in 1900 in which, as Steven Lukes explains, "He saw (the early) Pareto as seeking to 'justify the old abstract and ideological method of political economy and wanting to make it the general method of all the social sciences.'"[6] It is interesting that Parsons did not see to it that his dubious claim that all four men

6. Steven Lukes, *Emile Durkheim*, p. 405n78.

theorized unaware of the others was not deleted or muted some-what in the 1968 reprint edition of his book, two years after Tirya-kian's article came out. In any case, it is quite clear that Durkheim knew of Weber, and vice versa—more important, they may well have intentionally ignored each other because of nationalistic hos-tility or other reasons[7]—and that Durkheim knew at least one of Pareto's books well enough to review it. (From this it might also be surmised that Pareto knew of Durkheim's unfavorable review, in-asmuch as he read fluently in French and Italian and seemed to keep up with French intellectualism very closely; but this is not im-mediately important except in a general sense.) Yet the illusion per-sists among nonspecialists that Parsons's view is correct. Some un-certainty even exists as to whether or not Durkheim referred to Weber directly in his work, a debate which has produced, among other things, a letter from "Durkheim" himself.[8]

All these matters would be trivial except that misinformation be-comes a part of the sociological legacy, and descendants of the early giants write as if a given set of circumstances obtained, when they did not. More than that, as Tiryakian suggests:

> A more subtle question raised by all this is just what are the criteria used to determine what external stimuli (and by external we can in-clude a different culture or a different perspective) are cognized by a writer or a school as being relevant for their own creative develop-ment. Concretely, did Durkheim know of Weber's sociological writ-ings but ignore them because he considered them irrelevant for his own studies and *vice versa*? The practical consequences of this little problem in the intellectual history of sociology is that it can put us on our guards against perpetrating sins of omission. . . . Mental products are so related to their sociocultural setting that even the towering figures of the same social science may operate from suffi-ciently different presuppositions . . . that they will know of each other without knowing each other. (p. 336)

7. This is Edward Tiryakian's conclusion on pp. 335–336 of "A Problem for the Sociology of Knowledge." Durkheim also reviewed Marianne Weber's *Ehefrau und Mutter in der Rechtsentwickelung* [sic], rather unkindly, in his *Année Sociologigue* 11 (1906–1909): 363–369; translated in *Emile Durkheim on Institutional Analysis*, ed. Mark Traugott, pp. 139–144.

8. See Lukes, *Emile Durkheim*, p. 397n19: "(Tiryakian is mistaken to say that Durkheim nowhere refers to Weber: see 1913a (ii) (3), p. 26)." For rebuttal and ap-parent retraction, see "Durkheim confirme Tiryakian: un échange de correspon-dance," *European Journal of Sociology* 14 (1974): 354–355, an exchange between "Durkheim" and Lukes. "Durkheim" writes: "jamais le nom de Max Weber n'aura été évoqué dans mes écrits."

Following Tiryakian's lead into what he calls "the sociological salience of silence," let us review what is known about the possibility that Weber and Pareto knew of each other's work and decided to ignore it. Weber visited Italy often. He made at least twelve trips there between 1900 and 1914, many of them months in duration,[9] and from letters we know that he read Italian newspapers and followed "local" events carefully. During this period Pareto published 179 items, many of them in newspapers and political journals which Weber may have seen.[10] And if Weber did not read Pareto's work while in Italy, he could have seen it in Germany, since Pareto published no fewer than twenty-six book reviews for the *Zeitschrift für Sozialwissenschaft* between 1898 and 1902 (one of them in volume 1 [1898] of Emile Durkheim's *Le Suicide*, which solves the riddle of whether Pareto knew Durkheim's work).[11] All of this supports the general contention that Weber could have known that Pareto existed, either through his popular political analysis, his book reviews published in the *Zeitschrift*, his reputation as a political economist (international, according to Pareto experts), or from some other source. When it is remembered that Pareto published more than seven hundred items in English, French, Italian, and German, it becomes difficult to believe that Weber was ignorant of him.

The only scholar I know of who has made a definite statement on this matter is Gottfried Eisermann, a German sociologist who has published extensively on Pareto, including one brief book, *Vilfredo Pareto als Nationalökonom und Soziologe*,[12] in which he says, "One must immediately be impressed with the analogy of certain fundamental concepts of Pareto with those of Max Weber familiar to us" (p. 55). In trying to establish a connection where data are

9. They were as follows: 1900 (Corsica), 1901 (Rome and southern Italy), 1901 (Rome again), 1902 (Florence, having spent at least six months in Rome), 1902 December (Italian Riviera), 1903 (Rome), 1906 (Sicily), 1907 (Lake Como), 1908 (Florence), 1910 (Italy), 1911 spring (Italy), 1913 spring and autumn (Italy), 1914 spring (Italy). See, for documentation, either Marianne Weber, *Max Weber*, pp. 704–706, or Eduard Baumgarten, ed., *Max Weber*, pp. 696–704.
10. G. Busino, comp., "Les Ecrits de Pareto."
11. Not having seen a copy, I do not know if Pareto was as harsh in his review of Durkheim's work as Durkheim was of Pareto's two years later. The review appears on pp. 78–80 of the first volume of the journal.
12. Gottfried Eisermann's other relevant publications are "Vilfredo Pareto in Deutschland" and "L'Influence de Vilfredo Pareto en Allemagne."

slim, he continues, "One must therefore characterize as 'incomprehensible' that Max Weber knew a man like Vilfredo Pareto in name only. And an 'equally incomprehensible fact': Vilfredo Pareto knew Max Weber only by hearsay. So the two great 'Dioscuri' of modern sociology (like Castor and Pollux) thought, talked, wrote, taught, and discovered, who could have meant so much to each other, passed each other by" (p. 56). (Here Eisermann is taking issue with a remark Robert Michels made in his *Bedeutende Männer* [Leipzig: Verlag Quelle und Meyer, 1927], pp. 113–114.) "And it is equally inconceivable that Pareto knew Weber from only hearsay." Eisermann continues by musing that the two foremost representatives of modern sociology, with so much in common, could scarcely have been unaware of one another. As evidence, he introduces another remark by Michels, who quotes Weber as having voiced a high opinion of Gaetano Mosca, which indicates Weber's excellent Italian. Also, lest Pareto's German be suspect, Eisermann in a later sentence points to section 1580 of the *Trattato*, where Pareto translates material from the *Berliner Tageblatt*. And yet, after presenting much circumstantial evidence, Eisermann admits in a footnote that neither man referred to the other in their *Hauptwerke*, so nothing definitive can be claimed about the Pareto-Weber connection. This was Eisermann's opinion as late as 1975, when he published an article in the *Cahiers Vilfredo Pareto* on Pareto's influence in Germany. So far as I have been able to tell, this is where scholarly opinion remains, with very few writers any longer even considering the issue.

Though it is hard to believe, it seems no one heretofore, at least in English-language scholarship, has made a concrete connection between Pareto and Weber. A publisher in Milan, Società Editrice Libraria, inaugurated a series in 1903 called Biblioteca di Storia Economica (The Library of Economic History), the first "volume" of which consisted of 1,730 pages. Five other volumes appeared in staggered years until 1929, when the series apparently ended. Every single volume—even the last, which appeared six years after Pareto's death—bears this inscription on the title page, under the series title "Diretta dal Prof. Vilfredo Pareto," which means, of course, "edited by" Pareto. In these six bloated tomes (which total 7,000 pages) are included many book-length translations from the German, including the familiar names of Roscher, Knies, Eduard

Meyer, and Mommsen. After a 720-page part 1, on the title page of *Volume Secondo–Parte Seconda* are listed five works, the third of which is "M. Weber—La Storia Agraria Romana in Rapporto al Diritto Pubblico e Privato," a translation (no translator listed) of Weber's habilitation of 1891, "Die Römische Agrargeschichte." The entire work is translated, including the four surveying charts in the end, on pages 511–705.

What can we surmise from this? Given that Weber held the copyright to the habilitation (for it is so marked in the original edition), someone had to notify him or his publisher, Ferdinand Enke of Stuttgart, of their wish to reprint it. There may even have been royalties in question. It seems in any case inconceivable that a publisher would reprint a work of 195 pages without notifying its author, even if international copyright laws were such that no royalties would have to be paid. The social-science community of those days was certainly small enough that this courtesy would be extended. Thus it is most likely that Weber knew his work was selected, presumably by the general editor, Pareto, and printed in Milan in 1907 as part of an ambitious series. This is precisely when Weber was spending a great deal of time in Italy, and he may have even been contacted while there. Nowhere in the volumes is there the slightest hint that anyone but Pareto selected books for translation and inclusion. Unfortunately, though, he did not write an introductory essay, as would probably be called for today, so we cannot be *absolutely* sure of his familiarity with the work. But it is, at minimum, reasonable to assert that Pareto knew of Weber as a German social scientist important enough to be ranked in his series with the likes of Roscher and Mommsen. And the slightly more difficult extension can also be made that through this publication in 1907, Weber knew something of Pareto. It seems Eisermann's skepticism about their knowing each other "only by name" and through "hearsay" was well founded. Although we have established grounds for hypothesizing their mutual knowledge, however, this says virtually nothing about the quality or intensity of that mutual knowledge.[13]

13. A possible reason for the fact that Pareto's use of the Weber work in his series has not been noted before may be that bibliographies, even massive, nearly comprehensive ones like the Käsler for Weber, the Busino for Pareto, do not mention the Biblioteca and their respective affiliations with it. This omission I cannot

Unfortunately, the texts provide practically nothing to guide us. On page 238 of *Roscher and Knies*, Weber uses the word *residue* thus: "On p. 266 [of an article by Meinecke in the *Historische Zeitschrift* 6 (1891)] he describes this 'unknown quantity'—the irrational 'residue' [*dem irrationalen "Rest,"* 1922a, p. 46] of the personality—as the 'inner sanctuary' of the personality." While the use of the word closely resembles Pareto's own designation, this must be little more than an unconnected parallelism, for Weber, writing in 1905, would have preceded Pareto's usage by a decade. Other than this unimportant commonality, the texts indicate nothing in the way of explicit reference to one another.

On the first page of this chapter, it was asked, Why is Pareto a foil to Weber, rather than a directly compared referent? The answer is clear: one cannot compare theorists *directly* who refused to address one another. It is child's play, for instance, to evaluate Marx's opinion of Bruno Bauer, and vice versa, since neither of them was at all bashful about confrontation. Later on I asked, Is it possible that they wrote in conscious opposition to each other? This question, it will be remembered, was stimulated by Parsons's unjustified belief that Durkheim, Weber, and Pareto were insulated from one another. As the three leading social scientists of their respective countries, and for other reasons already mentioned, this putative mutual unawareness is clearly illusory. The case for conscious opposition is difficult to make, however. It is almost certainly true that had Pareto come across Weber's methodological essays of 1904–1907, particularly *Roscher and Knies*, he would have taken violent exception to some of Weber's opinions. And since Pareto oversaw the publication in his Library of Weber's work in 1907, is it unthinkable that he would have been attracted during his omnivorous reading (abetted by insomnia) to some of Weber's more current work? And yet, Pareto did not suffer from intellectual diffidence. Had he objected to Weber's formulations concerning "nonlogical" action, it seems reasonable that he would have attacked him in the

---

explain. For complete details on the Weber translation in Pareto's series, see Alan Sica, "Received Wisdom Versus Historical Fact." An Italian sociologist, Sandro Segré, has argued against my version of the story with special reference to Pareto's assistant, the historian Ettore Ciccotti, who played more of a role in producing the Biblioteca than Pareto did. See Segré's "Pareto and Weber," esp. pp. 248n6 and 258n76.

Trattato. But knowing as we now do (unlike Parsons in 1937) that Pareto reviewed Durkheim's *Suicide,* we must ask why he failed to bring any mention whatever of the Frenchman's work into his magnum opus, either in support of his own hypotheses or for critical dissection? It must be admitted, with a nod toward Parsons, that this is most strange. And it accentuates the urgency and continuing perplexity of Tiryakian's question about "the criteria used to determine what external stimuli . . . are cognized by a writer."

I *suspect* that Pareto and Weber knew of each other's works, read some of the same journals, physically crossed paths more than once on Italian soil, and each—for reasons that will earn permanent conjecture and an equally permanent indefiniteness—quite consciously decided not to tangle with the other over theoretical matters. Perhaps they (correctly) perceived in each other such radically different *Weltanschauungen,* epistemologies, and methodological skills that confrontation—and successful negotiation of the chasm between them—promised to call for more labor than the effort was worth. But in the final analysis these are private conjectures, nothing more.

For all these reasons, then, Pareto is the foil to Weber on irrationality: because Weber's analysis was more sensitive, Pareto's more rigorous; because Weber, not Pareto, is the one to overcome if changes in theory are desired; and because in spite of both these facts, Pareto's vision of human life and motivation can provide us with certain important realizations that Weber's half-completed theory cannot. Without developing a hermeneutically adequate understanding of Pareto's conceptualization of the irrational—which would require slightly, but only slightly, fewer pages than the analogous task for Weber—we might sketch a pre-hermeneutical portrait and, using it, propose some amendments to the Weberian approach.

First in *Roscher and Knies* (pp. 120ff.) and later on in a number of other places, Weber insisted that "freedom of the will" and "irrationality of the personality" stood in inalterable opposition. As so many of his personal students and later admirers have repeated, he was a champion of unfettered individualism at a time when the opportunities for its realization were dwindling. Pareto held precisely the same belief during his early adulthood (about 1866–1876, when Weber was between the ages of two and twelve) and in fact expended prodigious energy combatting what he saw as degenerate, antidemocratic, aristocratic rule in Italy. In 1882 he ran for office as a liberal from Florence, but did not succeed. Then in a four-year period (1889–1893, just as Weber was beginning his career), he published "167 articles, many of them scholarly, but the vast majority anti-government polemics."[14] At the same time his lectures to "the proletariat" were halted by police, and he became known to the government as a liberal troublemaker. This Pareto, it would seem, might easily share Weber's political sympathies and at the same time agree with him on the necessary relation between "rational action" and "freedom." Yet by around 1900, when he was fifty-two, Pareto had soured on the political fortunes of Italian liberalism and trade unionism. As might be expected, and as Robert Michels explained in *Political Parties* (1911), after becoming part of the political machinery and no longer a mere bodiless ideology these factions became in their own way as repressive of individual freedom as had the previous oligarchical government. And so, with perfect logic, Pareto became the enemy of those same forces— transformed, of course, by their rise to power—for whom he had done polemical battle for a dozen years. It is untrue, then (as Joseph Lopreato and others have shown),[15] that immediately upon being spurned by the electorate, Pareto became philosophically antidemocratic out of pique and "discovered" the "irrationality" of behavior, since that preceded by at least eighteen years his ideological change.

I believe it is fair to say, based on this evidence and other biographical and textual material, that Weber and Pareto shared a pre-intellectual or simply emotional fondness, even dedication, to individual autonomy. In his reports on Prussian agrarian workers Weber expressed the opinion that their dignity was greatly enhanced when they refused financial blandishments connected with agricultural rationalization, in order to retain whatever small measure of genuine autonomy was left them. Pareto entertained similar sentiments regarding the Italian working class and its struggle to organize politically in the face of stiff governmental resistance. Without doing undue violence to either of their intricate person-

14. *Vilfredo Pareto: Sociological Writings*, p. 10.
15. J. Lopreato, "Notes," p. 452.

alities and belief systems, we might argue that in this zealous defense of individualism from aggressors on both right and left, the two men conformed rather closely to the personality cynosure common to the cultured bourgeoisie of the period. But in the long run, Weber was more the conformist, for he remained steadfast in his enthusiasm for individual voluntaristic autonomy based on rational decisions and rational actions. While among the Stefan George circle and some other "deviants" such as Scheler this was not the prevalent attitude, with most other German intellectuals within Weber's ken his "philosophy of freedom" would have found ready acceptance. Harnack and Troeltsch, for instance, both of whom Weber respected, wrote from within precisely this ideology of liberal individualism.

Pareto, by contrast, when faced with repeated affronts to his political values during this heyday of European imperialism, retrenched, evaluated his own political convictions (and presumably the values they represented), and assumed a new posture. This later ideological viewpoint, which informed his last thirty-three years or so, is altogether more objective and detached from any particular set of values than was Weber's.[16] Supported by his inheritance, Pareto moved to his villa, nursed his health, wrote incessantly, and examined human behavior in all those manifestations about which he could find interpretable data. He observed as rigorously and systematically as one probably could given his self-entrapment in Celigny. Weber, with *his* inheritance, reentered the world of academy and politics and never regained the untrammeled freedom and lucidity he had enjoyed during the earlier days of detached existence (for instance, during his six-month stay in Rome between 1901 and 1902). Though it is true he was undergoing the final stages of his psychopathology, it is also the case

16. "As had been pointed out frequently, and particularly so by La Ferla, who described Pareto as a Voltairian character, Pareto had the unpleasant scoffing habit of the moralist who scrutinizes human beings and lays bare their vices rather than their virtues, their weaknesses, their vanity and stupidity, not in order to disprove or flay them, but in order *to enjoy the spectacle from above*. He did not have the makings of a moral reformer, nor those of a preacher, but he did have those of a moralist in the classical sense of the word, i.e., of the *dispassionate investigator of other people's passions*" (Norberto Bobbio, *On Pareto and Mosca*, p. 59; emphasis added). This "unpleasant" attitude existed to some degree in Weber's work, but much less so, and though Bobbio here presents it as a negative characteristic, for reasons given in the text, I view it differently.

that, as Germany geared up for the war Weber foresaw well in advance, his previously unmuddled objectivity became fouled somewhat by a tempered but potent nationalism. Of this there can be no doubt. While it is reckless to impugn his theoretical work in general on the grounds that he sometimes found it difficult to separate patriotic fervor from scholarly objectivity, it is worth pondering the fact that Pareto, during the same period, somehow eluded the call to nationalistic enthusiasm. In fact, he impudently refused late in life to respond to government requests that he submit certain trivial papers so he could be made a senator. A comparison of this combination of nonchalance and mockery with Weber's continuous official affiliation with government agencies and activities from 1914 until his death and his vigorous prosecution of official duties may indicate their relative capacities for unemotional observation and analysis.[17]

Enough said. By now at least this much should be clear: Weber was more subject to passionately motivated action than Pareto, and we must suppose that some connection obtains between this personality trait and scholarly perception. The shape of the relationship may not be definable, but its existence ought to be acknowledged. In addition, Weber refused to be associated in any positive theoretical way with irrationality, either that which infected the individual or the type which Weber, inspired by Gustave Le Bon, called "action conditioned by crowds."[18] In my opinion,

17. Factual information serving as background for my remarks over the several preceding pages can be gained, for Pareto, from Georges H. Bousquet, "Vilfredo Pareto (1848–1923)." Bousquet has written more biographical material about Pareto than anyone else, though memoirs about him abound. Of his forty or more publications about Pareto, only one other is in English: *The Work of Vilfredo Pareto*, 46 pages. Information for Weber's political beliefs and other biographical material came primarily from his wife's biography; the compilation by Baumgarten, *Max Weber;* Wolfgang Mommsen's two books on Weber's politics, *Max Weber und die deutsche Politik 1890–1920* and *The Age of Bureaucracy;* Ilse Dronberger's *The Political Thought of Max Weber;* and David Beetham's *Max Weber and the Theory of Modern Politics.*

18. Weber 1968a, 1: 23. In his introduction to a reprint edition of Gustave Le Bon's *The Crowd* (New York: Viking Press, 1960), Robert Merton identifies the classic as in some sense "a vogue book" (p. v) when it was published in 1895. I suspect that an additional reason for Weber's distaste for matters concerning irrationality (and one not mentioned heretofore) grew from his predisposition to view many actions of *hoi polloi* as intellectually indefensible, unreflective, and "common," hence irrational. Given the immense popularity throughout the nineteenth century for books that detailed examples of contagion and other irrational collective behavior (for instance, Charles Mackay's *Extraordinary Popular Delusions and the Madness of Crowds,* first published in 1841 and reprinted many times), it is likely that Weber was aware

Weber's private war with irrationality at its most horrifying had insured his permanent hostility toward it and toward any theorists who refused either (1) to condemn it as a primitive mental state leading to self-destructive action, or (2) to handle it in such a way that its impact was neutralized (which was Weber's strategy in his analysis of magic). This conclusion runs counter to the general consensus; moreover, Weber's analyses of religion are frequently invoked as evidence of his genuine interest in, even congeniality with, certain irrational states.

My reading of the materials in question, especially the early methodological essays, points to something in addition to this view. It shows a theorist who realized twenty years before his death that nonrational components of personality (and, by reasonable extension, of societies at large) were most important to human existence, but that the project for the (Kantian) theorist included bringing these rebellious, sometimes amoral components to heel— slipping them skillfully within the realm of reason. Between the period of *The Protestant Ethic* and the last lectures on economic history at Munich, this is the major undertaking I see Weber trying to accomplish. Although speaking from a position quite distinct from my own, Edward Tiryakian offers some support for my contention with this general reflection about Weber and Durkheim—an observation which does not pertain to Pareto's goals at all: "They rejected the evolutionary optimism prevalent in some liberal intellectual circles prior to the Great War since they both recognized that the absence of a religious grounding for modern society implied the loss of a secure foundation by means of which the *irrational potentialities* of mankind could be *harnessed* in constructive channels." [19] This hope that what the Frankfurt School knows as "the domination of nature" could be extended to human society was a grand bit of optimism for which Pareto had no patience.

What, then, is the Paretian alternative? Is it worth foregoing Weber's ingenious tack of *Verstehen* in order to partake of Pareto's

---

of "the mob" as an expression of the irrational about which he could have little serious interest. And in fact *Economy and Society* lacks anything like a compelling treatment of collective behavior. Needless to say, Pareto found these outbursts quite interesting and indicative of just those human characteristics most worthy of study.

19. Tiryakian, "Problem for the Sociology of Knowledge," p. 331 (emphasis added).

less instrumental approach to the problem? Perhaps we can ar-
range our program in such a way that valuable elements from both
men's theories can be remolded into a more useful, more realistic
theoretical move.

First, we must briefly consider what Pareto left us that still com-
mands attention. In 1935, at the height of the "Pareto craze," L. J.
Henderson wrote in the final paragraphs of his admiring book on
"the master," "This book [the *Trattato*] bears all the marks of the
spade-work of a pioneer. . . . Pareto's errors and omissions will
come to light if the work is continued, and this work is of the kind,
being scientific, that can be continued *by others*."[20] But by 1948
W. Rex Crawford, as part of an insufferably smug précis of Pareto's
work, apparently felt confident in writing, "The general attitude of
the work has a fructifying influence; but, specifically, it has pointed
out a road that is yet to be followed and, in our opinion, is unlikely
ever to be very productive."[21] While it is often noted that Parsons
and George Homans were both deeply influenced by Pareto's notion of equilibrium, the former even claiming that his "social system" idea originated with reading the *Trattato*, neither man can be
characterized as Paretian or even be credited with having advanced
the Paretian heritage. Aside from students of societal equilibrium,
elite theorists have profited from Pareto's ideas,[22] but here too his
actual theoretical apparatus (foxes, lions, and all) does not figure
importantly in current empirical work. But even if these two streams
of sociological research still heralded Pareto in the way Weber is
ritually called upon for legitimation of a given project, it would
matter little in the present context, for neither "equilibrium" nor
the "circulation of elites" is of much interest here, except to the
slight degree they bear upon the irrational.

In Chapter 1, I made hasty reference to the fact that Pareto had
been bypassed by contemporary researchers. At the same time I
hypothesized that his being ignored may have more to do with the
form of his work (or its style, to recall Bobbio's remarks about his
"Voltairian" tone) than its content. Let us consider three separate

20. L. J. Henderson, *Pareto's General Sociology*, pp. 58–59 (emphasis added).
21. W. Rex Crawford, "Representative Italian Contributions to Sociology,"
p. 568.
22. A tidy list of those influenced by Pareto appears in Nicholas S. Timasheff
and George A. Theodorson, *Sociological Theory*, pp. 138–139.

opinions, all written by men who claim special expertise vis-à-vis Pareto's sociology. First we may return to W. Rex Crawford's playful and condescending opening paragraphs to his article on Pareto:

> It must be remembered that even a man whose system is as a whole an ambitious but unacceptable failure . . . may have much influence. . . . This is not to say that the direct academic influence of the method of Pareto has been great. . . . The greatness of our author is the man rather than the method. Certain of his ideas are vital and meaningful, but the system as a whole seems fruitless. No one would today go to Thorstein Veblen for an answer to all the problems of economics; but once read him, and you will never forget certain things: in innumerable situations of your own life his theories will jump into your mind. . . . Pareto is like that. In spite of all the difficulty of language and form, there is something about Pareto that comes home to men's business and bosoms. . . . Treat him not as something to be studied but as a help in understanding the life that all of us lead.[23]

Such an evaluation of Pareto, appearing in one of the most influential postwar textbooks on the history of social thought, could have had pronounced impact on the post-Henderson reception of Pareto in the United States. And even if it literally did not, its message harmonized with subsequent opinion.

Crawford's approach to the *Trattato* (which, needless to say, leaves everything to be desired in terms of able hermeneutics) stands in blunt contradiction to that of Lopreato. In attacking an oft-heard criticism of the *Trattato* (that "the overwhelming bulk . . . consists of congeries of observations which put, in essence, anecdotal flesh on the taxonomy of residues and derivations")[24] Lopreato succeeds in isolating an entire body of "theories" that, in his opinion, conclusively demonstrate Pareto's talents in what later became concept formation and theory-building. Lopreato begins by reminding readers of the 200-page "specific theory" on religion and animism to be found in the *Trattato*, and then goes on to list the following: "Among other theories that come to mind are theories of law, censorship, revolution, social mobility, what today is known as 'status inconsistency,' protectionism, cooptation, deception, propaganda, population, nationalism, democracy, capitalism, exploitation [which Pareto called spoilation], manipulation and

23. Crawford, "Representative Italian Contributions to Sociology," pp. 555–556.
24. J. Lopreato, "Notes," p. 464.

image-production, bureaucracy, evolution, 'natural law,' morality, pornography" (ibid.).

Marion Levy supports Lopreato's claims and elaborates them to some extent with these observations:

> the critical contributions of Pareto in [sociology]—mind, not in the social sciences generally, for there we must include economics as well—fall under six headings, none of them which have been scrupulously followed or built upon by any considerable number of subsequent social scientists. These six are: (1) his statement about the scientific approach; (2) his careful drawing of the distinction between logical and non-logical conduct; (3) his demonstration of the limitations of strictly rational analysis in seeking solutions to problems; (4) his insistence on the interdependent social system; (5) the residue-derivation scheme (along with the derivatives); and (6) Pareto's specific empirical hypotheses.[25]

Levy continues concerning Pareto's "sixth" contribution to sociology: "There are empirical hypotheses—call them merely insights if you prefer—of this order of power scattered throughout the corpus of Pareto's work. If there are fewer than 1500 or 2000 such items I would be very much surprised" (ibid.).

Although Lopreato's and Levy's views are more recent than Crawford's, it is still reasonable to assume that in the United States the latter's opinion and prescription for Pareto usage prevails.[26] While I find Crawford's approach hermeneutically retarded, his charges are probably for the most part justified, and Lopreato and Levy are almost by necessity over-reacting to *some* extent (much as I sympathize with their positive reading of the *Trattato*). This is not the occasion for an analysis to explain Pareto's lack of American followers, a project which would have to take into consideration not only the intrinsic substantive, literary, philosophical, and epistemological aspects of his work but many external facts concerning American sociological scholarship and the reward system that propels it. What I want to establish, with these quotations from the three experts, is that the Pareto question is still alive and will con-

25. Marion Levy, "Sociologist Who Knew Science," p. 472.
26. One article comes to mind as a light in the darkness, John Carroll's "Pareto's Irrationalism," a brilliant work which not only takes Pareto's treatment of nonrationality seriously but also establishes a link between Pareto's thought and that of Nietzsche. This sort of Pareto scholarship is rare these days.

tinue to be at least until time is taken for a hermeneutically responsible interpretation of his entire sociological work, such that its relevance to contemporary interests and methodological tastes is demonstrated (or not, as the case may be).

What can also be gathered from their remarks is that Pareto's work is so sprawling that one may justifiably exercise editorial judgment in selecting those components that speak to a given empirical problem. Our empirical problem, of course, is to determine what place irrationality has in meaningful behavior (that is, meaning for the actor, not for the analyst) and, having done that, to proceed to develop a methodology, which in a manner not unlike the hermeneutical analysis of texts[27] and calling for similar cognitive skills, can order contemporary life without rending it to bits through methodological clumsiness or needless aggression. For the moment I can do little more than propose (again, without the necessary hermeneutical groundwork, thus seemingly by fiat), the ways Pareto's overall perception of social life can be used to augment (rather than supplant) Weber's theory of *soziales Handeln*.

First, we must address Pareto's method of assembling vast quantities of data (or, less elegantly, information), whether from ancient historians or daily newspapers (though his reliance upon popular sources has been exaggerated; most of his citations derive from perfectly respectable, often eminent, works).[28] Norberto Bobbio, who has given much thought to Pareto's style of data acquisition, writes thus:

> Between the moralists' analysis and that of Pareto there was nevertheless a difference in the observation material used. Pareto's neglected literary works; he did, it is true, examine theories in which men appear as the direct protagonists with their actions and feelings, sometimes openly confessed, sometimes only implied, but he was fond above all of examining the works of reflected thought, from the ancient cosmogonies to the theologies of the Christian era,

27. We may recall the lead offered by Paul Ricoeur's "The Model of the Text."

28. Pareto felt that sociology, if it hoped to become a true science, must interpret the present from the past and not reinterpret the past to suit present contingencies. As a consequence, he very consciously chose to use as a primary data source histories from Greece and Rome in search of material for documenting (as opposed to testing) his various analytic categories. These included, of course, not only six master and fifty-two minor types of "sentiments," but also four major and eighteen minor types of "derivations," plus a host of other explicative devices.

to the modern philosophies of history, from the theories of natural right to the recent theories of utilitarianism, socialism, solidarity, in which human action is the subject of a more or less rational interpretation and justification. Pareto had been struck, not only by the agitated play of passions in the theater of history, but also by the varying and captious way in which these passions had been hidden, simulated, masked by pseudo-rational constructions. The classical contrast between passion and reason no longer appeared to him as a contrast between the inferior and the superior part of the human soul [obviously Weber's position in his less circumspect moments], but between natural instinct and its falsification, between spontaneousness and fabrication. The function of reason was by no means that of dominating the passions, regarded as the servile part of man, but merely of disguising them in order to make them more acceptable (but not less offensive).[29]

Many critics (unlike Bobbio, whose critical estimate is appropriately subtle) have responded to the *Trattato* as a treasure trove of the trivially or grotesquely interesting, as a curiosity shop. The blame for this understandable but deficient reading falls with the author, who enjoyed taunting critics of his day when they objected to the format of the *Trattato* and especially to the outrageous footnotes. He was one to enjoy the sparkling story and included them by the score, not at times troubling himself with thematic continuity or coherence. Bobbio's comments suggest, however, that Pareto's learning and his willingness to plumb every conceivable source, historical, scientific, or philosophical, bring him very much into Weber's orbit in terms of sheer learning. In fact, I think it is demonstrable that while Weber's learning—that which shows in his published work, at any rate—was extraordinary regarding his specific research interests, Pareto possessed more bits of information, and not by any means all in unrelated batches. But this is relatively unimportant. What is at stake is my assertion that Pareto's methodology (while violating practically every canon of positivist induction as we now know it, and inciting critics to repeat ad nauseum that proof by example is not the same as proof through objective—statistical—test) still is worth emulating, perhaps more now than twenty years ago. Because this is today a rare claim, it requires elaboration.

29. Bobbio, *On Pareto and Mosca*, pp. 59–60.

A Curtain of Incomprehension:
Pareto and Contemporary Thought

Few historians of social thought were as difficult to impress or please as Pitirim Sorokin. Yet in his unique text, *Contemporary Sociological Theories*, he had this to say sixty years ago: "Pareto's treatise is the product of an original and outstanding scientific mind. It has been said to be as original and important as Vico's and Machiavelli's treatises. . . . In brief, Pareto's analysis of the correlation between the dynamics of the residue and that of action, and conclusions concerning the non-logical actions of human beings, represent, possibly, an unsurpassed analysis of human behavior."[30] Now, though, we live amid a dozen comfortable reasons to discount Pareto, as methodologist, substantive theorist, historian, ethical thinker, or political analyst. Already thirty years ago Peter Winch disposed of Pareto entirely in fifteen pages of his small, influential book, using hardly more words than fill some of Pareto's own footnotes.[31] Durkheim shared much with Pareto, but the former's admirers, practically numberless among sociologists today, disregard their master's momentary lapses into Paretian sentiment. For example, "Most social and ethical institutions are not, therefore, the result of reasoning and reckoning but of obscure causes, of subconscious feelings, and of motives which are unrelated to the effects they produce and which they then cannot explain."[32] With few exceptions (e.g., S. E. Finer, Joseph Lopreato, Charles Powers), social science has closed the book on Pareto, sometimes elegantly (Winch's Wittgensteinian attack), more often perfunctorily, without so much as a glance at his work.

Were Pareto still among us, how might he explain his extraordinary drop in credibility as an intellectual from the apogee of the 1930s, when Homans, Parsons, Sorokin, and many others stood in line to sing his praises, until the last generation or so when he became persona non grata among the right-thinking? He would surely point to the inevitable cycles of history and of thought; he

30. Pitirim Sorokin, *Contemporary Sociological Theories*, pp. 39, 52.
31. Peter Winch, *The Idea of a Social Science and Its Relation to Philosophy*, pp. 95–110.
32. Emile Durkheim, "The Positive Science of Ethics in Germany," p. 12.

might suggest a period of lions overtaken by foxes; he could even offer a technically adept set of equations that would describe the rise and fall of reputation just as he did for elites, stock prices, income, and other social phenomena. It would be easy for him to provide a thoroughly Paretian analysis of his decline, and tempting for his followers as well. But to do so would illustrate the weakness of his system as it is perceived today, because his special jargon would have to be applied and much of it rankles (e.g., "instinct"). Experts often explain by way of apologia that certain key Italian words (e.g., for "combinations" and "instinct") carry meanings that are more subtle and theoretically believable than their English cognates. But the Bongiorno/Livingston translation of the *Trattato* has so completely won over its readers that replacing their choices is no longer feasible. (Recall by comparison the healthy results of retranslating Weber after his "parsonization," so that, for instance, *Herrschaft* became menacing "domination" after a mild career as "authority.") In fact the entire apparatus of Pareto's theories appears utterly antique—was so even in 1935 when the translation appeared—and a study of contemporary life rigorously guided by Pareto's system would now seem as quaint as fiction that used dialogue à la Henry James. The appeal of such an enterprise would lie strictly in its aesthetic quality, in its success or failure at resuscitating a lost form of serious thought.

This brings up two barriers in understanding Pareto today, or perhaps any theoretical system constructed prior to the 1950s. The first has to do with scientism, the second with the goals of theorizing—which are, of course, closely related. It is extremely odd that Pareto must be defended against the common accusation that he was pre-scientific, since his education as a theoretical and applied scientist was top-notch, his adoration of the logico-experimental (scientific) method pure and uninterrupted, and his ability to make genuine scientific advances, especially in econometrics, unquestioned to this day. What is at stake is not "the" scientific method but "a" method. Pareto's was as clear and untroubled as J. S. Mill's, and he used it with confidence and skill. For Pareto there were social phenomena which were ipso facto nonlogical, from an informed point of view, and other social acts more or less in tune with causation as best we can know it or as he could know it. Rain dances do not promote rain so far as meteorology knows, and therefore to dance one with the hope of creating rain is nonlogical. It is not, of course, in the least irrational. To dance for rain with a war dance would be irrational and would probably be taken as a sure sign of psychopathology among tribe members who knew one dance from the other. Winch's arguments against Pareto on this score, his refusal to understand the meaning of social rituals for the people participating in them, is irrelevant to Pareto's larger concern. He did not care to improve or practice anthropology, except that of his own time. What did he care to do?

Science for an intellectual of his polymath tendencies and during his early adulthood (ca. 1875) was an instrument of clarification, a program designed to discover laws of nature and of the cosmos, and all for the purpose of bringing extra-human life and forces under control for the benefit of *Homo sapiens sapiens*. As an engineer he knew that equilibrium states could be predicted and maintained if the forces at work within them could be determined. After much reading, participation in Italian politics, and discussion with activist intellectuals, Pareto slowly began to see that the goals of enlightenment (those of early Christianity, the twelfth century, the eighteenth century, and socialism)—of all humanisms—with whose goals he initially sympathized, could not possibly guide social organization for an extended period, because human behavior collectively waxes and wanes like the tides; it undulates between extremes, and the truly scientific question is, Why? It is not, for Pareto, How can a society be designed to conform to certain moral principles? That is a nonlogical expression, as Weber would also have recognized. But whereas Weber grew increasingly despondent about the prospects of Western civilization saving itself from over-rationalized torpor, Pareto serenely fixed on a method that had served him excellently as an engineer and economist and began at the turn of the century collecting data which he thought might clarify his model of social change. If we view our own intellectual terrain and try mightily to evaluate theoretical voices dispassionately, we find an unabashed concern for specific moral ends. Neither Habermas, Giddens, nor the younger neo-Parsonsians worry about exposing their axiological interests—what used to be called cherished beliefs—as they spin their tales. They have put aside the scientistic ethos that prevailed among theory builders thirty years ago and instead keep one eye on the good society, suited to their particular tastes, and another on the logical strength of their case. Habermas receives plaudits because of his philosophical skill and sheer perseverance. But his work has not and cannot inspire field or empirical research, because it has this basic goal: to theorize what a sane social world might nowadays take in. Giddens has been more careful about speaking to research, but his many books have had only limited application to mainstream work.

With Pareto none of these utopian or quasi-utopian thought experiments are evident. When his political fortunes went sour, when he wearied of fighting with unions and collective demands over railroad and mining conditions, and when he began to understand the pusillanimous role of Italy's aristocracy in running the country in the 1890s, he dispensed with the thankless promulgation of another ideal scheme for social organization—which already littered library shelves during the nineteenth century. He took that "view from Mars" C. Wright Mills recommended to sociologists, gave up on all political programs, and settled down to the cool, even cold, enumeration and categorization of collective behavior through history.

It is not, however, this particular feature of his work that is worth retaining or using as a counterbalance to others today. The aloof posture is not itself valuable or even laudable anymore—it is a luxury of an aristocrat and an aristocratic age before daily life became routinely cataclysmic. In this way at least Habermas and Giddens have been correct in shedding the Paretian style of theorizing. But for his time and in order to gain the vantage point he wanted, Pareto wisely chose to distance himself from the passions of political life and to accumulate enormous data sets for the *Trattato*. In so doing he strengthened his aversion to emotionality and became, in Parsons's wonderful phrase, a "knocker" rather than a "booster."[33] As many have pointed out since, this smug detachment from Pareto's own history and that of everyone else ran heavily enough against the American spirit of joyous world domination after 1945 that his work began to be ignored, seen as Old World blues with no role to play in an America of boosterism.

If extraordinary self-distancing from human activities past and present is not Pareto's principal virtue—remember that many of

33. Talcott Parsons, *The Structure of Social Action*, p. 293.

the scientistic cult would say it is—are his conceptual categories still pertinent? This is not easy to answer, because no one has yet bothered to test his scheme of residues and derivations extensively enough to decide. They do not on their face seem promising today, because they are, up to a point, deterministic and would be hard to fit into conventional research regimens. They also seem to make analysis of social life too pat. When Pareto was working sleeplessly as a one-man bureau of social research, there were in the United States only a handful of universities with sociology departments, and fewer than a hundred bona fide sociologists. Now there are more than ten thousand in hundreds of departments in the United States alone. There must be something for them to do other than teach, so the search for fundable study becomes as important as (or more so than) any other activity among the professoriate. Because Pareto funded himself, he did not have to bend his interests to fit this or that agency during this or that political climate. He therefore did not have to ingratiate himself with bureaucrats or other academics by cagily worded proposals for money. So whereas now it is vital to all salaried academics to turn up "interesting" research topics year after year, strictly to meet their own financial needs and emotional desire for professional esteem, for Pareto the opposite held true: he wanted badly to finish a lifework before untimely death, so he could not afford to dally. Dalliance is precisely what modern social research does best. Every funded researcher wants to end the report of past work with the bankable phrase: "This clearly calls for further study before any definitive answer can be found." Part of this is self-serving hunger for money and status, part is not being as bright as Pareto (or Weber or Durkheim or Marx), and part is lack of imagination. Another component is the understandable hope that topics will last as long as one's career. No one wants to be a steel worker in Buffalo when steel has moved overseas. The rank and file of social science must do some work to justify their pay, so they refuse to hear that Pareto solved the mystery of human social organization in 1916. None of this is unknown to anyone, but it is not often mentioned. This fact itself would have amused Pareto and fitted into his description of a cycle during which genuine productivity drops and speculation becomes frenzied.

Other scholarly friends of Pareto have over the years heroically insisted upon his continued relevance to social analysis. But they have not succeeded in winning for him more readers than the occasional historian. If it was true that Mills wrote his *Power Elite* with Pareto in mind, that has not been the case for other important books in some years. When one finally does come to grips with Pareto's work, even in English translation, the manifest brilliance cannot be gainsaid; his precision of mind and crispness of expression stand in remarkable contrast to Weber's (or Parsons's) muddled phrases and endless sentence-paragraphs; his sympathies are perfectly reasonable given the historical circumstances of the time; and his willingness to go the distance in search of usable data at least equals Weber's. It becomes clear, then, that what his prospective readers are put off by is his aristocratic bearing, his repugnance at softheartedness whether within the working class or the ruling elite, his endless mockery of human follies—in short, because in print he does not seem a very pleasant man. But surely these are pre-, even anti-intellectual reasons for rejecting his ideas. Naturally derivations abound and are too easily fastened on by his critics, especially those who have not read him: he was a fascist inspiration; his method is poor; his data are arbitrarily gathered and arranged; his theoretical goal is to unseat reason, which is in itself reprehensible. All such objections are inane. His goal was simply and only to understand human life and its history. He was not in anyone's employ (sharing this happy state with Weber) and he believed in nothing except the virtue of sober inquiry. That he was full of passion (again, like Weber) and that it was carefully controlled and channeled into his work are equally obvious. But he was willing to say that some things are true and others not and then to document his claims, his inductions, as well as one man could. He was in essence and in a pure sense amoral, at least when building his scientific case.

Resistance to Pareto's mien and teaching is founded in just that nonlogical sphere of residues and the sentiments which sponsor them that he struggled to identify. It does not matter what we call them, whether Freud's approach is better, whether there really are *combinazioni* or aggregates in some nonnominal sense. What literature, art, the history of crime, war, sexuality, and all the other messy units of human endeavor show, even to the most blinded worshipper of scientism, is that the human animal has only recently discovered the process called giving just reasons, that many of its kind do not practice it very well yet, and that in the end what matter more than reasonable acts and their explanation are the harrowingly unpredictable, vicious, and self-adoring manners peculiar to our species. Consider, as in a film, the following scene: Anicius Manlius Severinus Boethius in his cell in 524, having just written the most beloved book of the next thousand years; the door opens, some men come in; they put a cord round his neck, twist it so that his eyes come out of the sockets, and then pound him to death with clubs. Make science of this.

Pareto's knowledge of ancient history was stupendous, the accumulation of a gifted, driven amateur. Surely he knew about Boethius's end, but when he refers to him, it is scientifically:

> For the very reason that we intend to remain strictly within logico-experimental bounds, we are not called upon to solve the metaphysical problem of Nominalism and Realism.[1] We do not presume to decide whether only the *individuum*, or only the *species*, exists, for the good reason, among others, that we are not sufficiently clear as to the precise meaning of the term "exist." We intend to study things and hence *individua*, and to consider species as aggregates of more or less similar things on which we determine ourselves for specified purposes. Further than that we choose not to go.
>
> [1]Familiar the language in which Boëthius, translating Porphyry, states the problem, *Isagogen Porphyrii commenta* I, 10 (Vienna, p. 159; Berlin, p. 25): *Mox de generibus et speciebus* . . . ("Next, as regards genera and species, I must be excused from deciding whether they are real or are mere conceptions of the mind, whether they are corporeal or incorporeal realities, and whether they are real apart from objects or are attributes of objects inseparable from them.") (*Trattato*, section 65)

The apparently odd juxtaposition—Boethius's bloody end (were they instructed to kill him painfully or was that simply their style, and were they told not to muss the manuscript or had it already been taken out of the cell?) and Pareto's tidy, conventional reference to an important philosophical argument which, had it not been for Boethius's own archival work in preserving ancient texts, may not have become a medieval standard—exemplifies Pareto's existential and scholarly dilemma. How can one mind take in and reflect seriously on the details of human history since Athens and Rome, then turn to an elaborate system of social scientific arranging and fill in the blanks? Surely part of Weber's greatness and his private anguish lay in trying to do just this, to carry on Mommsen's phenomenal tradition of historiography while helping give birth to its nemesis, social science. Stradivari did not write a "general theory of the violin"; he made them. His knowledge exceeded general theorizing and reached the pinnacle of specific requirements. A general theory of sound will not produce perfect timber. This is part of Pareto's paradoxical relation to us: he knew more about our past than we do (even within the limits of the texts he learned from) and stood in the midst of specificity, yet toed the scientific line almost religiously. As he put it:

> Now we are to study human conduct, the states of mind to which it corresponds and the ways in which they express themselves, in order to arrive eventually at our goal, which is to discover the forms of society. We are following the inductive method. We have no preconceptions, no *a priori* notions. We find certain facts before us. We describe them, classify them, determine their character, ever on the watch for some uniformity (law) in the relationships between them. (*Trattato*, section 145)

It would seem, then, that in order to throw out his conceptualizations we must analyze his data. And since very few, if any, social scientists today are capable of that, we have manufactured a simple dodge which is also applied regularly to Marx and Weber. We adopt, with little legitimate grounding, the definitions of proof provided in the 1920s by logical positivism, soften them just enough to allow social science its existence, and then argue that illustration or description is not proof. With that Pareto is dispatched. But nothing is ever proved in social science in a way that meets the most tempered positivist criteria. Until very recently it was taken as axiomatic that IQ and race were randomly related. It is now a "legitimate" area of research for some American academics to study whether what racists have always said was true: that American blacks cannot think as well as European whites. It was also accepted until about 1970 that women and men were different and that men were generally better at doing most of what industrial societies need done. Such an argument, neither proved nor disproved by science, is now anathema to most social scientists and a sizable share of the laity. What is this but more evidence for Pareto's cycles?

Besides being explained by the fact that today's audience lacks sufficient energy or information to challenge Pareto on his own grounds, his eclipse can be seen as a function—to speak in Parsons's voice—of purely psychological forces. If Pareto's theory of social action and cycles is even for the most part true, it rings the death knell for progress, political or intellectual. One cannot simultaneously accept a picture of humanity as forever treading a path of repetition (Vico's *ricorsi*) and at the same time see in its history some kind of progress. We have now several distinguished histories *of* progress, but how many compelling histories *as* progress? Today no philosopher or other acute observer of the human scene is making strong claims for the moral progress of contemporary societies, even if its mechanical improvements and innovations are obvious. Ever since Ogburn's *Social Change* (1922), practically everyone has been aware that as technology becomes ever more complicated and efficient, human organization walks a slower pace and often in a different direction. To many it seems incredible—but it would not have shocked Pareto—that the same culture to have perfected artificial birthing procedures in laboratories and clinics simultaneously listens with some sympathy to arguments against contraception based on ancient supernatural texts. Partisans of laboratory procreation view their enthusiasm as a stunning technical achievement and convenience. Each side finds its opponents incomprehensible. Both try to make rational arguments; neither has any basis in logic or reason; and the debate will continue until one side or the other becomes exhausted or extinguished. This in miniature is precisely the sort of human history Pareto found so intriguing and documented with data from a two-thousand-year period.

Another dimension to Pareto's lack of followers today is the political. It is not only that he was identified after his death in 1923 as a proto-fascist (an absurd charge) that makes him ideologically objectionable to social science today. He pointed out that elites always run societies and that those who refuse to employ force at some point lose control to those who do. He did not argue that this was a sound way of ordering the polity or that he found it a pleasant feature of social organization, but simply reported what his analysis of history told him. Messengers of bad news are not fondly treated. No study has shown Pareto wrong—in fact, quite the contrary, in a number of elite studies—but his "knocker" attitude to-

ward democracy repels even those members of mass society educated enough to read his work. Although Pareto always attacked
aristocratic privilege and what sociologists call ascribed statuses, his
distrust of mass democracy and its tendency toward "demagogic
plutocracy" allowed fascists and other enemies of republican sentiment to misuse Pareto. Mass democracy is not thus far a happily
conclusive experiment in government. Already in the 1890s Pareto
saw that elites who ran mass democracy relied on ever-increasing
national debts to finance their continued tenure in office. He could
scarcely imagine the size and importance of those debts now, only
sixty-five years after his death. Whether current forms of government in the West will endure is an open question, yet the data Pareto
amassed do not suggest an outcome welcome to those who think
well of current regimes.

Democracies foster much, especially hope. The "Machiavellians," identified by Burnham as "Defenders of Freedom" (Dante,
Machiavelli, Mosca, Sorel, Michels, Pareto),[34] do not trade in that
particular currency, because their experiences and learning taught
them to be wary of joyousness in the face of political life. Weber
(good friend of one Machiavellian, Michels) shared their realism/
skepticism, but did not close off hope. He did consider charisma to
be an opening into a less tragic era, as it had been so often in the
past. And a man who reveres Tolstoy's morality and art, as Weber
did, has not yet given up hope. Weber is the cautioning uncle of
modern times, pointing out the dangers ahead but in the end leaving his charges with some reason to go on. Pareto is the scoffing
grandfather, laughing at his young and forward-looking descendants for what they do not know and do not wish to know. Such
thinkers as Ernst Cassirer, Theodor Adorno, Hannah Arendt, and
Karl Jaspers have been stunned by this century's love affair with
the irrational at all levels of life and activity, but Pareto would
simply find them naive and ignorant of history. He did not recognize, for instance, that "*coincidentia oppositorum* between the irrational and rational forces in culture"[35] which Cassirer tried to demonstrate in his great work on myth.

Democracy keeps alive the illusion of openness and, along with

34. John Burnham, *The Machiavellians.*
35. John Michael Krois, *Cassirer*, p. 186.

that, the promise of knowledge advancing in some helpful way. If Jefferson suspected, as Vico had already propounded, that *upward* and *onward* are not the most accurate bywords of history, he suppressed this knowledge for the benefit of a utopian effort. Jefferson's historical persona is therefore easy to like. Pareto wanted to know what was true and what false, and such folk do not become utopian heroes. Absolute knowledge runs counter to democratic sensitivity, the wish for and belief in unending public debate—which is why Einstein and Mozart can be admired by democratic masses but never genuinely adored, since they single-handedly opened and closed an entire book of human enterprise. Pareto's *Trattato* is the Ninth Symphony of social theory. No one has surpassed Beethoven's monument, because it exhausts a form, using every known mechanism in achieving its desired end. A composer's reasonable response to the Ninth is to write miniatures, hoping there at least to say something interesting. Attempts to outdo Beethoven in the symphonic form (e.g., those of Mahler, Liszt, Bruckner) have uniformly failed. Yet the "Ode to Joy" is pleasant, exhilarating, even "supportive." Pareto's work of art is not. And the price paid for bringing bad news in such volume and detail is to be locked out of the party that humanity has been trying to carry on since the eighteenth century. It is for these and many other reasons that cannot be detailed here that Pareto's method or madness deserves emulation, even in modified form. To look unblinking at the facts of broad-scale cultural change and then attach to the results a philosophy of history that makes defensible sense within a stated realm of ultimate values: this is the lost task of social science, which Pareto carried so far toward completion.

The plain truth is that most sociologists do not *need* to know, and consequently do not know, much about anything beyond that which their methods can break apart and reduce to "explained variance." In fact, the words *intellectual* and, much less, *scholar* are no longer synonyms for *sociologist*, as they once were. As was explained at length above, this loss works against two ends: (1) sound hermeneutics of classical texts; and, more important, (2) avoidance of unnecessary and illegitimate conceptual fragmentation of the social world through micro analysis, the fruits of which are never reassembled into a comprehensive or holistic form. It is worthwhile, I believe, to reinstitute as a legitimate methodological device what might be called interpretative narrative, whether through historical materials (so successfully demonstrated by the Annales school in recent times) or through contemporary behavioral research. The mistake American sociologists have made is to take one aspect of Weber's work—the contentless nominalist typologies, too easily applicable to social phenomena of practically any type—and forget that the theoretical reliability of the typologies rests on and was generated by Weber's gigantic accretion of facts. Without the factual substrate and the qualifications it forced Weber to make whenever he generalized or constructed an ideal-type, the risk of applying purely arbitrary, even inaccurate concepts or systems of deductions becomes very great. While there is no guarantee that sizable agglomerations of facts will protect the researcher from conceptual fallacies, they can serve as a safeguard in an atmosphere of sociological research where few safeguards remain.

Having made the case for adopting in part Pareto's quasi-methodological technique, I must at the same time acknowledge that this style was hardly unique to him. Sorokin and Toynbee did much the same thing, as had Spencer and Comte before them. All have suffered at the hands of methodological specialists for their lack of rigor in selecting and grouping data but, of course, none of these specialists knew what the factual compilers knew. Is it ever possible, then, adequately to criticize a work such as Pareto's? Formal extrinsic critique is easily accomplished, but what of the more thorough internal criticism? Both Sorokin and Pareto produced philosophies of history which when viewed from on high seem to propose wave-motion patterns to historical change. There is little evidence that these particular patterns came to either theorist a priori. If we believe their own testimony and the testimony of their works, they seem to have appropriated wave motion in an effort to explain their data—certainly an innocent enough mode of analysis. If this is true, then is it not also possible that until Pareto's splendid compilation of information (or, at minimum, a substantial and *very* representative sample of it) is subjected to detailed investigation, his entire architectonic (of sentiments, derivations, and so on) will defy definitive assessment? Weber's comparative sociology of religion has received thorough study, such that by now almost all of his (amazingly few) errors are known and recorded. The same cannot be said for Pareto's work. Why is this the case? How much has it to do with the work itself, and how much with its present audience? Is the *Trattato* destined forever, as Crawford put it, "to remain a monument rather than a stepping stone"?[36]

In spite of these unanswered questions surrounding Pareto's masterpiece, for the moment we may leave completely aside Pareto's contentions about the nonlogical roots of behavior and the rationalizations attached to it post facto in the form of explanatory derivations.[37] I do not believe that to this point we have either shown them to be false or devised other theories which are very much better (including Freudianism). But proving them would be a thankless, perhaps impossible task given current standards of verification. In fact, what has contributed most to Pareto's eclipse, I believe, is not substantive or theoretical errors in his work but the difficulty of squeezing his "theorems," as he called them, into a fashionable methodological apparatus. His potential contributions to understanding irrationality will forever be blocked from entering discourse unless we are given respite from the methodological fetishism that now encumbers those interested in transmitting this sociological legacy accurately.

What *can* be learned from Pareto, whether or not his system is dealt with on its own complex terms, is this: those who would understand human behavior as thoroughly as they might cannot restrict themselves to the use of the rational model (even an enlightened version like Weber's, which takes account of deviation in a relatively perfunctory way through nonrational categories) without cutting the heart out of human thought, emotion, and activity. In the *Trattato* alone (merely a fraction of his work that added to sociological knowledge in one way or another), Pareto committed over 850,000 words to the demonstration, if not the proof, of this thesis. This he accomplished almost inadvertently, since his self-defined task—delineating the gap between rational explanation and nonlogical behavior—was not designed to investigate irrationality per se. If we are repulsed at his alleged "instinctivist psychol-

---

36. Crawford, "Representative Italian Contributions to Sociology," p. 568.

37. Though I am aware that Pareto scholars, following his lead, distinguish between *nonlogical* and *irrational*, I am collapsing the two for the moment, both because I see Pareto's distinction as somewhat forced and unnecessary and because I cannot here examine the nature of this difference, were it to be regarded as important to behavior.

262 *Irrationality in Social Life Reconsidered*

ogy," this reflects our insensitivity to Pareto's lexicon more than it does the inherent nature of his theory. As he explained to his students, "instincts" held no particular explanatory mystique for him (as they did for Freud). Rather, they designated a "regularity" which he perceived to be operating in human history and were to be thought of in the same terms as the "sentiments," that is, as thoroughly indescribable because of their unresponsiveness to positivist inquiry: as a given. Though in the professional sense, it is now ideologically impractical to invoke instinct as a causative, the turn away from *culture* as a universal explanation for behavior and toward sociobiology might prompt renewed interest in Pareto, even if for the wrong reason.[38]

In conclusion, I believe our Weberian perspective, nurtured from the first introductory course in sociology to the last graduate seminar, is doubtless a splendid vantage point from which to view certain portions of social reality; that, in fact, one can with considerable justification—and peer support—rest content within the boundaries of Weberianism through a lifetime of research, slightly altering this or that part of the entirety but leaving the edifice essentially as it was originally constructed. However, those few but, I believe, highly disruptive flaws in Weberian rationalism can be ameliorated tremendously by an infusion of the Paretian perspective. This includes the recognition that human rationality is a relatively rare event, not only because of intrinsic cognitive limits but because of insufficient information to plan truly rational action—something Pareto considered but Weber did not. As is often pointed out, "logical conduct" for Pareto is practically identical to Weber's "purpose-rational" type of social action. But whereas Weber unceremoniously relegates what he admits to be most of social action to the three other "lesser" types, Pareto quickly moves away from "logical conduct" and produces dozens of subdivided descriptive categories which deal comprehensively with behavior. His failures may be greater than Weber's, but so too were his ambitions and his attempted grasp. And this is the last lesson bequeathed by the Paretian legacy to those attentive to it.

38. My enthusiasm for sociobiology is quite limited, as I believe it would have been for Pareto. But my hope is that if the hegemony of *culture* as the master explanatory terms can be broken, then some of the objectionable surface features of Pareto's

Conclusion

It is not only out of concern for the accurate portrayal of classical theory that I have juxtaposed Weber and Pareto. And it is also not primarily because I have tremendous faith in or hope for a revitalized Paretian sociology. I have hinted at the probable benefits of a Paretian corrective to Weber's dominant theoretical expression, "the rational social act," since contemporary life is less and less characterized by action that is particularly "rational," however loosely defined. It is no secret (thanks to Weber himself, Nietzsche before him, and Lukács, Marcuse, Adorno, Mannheim, Habermas, and many others since), that rationalization at the civilizational level—the merciless coercion of behavior and thought into desiccated rationality and bureaucratic regulation—begets, at the extreme, irrational performances too horrible to discuss. Preliminary documentation of this comes from the literati—Kafka, Koestler, Beckett, Nabokov, Musil, and others. But their vision has somehow not worked out in the advanced West. Men do not wake up in their beds metamorphosed into ghastly, unloved insects, nor do they very often find themselves spirited away in the night by uniformed demons working for a political Mephistopheles. Rather, they "cope." Their means of coping, as undramatic and truly unheroic (in Weber's sense) as it is, frequently revolves around what Marxists have angrily called the "privatization of consciousness" or "of self." Indeed, there are those who celebrate the "freedom" which may, under fortuitous circumstances, blossom as a function of certain types of "privatization," especially those which break the bonds of constraining kinship or ethnic attachments. But for many—one would suppose, for the majority—the effect of all the sundry substantive irrationalities peculiar to advanced industrial societies, from the most trivial to the earth-shaking, is to drive people out of those very settings where rational action can be most rewarding. The political arena, for one, with the permanent passing of social movements, will never again be filled with the fundamental, spectacular power of the newly enlightened pursuing

---

writing may be ignored (as they were in the 1930s) and he may once again be taken seriously.

social change through calculated collective action and guided by liberating ideas, however poorly understood. One result of this emptying of meaning from the political realm, the "fall of public man,"[39] is potentially dangerous for nations who wish to survive what Habermas has aptly termed the "legitimation crisis." But the political sphere is not the only locus of action from which social actors have fled.

As I explained above, were one to use a conventional breakdown of social institutions in trying to locate what types of action occur where (using Weber's typology), I believe it could be shown that the "vital" institutions, as they were once termed (economic, political, stratificational, and—somewhat less "vital"—the educational and kinship) have receded as environments in which ordinary people can practice meaningful, rational action. The reasons for this, much too complex to disentangle here, are a formidable mix of the trivial, obvious, and well documented with the truly inscrutable. Since human beings tend to associate some forms of meaningfulness with their own satisfying public performances— that is, rational sorts of action—as these institutions become increasingly restrictive and exclusive of action that could be termed autonomous and rational they necessarily lose meaning.[40] Because man is the meaning-seeking animal, he gravitates to loci (or institutions) where meaning is likely to be found or created. The auxiliary or nonvital institutions (e.g., the supernatural, aesthetic, recreational) become *once again*, by default, the arenas in which social actors find their most meaningful experiences. I say "once again" since all three institutions seemed to be in eclipse—relative to previous historical periods—during the earlier part of this century and through much of the preceding one. Charles Morazé's noted history of the nineteenth century, *The Triumph of the Bourgeoisie*, is wisely titled, and the champions of capitalist accumulation cared very little for the church, the theater, or the gaming room. Their business was their life (remember Weber's father), and their need for meaning, however great or small, had to be met in the midst of

39. Richard Sennett, *The Fall of Public Man*.
40. For illustrative purposes, I repeat here Weber's contention that meaning is greatest in rational action, that is, when free of irrational constraints. Whether this is empirically true or is an artifact of liberal ideology is not in question.

secular, acquisitive rationalization at full tilt. While Oscar Wilde, Stefan George, Baudelaire, Mallarmé, and company registered their lonely protests, fortunes were being made by men whose instrumentalism and capacity for rational action knew few bounds.

Weber wondered, after visiting the frontier in this country, what would become of the American zest for opportunity and advancement when the open spaces closed. Perhaps in longing to proceed beyond *Wirtschaft und Gesellschaft* and into his sociology of the arts, he was subconsciously predicting where consciousness would necessarily flee when the cage of rationalization had become too rigid for actual escape. Had he not died prematurely, perhaps he would have provided us with an investigation of the irrational and the irrationalizable that would have spoken as brilliantly to our present situation as had *Wirtschaft und Gesellschaft* to that of his father.

Bibliography

SPECIAL BIBLIOGRAPHIES ON WEBER AND PARETO

Busino, Giovanni. "Bibliographie: chronologie des écrits de Vilfredo Pareto." In *Jubile du Professeur V. Pareto*, ed. Giovanni Busino, pp. 71–110. (1,027 entries.) Vol. 20 of *Oeuvres complètes de Vilfredo Pareto*, 21 vols. G. Busino, general editor. Geneva: Librairie Droz, 1975.

Gerth, Hans, and Hedwig Gerth. "Bibliography on Max Weber." *Social Research* 16, no. 1 (March 1949): 70–89.

Käsler, Dirk. "Max-Weber-Bibliographie." *Kölner Zeitschrift für Soziologie und Sozialpsychologie* 27 (December 1975): 703–730.

Seyfarth, Constans, and Gert Schmidt. *Max Weber Bibliographie: Eine Dokumentation der Sekundärliteratur.* (2,300 entries.) Stuttgart: Enke, 1977.

Tommissen, Piet. "Bibliographie des écrits sur V. P." In *Jubile du Professeur V. Pareto*, ed. Giovanni Busino, pp. 111–249. (1,845 entries.) Vol. 20 of *Oeuvres complètes de Vilfredo Pareto*, 21 vols, G. Busino, general editor. Geneva: Librairie Droz, 1975.

Weber, Marianne. "Chronologische Geordnetes Verzeichnis der Schriften von Max Weber." In *Max Weber: Ein Lebensbild*, pp. 715–719. Tübingen: Mohr, 1926.

Weiss, Johannes. "Literaturverzeichnis." In *Max Webers Grundlegung der Soziologie*, pp. 198–234. Munich: Verlag Dokumentation, 1975.

Winckelmann, Johannes, ed. *Soziologie. Weltgeschichtliche Analysen. Politik.* Stuttgart: A. Kröner, 1956.

WEBER'S MAJOR WORKS IN GERMAN, AND ALL ENGLISH TRANSLATIONS

1891   *Die römische Agrargeschichte in ihrer Bedeutung für das Staats- und Privatrecht.* Stuttgart: Enke. Reprinted Amsterdam: P. Schippers, 1962. Also reprinted in the "Ancient Economic History Series," ed. Moses Finley. Salem, N.H.: Ayer, 1980.

1892   "Die Verhältnisse der Landarbeiter im ostelbischen Deutschland." *Schriften des Vereins für Sozialpolitik* 55: 1–891.

1895–1896 "Die Ergebnisse der deutschen Börsenenquete." *Zeitschrift für das Gesammte Handelsrecht* 43: 83–219, 457–514; 44: 29–74; 45: 69–156.

1909   "Agrarverhältnisse im Altertum." In *Handwörterbuch der Staats-*

wissenschaften, ed. J. Conrad, pp. 52–188. Jena: Fischer. [Reprinted in 1924a: 1–288.]

1920–1921 *Gesammelte Aufsätze zur Religionssoziologie*. Mohr-Siebeck. 3 volumes: 1 (1920); 2, *Hinduismus und Buddhismus* (1921); 3, *Das antike Judentum* (1921). (Vol. 1, 6th printing: 1972; vol. 2, 5th printing: 1972; vol. 3, 6th printing: 1976.)

1921a   *Gesammelte politische Schriften*. Munich: Drei Masken Verlag. (2d edition: Mohr-Siebeck, 1958; 3rd edition: Mohr-Siebeck, 1971).

1921b   *Grundriss der Sozialökonomik*. Vol. 3: *Wirtschaft und Gesellschaft*. (Part 1.) Tübingen: Mohr-Siebeck.

1921c   *Die rationalen und soziologischen Grundlagen der Musik*. Munich: Drei Masken Verlag. (2d edition: 1924. New edition Tübingen: Mohr-Siebeck, 1972.)

1922a   *Gesammelte Aufsätze zur Wissenschaftslehre*. Tübingen: Mohr-Siebeck. (2d edition: 1951; 3rd edition: 1968; 4th edition: 1973.)

1922b   *Grundriss der Sozialökonomik*. Vol. 3: *Wirtschaft und Gesellschaft*. Ed. Marianne Weber. Tübingen: Mohr-Siebeck. (2d edition: 1925; 3rd edition: 1947.)

1923   *Wirtschaftsgeschichte: Abriss der universalen Sozial- und Wirtschafts-Geschichte*. Ed. S. Hellman and M. Palyi. Berlin: Duncker and Humblot. (2d edition Munich: Duncker and Humblot, 1924; 3rd edition: 1958.)

1924a   *Gesammelte Aufsätze zur Sozial- und Wirtschaftsgeschichte*. Tübingen: Mohr-Siebeck.

1924b   *Gesammelte Aufsätze zur Soziologie und Sozialpolitik*. Tübingen: Mohr-Siebeck.

1927   *General Economic History*. Trans. F. H. Knight. London: Allen and Unwin. (Reprinted Glencoe: Free Press, 1950; New York: Collier Books, 1961; New York: Free Press, 1966; New York: Transaction Books, 1981.)

1930   *The Protestant Ethic and the Spirit of Capitalism*. Trans. T. Parsons. London: Allen and Unwin. (Reprinted New York: Scribner's, 1958; London and New York: Allen and Unwin, 1986.)

1936   *Jugendbriefe*. Ed. Marianne Weber. Tübingen: Mohr-Siebeck.

1946   *From Max Weber: Essays in Sociology*. Trans., ed., and with an introduction by H. H. Gerth and C. Wright Mills. New York: Oxford University Press.

1947a   *Schriften zur theoretischen Soziologie, zur Sociologie der Politik und Verfassung*. Ed. M. Graf zu Solms. Frankfurt: Schauer.

1947b   *The Theory of Social and Economic Organization*. Trans. A. M. Henderson and T. Parsons. New York: Oxford University Press. (Reprinted New York: Free Press, 1964.)

1949   *The Methodology of the Social Sciences*. Trans. and ed. E. Shils and H. Finch. Glencoe: Free Press.

1950   "The Social Causes of the Decay of Ancient Civilization."

Trans. C. Mackauer. *Journal of General Education* 5: 75–88. (Reprinted in 1971b.)

1951   *The Religion of China.* Trans. and ed. H. Gerth. Glencoe: Free Press. (Reprinted New York: Free Press, 1968.)

1952   *Ancient Judaism.* Trans. and ed. H. H. Gerth and D. Martindale. Glencoe: Free Press. (Reprinted New York: Free Press, 1967.)

1954   *Max Weber On Law in Economy and Society.* Ed. and annotated by M. Rheinstein. Trans. M. Rheinstein and E. Shils. Cambridge, Mass.: Harvard University Press. (Reprinted New York: Simon and Schuster, 1967, pb.)

1956a   "Max Weber on Bureaucratization in 1909." In J. P. Mayer, *Max Weber and German Politics,* pp. 125–131. 2d edition. London: Faber and Faber.

1956b   *Soziologie. Weltgeschichtliche Analysen. Politik.* Ed. J. Winckelmann. Stuttgart: A. Kröner. (2d edition: 1960; 3d edition: 1964; 4th edition: 1968; 5th edition: 1973.)

1956c   *Staatssoziologie.* Ed. J. Winckelmann. Berlin: Duncker and Humblot. (2d edition: 1966.)

1956d   *Wirtschaft und Gesellschaft: Grundriss der verstehenden Soziologie.* Ed. J. Winckelmann. Tübingen: Mohr. (4th edition: 1964; 4th rev. edition: 1972; 5th rev. edition: 1976.)

1958a   *The City.* Trans. and ed. D. Martindale and G. Neuwirth. Glencoe: Free Press. (Reprinted New York: Free Press, 1966.)

1958b   *The Rational and Social Foundations of Music.* Ed. D. Martindale and J. Riedel. Trans. D. Martindale, J. Riedel, and G. Neuwirth. Carbondale: Southern Illinois University Press. (Reprinted 1969, pb.)

1958c   *The Religion of India.* Trans. and ed. H. H. Gerth and D. Martindale. Glencoe: Free Press. (Reprinted New York: Free Press, 1967, pb.)

1960   *Rechtssoziologie.* Ed. J. Winckelmann. Berlin: Hermann-Luchterhand. (2d edition: 1967.)

1962   *Basic Concepts in Sociology.* Trans. and introduction by H. P. Secher. New York: Philosophical Library. (Reprinted Secaucus: Citadel Press, 1972, pb.)

1963a   *Max Weber: Selections from His Work.* Ed. S. M. Miller. New York: Thomas Crowell.

1963b   *The Sociology of Religion.* Trans. E. Fischoff. Boston: Beacon Press. (Reprinted 1964, pb.)

1964   *Max Weber: Werk und Person.* Ed. Eduard Baumgarten. Tübingen: Mohr-Siebeck. (Includes about 143 pages of material unavailable elsewhere.)

1967   "A Letter from Max Weber." Trans. B. B. Frye. *Journal of Modern History* 39, no. 2 (June): 119–125 (unavailable elsewhere).

1968a   *Economy and Society: An Outline of Interpretive Sociology.* Partially trans. and ed. G. Roth and C. Wittich. 3 vols. New York: Bedminster Press. (Reprinted Berkeley and Los Angeles: University of California Press, 1979.)

1968b   *Max Weber on Charisma and Institution Building.* Ed. and introduction by S. N. Eisenstadt. Chicago: University of Chicago Press.

1968c   *Methodologische Schriften.* Ed. J. Winckelmann. Frankfurt: Fischer.

1968d   *Die protestantische Ethik.* Vol. 2: *Kritiken und Antikritiken.* Ed. J. Winckelmann. Munich: Siebenstern.

1970   "A Translation of Max Weber's 'Ueber einige Kategorien der verstehenden Soziologie' (Essay on Some Categories of Interpretive Sociology), with Introduction and Footnotes." M.A. thesis by E. E. Graber. Norman: University of Oklahoma.

1971a   "Max Weber on Race and Society." Trans. Jerome Gittleman; introduction by B. Nelson. *Social Research* 38: 30–41. (Trans. from 1924b: 456–462.)

1971b   *Max Weber: The Interpretation of Social Reality.* Ed. and introduction by J. E. T. Eldridge. New York: Scribner's. (Reissued Schocken, 1980.) (Contains a translation of some of Weber's industrial sociology unavailable elsewhere; and "Socialism.")

1972a   "Georg Simmel as Sociologist." Trans. and introduction by Donald N. Levine. *Social Research* 39, no. 1 (Spring): 155–163.

1972b   *Wirtschaft und Gesellschaft: Grundriss der verstehenden Soziologie.* 5th rev. edition in 1 volume. Ed. J. Winckelmann. Tübingen: Mohr-Siebeck.

1973   "Max Weber on Church, Sect, and Mysticism." Trans. J. Gittleman. *Sociological Analysis* 34, no. 2 (Summer): 140–149. (Trans. from 1924b: 462–470.)

1974   *On Universities: The Power of the State and the Dignity of the Academic Calling in Imperial Germany.* Trans., ed., and introduction by Edward Shils. Chicago: University of Chicago Press.

1975a   "Marginal Utility Theory and 'The Fundamental Law of Psychophysics.'" Trans. Louis Schneider. *Social Science Quarterly* 56, no. 1 (June): 21–36. (Trans. from 1922a: 384–399.)

1975b   *Roscher and Knies: The Logical Problems of Historical Economics.* Trans. and introduction by G. Oakes. New York: Free Press.

1976a   *The Agrarian Sociology of Ancient Civilizations.* Trans. and introduction by R. I. Frank. London: New Left Books.

1976b   *Wirtschaft und Gesellschaft: Grundriss der verstehenden Soziologie.* 5th rev. edition, plus 1 volume of annotations by J. Winckelmann. Tübingen: Mohr-Siebeck.

1977   *Critique of Stammler.* Trans. and introduction by G. Oakes. New York: Free Press.

1978a   "Anti-Critical Last Word on The Spirit of Capitalism." Trans. W. M. Davis. *American Journal of Sociology* 83, no. 5 (March):

1105–1131. (Trans. from *Die protestantische Ethik*, vol. 2, pp. 283–345.)

1978b *Max Weber: Selections in Translation*. Ed. W. G. Runciman; trans. E. Matthews. New York: Cambridge University Press. (About 38 pages of material are unavailable elsewhere.)

1979 "Developmental Tendencies in the Situation of East Elbian Rural Labourers." Trans. Keith Tribe. *Economy and Society* 8, no. 2 (May): 177–205.

1980 "The National State and Economic Policy (Freiburg Address)." Trans. Keith Tribe. *Economy and Society* 9, no. 4 (November): 428–449.

1981a *General Economic History*. Introduction by I. Cohen. New Brunswick: Transaction Books. (1927 F. H. Knight translation.)

1981b "Some Categories of Interpretive Sociology." Trans. E. Graber. *Sociological Quarterly* 22, no. 2: 151–180.

1982 *Max Weber Gesamtausgabe*. 33 volumes projected. Ed. H. Baier et al. Tübingen: J. C. B. Mohr (Paul Siebeck).

1984 "'Energetic' Theories of Culture." Trans. J. Mikkelson and C. Schwartz. *Mid-American Review of Sociology* 9, no. 2: 33–58.

1985 "Churches and Sects in North America." Trans. Colin Loader. *Sociological Theory* 3, no. 1 (Spring): 7–13.

1986 "The Reich President." Trans. Gordon Wells. *Social Research* 53, no. 1 (Spring): 128–132.

CITED WORKS

Abel, Theodore. "The Operation Called *Verstehen*." *American Journal of Sociology* 54 (1948): 211–218.

Adorno, Theodor. *Negative Dialectics*. Trans. E. B. Ashton. New York: Seabury Press, 1973.

Alexander, Franz. *Our Age of Unreason: A Study of the Irrational Forces in Social Life*. Philadelphia: Lippincott, 1951.

Althusser, Louis, and Etienne Balibar. *Reading Capital*. Trans. Ben Brewster. London: New Left Books, 1972.

Anderson, Charles. *The Sociology of Survival*. Homewood, Ill.: Dorsey, 1976.

Andreski, Stanislav. *Social Sciences as Sorcery*. New York: St. Martin's Press, 1973.

Antoni, Carlo. *From History to Sociology: The Transition in German Historical Thinking*. Trans. Hayden White. London: Merlin Press, 1962.

Antonio, Robert J., and Ronald Glassman, eds. *A Weber-Marx Dialogue*. Lawrence: University Press of Kansas, 1985.

Apel, Karl-Otto, et al. *Hermeneutik und Ideologiekritik*. Frankfurt: Suhrkamp, 1971.

Arendt, Hannah. *The Life of the Mind*. Vol. 1: *Thinking*; Vol. 2: *Willing*. New York: Harcourt Brace Jovanovich, 1978.

Aron, Raymond. "Interpreting Pareto: The Marx of the Bourgeoisie?" *Encounter* 47, no. 5 (November 1976): 43–53.

Badcock, C. R. *Madness and Modernity.* London: Blackwell, 1984.

———. *The Psychoanalysis of Culture.* London: Blackwell, 1980.

Barnes, Harry Elmer. *Historical Sociology.* New York: Philosophical Library, 1948.

Barnes, Harry Elmer, and Howard P. Becker. *Social Thought from Lore to Science.* Boston: D. C. Heath, 1938.

Barnett, H. G. *Innovation: The Basis of Cultural Change.* New York: McGraw-Hill, 1953.

Barthes, Roland. *S/Z.* Trans. Richard Miller. New York: Hill and Wang, 1975.

———. *Writing Degree Zero/Elements of Semiology.* Trans. A. Lavers and C. Smith. Boston: Beacon Press, 1970.

Baumgarten, Eduard, ed. *Max Weber: Werk und Person.* Tübingen: J. C. B. Mohr, 1964.

Becker, Ernest. *The Structure of Evil.* New York: Free Press, 1976.

Becker, Howard P. *Through Values to Social Interpretation: Essays on Social Contexts, Actions, Types, and Prospects.* Durham: Duke University Press, 1950.

Beetham, David. *Max Weber and the Theory of Modern Politics.* London: George Allen and Unwin, 1974.

Bell, Daniel. *The End of Ideology.* Glencoe: Free Press, 1960.

Bendix, Reinhard. *Kings or People: Power and the Mandate to Rule.* Berkeley and Los Angeles: University of California Press, 1978.

———. *Max Weber: An Intellectual Portrait.* New York: Anchor Books, 1962.

———. "Max Weber and Jacob Burckhardt." *American Sociological Review* 30, no. 2 (April 1965): 176–184.

———. "A Memoir of My Father." *Canadian Review of Sociology and Anthropology* 2 (1965): 1–18.

———. *Work and Authority in Industry.* New York: Harper and Row, 1963.

Bendix, Reinhard, and Guenther Roth. *Scholarship and Partisanship: Essays on Max Weber.* Berkeley and Los Angeles: University of California Press, 1971.

Benn, S. I., and G. W. Mortimore, eds. *Rationality and the Social Sciences.* London: Routledge and Kegan Paul, 1976.

Bergson, Henri. *Creative Evolution.* Trans. Arthur Mitchell. New York: Henry Holt, 1911.

Berk, Richard A., and Peter H. Rossi. "Doing Good or Worse: Evaluation Research Politically Reexamined." In *Evaluation Studies,* vol. 2, ed. Marcia Guttentag. Beverly Hills: Sage, 1977.

Bernstein, Richard J. *The Restructuring of Social and Political Theory.* New York: Harcourt Brace Jovanovich, 1976.

Bilous, Jaroslav, and John H. Quirk. "Interest in Pareto's Sociology: An Essay in the Quantitative History of Social Science." *Cahiers Vilfredo Pareto* 20 (February 1970): 145–164.

Blum, Alan. *Theorizing.* London: Heinemann, 1974.

Blumenberg, Hans. *The Legitimacy of the Modern Age*. Trans. Robert Wallace. Cambridge, Mass.: MIT Press, 1983.

————. *Work on Myth*. Trans. Robert Wallace. Cambridge, Mass.: MIT Press, 1985.

Bobbio, Norberto. *On Pareto and Mosca*. Geneva: Droz, 1972.

Bourke, Vernon. *History of Ethics*. New York: Anchor Books, 1970.

Bousquet, Georges H. *Pareto, le savant et l'homme*. Lausanne: Payot, 1960.

————. "Vilfredo Pareto (1848–1923): Biographical Notes on the Occasion of His Letters to Pantaleoni." *Banca Nazionale de Lavoro Quarterly Review* 58 (September 1961): 317–360.

————. *Vilfredo Pareto, le développement et la signification historique de son oeuvre*. Paris: Rivière, 1924.

————. *The Work of Vilfredo Pareto*. Hanover, Minn.: Sociological Press, 1928.

Breed, Warren. Review of Tomáš Masaryk's *Suicide and the Meaning of Civilization. Contemporary Sociology* 1, no. 3 (May 1972): 222.

Brown, Richard Harvey. *A Poetic for Sociology*. New York: Cambridge University Press, 1977.

————. *Society as Text: Essays on Rhetoric, Reason, and Reality*. Chicago: University of Chicago Press, 1987.

Brown, Richard, and Stanford Lyman, eds. *Structure, Consciousness, and History*. New York: Cambridge University Press, 1978.

Brubaker, Roger. *The Limits of Rationality: An Essay on the Social and Moral Thought of Max Weber*. Boston: Allen and Unwin, 1984.

Bruun, H. H. *Science, Values and Politics in Max Weber's Methodology*. Copenhagen: Munksgaard, 1972.

Bucolo, Placido, ed. *The Other Pareto*. New York: St. Martin's Press, 1980.

Burger, Thomas. *Max Weber's Theory of Concept Formation: History, Laws, and Ideal Types*. Durham: Duke University Press, 1976.

Burke, Peter. "Arnaldo Momigliano." In *20th Century Culture: A Biographical Companion*, ed. A. Bullock and R. Woodings. New York: Harper and Row, 1983.

Burnham, John. *The Machiavellians*. New York: John Day, 1943.

Burton, Robert. *Anatomy of Melancholy* [1628]. New York: Tudor Publishing, 1951.

Busino, Giovanni, comp. "Les Ecrits de Pareto." *Jubile du Professeur V. Pareto*. Geneva: Droz, 1975.

Carroll, John. "Pareto's Irrationalism." *Sociology* 7 (1973): 327–340.

Cassirer, Ernst. *The Logic of the Humanities*. Trans. Clarence Howe. New Haven: Yale University Press, 1960.

Chaudhuri, Nirad. *Scholar Extraordinary: The Life of Prof. Rt. Hon. Friedrich Max Müller*. London: Chatto and Windus, 1974.

Clecak, Peter. *Radical Paradoxes: Dilemmas of the American Left 1945–1970*. New York: Harper and Row, 1975.

Cohen, Ira H. *Ideology and Unconsciousness: Reich, Freud, and Marx*. New York: Columbia University Press, 1982.

Cohen, Jean. "Max Weber and the Dynamics of Rationalized Domination." *Telos,* no. 14 (Winter 1972): 63–86.

Collins, Randall. *Weberian Sociological Theory.* New York: Cambridge University Press, 1986.

Connerton, Paul, ed. *Critical Sociology.* Harmondsworth: Penguin, 1976.

Copleston, Frederick. *A History of Philosophy,* vol. 5. New York: Image Books, 1964.

Coser, Lewis, ed. *The Idea of Social Structure.* New York: Harcourt Brace Jovanovich, 1975.

Crawford, W. Rex. "Representative Italian Contributions to Sociology: Pareto, Loria, Vaccaro, Gini, and Sighele." In *An Introduction to the History of Sociology,* ed. Harry Elmer Barnes. Chicago: University of Chicago Press, 1948.

Cuddihy, John. *The Ordeal of Civility: Freud, Marx, Lévi-Strauss, and the Jewish Struggle with Modernity.* New York: Delta, 1976.

Curtin, Deane, ed. *The Aesthetics of Science.* New York: Philosophical Library, 1982.

Dallmayr, Fred, and Thomas McCarthy, eds. *Understanding and Social Inquiry.* Notre Dame: University of Notre Dame Press, 1977.

Dilthey, Wilhelm. *Dilthey: Selected Writings.* Trans. H. P. Rickman. Cambridge, Eng.: Cambridge University Press, 1976.

———. *Poetry and Experience. Selected Works,* vol. 5, ed. R. Makkreel and F. Rodi. Princeton: Princeton University Press, 1985.

Donoghue, Denis. *Ferocious Alphabets.* Boston: Little, Brown, 1981.

Draper, Hal. *Karl Marx's Theory of Revolution.* 2 vols. New York: Monthly Review Press, 1977.

Dronberger, Ilse. *The Political Thought of Max Weber: In Quest of Statesmanship.* New York: Appleton-Century-Crofts, 1971.

Dufrenne, Mikel. *The Phenomenology of Aesthetic Experience.* Evanston: Northwestern University Press, 1974.

Durkheim, Emile. "The Positive Science of Ethics in Germany." *History of Sociology* 6, no. 2; 7, no. 1–2 (1987): 191–251.

———. Review of Marianne Weber's *Ehefrau und Mutter in der Rechtsentwickelung* [sic]. In *Emile Durkheim on Institutional Analysis,* ed. Mark Traugott. Chicago: University of Chicago Press, 1978.

Dvorak, Max. *History of Art as the History of Ideas.* Trans. J. Hardy. Boston: Routledge and Kegan Paul, 1984.

Eisen, Arnold. "The Meanings and Confusions of Weberian 'Rationality.'" *British Journal of Sociology* 28, no. 1 (March 1978): 57–70.

Eisermann, Gottfried. "L'Influence de Vilfredo Pareto en Allemagne." *Cahiers Vilfredo Pareto* 13, no. 34 (1975): 155–173.

———. *Vilfredo Pareto als Nationalökonom und Soziologe.* Tübingen: Mohr, 1961.

———. "Vilfredo Pareto in Deutschland." *Kölner Zeitschrift für Soziologie und Sozialpsychologie* 8, no. 4 (1956): 647–652.

Eldridge, J. E. T. "The Rationalization Theme in Weber's Sociology." In *Max Weber,* ed. J. E. T. Eldridge. New York: Scribner's, 1971.

―――. "Weber's Approach to the Sociological Study of Industrial Workers." In *Max Weber and Modern Sociology,* ed. Arun Sahay. London: Routledge and Kegan Paul, 1971.

Eliaeson, Sven. "Some Recent Interpretations of Max Weber's Methodology." *Sociological Analysis and Theory* 7, no. 1 (February 1977): 21–72.

Endleman, Robert. *Psyche and Society: Explorations in Psychoanalytic Sociology.* New York: Columbia University Press, 1981.

Ewen, Stuart. *Captains of Consciousness: Advertising and the Social Roots of Consumer Culture.* New York: McGraw-Hill, 1976.

Ewen, Stuart, and Elizabeth Ewen. *Channels of Desire: Mass Images of the Shaping of American Consciousness.* New York: McGraw-Hill, 1982.

Ferkiss, Victor. *The Future of Technological Society.* New York: George Braziller, 1972.

Feyerabend, Paul. *Against Method.* London: New Left Books, 1975.

Finer, S. E., ed. *Vilfredo Pareto: Sociological Writings.* New York: Praeger, 1966.

Finley, Moses. *The Ancient Economy.* Berkeley and Los Angeles: University of California Press, 1973.

Fischoff, Ephraim. "The Protestant Ethic and the Spirit of Capitalism: History of a Controversy." *Social Research* 11 (February 1944): 53–77.

Fleck, Ludwik. *Genesis and Development of a Scientific Fact.* Chicago: University of Chicago Press, 1979.

Foucault, Michel. *The Birth of the Clinic: An Archaeology of Medical Perception.* Trans. A. M. Sheridan Smith. New York: Vintage Books, 1975.

―――. *Madness and Civilization: A History of Insanity in the Age of Reason.* Trans. Richard Howard. New York: Vintage Books, 1973.

Freund, Julien. *The Sociology of Max Weber.* Trans. Mary Ilford. New York: Vintage Books, 1969.

Freyer, Hans. *Soziologie als Wirklichkeitwissenschaften.* Leipzig: B. G. Teubner, 1930.

Friedrichs, Robert. *A Sociology of Sociology.* New York: Free Press, 1970.

Frings, Manfred. *Max Scheler.* Pittsburgh: Duquesne University Press, 1965.

Gabel, Joseph. *False Consciousness.* Trans. Margaret Thompson. New York: Harper and Row, 1975.

―――. "Hungarian Marxism." *Telos,* no. 25 (1975): 185–191.

Gadamer, Hans-Georg. *Philosophical Apprenticeships.* Trans. R. Sullivan. Cambridge, Mass.: MIT Press, 1985.

―――. "The Problem of Historical Consciousness." *Graduate Faculty Philosophy Journal* 5, no. 1 (Fall 1975): 8–52.

―――. *Truth and Method.* [Trans. not listed.] New York: Seabury Press, 1975.

Gardner, Howard. *Frames of Mind: The Theory of Multiple Intelligence.* New York: Basic Books, 1985.

Garfinkel, Harold. "The Rational Properties of Scientific and Common-sense Activities." In *Positivism and Sociology*, ed. A. Giddens. London: Heinemann, 1974.

Gay, Peter. *The Bourgeois Experience*. 2 vols. New York: Oxford University Press, 1984, 1986.

Geertz, Clifford. *The Interpretation of Cultures*. New York: Basic Books, 1973.

Gerth, Hans, and C. Wright Mills. *Character and Social Structure*. New York: Harcourt Brace and World, 1953.

Giddens, Anthony. *New Rules of Sociological Method*. New York: Basic Books, 1976.

————, ed. *Positivism and Sociology*. London: Heinemann, 1974.

Ginsberg, Morris. *Essays in Sociology and Social Philosophy*. Harmondsworth: Penguin, 1968.

————. *The Psychology of Society*. 9th ed. London: Methuen, 1964.

Godelier, Maurice. *Rationality and Irrationality in Economics*. Trans. Brian Pearce. New York: Monthly Review Press, 1974.

Goode, William J. *Explorations in Social Theory*. New York: Oxford University Press, 1973.

————. "A Theory of Role Strain." In *Explorations in Social Theory*. New York: Oxford University Press, 1973.

Goodwin, Robert E. *The Politics of Rational Man*. New York: John Wiley, 1976.

Gordon, Milton. *Human Nature, Class, and Ethnicity*. New York: Oxford University Press, 1977.

Gould, Carol, and Marx Wartofsky, eds. *Women and Philosophy*. New York: Putnam's Sons, 1976.

Gouldner, Alvin. *The Coming Crisis of Western Sociology*. New York: Avon Books, 1971.

————. "The Metaphoricality of Marxism and the Context-Freeing Grammar of Socialism." *Theory and Society* 1 (1974): 387–414.

Grab, Hermann J. *Der Begriff des Rationalen in der Soziologie Max Webers*. Karlsruhe: Braun, 1927.

Graber, Edith. "Interpretive Sociology Is Not Part of a Psychology." *Sociology Inquiry* 45, no. 4 (1975): 65–70.

————. "A Translation of Max Weber's 'Über einige Kategorien der verstehenden Soziologie,' with Introduction and Footnotes." M.A. thesis, University of Oklahoma, 1970.

Graff, Gerald. *Literature Against Itself: Literary Ideas in Modern Society*. Chicago: University of Chicago Press, 1979.

Graff, Gerald, and Reginald Gibbons, eds. *Criticism in the University*. Evanston: Northwestern University Press, 1985.

Gras, Vernon, ed. *European Literary Theory and Practice*. New York: Delta, 1973.

Green, Bryan S. "On the Evaluation of Sociological Theory." *Philosophy of the Social Sciences* 7, no. 1 (March 1977): 33–50.

Green, Martin. *The von Richthofen Sisters: The Triumphant and Tragic Modes of Love*. New York: Basic Books, 1974.

Habermas, Jürgen. *Knowledge and Human Interests.* Trans. Jeremy Shapiro. Boston: Beacon Press, 1972.

———. *Philosophical-Political Profiles.* Trans. F. Lawrence. Cambridge, Mass.: MIT Press, 1985.

———. "A Review of Gadamer's *Truth and Method.*" Trans. T. McCarthy. In *Understanding and Social Inquiry,* ed. Fred Dallmayr and Thomas Mc-Carthy. Notre Dame: University of Notre Dame Press, 1977.

———. "Rhetorik, Hermeneutik, und Ideologiekritik." In *Hermeneutik und Ideologiekritik,* Karl-Otto Apel et al. Frankfurt: Suhrkamp, 1971.

———. "The Universal Claims of Hermeneutics." Trans. D. Dickens from *Hermeneutik und Ideologiekritik,* Karl-Otto Apel et al. Frankfurt: Suhrkamp, 1971.

———. "Zur Logik der Sozialwissenschaften." In *Philosophische Rundschau,* vol. 5. Tübingen: Mohr, 1967.

———. *Zur Logik der Sozialwissenschaften.* Frankfurt: Suhrkamp, 1970.

Hartfiel, Günter. *Wirtschaftliche und soziale Rationalität: Untersuchungen zum Menschenbild in Ökonomie und Soziologie.* Stuttgart: Ferdinand Enke Verlag, 1968.

Hartman, Geoffrey. *Criticism in the Wilderness: The Study of Literature Today.* New Haven: Yale University Press, 1980.

Hauser, Arnold. *The Philosophy of Art History.* Evanston: Northwestern University Press, 1985.

———. *Social History of Art.* 4 vols. Trans. Stanley Godman, with the author. New York: Vintage Books, 1957.

———. *Sociology of Art.* Trans. K. J. Northcott. Chicago: University of Chicago Press, 1982.

Hegel, G. W. F. *The Philosophy of History.* Trans. J. Sibree. New York: Dover, 1956.

Heisenberg, Werner. *The Physical Principles of Quantum Theory.* New York: Dover, 1930.

———. *Physics and Philosophy: The Revolution in Modern Science.* New York: Harper and Row, 1958.

Hendel, Charles W. *Jean-Jacques Rousseau: Moralist.* New York: Bobbs-Merrill, 1934.

Henderson, L. J. *Pareto's General Sociology: A Physiologist's Interpretation.* Cambridge, Mass.: Harvard University Press, 1935.

Hertzler, Joyce. *American Social Institutions.* Boston: Allyn and Bacon, 1961.

Hinkle, Roscoe C., and Gisela J. Hinkle. *The Development of Modern Sociology: Its Nature and Growth in the United States.* New York: Random House, 1954.

Hodges, H. A. "Lukács on Irrationalism." In *Georg Lukács,* ed. G. H. R. Parkinson. New York: Vintage Books, 1970.

———. *The Philosophy of Wilhelm Dilthey.* London: Routledge and Kegan Paul, 1952.

———. *Wilhelm Dilthey: An Introduction.* 2d ed. London: Routledge and Kegan Paul, 1949.

Hollis, Martin. "The Limits of Irrationality." *European Journal of Sociology* 7 (1967): 265–271.

Hollis, Martin, and Edward J. Nell. *Rational Economic Man.* Cambridge, Eng.: Cambridge University Press, 1975.

Holton, George. *Thematic Origins of Scientific Thought: Kepler to Einstein.* Cambridge, Mass.: Harvard University Press, 1974.

Honigsheim, Paul. "Max Weber: His Religious and Ethical Background and Development." *Church History* 19 (1950): 219–239.

———. "Max Weber as Applied Anthropologist." *Applied Anthropology* 7, no. 4 (Fall 1948): 27–35.

———. "Max Weber as Historian of Agriculture and Rural Life." *Agricultural History* 23, no. 3 (July 1949): 179–213.

———. "Max Weber as Rural Sociologist." *Rural Sociology* 11, no. 3 (September 1946): 207–218.

———. *On Max Weber.* Trans. Joan Rytina. New York: Free Press, 1968.

Horkheimer, Max, and Theodor Adorno. *Dialektik der Aufklärung.* Amsterdam: Querido, 1947. Trans. as *Dialectic of Enlightenment*, trans. John Cumming. New York: Herder and Herder, 1972.

Huff, Toby. *Max Weber and the Methodology of the Social Sciences.* New Brunswick: Transaction Books, 1984.

Hughes, H. Stuart. *Consciousness and Society: The Reorientation of European Social Thought 1890–1930.* New York: Alfred A. Knopf, 1959.

Husserl, Edmund. *Logical Investigations.* 2 vols. Trans. J. N. Findlay. Atlantic Highlands: Humanities Press, 1970.

Ichheiser, Gustav. *Appearances and Realities: Misunderstanding in Human Relations.* San Francisco: Jossey-Bass, 1970.

Ingarden, Roman. *The Cognition of the Literary Work of Art.* Trans. Ruth Crowley and Kenneth Olson. Evanston: Northwestern University Press, 1973.

———. *The Literary Work of Art: An Investigation on the Borderlines of Ontology, Logic, and Theory of Literature.* Trans. George Grabowicz. Evanston: Northwestern University Press, 1973.

———. *Untersuchungen zur Ontologie der Kunst.* Tübingen: Niemeyer, 1961.

Israel, Marvin. Review of Alan Blum's *Theorizing. Contemporary Sociology* 5, no. 4 (July 1976): 517.

James, William. "The Sentiment of Rationality." *Mind* 4 (July 1879): 317–346.

Jameson, Fredric. Letter to the Editor. *New York Review of Books*, 5 August 1976, p. 45.

———. Review Essay on Erving Goffman's *Frame Analysis. Theory and Society* 3 (1976): 119–133.

———. "The Vanishing Mediator: Narrative Structure in Max Weber." *New German Critique* 1, no. 1 (Winter 1973): 52–89.

Janowitz, Morris. "Social Theory and Social Control." *American Journal of Sociology* 81, no. 1 (July 1975): 82–108.

Jarvie, I. C., and J. Agassi. "The Problem of Rationality in Magic." *British Journal of Anthropology* 18 (1967): 55–74.

Jaspers, Karl. *General Psychopathology.* 7th German ed. Chicago: University of Chicago Press, 1963.

———. *Three Essays: Leonardo, Descartes, Max Weber.* Trans. Ralph Manheim. New York: Harcourt Brace and World, 1964.

Jay, Martin. *The Dialectical Imagination.* Boston: Little, Brown, 1973.

Jones, Robert Alun. "On Understanding a Sociological Classic." *American Journal of Sociology* 83, no. 2 (September 1977): 279–319.

———. "Presentism, Anachronism, and Continuity in the History of Sociology: A Reply to Seidman." *History of Sociology* 6, no. 1 (Fall 1985): 153–172.

Kadushin, Charles. *The American Intellectual Elite.* Boston: Little, Brown, 1973.

Keat, R., and J. Urry. *Social Theory as Science.* London: Routledge and Kegan Paul, 1975.

Kelly, Louis. *The True Interpreter: A History of Translation Theory and Practice in the West.* New York: St. Martin's Press, 1979.

Kolegar, Ferdinand. "The Concept of 'Rationalization' and Cultural Pessimism in Max Weber's Sociology." *Sociological Quarterly* 5, no. 4 (Autumn 1964): 355–373.

Krieger, Murray. *Theory of Criticism.* Baltimore: Johns Hopkins University Press, 1976.

Krois, John Michael. *Cassirer.* New Haven: Yale University Press, 1987.

Kronman, Anthony T. *Max Weber.* (Jurists: Profiles in Legal Theory.) Stanford: Stanford University Press, 1983.

Kuhn, Thomas S. *The Structure of Scientific Revolutions.* 2d ed. Chicago: University of Chicago Press, 1970.

Kuhns, Richard. *Structures of Experience: Essays on the Affinity between Philosophy and Literature.* New York: Harper and Row, 1974.

Lacan, Jacques. *The Language of the Self: The Function of Language in Psychoanalysis.* Trans. A. Wilden. New York: Delta, 1975.

La Capra, Dominick. *Emile Durkheim: Sociologist and Philosopher.* Ithaca: Cornell University Press, 1972.

Lamprecht, Karl. *Deutsche Geschichte.* 12 vols. Berlin: Weidmann, 1902–1904.

Landmann, Michael. "Critiques of Reason from Max Weber to Ernst Bloch." *Telos,* no. 29 (Fall 1976): 187–198.

LaPiere, Richard T. *Social Change.* New York: McGraw-Hill, 1965.

Lasch, Christopher. *The Culture of Narcissism.* New York: W. W. Norton, 1979.

Lazarsfeld, Paul, and Anthony Oberschall. "Max Weber and Empirical Social Research." *American Sociological Review* 30, no. 2 (Spring 1965): 185–199.

Lecky, W. E. H. *History of the Rise and Influence of the Spirit of Rationalism in Europe* [1865]. London: Longmans, Green, 1910.

Lecourt, Dominique. *Marxism and Epistemology: Bachelard, Canquilhem, and Foucault*. Trans. B. Brewster. London: New Left Books, 1975.

Lenski, Gerhard. Review of I. Wallerstein's *The Modern World-System*. *Social Forces* 54, no. 3 (March 1976): 701–703.

Lentricchia, Frank. *After the New Criticism*. Chicago: University of Chicago Press, 1984.

———. *Criticism and Social Change*. Chicago: University of Chicago Press, 1984.

Leonard, Peter. *Personality and Ideology: Towards a Materialist Understanding of the Individual*. Atlantic Highlands: Humanities Press, 1984.

Levine, Donald. *The Flight from Ambiguity*. Chicago: University of Chicago Press, 1985.

Levy, Marion J., Jr. "A Sociologist Who Knew Science." *Social Science Quarterly* 54, no. 3 (December 1973): 469.

Lévy-Bruhl, Lucien. *Primitive Mentality*. Trans. Lilian Clare. London: Unwin, 1923.

Lichtman, Richard. *The Production of Desire: The Integration of Psychoanalysis into Marxist Theory*. New York: Free Press, 1982.

Lieberstein, Harvey. *Beyond Economic Man*. Cambridge, Mass.: Harvard University Press, 1975.

Lindblom, Charles E. *Politics and Markets: The World's Political-Economic Systems*. New York: Basic Books, 1977.

Lipton, David R. *Ernst Cassirer: Dilemma of a Liberal Intellectual in Germany 1914–1933*. Toronto: University of Toronto Press, 1978.

Little, David. *Religion, Order, and Law: A Study in Pre-Revolutionary England*. New York: Harper and Row, 1969.

Loewenstein, Karl. *Max Weber's Political Ideas in the Perspective of Our Time*. Amherst: University of Massachusetts Press, 1966.

Lopreato, Joseph. "Notes on the Work of Vilfredo Pareto." *Social Science Quarterly* 54, no. 3 (December 1973): 451–468.

Lopreato, Sally Cook. "Toward a Formal Restatement of Vilfredo Pareto's Theory of the Circulation of Elites." *Social Science Quarterly* 54, no. 3 (December 1973): 491–507.

Löwith, Karl. *Max Weber and Karl Marx*. Trans. H. Fantel. Boston: Allen and Unwin, 1982.

———. "Weber's Interpretation of the Bourgeois-Capitalistic World in Terms of the Guiding Principle of 'Rationalization.'" In *Max Weber*, ed. Dennis Wrong. Englewood Cliffs, N.J.: Prentice-Hall, 1970.

Luckmann, Thomas. "On the Rationality of Institutions in Modern Life." *Archives Européennes de Sociologie* 16, no. 1 (1975): 3–15.

Lukács, Georg. *Georg Lukács: Selected Correspondence 1902–1920*. Ed. J. Marcus and Z. Tar. New York: Columbia University Press, 1986.

———. *History and Class Consciousness: Studies in Marxist Dialectics*. Trans. Rodney Livingstone. Cambridge, Mass.: MIT Press, 1971.

———. *Soul and Form*. Trans. Anna Bostock. London: Merlin Press, 1974.

———. *The Theory of the Novel: A Historico-Philosophical Essay on the Forms of*

Great Epic Literature. Trans. Anna Bostock. Cambridge, Mass.: MIT Press, 1971.

———. *Die Zerstörung der Vernunft.* Berlin: Aufbau-Verlag, 1954. Trans. as *Destruction of Reason*, trans. P. Palmer. London: Merlin Press, 1980.

Lukes, Steven. *Emile Durkheim: His Life and Work.* New York: Harper and Row, 1972.

———. "Some Problems About Rationality." In *Rationality*, ed. Bryan Wilson. New York: Harper and Row, 1970.

Lüthy, Herbert. *From Calvin to Rousseau.* New York: Basic Books, 1970.

McCarthy, Thomas. "A Theory of Communicative Competence." *Philosophy of the Social Sciences* 3 (1973): 135–156.

MacIver, Robert. *Society: Its Structure and Changes.* New York: Ray Long and Richard R. Smith, 1932.

Mackay, Charles. *Extraordinary Popular Delusions and the Madness of Crowds* [1841]. New York: Noonday, 1974.

Madge, Charles. *Society in the Mind: Elements of a Social Eidos.* New York: Free Press, 1964.

Makkreel, Rudolf. *Dilthey: Philosopher of the Human Sciences.* Princeton: Princeton University Press, 1975.

Mann, Thomas. *Buddenbrooks.* Trans. H. T. Lowe-Porter. New York: Alfred A. Knopf, 1952.

———. *Doctor Faustus.* Trans. H. T. Lowe-Porter. New York: Alfred A. Knopf, 1948.

———. *Last Essays.* Trans. R. C. Winston and T. J. Stern. New York: Alfred A. Knopf, 1958.

———. *Stories of Three Decades.* Trans. II. T. Lowe-Porter. New York: Random House, 1936.

Mannheim, Karl. *Essays on the Sociology of Knowledge.* London: Routledge and Kegan Paul, 1968.

———. *From Karl Mannheim.* Ed. K. Wolff. New York: Oxford University Press, 1971.

———. *Man and Society in an Age of Reconstruction.* New York: Harcourt Brace and World, 1940.

———. "On the Interpretation of Weltanschauung." In his *Essays on the Sociology of Knowledge.* London: Routledge and Kegan Paul, 1968.

Marcus, Steven. *Engels, Manchester, and the Working Class.* New York: Vintage Books, 1975.

Marcuse, Herbert. "The Affirmative Character of Culture." In *Negations*, trans. J. Shapiro. Boston: Beacon Press, 1968.

———. *Eros and Civilization.* Boston: Beacon Press, 1955.

———. "Industrialization and Capitalism in the Work of Max Weber." In *Negations*, trans. J. Shapiro. Boston: Beacon Press, 1968.

———. *Negations.* Trans. J. Shapiro. Boston: Beacon Press, 1968.

———. *One-Dimensional Man: Studies in the Ideology of Advanced Industrial Societies.* Boston: Beacon Press, 1964.

Marshall, Gordon. *In Search of the Spirit of Capitalism: An Essay on Max Weber's*

Protestant Ethic Thesis. New York: Columbia University Press, 1982.

Marx, Karl. "Contribution to the Critique of Hegel's Philosophy of Right." In *Marx/Engels: Collected Works,* vol. 3. New York: International Publishers, 1975.

Masaryk, Thomas. *Suicide and the Meaning of Civilization* [1881]. Trans. W. Weist and R. Batson. Chicago: University of Chicago Press, 1970.

Masur, Gerhard. *Prophets of Yesterday: Studies in European Culture 1890–1914.* New York: Harper and Row, 1966.

Mayer, J. P. *Max Weber and German Politics: A Study in Political Sociology.* 2d ed. London: Faber and Faber, 1956.

Menger, Carl. *Problems of Economics and Sociology.* Trans. F. J. Nock. Urbana: University of Illinois Press, 1963.

Merleau-Ponty, Maurice. *The Essential Writings of Merleau-Ponty.* Ed. Alden Fisher. New York: Harcourt Brace and World, 1969.

———. *The Primacy of Perception.* Ed. J. M. Edie. Evanston: Northwestern University Press, 1964.

Merton, Robert K. "The Ambivalence of Le Bon's *The Crowd.*" Introduction to Gustave Le Bon, *The Crowd.* New York: Viking Press, 1960.

———. "The Historicist/Presentist Dilemma: A Composite Imputation and a Foreknowing Response." *History of Sociology* 6, no. 1 (Fall 1985): 137–151.

———. *On the Shoulders of Giants.* New York: Harcourt Brace Jovanovich, 1965.

———. "On the History and Systematics of Sociological Theory." In his *Social Theory and Social Structure,* enlarged ed. New York: Free Press, 1968.

Merton, Robert K., and Matilda White Riley, eds. *Sociological Traditions from Generation to Generation.* Norwood, Conn.: Ablex, 1980.

Michels, Robert. *Political Parties.* Trans. E. Paul and C. Paul. New York: Free Press, 1962.

Mills, C. Wright. *Power, Politics, and People.* New York: Oxford University Press, 1967.

Misgeld, Dieter. "Critical Theory and Hermeneutics: The Debate Between Habermas and Gadamer." In *On Critical Theory,* ed. John O'Neill. New York: Seabury Press, 1976.

Mitroff, Ian. Review of P. Feyerabend's *Against Method. Contemporary Sociology* 5, no. 3 (1976): 236–237.

Mitzman, Arthur. *The Iron Cage: An Historical Interpretation of Max Weber.* New York: Grosset and Dunlap, 1971.

———. *Sociology and Estrangement: Three Sociologists of Imperial Germany.* New York: Alfred A. Knopf, 1973.

Momigliano, Arnaldo. *Essays in Ancient and Modern Historiography.* Middletown, Conn.: Wesleyan University Press, 1982.

———. "Max Weber and Edward Meyer." In Arnaldo Momigliano, *Sesto Contributo alla Storia degli Studi Classici e del Mondo Antico,* vol. 1. Rome: Edizioni di Storia e Litteratura, 1980.

———. *Studies in Historiography.* New York: Harper and Row, 1966.

Mommsen, Wolfgang. *The Age of Bureaucracy: Perspectives on the Political Sociology of Max Weber.* New York: Harper and Row, 1977.

———. *Max Weber and German Politics.* Trans. Michael Steinberg. Chicago: University of Chicago Press, 1984.

———. *Max Weber und die deutsche Politik 1890–1920.* Tübingen: Mohr, 1959.

Moore, Barrington. *Injustice: The Social Bases of Obedience and Revolt.* New York: M. E. Sharpe, 1978.

———. *Privacy: Studies in Social and Cultural History.* New York: M. E. Sharpe, 1984.

Moravec, Jaroslav. Letter to the Editor. *Contemporary Sociology* 5, no. 4 (July 1976): 399–400.

Morawski, Stefan. *An Inquiry into the Fundamentals of Aesthetics.* Cambridge, Mass.: MIT Press, 1974.

Morazé, Charles. *The Triumph of the Bourgeoisie.* New York: Anchor Books, 1968.

Munch, Peter. "'Sense' and 'Intention' in Max Weber's Theory of Social Action." *Sociological Inquiry* 45, no. 4 (1975): 59–65.

Nabokov, Vladimir. *Bend Sinister.* London: Weidenfeld and Nicolson, 1960.

Nakamura, Hajime. *Ways of Thinking of Eastern Peoples.* Honolulu: University Press of Hawaii, 1964.

Natanson, Maurice. *The Journeying Self: A Study in Philosophy and Social Role.* Reading, Mass.: Addison-Wesley, 1970.

Nelson, Benjamin. "Max Weber's 'Author's Introduction' (1920): A Master Clue to His Main Aims." *Sociological Inquiry* 44, no. 4 (1974): 269–278.

———. "Max Weber's *The Protestant Ethic:* Its Origins, Wanderings and Foreseeable Future." In *Beyond the Classics: Essays in the Scientific Study of Religion,* ed. C. Y. Glock and P. E. Hammond. New York: Harper and Row, 1973.

Neumann, Franz. *Behemoth: The Structure and Practice of National Socialism 1933–1944.* New York: Oxford University Press, 1942.

Nietzsche, Friedrich. *Basic Writings of Nietzsche.* Trans. and ed. Walter Kaufman. New York: Modern Library, 1968.

———. *The Birth of Tragedy.* New York: Anchor Books, 1956.

Nisbet, Robert. *Sociology as an Art Form.* New York: Oxford University Press, 1976.

Nolte, Ernst. *Three Faces of Fascism: Action Française, Italian Fascism, National Socialism.* New York: Mentor, 1969.

Northrop, F. S. C. *The Meeting of East and West.* New York: Macmillan, 1946.

Oberschall, Anthony. *Empirical Social Research in Germany 1848–1914.* New York: Basic Books, 1965.

Ogburn, William. *Social Change.* New York: B. W. Huebsch, 1922.

O'Neill, John, ed. *On Critical Theory.* New York: Seabury Press, 1976.

———. *Sociology as a Skin Trade.* New York: Harper and Row, 1972.

Otsuka, Hisao. *The Spirit of Capitalism: The Max Weber Thesis in an Economic Historical Perspective.* Tokyo: Iwanami Shoten, 1982.

Otto, Rudolf. *The Idea of the Holy: An Inquiry into the Nonrational Factor in the*

Idea of the Divine and Its Relation to the Rational. Trans. John W. Harvey. New York: Oxford University Press, 1958.

Palmer, Richard E. *Hermeneutics: Interpretation Theory in Schleiermacher, Dilthey, Heidegger and Gadamer.* Evanston: Northwestern University Press, 1969.

Pareto, Vilfredo. *Compendium of General Sociology.* Ed. E. Abbott. Minneapolis: University of Minnesota Press, 1980.

―――. *Cours d'économie politique professé à l'Université de Lausanne.* 2 vols. Paris: Pichon, 1896–1897.

―――. *Manuel d'économie politique.* Paris: Giard and Brière, 1909.

―――. *Manual of Political Economy.* Trans. Ann S. Schweir. New York: A. M. Kelley, 1971.

―――. *The Mind & Society,* vols. 1–4. Trans. Andrew Bongiorno and Arthur Livingston. New York: Dover, 1963.

―――. "Part IV. Circulation of Elites: Spoilation." [From *Les Systèmes socialistes.*] In *Italian Fascisms: From Pareto to Gentile,* ed. Adrian Lyttelton. New York: Harper and Row, 1975.

―――. *The Rise and Fall of the Elite: An Application of Theoretical Sociology.* Intro. by Hans L. Zetterberg. [Trans. not listed.] Totowa, N.J.: Bedminister Press, 1968.

―――. *The Ruling Class in Italy Before 1900.* [Trans. not listed.] New York: Howard Fertig, 1974.

―――. *Vilfred Pareto: Sociological Writings.* Ed. S. E. Finer. Trans. Derick Mirfin. New York: Praeger, 1966.

Parkinson, G. H. R., ed. *Georg Lukács.* New York: Vintage Books, 1970.

Parsons, Talcott. *Social Structure and Personality.* New York: Free Press, 1964.

―――. *The Social System.* New York: Free Press, 1964.

―――. *The Structure of Social Action* [1937]. 2 vols. New York: Free Press, 1968.

Parsons, Talcott, and Edward Shils, eds. *Toward a General Theory of Action.* New York: Harper and Row, 1962.

Patterson, Orlando. *Slavery and Social Death.* Cambridge, Mass.: Harvard University Press, 1982.

Pen, Jan. *Income Distribution.* New York: Penguin, 1971.

Phillips, Derek. *Abandoning Method.* San Francisco: Jossey-Bass, 1974.

Pirsig, Robert. *Zen and the Art of Motorcycle Maintenance.* New York: Morrow, 1974.

Poggi, Gianfranco. *Calvinism and the Capitalist Spirit.* Amherst: University of Massachusetts Press, 1983.

Poster, Mark. *Existential Marxism in Postwar France.* Princeton: Princeton University Press, 1975.

Prechel, Harland, and Alan Sica. "Demonstrating Dependency: A Critique of Ideologies, Educational Development, and Quantitative Test." *Political Power and Social Theory: A Research Annual* 6 (1986).

Racca, Vittorio. "Working with Pareto." *Virginia Quarterly Review* 11 (1935): 375–382.

Radden, Jennifer. *Madness and Reason*. Boston: Allen and Unwin, 1985.

Radhakrishnan, S. *Eastern Religions and Western Thought*. New York: Oxford University Press, 1939.

Rawls, John. *A Theory of Justice*. Cambridge, Mass.: Harvard University Press, 1971.

Rhea, Buford, ed. *The Future of the Sociological Classics*. London: Allen and Unwin, 1981.

Rheinstein, Max. Introduction to *Max Weber On Law in Economy and Society*. New York: Simon and Schuster, n.d.

Rickert, Heinrich. *Science and History*. Trans. G. Riesman. Princeton: Van Nostrand Reinhold, 1962.

Ricoeur, Paul. *The Conflict of Interpretations: Essays on Hermeneutics*. Evanston: Northwestern University Press, 1974.

———. *Freud and Philosophy: An Essay on Interpretation*. Trans. Denis Savage. New Haven: Yale University Press, 1970.

———. "The Model of the Text: Meaningful Action Considered as a Text." *Social Research* 38 (Autumn 1971): 529–562.

Ringer, Fritz K. *The Decline of the German Mandarins: The German Academic Community, 1890–1933*. Cambridge, Mass.: Harvard University Press, 1969.

Robertson, H. M. *Aspects of the Rise of Economic Individualism*. Cambridge, Mass.: Cambridge University Press, 1933.

Roth, Guenther. "History and Sociology in the Work of Max Weber." *British Journal of Sociology* 27, no. 3 (September 1976): 306–318.

———. Review of *Wirtschaft und Gesellschaft*, 5th ed. *Contemporary Sociology* 6, no. 5 (September 1977): 619–620; *American Journal of Sociology* 83, no. 3 (November 1977): 766–769.

Rothenberg, Albert. *The Emerging Goddess: The Creative Process in Art, Science, and Other Fields*. Chicago: University of Chicago Press, 1979.

Sabine, George. *A History of Political Theory*. New York: Henry Holt, 1937.

Sahay, Arun, ed. *Max Weber and Modern Sociology*. London: Routledge and Kegan Paul, 1971.

———. *Sociological Analysis*. London: Routledge and Kegan Paul, 1972.

Said, Edward. *The World, the Text, and the Critic*. Cambridge, Mass.: Harvard University Press, 1983.

Samuels, Warren J. *Pareto on Policy*. Amsterdam: Elsevier, 1974.

Sanders, Scott. Review of S. Morawski's *An Inquiry into the Fundamentals of Aesthetics*. *Telos*, no. 27 (Spring 1976): 195–199.

Scheler, Max. *Formalism in Ethics and Non-Formal Ethics of Values*. Trans. M. Frings and R. Funk. Evanston: Northwestern University Press, 1973.

———. *Man's Place in Nature*. Trans. H. Meyerhoff. Boston: Beacon Press, 1961.

———. *The Nature of Sympathy*. Trans. Peter Heath. Hamden, Conn.: Shoe String Press, 1970.

————. *On the Eternal in Man.* Trans. B. Noble. Hamden, Conn.: Shoe String Press, 1972.

————. *Ressentiment.* Trans. W. Holdheim. New York: Schocken Books, 1972.

————. *Die Wissensformen und die Gesellschaft.* Bern: Franke Verlag, 1960. Partially trans. M. Frings as *Problems of a Sociology of Knowledge.* Boston: Routledge and Kegan Paul, 1980.

Schelting, Alexander von. *Max Webers Wissenschaftslehre.* Tübingen: Mohr, 1934.

Schiller, Friedrich. *The Aesthetic Education of Man.* Trans. Reginald Smith. New York: Frederick Ungar, 1965.

Schilpp, Paul A., ed. *The Philosophy of Karl Jaspers.* New York: Tudor, 1957.

Schmidt, Gert. "Max Weber and Modern Industrial Sociology: A Comment on Some Recent Anglo-Saxon Interpretations." *Sociological Analysis and Theory* 6, no. 1 (February 1976): 47–73.

Schroeter, Gerd. "A Conversation Between Joseph Schumpeter and Max Weber." *History of Sociology* 6, no. 1 (Fall 1985): 161–172.

————. "Exploring the Marx-Weber Nexus." *Canadian Journal of Sociology* 10, no. 1 (1985): 69–89.

Schumpeter, Joseph. *History of Economic Analysis.* Ed. E. Schumpeter. New York: Oxford University Press, 1954.

Schutz, Alfred. *The Phenomenology of the Social World.* Trans. George Walsh and F. Lehnert. Evanston: Northwestern University Press, 1972 (paperback ed.).

Schwendinger, Herman, and Julia Schwendinger. *Sociologists of the Chair.* New York: Basic Books, 1974.

Scitovsky, Tibor. *The Joyless Economy: An Inquiry into Human Satisfaction and Consumer Dissatisfaction.* New York: Oxford University Press, 1976.

Segré, Sandro. "Pareto and Weber: A Tentative Reconstruction of Their Intellectual Relationship with an Excursus on Pareto and the German Language." *Cahiers Vilfredo Pareto* 20 (1982): 247–271.

Seidman, Steven. "Classics and Contemporaries: The History and Systematics of Sociology Revisited." *History of Sociology* 6, no. 1 (Fall 1985): 121–135.

Sennett, Richard. *The Fall of Public Man: On the Social Psychology of Capitalism.* New York: Vintage Books, 1978.

Seyfarth, Constans, and Gert Schmidt. *Max Weber Bibliographie: Eine Dokumentation der Sekundärliteratur.* Stuttgart: Enke, 1977.

Shapiro, Gary, and Alan Sica, eds. *Hermeneutics: Questions and Prospects.* Amherst: University of Massachusetts Press, 1984.

Sica, Alan. "Hermeneutics and Social Theory: The Contemporary Conversation." *Current Perspectives in Social Theory* 2 (1981): 39–54.

————. "The Problem of Irrationality and Meaning in the Work of Max Weber." Ph.D. dissertation, University of Massachusetts, 1978.

————. "Reasonable Science, Unreasonable Life: The Happy Fictions of Marx, Weber, and Social Theory." In *A Weber-Marx Dialogue,* ed. Robert J.

Antonio and Ronald Glassman. Lawrence: University Press of Kansas, 1985.

———. "Received Wisdom Versus Historical Fact: On the Mutual Awareness of Weber and Pareto." *Journal of the History of Sociology* 1, no. 2 (Spring 1979): 17–34.

———. Review of Max Scheler's *Problems of a Sociology of Knowledge. Journal of the History of Sociology* 4, no. 1 (Spring 1982): 100–104.

———. "The Unknown Max Weber: A Note on Missing Translations." *Mid-American Review of Sociology* 9, no. 2 (Winter 1984): 33–58.

Simmel, Georg. *Georg Simmel on Individuality and Social Forms.* Ed. Donald Levine. Chicago: University of Chicago Press, 1971.

———. *Goethe.* Leipzig: Klinkhardt and Biermann, 1913.

———. *The Problems of the Philosophy of History.* Trans. Guy Oakes. New York: Free Press, 1977.

———. *Rembrandt: Ein Kunstphilosophischer Versuch.* Leipzig: Kurt Wolff, 1916.

———. *Schopenhauer und Nietzsche.* Leipzig: Duncker and Humblot, 1907. Trans. by H. Loiskandl et al. as *Schopenhauer and Nietzsche.* Amherst: University of Massachusetts Press, 1986.

Smelser, Neil. *Comparative Methods in the Social Sciences.* Englewood Cliffs, N.J.: Prentice-Hall, 1976.

Solms-Roedelheim, Max Ernst Graf zu, ed. *Aus den Schriften zur Religionssoziologie (Max Weber).* Frankfurt: Schauer, 1948.

Sorokin, Pitirim. *Contemporary Sociological Theories.* New York: Harper and Row, 1928.

———. *Social and Cultural Dynamics.* 4 vols. [1937–1941]. New York: Bedminister Press, 1962.

———. *Society, Culture and Personality.* New York: Harper Brothers, 1947.

———. *Ways and Power of Love.* Boston: Beacon Press, 1954.

Spiegelberg, Herbert. *The Phenomenological Movement.* 2d ed. The Hague: Nijhoff, 1965.

Spykman, Nicholas J. *The Social Theory of Georg Simmel.* New York: Atherton, 1966.

Stammer, Otto, ed. *Max Weber and Sociology Today.* Trans. Kathleen Morris. New York: Harper and Row, 1972.

Stark, Werner. *The Sociology of Knowledge: An Essay in Aid of a Deeper Understanding of the History of Ideas.* London: Routledge and Kegan Paul, 1958.

———. *The Sociology of Religion.* 5 vols. New York: Fordham University Press, 1973.

Staude, John. *Max Scheler: An Intellectual Portrait.* New York: Free Press, 1967.

Steiner, George. *After Babel: Aspects of Language and Translation.* New York: Oxford University Press, 1975.

Stirling, James. *The Secret of Hegel.* London: Longman, Green, Longman, Roberts, and Green, 1865.

Struve, Walter. *Elites Against Democracy: Leadership Ideals in the Bourgeois Po-*

litical Thought in Germany 1890–1933. Princeton: Princeton University Press, 1973.

Swidler, Ann. "The Concept of Rationality in the Work of Max Weber." *Sociological Inquiry* 43 (1973): 35–52.

Tarascio, Vincent. *Pareto's Methodological Approach to Economics.* Chapel Hill: University of North Carolina Press, 1968.

Tashjean, John E. "Interest in Pareto's Sociology: Reflections on a Bibliography." *Cahiers Vilfredo Pareto* 20 (February 1970): 141–143.

Thomas, Keith. *Religion and the Decline of Magic.* New York: Scribner's, 1971.

Thompson, John B. *Critical Hermeneutics: A Study in the Thought of Paul Ricoeur and Jürgen Habermas.* New York: Cambridge University Press, 1981.

Timasheff, Nicholas S. and George A. Theodorson. *Sociological Theory: Its Nature and Growth.* 4th ed. New York: Random House, 1976.

Tiryakian, Edward A. "A Problem for the Sociology of Knowledge: The Mutual Unawareness of Emile Durkheim and Max Weber." *European Journal of Sociology* 7, no. 2 (1966): 330–336.

Tönnies, Ferdinand. *Community and Society.* Trans. Charles P. Loomis. New York: Harper and Row, 1963.

Torrance, John. "Max Weber: Methods and the Man." *Archives Européenes de Sociologie* 15, no. 1 (1974): 127–165.

———. "Rationality and the Structural Analysis of Myth." *European Journal of Sociology* 8 (1967): 272–281.

Treitschke, Heinrich von. *Politics.* Ed. Hans Kohn. New York: Harcourt Brace and World, 1963.

Truzzi, Marcello, ed. *Verstehen: Subjective Understanding in the Social Sciences.* Reading, Mass.: Addison-Wesley, 1974.

Turner, Bryan S. *Weber and Islam: A Critical Study.* London: Routledge and Kegan Paul, 1974.

Turner, Stephen. "Weber Agonistes." *Contemporary Sociology* 15, no. 1 (January 1986): 47–50.

Vucinich, Alexander. *Social Thought in Tsarist Russia: The Quest for a General Science of Society 1861–1917.* Chicago: University of Chicago Press, 1976.

Wallerstein, Immanuel. *The Modern World-System: Capitalist Agriculture and the Origins of the European World-Economy in the 16th Century.* New York: Academic Press, 1974.

Walzer, Michael. *The Revolution of the Saints: A Study in the Origins of Radical Politics.* New York: Atherton, 1968.

Wardell, Mark, and Stephen Turner, eds. *Sociological Theory in Transition.* Boston: Allen and Unwin, 1986.

Weber, Marianne. "Academic Conviviality." *Minerva* 15, no. 2 (Summer 1977): 214–246.

———. *Max Weber: A Biography.* Trans. Harry Zohn. New York: John Wiley and Sons, 1975.

Weinstein, Fred, and Gerald Platt. *Psychoanalytic Sociology*. Baltimore: Johns Hopkins University Press, 1973.

——. *The Wish to Be Free: Society, Psyche, and Social Change*. Berkeley and Los Angeles: University of California Press, 1969.

Weintraub, Karl. *Visions of Culture*. Chicago: University of Chicago Press, 1966.

Wellek, René, and Austin Warren. *Theory and Literature*. 3d ed. New York: Harcourt Brace and World, 1962.

Wellmer, Albrecht. "Communications and Emancipation." In *On Critical Theory*, ed. John O'Neill. New York: Seabury Press, 1976.

——. *Critical Theory of Society*. Trans. John Cumming. New York: Seabury Press, 1974.

Whitehead, Alfred North. *Interpretation of Science*. Indianapolis: Bobbs-Merrill, 1961.

——. *Process and Reality: An Essay in Cosmology* [1929]. New York: Macmillan, 1977 (corrected edition).

——. *Science and the Modern World*. New York: Macmillan, 1925.

Wiley, Norbert. Review of Randall Collins's *Conflict Sociology*. *Contemporary Sociology* 5, no. 3 (May 1976): 237.

Willey, Thomas E. *Back to Kant: The Revival of Kantianism in German Social and Historical Thought 1860–1914*. Detroit: Wayne State University Press, 1978.

Williams, Robin. *American Society: A Sociological Interpretation*. New York: Alfred A. Knopf, 1960.

Wilson, Bryan R., ed. *Rationality*. New York: Harper and Row, 1971.

Winch, Peter. *The Idea of a Social Science and Its Relation to Philosophy*. London: Routledge and Kegan Paul, 1960.

Winckelmann, Johannes. *Legitimität und Legalität in Max Webers Herrschaftssoziologie*. Tübingen: Mohr, 1952.

Winckelmann, Johannes, ed. *Max Weber: Die protestantische Ethik*. 2 vols. Munich: Siebenstern Taschenbuch, 1968.

Wolff, Kurt, ed. *The Sociology of Georg Simmel*. New York: Free Press, 1950.

Wolff, Robert Paul. "Man as a Rational Political Agent." In *Women and Philosophy*, ed. Carol Gould and Marx Wartofsky. New York: Putnam's, 1976.

Wölfflin, Heinrich. *Principles of Art History*. New York: Dover, 1950.

Wrong, Dennis, ed. *Max Weber*. Englewood Cliffs, N.J.: Prentice-Hall, 1970.

Zeitlin, Irving. *Ideology and the Development of Sociological Theory*. Englewood Cliffs, N.J.: Prentice-Hall, 1968.

Znaniecki, Florian. *Cultural Reality*. Chicago: University of Chicago Press, 1919.

——. *The Social Role of the Man of Knowledge*. New York: Harper and Row, 1968.

Index

Compositor: G&S Typesetters, Inc.
Text: 10/13 Palatino
Display: Palatino
Printer: Braun-Brumfield, Inc.
Binder: Braun-Brumfield, Inc.